ENVIRONMENTAL MANAGEMENT ACCOUNTING

Sustainable development will not happen without substantial contributions from and leading roles of companies and business organisations. This requires the provision of adequate information on corporate social and ecological impacts and performance. For the last decade, progress has been made in developing and adapting accounting mechanisms to these needs but significant work is still needed to tackle the problems associated with conventional accounting.

Until recently, research on environmental management accounting (EMA) has concentrated on developed countries and on cost–benefit analysis of implementing individual EMA tools. Using a comparative case study design, this book seeks to redress the balance and improve the understanding of EMA in management decision-making in emerging countries, focussing specifically on South-East Asian companies. Drawing on 12 case studies, taken from a variety of industries, *Environmental Management Accounting: Case Studies of South-East Asian Companies* explores the relationship between decision situations and the motivation for, and barriers to, the application of clusters of EMA tools as well as the implementation process itself.

This book will be useful to scholars interested in the environmental and sustainability management accounting research field and those considering specific approaches to EMA within emerging economies.

Christian Herzig is Lecturer at Nottingham University, UK.

Tobias Viere is Research Fellow at Leuphana University of Lüneburg, Germany.

Stefan Schaltegger is Professor at Leuphana University of Lüneburg, Germany.

Roger L. Burritt is Professor at University of South Australia, Australia.

ENVIRONMENTAL MANAGEMENT ACCOUNTING

Case studies of South-East Asian companies

Christian Herzig, Tobias Viere, Stefan Schaltegger and Roger L. Burritt

Routledge
Taylor & Francis Group

LONDON AND NEW YORK

First published 2012
by Routledge
2 Park Square, Milton Park, Abingdon, Oxon OX14 4RN

Simultaneously published in the USA and Canada
by Routledge
711 Third Avenue, New York, NY 10017

Routledge is an imprint of the Taylor & Francis Group, an informa business

British Library Cataloguing in Publication Data
A catalogue record for this book is available from the British Library

Library of Congress Cataloging in Publication Data
Environmental management accounting : case studies in South-East
Asian companies / Christian Herzig ... [et al.].
p. cm.
Includes bibliographical references and index.
 1. Environmental auditing—Southeast Asia—Case studies. 2.
Agricultural industries—Environmental aspects—Southeast Asia.
3. Industries—Environmental aspects—Southeast Asia. I. Herzig,
Christian.
TD194.7.E5975 2012
333.70959–dc23
2011036757

ISBN: 978–0–415–69431–5 (hbk)
ISBN: 978–0–415–50678–6 (pbk)
ISBN: 978–0–203–12536–6 (ebk)

Typeset in Bembo
by Prepress Projects Ltd, Perth, UK

CONTENTS

FIGURES

TABLES

ABOUT THE AUTHORS

Christian Herzig is Lecturer in Sustainability Accounting and Reporting at the International Centre for Corporate Social Responsibility (ICCSR) at Nottingham University Business School, UK. Christian has held previous postdoctoral appointments in Germany, Australia, and the UK.

Tobias Viere is Research Fellow of the Centre for Sustainability Management (CSM), Leuphana University of Lüneburg, Germany, and Research and Development Representative of ifu Hamburg GmbH, Germany. He is also a member of the ISO international expert working group on Material Flow Cost Accounting.

Stefan Schaltegger is Professor of Management and Head of the Centre for Sustainability Management (CSM) and the MBA Sustainability Management, Leuphana University of Lüneburg, Germany. He is the chairman of Environmental Management Accounting Network (EMAN) Europe and Global and is the co-author with Roger Burritt of *Contemporary Environmental Accounting: Issues, Concept and Practice* (2000, Greenleaf).

Roger L. Burritt is Professor of Accounting and Director of the Centre for Accounting, Governance and Sustainability, University of South Australia, Australia. He is the founder of the Asia-Pacific Centre for Environmental Accountability (APCEA) and chairman of EMAN Asia Pacific. He is co-author of the book *Contemporary Environmental Accounting: Issues, Concept and Practice* (2000, Greenleaf) and is editor-in-chief of the book *Environmental Management Accounting and Supply Chain Management*.

FOREWORD

Craig Deegan, Professor of Accounting, RMIT University, Melbourne, Australia

It has never been more critical for organisations of all sizes and across all sectors to monitor and control the social and environmental implications of their operations. To enable various stakeholders, such as investors, consumers, employees, local communities, government, and so forth, to make informed decisions about whether they should support particular organisations, they need information about the performance of an organisation, including information about social and environmental performance. The accountant is central to this role.

Similarly, with increasing pressure to control negative social and environmental impacts of an organisation, managers require timely information about various aspects of their operation beyond those reflected in the organisation's financial performance. Central to information managers' needs are well-designed environmental management accounting (EMA) systems – something that this valuable book addresses.

Although the case for EMA is clear, experience indicates that management generally have little understanding of the environmental costs they generate – often because their accounting systems fail to supply them with such information. Accountants need to respond and find ways to incorporate environmental costs within their accounting systems. EMA facilitates this.

Because EMA is typically established for internal decision-making it is difficult for interested people, outside the organisations, to obtain information about the internal accounting processes. Bringing together a knowledgeable team of researchers and practitioners, the authors of this book are able to enter organisations across South-East Asia to provide valuable insights that would not otherwise be available.

Prior to providing case study-specific information the book provides a very useful introductory chapter which gives a general overview of EMA. As is clearly indicated, EMA systems – if properly developed – fulfil dual goals of reducing environmental impacts and enhancing economic performance. As the introductory material also explains, EMA systems range in complexity, but often an EMA system can be introduced without significant or costly changes being made to existing management accounting systems. As the United Nations Division Sustainable Development stated some years ago (UN DSD 2001: 3):

> Doing environmental management accounting is simply doing better, more comprehensive management accounting, while wearing an 'environmental' hat that opens the eyes for hidden costs.

Although the implementation of a well-designed EMA system will help achieve a number of environmental and financial aims, there will be various factors that at times might hinder, or support, the implementation of an EMA system. The 12 exploratory case studies provided in this text provide us with rich insights into various issues that confronted various organisations within South-East Asia – an area that has not previously been the subject of a large body of published EMA research. A number of the organisations encounter factors that are quite specific to their locality (as well as some issues that have applicability internationally). By providing information about how these organisations have addressed various issues within the South-East Asian context this book provides a valuable resource for both organisations and accounting researchers. As is clearly demonstrated, different organisational environments (with differences in cultures, technologies, and economic standing) and institutional settings (with different regulatory, legal, and political environments) will provide different pressures for organisations. As this book demonstrates, well-designed EMA systems take these factors into account.

The authors of this text have a wealth of experience and are known experts in the field of EMA. It is immensely pleasing that they have put this series of case studies together and I wholeheartedly recommend this book to people who are concerned about improving the environmental and financial performance of their organisations. I also recommend it to accounting researchers, research students, and others with an interest in issues associated with the broad area of management accounting.

Reference

UN DSD (United Nations Division for Sustainable Development) (2001) *Environmental Management Accounting. Procedures and Principles*, New York: UN DSD.

FOREWORD

*James M. Sylph, Executive Director, Professional
Standards, IFAC, New York, United States*

I am pleased to recommend this book on environmental management accounting in South-East Asia to accounting researchers and practitioners, whom it encourages to strive for sustainable development of business and society.

Such striving is a core challenge for businesses all over the world. Management and other accountants are becoming key players in this process. They fulfil a range of important tasks. These include preparation, verification, and assurance of sustainability and integrated reports, gathering and analysis of information on corporate sustainability performance, developing product and corporate carbon footprints, and scrutinising and refining sustainability business strategies.

The International Federation of Accountants (IFAC) is committed to sustainability within and through the work of the global accounting community. In 2005, IFAC published the only *International Guidance Document on Environmental Management Accounting*. Engagement in this area has since been extended through the development of a *Sustainability Framework* published by IFAC's Professional Accountants in Business Committee addressing how to embed sustainability within the DNA of an organisation. Most recently, IFAC joined with the Prince's *Accounting for Sustainability* project in the UK and others, to establish the *International Integrated Reporting Committee* to create a globally accepted integrated reporting framework which brings together financial, environmental, social, and governance information in a clear, concise, consistent, and comparable format (http://www.theiirc.org). The aim is to help with the development of more comprehensive and comprehensible information about organisations, prospective as well as retrospective, to meet the needs of a more sustainable, global economy.

The detailed case book with case studies on environmental management accounting in South-East Asia offers profound insights into the implementation aspects of environmental management accounting. The focus on small and medium-sized companies in four emerging economies of South-East Asia makes this book unique and crucially important as a basis for developing a global approach to sustainability issues. Without the inclusion of small and medium-sized enterprises and companies from developing and newly industrialised countries, sustainable business development will not be comprehensive and will miss very important sections of the business community and the embedding of environmental awareness and information flows in everyday thinking and actions. To my further pleasure the book draws on one of IFAC's 2002 Articles of Merit, the conceptualisation of a comprehensive framework of Environmental Management Accounting, to highlight the multitude of decision settings and available tools within this field. Taken together, *Environmental Management Accounting: Case Studies of South-East Asian Companies* is a very useful and most welcome addition to research, policy-making, professional education, and practice in the area.

FOREWORD

Richard Welford, Chairman CSR Asia and Professor at AIT Bangkok, Thailand

In a world characterised by rapid change and uncertainty there is a growing business need for support in understanding the complexity of environmental issues and their economic implications, and for decisions which address problems such as resource scarcity, carbon emissions reduction and increasing energy costs. This book offers insights into the critical role that environmental management accounting has to offer in facilitating the integration of environmental considerations into management decision-making and fostering economically viable and environmentally sound business. The book's greatest value lies in the rich set of case study examples and the synthesis provided from South-East Asian companies. It gives practitioners, academics, policymakers, and students the guidance they need to understand the multiple uses of environmental management accounting.

In spite of progress made recently in enhancing environmentally sound business in emerging and less developed countries, there remains significant work to be accomplished. Thus, *Environmental Management Accounting: Case Studies of South-East Asian Companies* is a much-needed and welcome book addressing a region in which companies face different motivations and barriers for undertaking environmentally sound, economically viable business. It also reflects specific business environments, organisational contexts, and operational and investment settings in emerging and less developed countries and provides guidance for improving accounting practice in order to reduce environmental impacts and improve monetary benefits.

The distinguishing feature of this publication is its systematic framework and approach to investigating the usefulness of environmental management accounting for corporate decision-makers. The book compares different decision situations and institutional settings related to environmental issues within and across 12 organisations in four South-East Asian countries. Investigation and comparison of the various ways in which managers can implement environmental management accounting tools to improve management accounting and control makes the book a cutting-edge source of information for audiences with a concern to learn about sustainability, corporate social responsibility, environmental management and their impacts on business.

It is my hope that with this book as a guide, given its richness of content, potential reach, and focus on actions taken, the emerging community of environmentally sound businesses in Asia will be strengthened and expanded, the region's competitiveness enhanced and progress made in tackling major environmental issues faced by society today. *Environmental Management Accounting: Case Studies of South-East Asian Companies* will support close thinking about accounting needed to support management decision-making, future planning, and sustainable development.

ACKNOWLEDGEMENTS

This book is the result of a series of company visits and consultations in Indonesia, the Philippines, Thailand, and Vietnam, and numerous discussions among the authors and others. It would not have been possible without the help of many people from South-East Asia, Australia, Germany, and the United Kingdom.

Our sincere thanks go to all involved in the Environmental Management Accounting – South-East Asia (EMA-SEA) programme and who supported and encouraged us to conduct case study research in the South-East Asian region.

- Deutsche Gesellschaft für Internationale Zusammenarbeit (GIZ) GmbH (former InWent Capacity Building International), Bonn, Germany (http:// www.giz.de), for initialising, funding, and managing the EMA-SEA programme and, in particular, Guenter Tharun, Petra Kontny, Karena Kimmel, and Karen Pacheco.
- The Asian Society for Environmental Protection, Bangkok, Thailand (ASEP, http://www.asepinfo.org), for managing the EMA-SEA programme in the region, their hospitality, and support in cross-cultural learning. Our thanks go to two presidents of ASEP, Raymond Leung and Boonyong Lohwongwatana, and ASEP's administrative manager, Tatchanok Siriwipanan, as well as Brenda Cabahug and Anthony Guirnela.
- The Indonesian Society of Environmental Professionals (IPHLI), particularly Paul Louis Coutrier, and the Indonesian Cleaner Production Center (PPBN – Pusat Produksi Bersih Nasional, http://ppbn.or.id/ site/index.php), particularly Sri Handayani Abdullah and Aris Ika Nugrahanto. Furthermore, we thank Fani Cahyandito, Faisal Djalal,

Dido Harisoesyanto, Maria E. Hastuti, Anhar Kramadisastra, Zulkifli Nasution, Purwatiningsih Lisidono, Moses Singghi, Tigor Tambunana, Ario Tranggono, Wiesje Astrid Rondonuwu, and Chandra Wirman.

- In the Philippines, our thanks go to Edwin J. Calilung and Alvin Culaba for the organisation of the EMA-SEA activities. We are also grateful for the support and collaboration of Hazel Alfon, Dioscoro Baylon, Augusto D. Camba, Elmer Dadios, Ricardo Danlag, Rosana E. Espiritu, Fe K. Gloria, Ariel Nones, Christine D. Olairez, Eric E. Raymundo, Clarencia S. Reyes, Fatima Reyes, Bernado D. Tadeo, Barbara Tio, and Richard Bryan C. Uy.

- In Thailand, the organisation of EMA-SEA events was supported by the Thai Environmental Institute (TEI, http://www.tei.or.th), and especially Watcharapong Silalertraksa, Sutee Smudraprabhud, and Sumon Sumetchoengprachya. We would also like to acknowledge the hospitality and support of Sopida Boonaneskap, Suchada Chaisawadi, Somporn Kamolsiripichaiporn, Chongprode Kochaphum, Kularb Kimsri, Duangmanee Komaratat, Pongvipa Lohsomboon, Jiraprapa Prasopsorn, Malinee Suksuart, and Soydoa Vinitnantharat.

- In Vietnam, the EMA-SEA programme would not have been successful at all without the support of the Viet Nam Cleaner Production Centre (VNCPC, http://vncpc.vn), particularly Le Thu Ha, Tang Thi Hong Loan, Ngo Thi Nga, and Tran Van Nhan. EMA-SEA was also supported by Tran An, Ding Dung Duong, Tran Tien Dung, Le Thu Hoa, Le Thanh Loan, Nguyen Thanh Ngan, Nguyen Dang Anh Thi, Tu Anh Ha Thi, Nguyen Chau Tran, and Vu Thuy.

- We would like to thank all participants of the EMA-SEA 'training of trainers' seminars for ongoing promotion and dissemination of information in the South-East Asian region. A list of EMA trainers and consultants in the region including their contact details can be found on the Global Campus 21 website (http://gc21.inwent.org/EMAportal).

We would like to thank all the companies involved for their cooperation and participation in our research. In particular we would like to thank a number of people who were involved in various ways in conducting the case study research leading to this book:

- Aris Salim, Ignatio Y. Suyanto, and Chandra Wirman – Indah Jaya;
- Zulkifli Nasution and Nugraha Sumpena – Bisma Jaya;
- Rhoda Natividad and Eric E. Raymundo – JBC Food;
- Bernardo D. Tadeo, Rosana E. Espiritu, and Hanshel Z. Layaoen – Oliver Enterprises;
- Richard Bryan C. Uy and Evangeline Manlangit – Well-Ever Electroplating Shop;

- Khun Wanna Ongthanawat, Khun Sawanee Tonyoopaiboon, Burghard Rauschelbach, and Khun Suparp Pisuraj – Classic Crafts;
- Khun Thanes Somboon and Umaporn Phanaphon – Thai Cane Paper.
- Tran Tien Dung and Nguyen Dang Anh Thi – Chau Thanh Tam Shrimp Farm, Tan Loc Food, and Sai Gon Beer;
- Jan von Enden – Neumann Coffee Vietnam;

We offer our thanks to staff at the Centre for Accounting, Governance and Sustainability, School of Commerce, University of South Australia, for their proofreading and administrative assistance: Dr Amanda Carter, Rainbow Shum, and Stacey Truran. We also thank Aino Martikainen, Kulawal Supesuntorn, Niko Schäpke, and Cornelia Fermum of the Centre for Sustainability Management, Leuphana University of Lüneburg, Germany, as well as all researchers who improved the quality of our research by contributing to discussions on the case studies and general content of the book. We would also like to thank the International Centre for Corporate Social Responsibility, Nottingham University Business School, UK.

The case study research in South-East Asian companies was a precious experience and great challenge for all of us. We are grateful to have had the possibility to immerse ourselves in the South-East Asian business culture and to gain new insights into the role, implementation, and use of environmental management accounting (EMA). To share our experiences and knowledge gained through the conduct of our study with agents of sustainable development, including researchers, managers, accountants, consultants, and practitioners, is the prime objective of this book. We are confident that it will contribute to better understanding of the requirements and capabilities of actual implementation of EMA in emerging economy countries. We hope that it supports and facilitates sustainable business development in the South-East Asian region and beyond.

Roger L. Burritt, Christian Herzig, Stefan Schaltegger, and Tobias Viere
Adelaide, Lüneburg, Nottingham, June 2011

ABBREVIATIONS

ABC	activity-based costing
ACS	automated carbonisation system
ADB	Asian Development Bank
ASEP	Asian Society for Environmental Protection
BOD	biochemical oxygen demand
BSCI	Business Social Compliance Initiative
BSE	bovine spongiform encephalopathy
BSI	British Standards Institution
CDM	clean development mechanism
CERs	certified emission reductions
CIA	Central Intelligence Agency
CO_2eq	carbon dioxide equivalents
Co.	company
COD	chemical oxygen demand
Corp.	corporation
CRH	carbonised rice husk
CTT	Chau Thanh Tam Shrimp Farm
CV	type of Indonesian business entity (from Dutch: *commanditaire vennootschaap*)
DAO	DENR Administrative Order
DENR	Department of Environment and Natural Resources, Philippines
DEQP	Department of Environmental Quality Promotion, Thailand
DILG	Department of the Interior and Local Government, Philippines
DOC	dissolved oxygen content

ECC	Environmental Compliance Certificate
EFA	environmental financial accounting (or external monetary and physical environmental accounting)
EIA	Energy Information Administration
EMA	environmental management accounting
EMA-SEA	Environmental Management Accounting in South-East Asia
EMB	Environmental Management Bureau
EPA	Environmental Protection Agency
EPI	environmental performance indicator
EPLCA	European Platform on Life Cycle Assessment
ERP	enterprise resource planning or emergency response procedure
EU	European Union
FAO	Food and Agriculture Organization of the United Nations
FASB	Financial Accounting Standards Board
GDP	gross domestic product
GIZ	Deutsche Gesellschaft für Internationale Zusammenarbeit [German Association for International Cooperation]
GmbH	type of German business entity [*Gesellschaft mit beschränkter Haftung*]
GTZ	Deutsche Gesellschaft für Technische Zusammenarbeit [German Technical Cooperation, now GIZ]
GWP	global warming potential
HACCP	hazard analysis and critical control point
HSE	health, safety, and environment
IASB	International Accounting Standards Board
IASC	International Accounting Standards Committee
ICAA	Institute of Chartered Accountants in Australia
ICFPA	International Council of Forest and Paper Associations
ICLEI	International Council for Local Environmental Initiatives
ICO	International Coffee Organization
IDR	Indonesian rupiah
IFAC	International Federation of Accountants
IGES	Institute for Global Environmental Strategies
InWEnt	Internationale Weiterbildung und Entwicklung [Capacity Building International, now GIZ]
IPCC	Intergovernmental Panel on Climate Change
ISO	International Organization for Standardization
JBC	JBC Food Corporation
LCA	life cycle assessment
LDC	less developed countries
LPG	liquefied petroleum gas
Ltd	Limited (type of company)

MEMA	monetary environmental management accounting
METI	Japanese Ministry of Economy, Trade and Industry
MFCA	material flow cost accounting
NPV	net present value
NZBCSD	New Zealand Business Council for Sustainable Development
OTOP	One Tambon One Product
PAS	publicly available specification
PCO	Pollution Control Officer
PD	Presidential Decree
PEMA	physical environmental management accounting
PET	polyethylene
PHP	Philippine pesos
PhilRice	Philippine Rice Research Institute
PIA	Philippine Information Agency
PLC	public limited company
PT	type of Indonesian business entity (from Bahasa Perseroan Terbatas)
SA 8000	Social Accountability International's SA 8000 Standard
SAP	system application programme
SMEs	small- to medium-sized enterprises
THB	Thai baht
tPHP	thousand PHP
TSS	total suspended solids
UN	United Nations
UNDSD	United Nations Division of Sustainable Development
UNEP	United Nations Environment Programme
UNEP RRC.AP	UNEP Regional Resource Centre for Asia and the Pacific
UNESCAP	United Nations Economic and Social Commission for Asia and the Pacific
UNFCCC	United Nations Framework Convention on Climate Change
UNStat	United Nations Statistics Division
US	United States
USAID	United States Agency for International Development
USD	United States dollar (US$)
VOCs	volatile organic compounds
VND	Vietnamese dong
WBSCD	World Business Council for Sustainable Development
WRI	World Resources Institute

1

INTRODUCTION AND STRUCTURE OF THE BOOK

Introduction

Environmental management accounting (EMA) is a concept of sustainability management which comprises a set of accounting tools and practices to support managerial decision-making on environmental and economic performance. EMA primarily supports internal decision-making; therefore, it is comparatively difficult to gather reliable information on the actual drivers, practice, state, and quantity of EMA applications in companies and other organisations.

To date, case study research on EMA has focussed mainly on single applications in large companies in industrialised countries. This research book provides new insights into the implementation of EMA through a comparative case study consisting of 12 exploratory case studies conducted in small, medium, and large companies in four emerging economy countries of South-East Asia: Indonesia, the Philippines, Thailand, and Vietnam. The study seeks to explore various decision situations and institutional settings and the way these are linked with types of EMA information, as well as the uses of, and linkages between, a large range of tools which support decision-making at different management levels and company contexts. The book analyses the applicability of EMA and its related tools contingent on the decision-making context within the company.

Motivation for this collection of case studies

In 2003, InWent Capacity Building International (now GIZ Deutsche Gesellschaft für Internationale Zusammenarbeit GmbH), Germany, commissioned the Centre for Sustainability Management of Leuphana University Lüneburg, Germany, to conduct a capacity development programme on

Environmental Management Accounting in South-East Asia (EMA-SEA). The programme operated from late 2003 to early 2008 and was financed by the German Federal Ministry for Economic Cooperation and Development and supported by two non-profit organisations: the previously mentioned InWent, as international coordinator, and the Asian Society for Environmental Protection, as the main regional partner for Indonesia, the Philippines, Thailand, and Vietnam. The Centre for Sustainability Management provided the programme content and conducted a series of information workshops, training seminars, internet-based seminars, and 'training of trainers' workshops for managers, engineers, consultants, and other business-related persons, as well as representatives from governments, local authorities, and academia in the South-East Asian region. During the project the Centre for Sustainability Management worked closely with the Centre for Accounting, Governance and Sustainability, University of South Australia.

The EMA-SEA programme aimed at developing individual and institutional EMA capacity in the region and continues in a voluntary way now that the supported part of the programme has been completed. An internal survey among the participants of EMA-SEA 'training of trainers' seminars revealed that about half were integrating EMA in their daily work as consultants, environmental engineers, managers, lecturers, and researchers. More than 40 cases of EMA implementation leading to substantial financial savings and environmental improvements were reported in 2006 and 2007. In those cases where the interviewees quantified savings and improvements, the average annual financial saving was about €23,100 and the average reduction in annual CO_2 equivalents of 1,700 tonnes per company (the survey can be found in the downloads and links page of http://gc21.inwent.org/EMAportal).

The didactic concept of the different types of EMA seminars was based on the project casework training approach (Tharun 1995a,b). The approach combines lectures, group work, and discussion and is based on realistic examples. At the beginning of the EMA-SEA programme, the Centre for Sustainability Management developed several South-East Asian company examples to support the project casework training approach and the development of training materials. This experience strengthened the authors' desire to conduct comprehensive research beyond the scope and duties of the EMA-SEA programme. The result of this research is manifested in this book, which introduces 12 embedded case studies as part of an overall comparative case study. The structure of the case study book is explained next.

Structure of the book

This introductory section precedes Part I of the book. Part I includes an overview of conventional and environmental accounting which constitutes the basis for EMA definition (see Figure 1.1). A framework for the characterisation

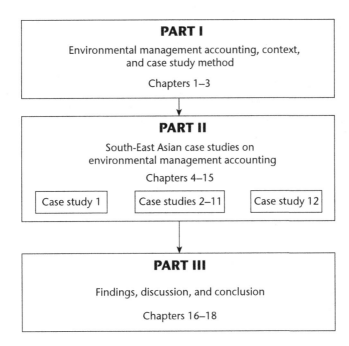

FIGURE 1.1 Structure of the book.

and systematisation of EMA decision settings and tools is then explained, followed by a description of individual EMA tools.

In the remainder of Part I, research method and design are elaborated. First, the economic and environmental importance of the South-East Asian region is described briefly. The authors then explain the usefulness of the EMA concept as well as the state of EMA implementation in the South-East Asian context. Against this background, the purpose and the methodology of the EMA study is defined, followed by a brief general introduction to case study research, reasons for conducting case studies, and types of case studies. Finally, this part of the book outlines the specific case study design for studying companies' decision situations, institutional settings and implementation of EMA in South-East Asia and concludes with an overview of the 12 South-East Asian company case studies that constitute the comparative case study.

Part II presents each embedded case study in detail. Each of the 12 cases from Indonesia, the Philippines, Thailand, and Vietnam then forms a separate chapter in Part II.

The findings of the comparative case study are discussed in Part III of the book, which concludes with an outlook for future EMA research and implementation.

References

Tharun, G. (1995a) *The project casework (PCW) concept in brief: its rationale, structure, function, development and origin in 42 Statements*, Bangkok: Carl Duisberg Gesellschaft.

Tharun, G. (1995b) *Training für das Management von Umweltprojekten: Fortbildungsmaßnahmen für Führungskräfte aus Wirtschaft und Verwaltung als Lösungsansatz zur Bewältigung von Umweltproblemen in Entwicklungsländern [Training for the management of environmental projects: further education for business and public administration executives on tackling environmental problems in developing countries]*, Frankfurt: Peter Lang.

Part I

Introduction to environmental management accounting

2

ENVIRONMENTAL MANAGEMENT ACCOUNTING

Introduction to environmental and conventional accounting

Environmental accounting is a specific type of accounting which brings together monetary and physical information to (i) provide support for decision-making by managers, and (ii) facilitate accountability through feedback from reports made to internal and external stakeholders (Burritt, Hahn, and Schaltegger 2002). Accounting supports decision-making processes. Accounting involves collecting, recording, classifying, and reporting purpose-orientated information, predominantly in monetary units, and is often based on physical information, such as items of semi-manufactured products, production schedules, or kilograms of raw materials (Schaltegger and Burritt 2000). The accounting process can also provide an important foundation for improving the environmental records of businesses, for example in relation to making transparent cost and environmental savings from the reduction of waste. The provision of monetary and physical information to management and external stakeholders about the environmental impacts of business and the financial consequences of environmentally relevant business activities is expressed by the term 'corporate environmental accounting' (Schaltegger and Burritt 2000).

Environmental management accounting (EMA) information is available for use by corporate decision-makers to reduce environmental impacts and enhance economic performance (Schaltegger and Müller 1997; Burritt *et al.* 2002; IFAC 2005; Wagner and Enzler 2006). Management may also decide to use EMA as the foundation for disclosures to external parties.

Management still has discretion in deciding which environmental issues to recognise, how to measure and what to disclose, but if the accounting system highlights the monetary benefits from certain environmentally helpful activities, no manager would be likely to refuse to take action. Environmental management during the 1990s became an increasingly important issue in financial markets, hitherto a very conservative sector of the world economy as far as environmental issues are concerned. Growth in the socially responsible investment sector adds to this momentum (Kurtz 2008). The importance of environmental accounting for other stakeholders cannot be overestimated either. Management, non-government organisations, shareholders, governments, and other groups are seeking information about the environmental risks and returns from business (Schaltegger, Burritt, and Petersen 2003) – information that environmental accounting systems are designed to capture, track, and report. In the following sections, the functions of conventional accounting and accounting processes are outlined before environmental accounting systems are introduced and differences outlined.

Accounting and purpose-orientated information

To appreciate the significance of EMA it is first necessary to gain an understanding of conventional accounting and why it does not serve managers well in the context of environmental matters. Accounting fulfils a number of functions in an organisation. First, it provides feedback to stakeholders about performance: some stakeholders, such as managers, can be thought of as internal to the business, whereas others, such as shareholders and regulators, are seen as external (see Figure 2.1).

Accounting provides information to managers at all levels to support the decisions that they need to make. This includes decisions such as determining (i) the short-run price of their products, (ii) the mix of products and services to offer customers, and (iii) the quality of products. The making of long-run decisions is also supported by accounting information such as those about capital investment, whether to enter a market, or to close down a business, or a segment of a business.

Directors and managers are accountable to shareholders for the use of corporate resources; they have a position of stewardship over resources entrusted to them. Accounting information provides feedback to internal (e.g. employees) and external stakeholders (e.g. shareholders) about stewardship of these resources. In practice, the distinction between internal and external stakeholders is blurred as managers may own shares or share options – they have both internal and external perspectives on the business.

Second, accounting also acts as a record of organisational memory. It stores knowledge about the organisation, knowledge that can be lost completely if left to reside in the minds of people employed by the business, and knowledge that can be transferred to others in the business. Such knowledge may relate to past customers, the success or failure of products to generate value for the

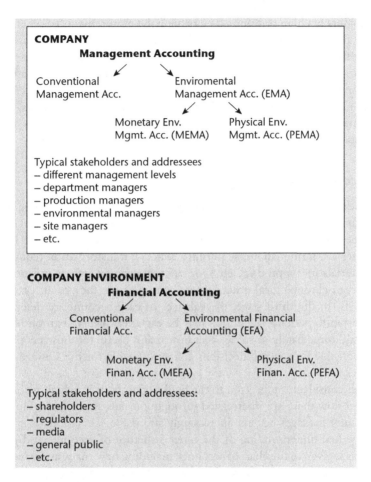

FIGURE 2.1 Accounting systems and stakeholders.

business, or the development of processes within the business that can help protect the environment while improving the financial bottom line. All of this knowledge can be recorded in a formal accounting system.

Finally, accounting also acts as an instrument for tracking where a business has been, where it is at present, and, through extrapolation, where it plans to be in the future (stewardship). It is, in effect, a classification, recording, and reporting device, the product of which can be used by internal and external stakeholders.

Corporate managers make decisions and act in the present, usually guided by their experience and information available to them about the past and present. The aim of their decisions and actions is to achieve objectives that are established for the future of their organisations. Such objectives are usually complex but, for commercial corporations, the pursuit of monetary gain for shareholders is a high priority, as is satisfying the requirements of other stakeholders, particularly compliance with legal requirements (e.g. health, safety and environment legislation) and economic performance. As the future is uncertain, managers need access to all relevant information obtainable at a reasonable cost about alternative courses of action available to them (Chambers 1957: 3). In this context, information provides purpose-orientated data for users, that is, information about how a desired future state might be achieved. If the desired future state relates to sustainability, then accounting has a part to play.

The accounting process

Accounting records data in a logical, rigorous, meticulous way in three stages. In the first stage, the main accounts are identified and classified in a chart of accounts. Second, signs, signals or characteristics of a transaction (e.g. buying raw materials, hiring labour, acquiring a factory), transformation (converting raw materials into a product, etc.), or external events (such as inflation) are recorded in chronological order, generally at the time they occur or shortly afterwards. In the third stage, the balances of each account are determined from period to period. The period may be each year, every six months, each week, day, immediately, or some other time that is useful for those people who are responsible for making decisions and accountable for the stewardship of resources.

Much consideration is given to the books of account in which records are kept, and how these are interrelated through journals and ledgers. However, as computer packages become increasingly affordable, less emphasis is placed on individual understanding of the inner structure of accounts and greater emphasis is given to the chart of accounts, including how many and what types of categories are included, as well as the interpretation of statements that can be derived from account balances at the third stage of the accounting process.

The process of recording accounting data using computers is quite simple and can be undertaken by most people with little training being required, for example through an enterprise resource planning (ERP) system; however, the data gathered change over time as information and knowledge about different issues are considered to be relevant. For example, conventional accounting records monetary information about the financial position and changes in financial position (the financial performance) of the business because the legal system, often through a companies act, requires such information to be collected and disclosed. However, accounting also records other types of information. With the growing importance of environmental issues to business, considerable attention has been given to the need for recording environmental information in the chart of accounts and so some computer packages have been developed to accommodate this need. For example, several providers of

ERP systems have started to integrate energy and carbon accounting in their solution packages. In contrast, the US Environmental Protection Agency developed specific pollution prevention accounting software for conducting financial evaluations of current and potential investments. The German Institute for Standardisation released a technical rule (Publicly Available Specification, PAS 1025) which specifies the data exchange between ERP systems and environmental information systems (Lang, Rey, Wohlgemuth, Genz, and Pawlytsch 2003).

Today, a large number of companies in emerging countries collect, use, and distribute information related to the natural environment. This reflects a fundamental change from two decades ago (see, for example, Gray, Owen, and Adams 1996; Schaltegger and Burritt 2000). There is increasing pressure from stakeholders concerned about the impact of corporate activities on the environment. Also, the costs of environmental impacts have risen substantially, for example through penalties established in new environmental legislation, investments in environmentally benign processes and products encouraged by tighter environmental regulation, and the growing recognition of global environmental problems such as global warming and the reduction of carbon emissions.

Such pressures have led to the emergence of various perceptions of the concept and practices of environmental accounting (for example, Gray, Bebbington, and Walters 1993; Schaltegger and Stinson 1994; EPA 1995; Gray *et al.* 1996; Schaltegger 1996; Burritt 1997; Parker 1999; Schaltegger and Burritt 2000; Lohmann 2009). These perceptions are considered in the following sections.

Conventional corporate accounting

Conventional corporate accounting provides separate information about monetary and physical aspects of the company's activities. Such systems, expressed in monetary units, include:

- financial accounting which serves to provide external corporate stakeholders with information on a regular basis about the company's dated financial position, changes in the financial position for specified periods of time, and cash flow; and
- management accounting (sometimes called managerial accounting) designed to satisfy internal needs of corporate decision-makers about short-term cost and revenue, long-term investments and internal accountability.

Each of these two types of accounting is considered in turn below.

Conventional financial accounting

Financial accounting is the branch of accounting that provides information to people outside the business (Horngren, Foster, and Datar 2000). Such information is gathered, measured, recorded, and reported. The International Accounting Standards Board identifies that '[t]he objective of financial statements is to provide information about the financial position, performance, and changes in the financial position of an enterprise that is useful to a wide range of users in making economic decisions' (IASB 2011: A379). The purpose of financial accounting is to generate financial information about a company in order to provide a basis for transparency and accountable relationships with stakeholders such as shareholders, creditors, investors, and non-government organisations. Financial reporting is used by managers to communicate the dated financial information to external parties. In particular, information reported reflects the financial position and changes in financial position of a company's dated accrual-based information, and additional information considered beneficial for stakeholders to receive, for example the cash balance. Accrual-based accounting is accounting that recognises and records the impact of a business transaction, transformation, or event as it occurs, regardless of whether cash is affected (e.g. purchases on credit). One important aspect of accrual accounting is that it recognises assets and liabilities of the business, unlike cash accounting, which only recognises one asset: cash.

Financial accounts are reported to the public and, hence, there has been considerable discussion and pressure on the accounting profession and business for such information about actual economic performance to be reported in a 'true and fair' way to make sure that similar transactions, transformations, and external events are treated in the same way. The relationship between stakeholders and management is characterised by information asymmetry. Managers have control of the information shareholders require. Furthermore, managers have every incentive to present economic results in the way that most favours themselves. Hence, standard-setting bodies and regulatory agencies have been established to make sure that standard information is supplied to stakeholders by managers in an unbiased way. Professional, independent financial auditors review company accounting books and financial reports on the basis of standards and associated guidance notes and interpretations, thereby maintaining credibility of the reported information and the public reporting process.

Financial accounting and reporting standards have, therefore, a big influence on the type of information collected, analysed, and considered for disclosure by management (for a discussion of the role of standards in facilitating communication, see Blankart and Knieps 1993). This is one reason why it is so important for monetary aspects of environmental issues to be adequately covered in financial accounting standards and conventions. In recent years the importance of external reporting of non-financial information about social, environmental, and governance aspects of a business has received recognition, for example through the development of notions such as broad-based business reporting (ICAA 2008), the European Commission's (2011) public consultation process conducted on disclosure of non-financial information by companies and the integrated reporting initiative (IIRC 2011).

Conventional management accounting

In practice, management accounting provides the foundation for all other accounting systems. The management accounting process has long been recognised as involving 'the identification, measurement, accumulation, analysis, preparation, and interpretation of information that assists executives in fulfilling organizational objectives' (Horngren, Foster, Datar, Rajan, and Ittner 2008: 2). It thus primarily focuses on internal accounting and reporting. Horngren and colleagues (2000: 888) recognise that '[m]anagement accounting measures and reports financial and non-financial information that helps managers make decisions to fulfil the goals of an organization'. Conventional management accounting includes information expressed in physical units such as for production planning which outlines production schedules, inventory and material accounting, and quality management (see IFAC 2009a). Although management accounting has always been concerned with financial and non-financial information, the importance of non-financial matters has changed with the emerging emphasis on social and environmental issues (Burritt et al. 2002).

Conventional management accounting does not normally give explicit, separate recognition to company-related environmental impacts. Instead, it is mainly designed to satisfy the needs of managers seeking information about the economic performance of the company as a basis for decision-making (Burritt et al. 2002). From a pragmatic perspective, the critical test for any accounting system is whether it produces information, such as environmental information, that is useful to stakeholders (e.g. managers) for evaluating their own ends (Chambers 1966; Schaltegger and Burritt 2000). Hence, management accounting systems should be designed to satisfy the fact that different managers may require different information, including different information about the environment – as moral or external pressure mounts on managers to comply with tighter environmental legislation and to be aware of corporate environmental impacts on stakeholders (Schaltegger and Burritt 2000). For example, senior managers may be interested in monetary information that shows material effects on shareholder value, including environmentally related impacts on the economic situation of companies. Corporate environment managers (see Parker 1999), on the other hand, may be interested in various waste and pollution figures expressed in physical units, such as CO_2 emissions, and generally have no direct interest in whether the costs of pollution abatement or waste reduction measures are capitalised or considered as expenses in the monetary account.

The main stakeholders in management accounting hold different management positions (e.g. top, product, and site managers). Because it provides internal information, management accounting and accounts are subject to almost no external regulation. The United States is one exception where a series of cost accounting standards have been introduced to guide, for example, ways of linking costs to transactions made between the government and the private sector. The intention is to stop management loading up onto government contracts costs associated with conducting commercial business, especially in industries such as defence where contracts are for very large amounts of money.

Environmental accounting

The main difference between conventional and environmental accounting is that the latter specifically identifies, measures, analyses, and interprets information about environmental aspects of company activities. Within the conventional approach this distinction is somewhat unclear. Yet, if environmental information is potentially important, differences in the units of measurement, data quality, and sources cannot simply be neglected if purpose-orientated information is to be provided for different managers. There is a wide consensus that there are two main groups of environmental impacts related to company activities (Schaltegger and Burritt 2000: 58): environmentally related impacts on the economic situation of companies, and company-related impacts on environmental systems.

Environmentally related impacts on economic systems are reflected through monetary environmental information (Figure 2.2). Monetary environmental information addresses all company-related impacts on its past, present, or future financial stocks and flows, and is expressed in monetary units (e.g. measures expressed in expenditure on cleaner production, cost of fines for breaching environmental laws, monetary values of environmental assets). Monetary environmental accounting systems can be considered as a broadening of the scope, or a further development or refinement, of conventional accounting in monetary units as they are based on the methods of conventional accounting systems.

Related impacts of corporate activities on environmental systems are reflected in physical environmental information, thus enlarging the conventional accounting perspective (see Figure 2.2). Thus, at the corporate level, physical environmental information includes all past, present, and future material and energy amounts that have an impact on the environment. Physical environmental information is always expressed in physical units, such as tonnes, kilograms, cubic metres, or joules (e.g. tonnes of carbon dioxide

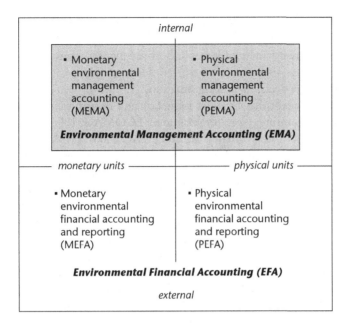

FIGURE 2.2 Environmental accounting systems (modified from Bartolomeo, Bennett, Bouma, Heydkamp, James, and Wolters 2000: 33).

equivalent emissions, kilograms of material per customer served, joules of energy used per unit of product).

Hence, incorporation of environmental information in accounting systems leads to the need for development of comprehensive environmental accounting systems. These can be divided in two: EMA and external monetary and physical environmental financial accounting (EFA) (Figure 2.2). EFA is not of primary concern for this book and so attention now turns to EMA (but links to external uses of EMA information will be discussed in a few case studies).

Environmental management accounting: framework and tools

Environmental management accounting (EMA) is 'the management of environmental and economic performance through the development and implementation of appropriate environment-related accounting systems and practices' (IFAC 1998: para. 1). It identifies, collects, analyses, and uses two types of information: physical information on the flows, stocks, and conversion of materials and energy, and environmentally induced monetary information (UNDSD 2001). EMA supports companies in analysing and improving environmental and economic performance and also links these two types of performance by identifying win–win situations, that is, improvements and innovations that lead to less environmental impact and increased competitiveness simultaneously (Schaltegger and Burritt 2000). Corporate decisions are made on a great variety of issues and, consequently, many different managers and business functions are involved. Hence, various tools are required depending on the decision-making situation.

EMA is a concept that includes monetary and non-monetary approaches to internal accounting (see, for example, ECOMAC 1996; Bennett and James 1998; IFAC 1998; Burritt *et al.* 2002; IFAC 2005). EMA can be defined as a generic term that includes both monetary environmental management accounting (MEMA) and physical environmental management accounting (PEMA) (see Figure 2.2). The United Nations Division for Sustainable Development launched an initiative to support governments in promoting EMA (Schaltegger, Hahn, and Burritt 2001). The initiative was later taken up by the International Federation of Accountants (IFAC 2005), which produced detailed guidance for organisations wishing to introduce EMA. IFAC (2009a) has also integrated aspects of EMA (the internal management perspective) into its broader sustainability framework. Hence, when dealing with carbon emissions, IFAC (2009b) suggests professional accountants should understand (i) its strategic importance for the organisation, (ii) the internal management and measurement perspective, (iii) the external reporting of carbon emissions, and (iv) engagement with wider stakeholders in considering an organisation's long-term carbon footprint.

MEMA deals with environmental aspects of corporate activities expressed in monetary units and generates information for internal management use (e.g. costs of fines for breaking environmental laws and investment in capital projects that improve the environment). In terms of its methods, MEMA is based on conventional management accounting that is extended and adapted for environmental aspects of company activities. It is the central, pervasive tool providing, as it does, the basis for most internal management decisions, as well as addressing the issue of how to track, trace, and treat costs and revenues that are incurred because of the company's impact on the environment (Schaltegger and Burritt 2000: 59). MEMA contributes to strategic and operational planning, provides the main basis for decisions about how to achieve desired goals or targets, and acts as a control and accountability device (Schaltegger and Burritt 2000: 90). MEMA also can be adapted to conventional management accounting systems as explained by IFAC (2009b). Environmental costs can be better understood through different costing systems such as (i) activity-based costing (ABC), activity-based management and activity-based budgeting (see Burritt and Schaltegger 2001), or alternatives such as resource consumption accounting, (ii) environment/life cycle design and/or life cycle assessment/life cycle costing, or (iii) full cost accounting (IFAC 2009a).

PEMA also serves as an information tool for internal management decisions. However, in contrast with MEMA it focuses on a company's impact on the natural environment, expressed in terms of physical units such as kilograms. PEMA tools are designed to collect environmental performance and impact information in physical units for internal use by management (Schaltegger and Burritt 2000: 61–63). According to Schaltegger and Burritt (2000: 261), PEMA as an internal environmental accounting approach serves as:

- an analytical tool designed to detect ecological strengths and weaknesses;
- a decision-support technique concerned with highlighting relative environmental quality;
- a measurement tool that is an integral part of other environmental measures such as eco-efficiency;
- a tool for direct and indirect control of environmental consequences;
- an accountability tool providing a neutral and transparent base for internal and, indirectly, external communication; and
- a tool with a close and complementary fit to the set of tools being developed to help promote ecologically sustainable development.

Relevance and benefits of EMA

Environmental issues increasingly influence the economic performance of companies and organisations. Growth in environmental regulations, rising costs of electricity, fuel, and raw materials, the demand for environmental information by investors, and requirements of business and private customers for environmentally benign products provide several important examples. Thus, managers need to incorporate environmental considerations into their regular decision-making activities and processes. The financial impact of environmentally-related decisions is often underestimated or not even considered at all (e.g. Burritt, Schaltegger, and Zvezdov 2010). One main reason is the lack of adequate information. Through conventional accounting processes, environmental costs are often hidden as part of overhead costs and are not, or at best only inaccurately, related to products, processes, and activities. A popular way to illustrate this is with the picture of an iceberg in which most environmental costs are hidden under the water line. Furthermore, conventional accounting does not consider environmental impacts as long as they have no immediate financial consequences or regulators require them to be taken into consideration. For instance, the impact of a company's air emissions on the health of neighbouring communities might not be accounted for at all until it suddenly leads to problems with those communities and authorities.

EMA addresses these inadequacies. It provides tools and methods to help managers assess the impact of measures taken to improve both corporate financial and environmental performance. EMA can systematically integrate environmental aspects of the corporation into management accounting and decision-making processes. In particular, it helps to reveal financial benefits and potential cost savings that can be gained from addressing environmental considerations facing the business. At the same time, it highlights and quantifies the environmental benefits and improvements from such measures.

The importance of EMA for businesses is widely acknowledged. As mentioned above, since the 1990s IFAC has promoted EMA and has published international guidelines on EMA (IFAC 2005) as part of its approach to sustainability accounting (IFAC 2009a,c). Such documentation emphasises the inclusion of adequate material and energy flow information into cost accounting. This is also reflected in the International Organization for Standardization (ISO) efforts to standardise the material flow-based cost accounting approach as ISO 14051 on material flow cost accounting (MFCA) (Kokubu, Campos, Furukawa, and Tachikawa 2009). Most case studies on EMA focus on these specific EMA applications too, but some also highlight other important areas and applications of EMA such as its link to life cycle analysis, strategic planning, or budgeting (for instance, Bennett, Bouma, and Wolters 2002; Bennett, Rikhardsson, and Schaltegger 2003; Rikhardsson, Bennett, Bouma, and Schaltegger 2005; Schaltegger, Bennett, and Burritt 2006; Schaltegger, Bennett, Burritt, and Jasch 2008 for a wide collection of EMA case studies; Burritt 2004 for an overview of EMA challenges beyond MFCA).

Conceptual framework for EMA

Burritt and colleagues (2002) develop a framework for EMA which classifies different EMA tools, such as environmental investment appraisal, environmental cost accounting, or life cycle costing, according to the associated decision-making situation. The EMA framework provides a basis for managers and other decision-makers to choose an appropriate tool depending on their particular concern and objective.

Figure 2.3 categorises these EMA systems according to two dimensions: monetary versus physical. Different types of managers rely on and have their performance assessed using either physical, or monetary, or both types of information. For example, managers in the corporate environmental department have various goals including:

- identifying environmental improvement opportunities;
- prioritising environmental actions and measures;
- environmental differentiation in product pricing, mix, and development decisions;
- transparency about environmentally relevant corporate activities;
- meeting the claims and information demands of critical environmental stakeholders, to ensure resource provision and access; and

		Monetary EMA		Physical EMA	
		Short-term	Long-term	Short-term	Long-term
Past-oriented	Routinely generated	Environmental cost accounting [1]	Environment-induced capital expenditure and revenue [2]	Material and energy flow accounting [9]	Environmental capital impact accounting [10]
Past-oriented	Ad hoc	Ex-post assessment of relevant environmental costing decisions [3]	Ex-post inventory assessment of projects (including life cycle costing-LCC) [4]	Ex-post assessment of short-term environmental impacts [11]	Ex-post inventory appraisal of physical environmental investments (including life cycle assessment-LCA) [12]
Future-oriented	Routinely generated	Monetary environmental budgeting [5]	Environmental long-term financial planning [6]	Physical environmental budgeting [13]	Environmental long-term physical planning [14]
Future-oriented	Ad hoc	Relevant environmental costing [7]	Monetary environmental investment appraisal [8]	Tools designed to predict relevant environmental impacts [15]	Physical environmental investment appraisal [16]

FIGURE 2.3 Environmental management accounting (EMA) decision settings and tools (based on Burritt *et al.* 2002).

- justifying environmental management division and environmental protection measures.

Three additional dimensions of EMA decision settings are important:

- Time frame being addressed in the decision setting: does the decision require information concerning the past (e.g. the material flow records of last month) or does it require future-orientated information (e.g. predicted cost savings caused by a potential cleaner production measure)?
- Length of time frame: does the decision setting involve information concerning several years (long-term, often strategic focus) or does it cover a few months, weeks, days only (short-term, often operational focus)?
- Routineness of information provision: is the required information gathered regularly or does it have to be collected ad hoc, for this single instance only?

Different managers have different time frames and demands for routine or ad hoc information. For example, senior managers tend to have a longer time frame and need ad hoc information for critical decisions. In consequence, a wide range of EMA tools is available. Each tool is likely to be of use to different managers, given their particular level in the business and their own specialisation. A group of tools is illustrated in Figure 2.3. The framework provides guidance about tools available to support a range of decisions:

- product and production managers taking green opportunities when these are available;
- eco-efficiency improvements that reduce the volume of environmentally harmful materials used;
- use of environmental performance indicators to appraise staff;
- the extent of subsidies from government that are environmentally damaging and which may be removed in the future;
- potential corporate impacts of environmental taxes and tightening regulations, designed to bring corporations closer to tracking the full cost of their activities;
- divisional impacts on environmental capital such as biodiversity, land, water, and air quality; and
- corporate impacts on the goal of sustainable society.

The following section aims to give an overview of the major EMA tools presented in the EMA framework in Figure 2.3.

Decision settings and tools of the EMA framework

Decision settings and related tools can be conveniently classified into four groupings representing: past-orientated, routinely generated information; past-orientated, ad hoc information; future-orientated, routinely generated information; and future-orientated, ad hoc information. Each of these four groupings is examined below. An overview is provided in Figure 2.3.

Past-orientated, routine information

Routine approaches include tools for monetary as well as physical environmental management accounting (MEMA and PEMA) which are applied on a regular basis. EMA tools can be based either on monetary or on physical data (the box numbers in the following list refer to the box numbers in Figure 2.3).

MEMA tools

Box 1. Environmental cost accounting as considered in the context of corporate management helps in the planning, management and control of operations (Schaltegger and Burritt 2000; Bebbington, Gray, Hibbitt, and Kirk 2001; Howes 2002; IFAC 2005; Jasch 2009). Cost accounting is past-orientated and has a short-term focus. In the past decade a number of important conceptual developments have taken place in the field of environmental cost accounting (Schaltegger and Müller 1997; Fichter, Loew, and Seidel 1997; Bennett *et al.* 2002; IFAC 2005; Jasch 2009; IFAC 2009c). These include, for example, the use of variable costing, absorption costing, activity-based, and resource consumption costing methods. Generally, the different approaches to environmental cost accounting can be classified based on the definition of environmental costs and the accounting method adopted (e.g. full cost accounting, direct costing, or process costing) (Schaltegger and Burritt 2000).

One possible system for addressing environmental cost accounting is the application of a form of process costing. Process costing is also often referred to as ABC or activity-based accounting. When using the term 'process costing', the cost object is usually a specific technical process or process step, whereas, with activity-based costing/accounting, the cost object tends to be the activity being undertaken by individual employees, groups of employees, machines, or computers, but the essential ideas behind both are the same. ABC focuses on costing activities and then allocating the cost of activities to products on the basis of the individual product's demand for those activities (Horvath and Mayer 1989; Parker 1999). One specific variant of process costing is that of MFCA (see Kokubu *et al.* 2009). The approach is also known under different names such as material flow-orientated ABC (see, for example, Schaltegger and Burritt 2000), material flow-orientated process costing, internal environmental accounting, flow cost accounting (see, for example, Jasch 2009), flow-orientated environmental accounting, resource efficiency accounting, and environmentally orientated process cost accounting. One of the main advantages of using activity-based costing to assess environmental costs – apart from the advantages concerning environmental full cost accounting (Bebbington *et al.* 2001) – is the integration of environmental cost accounting into the strategic management process and its link to management objectives and activities.

Example: The production manager's continuous search for efficiency gains and productivity increases is supported by quarterly reports on environmental costs and revenues provided by the accounting department.

Box 2. Environmentally induced capital expenditure and revenues represent routinely generated information with a long-term focus which is past-orientated (Schaltegger *et al.* 2001). By definition environmentally induced capital expenditure and revenues are part of MEMA. Environmentally induced revenues can stem from the sale of recyclables or higher contribution margins of eco-products, whereas environmentally induced costs can be seen as internal costs (including opportunity costs) of a business, the economic costs, or all costs to society, including external costs (Schaltegger and Burritt 2000). Environmental expenses are environmentally related costs that have provided a benefit that has now expired (Schaltegger and Burritt 2000). Such expenses are matched against revenues in the profit-and-loss account (income account or statement of financial performance). This information is also of relevance for financial accounting. Despite the magnitude of environmental expenses in many industries (see, for example, Fichter *et al.* 1997), no financial accounting standard requires their separate recognition, although company law does lay down some disclosure rules (e.g. in Australia under s. 215 of the Corporations Act 2001). Environmental issues are clearly part of the risk structure of a company (Burritt 2005) and, where important, should be disclosed separately if environmentally induced financial risks are to be made transparent, for example for investors (EU 2003).

Example: for each financial year expired, the Chief Financial Officer assesses the contribution of the company's environmental assets (end of pipe facilities such as the wastewater treatment plant, energy efficiency equipment such as heat exchangers, rejects reprocessing units, etc.) to the overall business success in terms of raw material and energy expenses, reduced legal expenses and liabilities, and additional revenues of less polluting products. This environmental return on assets serves as basis for budgeting and capital expense-related decisions.

PEMA tools

One important reason for management to apply PEMA tools is that monetary approaches to EMA often depend on prior physical information about material, energy, waste, and emission flows. Some managers only seek out physical information for their activities, for example environmental managers with a responsibility to check that the company complies with environmental legislation which requires movement of particular chemicals to be tracked. Research and development managers may also need physical environmental information to support innovation management processes, for example when they are developing new products or processes. Other managers need physical information in order to place a monetary value on it, such as a carbon manager seeking to predict the expected loss for selling carbon credits because the company has emitted larger volumes of CO_2 equivalents than permitted by regulation.

Box 9. Material and energy flow accounting can be defined in general as accounts in physical units (usually in terms of kg or tonnes, and kWh) which comprise the extraction, production, transformation, consumption, recycling, and disposal phases of materials, a number of material flow-accounting activities at the level of plants or businesses, and the generation, transformation, use, and recycling of energy (Liedtke, Manstein, Bellendorf, and Kranendonk 1994). Material and energy flow accounting (IFAC 2005; Wagner and Enzler 2006; Jasch 2009) is a widely used and well-known approach in comparison with some other PEMA tools. Material and energy flow charts are commonly used to depict a production system, product life cycle, and so forth. For each process or step within these flow charts, input/output tables are derived which aim at balancing the physical inputs and outputs and explain the material and energy transformation which occurs in that particular process. This approach enables a detailed view and analysis of drivers of material and energy flow-related performance and replaces an environmental black-box perspective of a company or production line, where only total inputs and outputs are known and treated like overheads.

Material and energy flow accounting is past-orientated, that is, it focuses on material and energy flows that took place in the past. It is also short-term, in that it focuses on short-term impacts on the environment at the product, site, division, and company levels (see, for example, Schaltegger and Burritt 2000). In its original sense, material and energy flow accounting is a routine activity, therefore generating regular information. When introduced, the approach mostly relates to projects; however, this changes to routine use once it is established in the company. Depending on national and international laws, the accounting for certain hazardous and harmful materials and substances is a legal requirement.

Example: The maintenance team is monitoring machinery-specific energy consumption and rejects on a daily basis to detect problems in a timely way.

Box 10. A complement to material and energy-flow accounting is environmental (or natural) capital impact accounting. Capital can be viewed as a stock that provides a flow of valuable goods or services into the future. Natural capital is, then, the stock of natural ecosystems that provides a flow of valuable ecosystem goods or services into the future. An example is fish stocks in the ocean which provide a flow of new fish which can be sustained. Long-term sustainable development is seen to depend upon the maintenance of natural capital, hence environmental capital impact accounting is a tool with a long-term focus. However, it still is past-orientated and is based on physical measures (i.e. it remains part of physical environmental management accounting). It also generates information in a routine way. At the organisational level natural capital refers to the natural resources (energy and matter) and processes needed to produce products and deliver services (Forum for the Future 2003: 8). These resources include sinks that absorb, neutralise, or recycle wastes; resources, some of which are renewable (e.g. timber, grain, fish, and water), whereas others are not (e.g. fossil fuels); and processes, such as climate regulation and the carbon cycle, which enable life to continue in a balanced and healthy way.

Environmental capital impact accounting assesses the damage to ecological capital. Maintenance of natural capital is seen by supporters of strong sustainability as being the minimum acceptable position, whereas proponents of weak sustainability accept the possibility of substitution between human-made and natural capital and therefore a reduction in natural capital as acceptable (Ekins, Simon, Deutsch, Folke, and De Groot 2003). However, companies concerned about natural capital impact accounting will manage their impacts on natural capital in line with company environmental policy to, as a minimum, maintain such capital or to, say, reduce waste to zero and minimise their ecological footprint. The alternative but less credible position is to destroy natural capital and argue the case for human capital substitution (Schaltegger and Burritt 2000). A list of natural capital impact accounting matters is outlined by Forum for the Future (2003) and includes:

- substitute abundant minerals for those that are scarce in nature;
- ensure that all mined materials are used efficiently within cyclic systems, systematically reduce dependence on fossil fuels and use renewable resources instead;
- eliminate the accumulation of human-made substances and products in nature – substitute all persistent and unnatural compounds with substances that can be easily assimilated by natural systems;
- eliminate waste, re-use, recycle, or re-manufacture where possible;
- prevent the physical degradation of nature and protect and enhance biodiversity and ecosystem functions;
- draw renewable resources only from well-managed ecosystems that restore themselves;
- systematically pursue the most productive and efficient use of resources and land;
- adopt the precautionary principle in any situation that may result in the modification of nature; and
- limit and reduce over time the use of substances extracted from the Earth's crust.

Example: The head of a textile company's purchasing department is examining a time series of past results about the company's environmental impacts, in particular resource and water depletion. The benchmark is part of a decision whether or not to become a member of a local organisation called 'Water Watch' aiming to monitor long-term supplies of drinkable water from a river used by the company.

Past-orientated, ad hoc information

Ad hoc approaches include tools for monetary as well as physical environmental management accounting that are applied in specific situations or cases.

MEMA tools

Box 3. Ex-post assessment of relevant environmental costing decisions is a monetary calculation made in relation to environmental costs after they have been incurred. Ex-post analysis is carried out after the production of goods or services. This allows management to make use of a revised monetary calculation in relation to material and energy flow costs based on the actual costs incurred (Schaltegger *et al.* 2003; Burritt, Herzig, and Tadeo 2009). An ex-post calculation exercise also provides a valuable basis for calculations of future environmental costs for short-term decision-making. Carrying out ex-post calculation exercises or product-costing analyses focussing on environmental costs is a short-term exercise for the purpose of assessing the success of previous ad hoc decisions (e.g. green product mix, special orders, and short-term outsourcing costing exercises).

Example: The product manager is checking last month's sales to decide whether to continue the new marketing campaign for a certain product that highlights the environmental friendliness of this product in the mix.

Box 4. Ex-post inventory appraisal of physical environmental investments such as life cycle costing is a method in which all costs of a product (or a process or activity) throughout its lifetime, from raw material acquisition to disposal, are identified (Hunkeler, Lichtenvort, and Rebitzer 2008; see also Schaltegger and Burritt 2000). Life cycle costing can focus on internal costs, or it can attempt to consider both internal and external costs of a business. In both cases, it attempts to measure the costs of a product or process during its life-time in monetary terms. In contrast to conventional life cycle costing, which is mainly interested in the monetary gain of a product or process during its life cycle, environmental life cycle costing aims at making transparent all life cycle-related costs including those to be borne by society. Another tool which falls under this category is ex-post assessment of individual investments. It also links with the life cycle notion.

Example: The Chief Financial Officer is demanding a report on the actual annual revenues from the three-year-old wind power station in order to approve or reject the environmental department's plans to construct a second station.

PEMA tools

Box 11. Ex-post assessment of short-term environmental impacts is the physical equivalent of a monetary ex-post calculation exercise (see above regarding ex-post assessment of relevant environmental costing decisions). It is expressed in physical terms, and is past-orientated, since it is carried out ex-post. Also it is short-term, since it focuses on short-term environmental impacts, for example of a site or a product.

Example: The legal department wants to know whether last month's small oil spill caused any damage to the nearby lake.

Box 12. Ex-post inventory appraisal of physical environmental investments such as life cycle assessment (LCA) as defined in ISO 14040/44 is the key tool that produces physical ad hoc information about products and projects. Where LCA is carried out ex-post (e.g. after a product has already been introduced to the market), it is past-orientated. In this sense it is the equivalent of monetary post-investment assessment (i.e. it is a form of physical environmental post-investment appraisal). Even though it is applied ex-post, LCA is long-term in the sense that it addresses long-term environmental impacts, rather than having an orientation towards short-term impacts. Often, major environmental impacts occur outside the boundaries of a business. Giving recognition to these external effects is not accepted within conventional management and accounting philosophies as long as the costs of such environmental impacts need not be borne by the firm.

Example: To synthesise their basic intermediate, a chemical company can apply diverse methods involving different processes and raw materials. The process manager wants to know which method is the least environmental harmful one.

Future-orientated, regular information

MEMA tools

Box 5. Monetary environmental (operational and capital) budgeting present another important approach of EMA. A budget can be defined as a quantitative expression of a proposed plan of action by management for a future time period and aids to its coordination and implementation (Horngren *et al.* 2008). In practice, corporate budgets are used for a number of purposes, such as assisting in achieving a firm's business objectives, authorising managers to spend defined amounts of money in a specified period of time, forecasting events over which no control is exercised, or making an attempt to affect factors which are open to influence and control. Monetary environmental operational budgeting (focussing on material and energy flows) and monetary environmental capital budgeting (concentrating on corresponding stocks of energy and materials) are two complementary instruments that 'encourage a proactive use of budgetary control that is based on a management philosophy designed to eliminate adverse corporate environmental effects' (Burritt and Schaltegger 2001: 164). Both instruments are future-orientated (as they focus on future costs) and short-term (since they relate to defined time horizons corresponding to the chosen budget period). Standard environmental costing, which complements operational budgeting in production, can be used to provide information for short-term planning.

Example: Based on MFCA assessment results which revealed high waste-related costs, the plant manager provides next year's budget for expenditure on employee training about waste reduction and energy efficiency.

Box 6. Environmental long-term financial planning is by definition future-orientated. It is especially concerned with future environmental costs and cost savings. Based on the general definition of environmental costs as costs intended to protect the environment, some authors propose that potential or future costs should also be assessed (Schaltegger and Burritt 2000). Since an important use of management accounting information is to assist planning for the future, extending environmental costing approaches to include financial planning is, therefore, a natural process for full cost, direct cost and activity-based approaches because the future consequences for the environment are required to be taken into account if managers use these methods. Apart from the pros and cons mentioned above, any consideration of future consequences faces quite substantial problems when trying to estimate future costs and cost savings. Estimation of the future costs of pollution prevention and environmental liabilities is particularly difficult as neither future technologies nor future demands of stakeholder groups are known.

Example: Based on forecasts of energy and raw material scarcity and development of prices for the next 10 years, the production planning department regularly revises projections on the layout, capacities, and costs of its pharmaceutical processing network including heat-exchanging and waste separation devices.

PEMA tools

Box 13. Physical environmental budgeting is based on material and energy flow activities and expressed in physical units (Schaltegger and Burritt 2000). The material and energy flow activities are abstracted in environmental resources or issues, such as climate stability, land, or water, which are broken down to environmental indicators (ICLEI 2003). Whereas materials and energy flow accounting as well as environmental capital impact accounting are instruments orientated towards the past, physical environmental budgeting of flows and stocks is a future-orientated short-term tool that is routinely applied to generate information.

Physical environmental budgeting aims to provide a framework for managing natural resources. It is a tool with great relevance to the management of natural resources and to the saving of natural resources because it tries to assess the total environmental impact during the budget period (ICLEI 2003). As budgets are prepared, limits are defined for environmental impacts such as CO_2 emissions. The aim is budgeting to achieve the short-run physical environmental targets of an organisation (ICLEI 2003).

Example: To achieve the company's annual environmental targets, the environmental managers arrange quarterly meetings where managers from all relevant departments agree upon the maximum limits for their energy consumption, carbon emissions, and waste generation in the quarter ahead.

Box 14. Environmental long-term physical environmental planning comentments environmental impact capital accounting (Box 10) by estimating future impacts and links with decisions to reduce or control such impacts in the future.

Example: The finance, research and development, environmental, and production planning managers retreat to simulate the CEO's vision of a zero-emission plant within five years.

Future-orientated, ad hoc information

MEMA tools

Box 7. Relevant environmental costing provides information on future costs and revenues of short-term measures. This includes the estimated costs of special orders (e.g. job costing) as well as the simulation of product mix choices under capacity constraints.

Example: A printing plant's customer would like its catalogue printed on Forest Stewardship Council-approved paper without using ink that contains high levels of volatile organic compounds (VOCs cause health as well as environmental impacts). The printing plant's sales manager has to derive a price for this special order.

Box 8. Monetary environmental (project) investment appraisal, environmental life cycle budgeting, and target pricing are three tools developed to address corporate environmental issues in a future-orientated manner and with a long-term focus. The basic idea of target pricing is to determine a target price for which effective demand exists in the market and then, on the basis of this, to find the acceptable maximum costs of the product. Applied to environmental costs this means that the acceptable future price for a product would be established and then (after deducting an appropriate profit margin and other relevant costs) the maximum acceptable environmental costs would be determined. Given the need for acceptable margins, new product development would then have to take account of this maximum cost level when designing, producing, and disposing of the product, in other words the product would have to be designed and manufactured in a way that the maximum acceptable level of environmental costs would not be exceeded. As with any investment appraisal, monetary environmental investment appraisal has the basic goal of calculating the net effect of the costs and benefits of different investment alternatives. In doing so it has a particular focus on environmental costs including quantifiable environmental benefits caused by cost savings (Schaltegger and Burritt 2000). Although calculation of direct costs forms a necessary part of any method of investment appraisal, environmentally related costs are sometimes hidden in the general overhead costs of a business and therefore may not be separately considered. Nevertheless, these costs can significantly affect the cost structure and thus the profitability of an investment. Another aspect of monetary environmental project investment appraisal is to extend the time horizon and use long-term financial indicators, since environmental investments often have longer payback periods than other investments. Calculation of long-term financial indicators such as net present value and option value can help managers to consider future financial impacts induced by environmental impacts.

Example: The engineer in charge of utilities suggests investing in a device to convert exhaust heat into electric power, a so-called organic Rankine cycle. An alternative option would be the purchase of a less expensive heat exchanger to heat the office building during the cold months of the year. The plant managers compare both options in terms of payback and net present value.

PEMA tools

Box 15. Tools designed to predict relevant (physical) environmental impacts are very similar to those used in ex-post assessment of short-term environmental impacts of, for example, a site or a product. Both are based on physical calculations and are therefore part of physical environmental management accounting. Both have a short-term focus (e.g. they provide a projection or assessment of environmental impacts given short-run constraints on the company's activities). However, there is a crucial difference in scope. Whereas the assessment of short-term environmental impacts is ex-post, the assessment of relevant environmental impacts is ex-ante, that is, it is future-orientated. This means it focuses on the short-term environmental impacts of future activities of the business.

Example: The environmental managers need to decide whether to use the budget for replacing all old light bulbs on energy-saving ones or on an automatic switch-off device for the assembly line when it is not used. They want to know which option is more beneficial in terms of energy saving and global warming contribution.

Box 16. The same tools (LCA and environmental investment assessment) used for ex-post physical environmental investment appraisal are used for long-term, future-orientated physical environmental investment assessment in physical terms. The introduction of an effective environmental information system is a precondition for the success of any reform in this area, which is why several authors have called for a survey of all discharges over the whole life cycle of products (Fava, Denison, Jones, Curran, Vigon, Selke, and Barnum 1991; Fava, Jensen, Pomper, De Smet, Warren, and Vignon 1992; Environment Canada 1995; Lave, Cobas-Flores, Henderson, and McMichael 1995). LCA is considered to be one of the most promising tools for such a survey (see, for example, Pidgeon and Brown 1994) since it takes a broad view of product life cycles and largely corresponds with the philosophy of deep greens (see, for example, Maunders and Burritt 1991). LCA basically calculates environmental impacts in physical terms. Future-orientated LCA, like environmental investment appraisal, is carried out ex-ante (e.g. during new product development, but before the product is introduced to the market). A number of environmental considerations have been proposed for incorporation into ex-ante environmental investment appraisal (see, for example, Schaltegger and Burritt 2000), including expansion of the cost inventory, comprehensive allocation of impacts, extension of the time horizon and the use of long-term environmental indicators.

Example: The research and development department has developed a new insulation material that consists of several renewable materials. To demonstrate its superiority the department compares the environmental impacts of the material's production and disposal with the environmental benefits, in particular energy savings, of its use phase.

The cases examined in this research book provide an opportunity to shed light on the role and use of the 16 boxes (tools) introduced above. In the next section, the prerequisites for a comparative case study in South-East Asian companies are introduced.

Usefulness of EMA information in the South-East Asian context

South-East Asia is known for its part in economic expansion of the region. In parallel, the region also is associated with an environmental crisis that is partly associated with the rapid economic expansion of industry and population. This chapter continues with an examination of (i) the economic growth and environmental crisis in South-East Asia, (ii) the role of EMA in the South-East Asian context, and (iii) the purpose of investigating the application of EMA through a comparative case study of 12 companies in four countries in South-East Asia: Indonesia, the Philippines, Thailand, and Vietnam.

Economic and environmental importance of South-East Asia

The South-East Asian region is home of some of the fastest-growing economies in the world (McDonald, Robinson, and Thierfelder 2008). In spite of the Asian financial crisis in 1997, many countries have shown significant annual gross domestic product (GDP) growth rates in recent years (UNESCAP 2006; CIA 2010). Rapid economic growth has been fuelled by the Asian region's rising status as a global production centre (UNESCAP 2006).

Accompanying economic growth has been an increase in energy consumption, volume of traffic, and disposal of waste; hence the South-East Asian region is also characterised by increasing environmental problems (Bryant and Parnwell 1996). Industrial activities with potentially negative environmental impacts include rapidly growing, highly polluting industries, such as the manufacture of transport equipment, crude steel, chemicals, petroleum, rubber, and plastic products (UNESCAP 2006). Economic dependency on energy is increasing in the Philippines, Thailand, and Indonesia, since the amount of energy to produce one unit of GDP rose between 1990 and 2002 (Balce, Tjaroko, and Zamora 2003; UN 2005; UNESCAP 2006). Electricity demand is expected to more than quadruple between 2000 and 2020. Energy-intensive sub-sectors in South-East Asia have experienced one of the fastest growth rates in per capita energy consumption worldwide, which, inter alia, is responsible for rising air pollution loads (UNESCAP 2006) and has implications for global warming. Absolute CO_2 emissions have grown rapidly on a per capita basis from 1990 to 2006, although per capita CO_2 emissions in the Philippines and Indonesia have declined slightly (UNSD 2006). Meanwhile Indonesian and Vietnamese business depends heavily on the exploitation of natural resources including oil and gas, plywood, mining, chemical fertilisers, rubber, and palm oil as main exports (CIA 2010). UNESCAP (2006) considers the extraction and processing of raw materials as inputs to manufacturing as one of the main sources of pressure on environmental resources. Finally, agriculture and aquaculture remain important pillars of the national economies in South-East Asia for domestic consumption and exports (UNESCAP 2006), but these industries have their own unique environmental and biodiversity problems. In short, economic expansion goes hand in hand with environmental problems associated with increasing demand for natural resources and land, an increase in manufacturing processes, energy, and water consumption.

Further environmental impacts are caused by poverty in the South-East Asian region: 670 million people live on less than US$1 per day and lack food to meet their daily needs (UN 2005). Increasing pressure is being placed on the limited carrying capacity of ecosystems (UNESCAP 2006). Income inequality has risen or remained high in countries such as Thailand and the Philippines (World Bank 2006) because economic growth is not shared equally among the population. Poverty remains a fundamental problem in some regions, for example in Indonesia, where the incidence of poverty ranges from 1.3 per cent of the population in Jakarta to 46 per cent in West Nusa Tenggara (Chowdhury and Islam 2001).

On the basis of environmental footprint measures, the region is already living above its environmental means and environmental sustainability is at serious risk (UNESCAP 2006; Global Footprint Network 2010). Clapp and Dauvergne (2003: 19) state that a 'decade of rapid economic growth with few environmental safeguards left South-East Asia as one of the most polluted and degraded regions in the world'. Decoupling environmental impacts from economic growth, a prerequisite for sustainable development (von Weizsäcker, Lovins, and Lovins 1997), seems to be a distant prospect as 'incremental improvements in environmental regulatory policy typically have been over-ridden by the scale effects of increased production, consumption and resource use' (Angel and Rock 2003: 4).

Environmental and social impacts of companies in the region are likely to increase further if the relationship between corporate environmental and financial performance is either not known or not taken into account in decision-making processes. To improve company awareness, and to enable companies to reduce their environmental impacts and create financial benefits from environmental measures, consideration needs to be given to the gathering and generation of physical environmental information and environment-related financial information through EMA.

Usefulness of EMA information

EMA is designed to identify and measure the benefits related to economic and environmental effects of corporate activities and increase transparency to decision-makers in the company (Schaltegger and Burritt 2000; Burritt *et al.* 2002). The voluntary application of EMA tools makes information on environmental and environment-related financial performance available to decision-makers.

As described above, EMA has two particular strengths: (i) EMA tools provide the opportunity to analyse environmental impacts of the company on the natural environment, and (ii) EMA provides information to help managers become aware and address environmentally driven monetary impacts on the company. EMA supports contextual integration by combining ecological effectiveness and efficiency with economic performance (e.g. Schaltegger 1998). By doing so, EMA can help avoid the situation where environmental responsibilities are placed in separate organisational 'silos', leading to inadequate attention being given to the identification of complementarities and conflicts with other organisational activities and parts of the organisation. EMA helps overcome such a silo mentality, which, if unchecked, can lead to a total or partial failure to address environmental issues. It also places a focus on combining measures of economic and environmental performance as the basis for decision-making.

By linking environmental issues with conventional management tools, EMA also avoids the establishment of environmental management systems and tools that are unconnected with day-to-day business and which only run in parallel with existing corporate management systems called instrumental integration (Burritt *et al.* 2002). In the past, environmental aspects of a company's activities tended to be segmented in parallel organisational structures and departments separate from conventional business management. In contrast, EMA, and particularly monetary EMA, supports instrumental integration by integrating accounting for environmental issues and conventional management accounting (see Burritt *et al.* 2002; Schaltegger and Burritt 2005, 2010).

The instrumental integration capability of EMA, with its concepts and tools, is of particular interest to small and medium-sized enterprises (SMEs) because of their scarce resources (time, personnel, and finance), lower tolerance for failure (Herzig and Schaltegger 2004), and attitude to risk and risk management (Burritt 2005) compared with larger firms (see also de Bruijn and Hofman 2002: 195). It is all the more promising because in emerging economy countries small and medium-sized enterprises make an important and dynamic contribution to economic development as well as leading to environmental degradation. For specific environmental impacts, the cumulative contributions of SMEs may even exceed those of multinational enterprises because of relatively inefficient production techniques and operations such as metal finishing, textile manufacture, electroplating, and food processing (Hobbs 2000; Scott 2000). Therefore, moving towards sustainability cannot be achieved solely by encouraging and enabling large companies to assess net realisable benefits from implementing profitable activities that improve the environment and social wellbeing. Hence, whether small, medium-sized, or large, all enterprises play an important and complementary role in moving towards the reduction of corporate environmental impacts. Likewise, all sizes of companies can potentially gain from implementing eco-efficient and eco-effective activities designed to improve economic value as well as reduce the company's environmental impact added (Schaltegger and Burritt 2000). EMA provides information that facilitates managers in their search for corporate eco-efficient and eco-effective activities. The questions are whether companies in South-East Asia are aware of the opportunities which can lead to greater eco-efficiency and eco-effectiveness and whether EMA can be used in emerging countries when it has largely been rolled out by large companies in developed countries.

EMA in South-East Asia

At the time this comparative case study started, EMA application in the South-East Asian region was in its early stages. The Philippines constituted an exception in this regard. Mainly driven by the country's organisation of accountants, through the Philippines Institute of Certified Public Accountants, some aspects of EMA have been integrated into undergraduate accountancy education and continuing professional development (Reyes 2001, 2002), thereby promoting education and practice. Furthermore, a Philippine guidebook on environmental management has been published and distributed (EMB 2003). Research in environmental and social accounting in Thailand has revealed an overall positive attitude towards social and environmental accounting amongst accountants, auditors, and accounting-related professionals (Kuasirikun 2005). Some company projects on environmental cost accounting have also been conducted in Philippine and Thai industries. However, in only a few cases are documentation and reports dealing with the application of EMA available, and these case studies have mostly been carried out in cooperation with large and multinational companies (Setthasakko 2010). In comparison with the Philippines and Thailand, the dissemination of EMA in the other two case study target countries, Indonesia and Vietnam, is still less advanced. In these countries institutionalisation has taken place slowly and only a few large companies have begun to apply EMA in recent times. In general, the research on corporate social and environmental accounting in all four countries can be seen as being underdeveloped (Kuasirikun 2005; Kuasirikun and Sherer 2004; Herzig, Viere, Burritt, and Schaltegger 2006).

As EMA is not common in South-East Asia and little documentation about EMA applications has been available, special attention has been paid to company case study research on EMA. To work out how EMA can be applied successfully in South-East Asian companies, 20 companies have been visited and 12 in-depth company case studies on EMA have been carried out by the four authors of the book. The single case studies act as pieces of a conceptual puzzle which results in a comparative research study revealing, and contributing to a better understanding of, specific decision-making situations relating to EMA implementation in South-East Asian businesses. The research was motivated by the fact that, when it comes to environmental and sustainability management, the average South-East Asian company is in a different situation from companies operating in industrialised countries. Emerging countries face greater difficulties than developed countries because they usually do not have the institutional capacity in place to promote environmental protection or encourage the inclusion of environmental costs in decision-making (Davy 1997: 179). Moreover, predominantly SMEs have been included in the study as they have been neglected in EMA research for many years, despite the fact that smaller organisations face greater difficulties than larger organisations for a number of reasons, including being time-poor and short of appropriate specialised human resources (Hillary 2000: 352). In the next chapter, the research design is described.

References

Angel, D.P. and Rock, M.T. (2003) 'Industrial transformation in East Asia: assessing policy approaches to improving the environmental performance of industry within rapidly industrialising economies', *IHDP: Newsletter of the International Human Dimensions Programme on Global Environmental Change* 01/2003: 4–6.

Balce, G.R., Tjaroko, T.S., and Zamora, C.G. (2003) *Overview of biomass for power generation in Southeast Asia*, Jakarta: ASEAN Center for Energy.

Bartolomeo, M., Bennett, M., Bouma, J.J., Heydkamp, P., James, P., and Wolters, T. (2000) 'Environmental management accounting in Europe: current practice and future potential', *European Accounting Review*, 9: 31–52.

Bebbington, J., Gray, R., Hibbitt, C. and Kirk, E. (2001) *Full cost accounting: an agenda for action*, London: ACCA.

Bennett, M. and James, P. (1998) 'The green bottom line', in Bennett, M. and James, P. (eds) *The green bottom line: environmental accounting for management – current practice and future trends*, Sheffield: Greenleaf Publishing, pp. 30–60.

Bennett, M., Bouma, J.J., and Wolters, T. (2002) *Environmental management accounting: informational and institutional developments*, Dordrecht: Kluwer Academic Publishers.

Bennett, M., Rikhardsson, P., and Schaltegger, S. (eds) (2003) *Environmental management accounting: purpose and progress*, Rotterdam: Kluwer Academic Publishers.

Blankart, C.B. and Knieps, G. (1993) 'State and standards', *Public Choice*, 1: 39–52.

de Bruijn, T.J.N.M. and Hofman, P. (2002) 'Pollution prevention: increasing environmental capabilities of SMEs through collaboration', in de Bruijn, T.J.N.M. and Tukker, A. (eds) *Partnership and leadership: building alliances for a sustainable future*, Dordrecht: Kluwer Academic Publishers, pp. 195–215.

Burritt, R.L. (1997) 'Corporate environmental performance indicators: cost allocation – boon or bane?', *Greener Management International*, 17: 89–100.

Burritt, R.L. (2004) 'Environmental management accounting: roadblocks on the way to the green and pleasant land', *Business Strategy and the Environment*, 13: 13–32.

Burritt, R.L. (2005) 'Environmental risk management and environmental management accounting: developing linkages', in Tukker, A., Rikhardsson, P.M., Bennett, M., Bouma, J.J., and Schaltegger, S. (eds) *Implementing environmental management accounting: status and challenges*, Dordrecht: Kluwer Academic Publishers, pp. 123–141.

Burritt, R.L. and Schaltegger, S. (2001) 'Eco-efficiency in corporate budgeting', *Environmental Management and Health*, 12: 158–174.

Burritt, R.L., Hahn, T., and Schaltegger, S. (2002) 'Towards a comprehensive framework for environmental management accounting: links between business actors and environmental management accounting tools', *Australian Accounting Review*, 12: 39–50.

Burritt, R.L., Herzig, C., and Tadeo, B. (2009) 'Environmental management accounting for cleaner production: the case of a Philippine rice mill', *Journal of Cleaner Production*, 17: 431–439.

Burritt, R.L., Schaltegger, S., and Zvezdov, D. (2010) *Carbon management accounting: practice in leading German companies*, Centre for Accounting, Governance and Sustainability Occasional Working Papers, No. 2, May, University of South Australia, Adelaide.

Bryant, R.L. and Parnwell, M.J. (1996) 'Introduction: politics, sustainable development and environmental change in South-East Asia', in Parnwell, M.J. and Bryant, R.L. (eds) *Environmental change in South-East Asia: people, politics and sustainable development*, London: Routledge, pp. 7–19.

Chambers, R.J. (1957) *Accounting and action*, Sydney: The Law Book Company of Australasia.

Chambers, R.J. (1966) *Accounting, evaluation and economic behavior*, Houston: Scholars Book Co.

Chowdhury, A. and Islam, I. (2001) *The political economy of East Asia*, Oxford: Oxford University Press.

CIA (Central Intelligence Agency) (2010) *The world factbook* [online – accessed on 29 October 2010]. Available from Internet: https://www.cia.gov/library/publications/the-world-factbook/geos/ha.html.

Clapp, J. and Dauvergne, P. (2003) 'Environment, development, and security in Southeast Asia: exploring the linkages', in Dewitt, D.B. and Hernandez, C.G. (eds)

Development and security in Southeast Asia volume I: the environment, Aldershot, England: Ashgate, pp. 19–32.

Davy, A. (1997) 'Environmental management systems: ISO 14001 issues for developing countries', in Sheldon, C. (ed.) *ISO 14001 and beyond: environmental management systems in the real world*, Sheffield: Greenleaf, pp. 169–182.

ECOMAC (1996) *Synreport: eco-management accounting as a tool of environmental management (the Ecomac project)*, Zoetermeer: EIM Small Business Research and Consultancy.

Ekins, P., Simon, S., Deutsch, L., Folke, C., and De Groot, R. (2003) 'A framework for the practical application of the concepts of critical natural capital and strong sustainability', *Ecological Economics*, 44: 165–185.

EMB (Environmental Management Bureau) (2003) *Guidebook on environmental management system, pollution prevention/cleaner production and environmental cost accounting*, Quezon City, Philippines: EMB.

Environment Canada, Solid Waste Management Division (1995) 'The life cycle concept: backgrounder', *Ecocycle*, 1: 6.

EPA (US Environmental Protection Agency) (1995) *Introduction to environmental accounting*, Washington, DC: US EPA.

EU (European Union) (2003) 'Directives 2003/51/EC of the European Parliament and of the council of 18 June 2003 amending Directives 78/660/EEC, 83/349/EEC, 86/635/EEC and 91/674/EEC on the annual and consolidated accounts of certain types of companies, banks and other financial institutions and insurance undertakings', *Official Journal of the European Union*, L178/16.

European Commission (2011) *Public consultation on disclosure of non-financial information by companies* [online – accessed on 29 November 2011]. Available from Internet: http://ec.europa.eu/internal_market/consultations/2010/non-financial_reporting_en.htm.

Fava, J., Jensen, A., Pomper, S., DeSmet, B., Warren, J., and Vignon, B. (eds) (1992) *Life cycle assessment data quality: a conceptual framework,* Wintergreen: SETAC.

Fava, J., Denison, R., Jones, B., Curran, M., Vigon, B., Selke, S., and Barnum J. (eds) (1991) *A technical framework for life cycle assessment*, Smugglers Notch, VT: SETAC.

Fichter, K., Loew, T., and Seidel, E. (1997) *Betriebliche Umweltkostenrechnung*, Berlin: Springer.

Forum for the Future (2003) *The SIGMA guidelines: toolkit*, London: Forum for the Future.

Global Footprint Network (2010) *Ecological footprint atlas 2010* [online – accessed on 7 July 2011]. Available from Internet: http://www.footprintnetwork.org/gfn_sub.php?content=books.

Gray, R.H., Bebbington, J., and Walters, D. (1993) *Accounting for the environment*, London: Chapman Publishing.

Gray, R., Owen, D., and Adams, C. (1996) *Accounting and accountability: changes and challenges in corporate social and environmental reporting*, London: Prentice Hall Europe.

Herzig, C. and Schaltegger, S. (2004) 'Nachhaltiges Unternehmertum im Handwerk: wie kann nachhaltiges Wirtschaften in kleinen und mittleren Unternehmen gefördert werden?' [Sustainable entrepreneurship in trade: how can business in small and medium-sized enterprises be sustained?], in Merz, J. and Wagner, J. (eds) *Perspektiven der Mittelstandsforschung: ökonomische Analysen zu Selbständigkeit, freien Berufen und KMU*, Münster: Lit, pp. 361–387

Herzig, C., Viere, T., Burritt, R., and Schaltegger, S. (2006) 'Understanding and supporting management decision-making: South-East Asian case studies on environmental management accounting', in Schaltegger, S., Bennett, M., and Burritt, R. (eds) *Sustainability Accounting and Reporting*, Dordrecht: Springer, pp. 491–508.

Hillary, R. (2000) *Small and medium-sized enterprises and the environment: business imperatives*, Sheffield: Greenleaf.

Hobbs, J. (2000) 'Promoting cleaner production in small and medium-sized enterprises', in Hillary, R. (ed.) *Small and medium-sized enterprises and the environment: business imperatives*, Sheffield: Greenleaf, pp. 148–157.

Horngren, C.T., Foster, G., and Datar, S.M. (2000) *Cost accounting: a managerial emphasis*, Upper Saddle River, NJ: Prentice Hall International.

Horngren, C.T., Foster, G., Datar, S.M., Rajan, M.V., and Ittner, C. (2008) *Cost accounting: a managerial emphasis*, Upper Saddle River, NJ: Pearson Prentice Hall.

Horvath, P. and Mayer, R. (1989) 'Prozesskostenrechnung: der neue Weg zu mehr Kostentransparenz und wirkungsvolleren Unternehmensstrategien' [Process costing: the new way to cost transparency and effective corporate strategies], *Controlling*, 1: 214–219.

Howes, R. (2002) *Environmental cost accounting: an introduction and practical guide*, London: Elsevier.

Hunkeler, D., Lichtenvort, K., and Rebitzer G. (eds) (2008) *Environmental life cycle costing*, Boca Raton, FL: CRC Press.

IASB (International Accounting Standards Board) (2011) *International Accounting Standard 1: presentation of financial statements*, London: IFRS Foundation/IASB.

ICAA (Institute of Chartered Accountants in Australia) (2008) *Broad based business reporting: the complete reporting tool*. Adelaide: ICAA.

ICLEI (International Council for Local Environmental Initiatives) (2003) *Eco-budget: a model of environmental budgeting* [online – accessed on 3 June 2008]. Available from Internet: http://www.iclei.org/europe.

IFAC (International Federation of Accountants) (1998) *Environmental management in organizations: the role of management accounting*, New York: Financial and Management Accounting Committee, IFAC.

IFAC (International Federation of Accountants) (2005) *International guidance document of EMA*. New York: Professional Accountants in Business Committee, IFAC.

IFAC (International Federation of Accountants) (2009a) *Evaluating and improving costing in organisations*, New York: Professional Accountants in Business Committee, IFAC.

IFAC (International Federation of Accountants) (2009b) *Sustainability framework*, New York: Professional Accountants in Business Committee, IFAC.

IFAC (International Federation of Accountants) (2009c) *Evaluating the costing journey: a costing levels continuum maturity model*, New York: Professional Accountants in Business Committee, IFAC.

International Integrated Reporting Committee (2011) *Towards integrated reporting: communicating value in the 21st century* [online – accessed on 29 October 2011]. Available from Internet: http://www.theiirc.org.

Jasch, C. (2009) *Environmental and material flow cost accounting: principles and procedures*, Berlin: Springer.

Kokubu, K., Campos, M.K.S., Furukawa, Y., and Tachikawa, H. (2009) 'Material flow cost accounting with ISO 14051', *ISO Management Systems*, January–February: 15–18.

Kuasirikun, N. (2005) 'Attitudes to the development and implementation of social and environmental accounting in Thailand', *Critical Perspectives on Accounting*, 16: 1035–1057.

Kuasirikun, N. and Sherer, M. (2004) 'Corporate social accounting disclosure in Thailand', *Accounting, Auditing & Accountability Journal*, 17: 629–660.

Kurtz, L. (2008) 'Socially responsible investment and shareholder activism', in Crane, A., McWilliams, A., Matten, D., Moon, J., and Siegel, D.S. (eds) *The Oxford handbook of corporate social responsibility*, Oxford: Oxford University Press, pp. 568–576.

Lang, C., Rey, U., Wohlgemuth, V., Genz, S., and Pawlytsch, S. (2003) *PAS 1025 – Austausch umweltrelevanter Daten zwischen ERP-Systemen und betrieblichen Umweltinformationssystemen* [Data exchange between ERP systems and environmental information systems], PAS 1025:2003–12, Berlin: Beuth.

Lave, L.B., Cobas-Flores, E., Henderson, C.T., and McMichael, F.C. (1995) 'Life cycle assessment: using input–output analysis to estimate economy-wide discharges', *Environmental Science and Technology*, 29: 420A–426A.

Liedtke, C., Manstein, C., Bellendorf, H., and Kranendonk, S. (1994) *Oeko-Audit und Ressourcenmanagement erste Schritte in Richtung eines EU-weit harmonisierungsfaehigen Umweltmanagementsystems [Eco-audits and resource management initial steps towards an EU-wide environmental management system that can be harmonized]*, Wuppertal, Germany: Wissenschaftszentrum Nordrhein-Westfalen Wuppertal Institut fuer Klima, Umwelt, Energie.

Lohmann, L. (2009) 'Toward a different debate in environmental accounting: the cases of carbon and cost–benefit', *Accounting, Organizations and Society*, 34: 499–534.

Maunders, K. and Burritt, R.L. (1991) 'Accounting and ecological crisis', *Accounting, Auditing & Accountability Journal*, 4: 9–26.

McDonald, S., Robinson, S., and Thierfelder, K. (2008) 'Asian growth and trade poles: India, China, and East and Southeast Asia', *World Development*, 36: 210–234.

Parker, L. (1999) *Environmental costing: an exploratory examination*, Australian Society of Certified Practising Accountants, Melbourne, Australia, February.

Pidgeon, S. and Brown, D. (1994) 'The role of lifecycle analysis in environmental management. a general panacea or one of several useful paradigms?', *Greener Management International*, 7: 36–44.

Reyes, M.F. (2001) 'Environmental management accounting education in the Philippines: the accountancy profession as a medium for change', *Journal of the Asia Pacific Centre for Environmental Accountability*, 7: 7–11.

Reyes, M.F. (2002) 'The greening of accounting: putting the environment onto the agenda of the accountancy profession in the Philippines', in Bennett, M., Bouma, J.J., and Wolters, T. (eds) *Environmental management accounting: informational and institutional developments*, Dordrecht: Kluwer, pp. 215–220.

Rikhardsson, P.M., Bennett, M., Bouma, J.J., and Schaltegger, S. (eds) (2005) *Implementing environmental management accounting: status and challenges: eco-efficiency in industry and science*, Dordrecht: Kluwer.

Schaltegger, S. (1996) *Corporate environmental accounting*, London: John Wiley and Sons.

Schaltegger, S. (1998) 'Accounting for eco-efficiency', in Nath, B., Hens, L., Compton, P., and Devuyst, D. (eds) *Environmental management in practice. Volume I: Instruments for environmental management*, London: Routledge, pp. 272–287.

Schaltegger, S. and Burritt, R.L. (2000) *Contemporary environmental accounting: issues, concepts and practice*, Sheffield: Greenleaf Publishing.

Schaltegger, S. and Burritt, R. (2005) 'Corporate sustainability', in Tietenberg, T. and Folmer, H. (eds) *The international yearbook of environmental and resource economics 2005/2006*, Northampton, MA: Edward Elgar Publishing.

Schaltegger, S. and Burritt, R.L. (2010) 'Sustainability accounting for companies: catchphrase or decision support for business leaders?', *Journal of World Business*, 45: 375–384.

Schaltegger, S. and Müller, K. (1997) 'Calculating the true profitability of pollution prevention', *Greener Management International*, 17: 53–68.

Schaltegger, S. and Stinson, C. (1994) *Issues and research opportunities in environmental accounting*. WZZ – Discussion Paper, No. 9423, Berlin: WZZ.

Schaltegger, S., Bennett, M., and Burritt, R. (eds) (2006) *Sustainability accounting and reporting*, Dordrecht: Springer.

Schaltegger, S., Burritt, R., and Petersen, H. (2003) *An introduction to corporate environmental management: striving for sustainability*, Sheffield: Greenleaf Publishing.

Schaltegger, S., Hahn, T., and Burritt, R. (2001) 'Environmental management accounting: overview and main approaches', in Seifert, E. and Kreeb, M. (eds) *Information, organisation and environmental management accounting*, Rotterdam: Kluwer.

Schaltegger, S., Bennett, M., Burritt, R.L., and Jasch, C. (2008) *Environmental management accounting for cleaner production*, Dordrecht: Springer.

Scott, A. (2000) 'Small-scale enterprises and the environment in developing countries', in Hillary, R. (ed.) *Small and medium-sized enterprises and the environment. business imperatives*, Sheffield: Greenleaf, pp. 276–288.

Setthasakko, W. (2010) 'Barriers to the development of environmental management accounting: an exploratory study of pulp and paper companies in Thailand', *EuroMed Journal of Business*, 5: 315–331.

UN (United Nations) (2005): *The Millennium Development Goals report 2005*, New York: United Nations.

UNDSD (United Nations Division for Sustainable Development) (2001) *Environmental management accounting, procedures and principles*, New York: UNDSD.

UNSD (United Nations Statistics Division) (2006) *The official United Nations site for the Millennium Development Goals Indicators* [online – accessed on 25 February 2007]. Available from Internet: http://mdgs.un.org/unsd/mdg/Default.aspx.

UNESCAP (United Nations Economic and Social Commission for Asia and the Pacific) (2006) *State of the environment in Asia and the Pacific 2005*, Bangkok: UNESCAP.

von Weizsäcker, E.U., Lovins, A.B., and Lovins, L.H. (1997) *Factor 4: doubling wealth – halving resource use: the new report to the Club of Rome*, Sydney: Allen & Unwin.

Wagner, B. and Enzler, S. (eds) (2006) *Material flow management*, Heidelberg: Physica-Verlag.

World Bank (2006) *Corporate environmental and social responsibility in the East Asia and Pacific region: review of emerging practice*, Washington, DC: World Bank.

3

COMPARATIVE CASE STUDY ON EMA IN SOUTH-EAST ASIA

Purpose and research questions for the EMA research study

To date, the majority of case studies on environmental management accounting (EMA) have focussed on the application of a single tool. In a few cases, emphasis has been on a combination of two or more tools. The goal of these case studies is to show that an EMA tool, such as the physical environmental management accounting (PEMA) tool 'material and energy flow accounting', or the monetary environmental management accounting (MEMA) tool 'environmental cost accounting', can be applied in different companies in a country or an industry, or how internal implementation of a particular corporate EMA tool can be undertaken, or what the costs and benefits are of the application of an EMA tool (e.g. Ditz, Ranganathan, and Banks 1995; Bartolomeo, Bennett, Bouma, Heydkamp, James, and Wolters 2000; Letmathe and Doost 2000; Jasch 2009; Scavone 2006).

In contrast, this study adopts a broader perspective. The purpose is to examine different decision situations which depend on different company contexts and management levels and the way these particular decisions and associated internal accountability processes are linked with different types of EMA information, in particular through the use of monetary and physical measures. The study intends to identify contexts which influence the application of specific EMA tools that are used to provide necessary information for decision-making. Depending on the particular decision-making contexts, generic patterns of EMA tools are expected to facilitate the integration of environmental considerations into management decision-making.

Overall, the study seeks to provide a holistic perspective on the large range of tools which can be used for management decision-making and accountability by different groups of management, in different organisations. It analyses the applicability of the EMA framework and related tools depending on the decision-making context within the company. The findings of the study provide answers to the questions developed below.

Factors influencing the implementation of EMA

The stakeholder view of the firm (Freeman 1984) implicitly acknowledges a multitude of interests, objectives, and rationales among internal as well as external stakeholders. It questions the one-dimensionality of the shareholder value concept that often continues to be associated with mainstream accounting thought. However, accounting research also acknowledges that management accounting can serve different and even contradictory rationalities. For instance, in a longitudinal field study on the use of cost accounting data in US military repair facilities, Ansari and Euske (1987) explored a need to incorporate other forms of rationality in management accounting and distinguished:

> three alternative theoretical perspectives on the use of accounting data in organizations: (i) technical-rational, which is driven by considerations of efficiency; (ii) socio-political, which is the pursuit of power and influence, and (iii) institutional, which stems from the need to put on an appropriate facade for the world to see.
>
> *(Ansari and Euske 1987: 553)*

A major difference associated with their socio-economic rationality approach is the role of corporate objectives. Socio-economic rationality addresses a multitude of objectives which need to be considered in a rational way. Ansari and Euske's (1987) research found that stated objectives were of a technical-rational nature and that other uses 'infiltrate' or even contradict the original purpose. Internal stakeholder rationales might not necessarily fit organisational rationales and objectives or they might not even act in a rational way at all.

Schaltegger and Sturm (1990) developed a concept that aligns stakeholder thinking with overarching corporate objectives and strategies. Their concept of socio-economic rationality, which also relates to the work of Hill (1991), recognises that a company is embedded in a social environment with various stakeholders pursuing different goals and acting on the basis of different assumptions, values, and goals being pursued. As a consequence, managers needs to consider these different values and goals pursued by these stakeholders if they want to secure support and continue collaboration with these stakeholders. This, furthermore, leads to the requirement that managers should pursue several goals in order to be successful in establishing relationships with the stakeholders. However, the means available to a company are scarce, which raises the question of how to consider these different requirements. The argument is that balanced management of these objectives is required. Corporate objectives are grouped into five spheres: scientific-technological, economic, legal, socio-cultural, and political. Each sphere differs in terms of criteria for success and type of rationality. For instance, whereas the success criterion in the economic sphere is efficiency as the core goal of economic rationality, success in the socio-cultural sphere depends on achieving legitimacy, implying normative or communicative rationality (for a summary of the concept see Schaltegger, Burritt, and Petersen 2003: ch. 7).

From the point of view of socio-economic rationality it is argued that EMA might be used not only to achieve efficiency but also to gain effectiveness, legitimacy, compliance/legality, and freedom of action depending on the specific institutional settings and organisational environments in which it operates. Our analysis of the 12 case studies aims at considering specific stakeholder roles and rationalities and includes all spheres of socio-economic rationality to help understand distinct organisational environments and institutional settings and how they influence the implementation of EMA. More specifically, the five spheres of influence are distinguished and analysed: economic, technical and technological, legal and regulatory; socio-cultural, and political, thereby leading to the first research question:

RQ1: How do different organisational environments and institutional settings influence the implementation of EMA in South East Asia?

Patterns of EMA use

Burritt, Hahn, and Schaltegger's (2002) conceptual framework for EMA encompasses a large range of different EMA tools that serve different needs depending on the decision context, purpose, and management level (see Chapter 2 and Figure 2.3). The framework suggests that different EMA tools can be assigned according to the decision or internal accountability settings, and that managers need different types of information when making decisions. A comparative empirical investigation of the applicability of the conceptual framework has not previously been undertaken (but see Burritt and Saka 2006). Moreover, EMA tools may be linked in various ways and interact when applied in corporate practice (identified through patterns in the use of EMA tools).

First, to be well informed, many decision situations require the joint application of both the monetary and comparable PEMA tools. An example is material flow cost accounting (MFCA), which is a tool that provides regularly generated, short-term and past-orientated information about physical material flows and related cost figures. It became an environmental management standard (ISO 14051) in late 2011 (see Kokubu, Campos, Furukawa, and Tachikawa 2009). Similarly, the consideration of potential future costs of an investment is based initially on information about expected future physical impacts on the environment. Both PEMA and MEMA tools corresponding to this decision situation are future-orientated and ad hoc in kind.

Second, MEMA and PEMA can also be linked for particular eco-efficiency analyses. Eco-efficiency is defined as the ratio between economic performance and environmental impact added (e.g. value added per unit of environmental impact added; see, for example, Schaltegger and Sturm 1992; Schaltegger 1998; Schaltegger and Burritt 2000). One purpose of such eco-efficiency analyses can be to discuss portfolio considerations (e.g. Ilinitch and Schaltegger 1995; Schaltegger and Burritt 2000; Saling, Kicherer, Dittrich-Krämer, Wittlinger, Zombik, and Schmidt 2002) supporting strategic management and product portfolio development. Another consideration is often to optimise the costs per kilogram of carbon dioxide or other environmental impacts being reduced (e.g. Schaltegger 1998). Without going in depth into the various possible reasons and applications for analysing eco-efficiency, this field of application needs to be emphasised as it is increasingly used to support decision-making in industry.

Third, MEMA and PEMA can be brought together to help emphasise economic/ecological (eco-)effectiveness of organisations, or parts of organisations. Eco-effectiveness relates to whether goals for the organisation about desired economic and environmental targets, standards, or budgets are met. Hence, effectiveness and efficiency are two matters into which EMA can provide insights.

Fourth, EMA provides all levels of organisational decision-makers with additional decision-making power, by focussing on measurements of environmental and economic performance in similar, comparable terms. Relative (ratio) analysis is used to facilitate the comparison between different alternatives in relation to how to increase eco-efficiency and improve eco-effectiveness. Finally, apart from these links between MEMA and PEMA, many interactions between the past and future as well as between ad hoc and routine EMA approaches are likely to exist.

From prior research little information is available about possible interactions between these tools and how institutional settings influence their implementation. This leads to the following research question:

RQ2: How do EMA tools interact and complement each other to support managers in decision-making?

The case study approach

The case study approach has been chosen as the foundation for addressing the research questions. Case study research is a well-established approach with a long history, and is particularly applied in the social sciences (Yin 2003). In the following section the purpose and characteristics of research case studies are described and the reason why this method is seen to provide useful answers to the questions is explained.

Purpose and characteristics of case studies

Besides their widespread application for teaching purposes, case studies have become quite common in management accounting research in general (Ryan, Scapens, and Theobald 2002), and in EMA research (e.g. Ditz *et al.* 1995; Burritt 2004) and related approaches such as eco- or sustainability management control (e.g. Schaltegger and Sturm 1998; Moon, Gond, Grubnic, and Herzig 2011) and the sustainability balanced scorecard (e.g. Schaltegger and Dyllick 2002), particularly in recent years. In the literature, however, there is still no precision in the terminology associated with case studies. In some situations cases are recognised as a research method (e.g. Ryan *et al.* 2002) whereas others stress that case studies are not a specific and isolated method of empirical sociological research (e.g. Witzel 1982; Lamnek 1995). From this perspective a case study includes, in principle, the whole spectrum of sociological research methods; in other words a case study is a manifold methodical approach (Witzel 1982) that brings the theoretical specification of a methodology into practical action without in itself being a research method (Lamnek 1995). Therefore, case studies are seen as being located between an actual research method and a methodological paradigm. However, it is commonly understood that case studies are not a methodology (Ryan *et al.* 2002). Rather case studies can be used for research and teaching in combination with different methodological approaches (Ryan *et al.* 2002). Yin (2003: 13) defines the case study as 'an empirical inquiry that investigates a contemporary phenomenon within its real-life context, especially when the boundaries between phenomenon and context are not clearly evident'. Hence, following Yin (2003), case studies are seen here as a research strategy comprising the logic of design, data collection techniques, and specific approaches to data analysis.

Choosing case studies as the research method does not imply a qualitative (interpretive) research methodology, as case study research can support both interpretive as well as positivistic approaches (Ahrens and Chapman 2006, drawing on Silverman 1993; see also Walsham 1995). The aim is to answer the research questions in a holistic manner that embraces interpretive as well as positivistic methodology: '[w]ithout the specifics of qualitative studies, the general assertions of positivistic research would be hollow. Likewise, the specific investigations of qualitative research question and refine the general statements of positivistic studies' (Ahrens and Chapman 2006: 19).

Why a case study?

Case studies can be seen as a guide to establishing a frame for data collection in a particular piece of research, thereby seeking to cover contextual conditions which might be relevant for the phenomenon being studied. Case studies are particularly suitable for research areas where there are few prior theoretical pieces of literature or empirical research work (Eisenhardt 1989) and the most appropriate research questions are those asking 'how' and 'why' (Yin 2003) rather than those requiring broad statistical analysis. Kloot (1997) observes that there have been numerous calls for case studies to be undertaken to study accounting in practice as well as to gain rich descriptions of actual situations (e.g. Kaplan 1986; Scapens 1990) and a fuller understanding of the context and factors which shape contemporary management practices (e.g. Parker 1999).

The present study seeks to illuminate different decision-making contexts in South-East Asian companies which are related to environmental issues, and to analyse ways in which managers in different industries and from different departments and levels depend on EMA information. Thus case studies are used here as a research strategy to analyse decision-making and internal accountability processes, how environmental information influences these processes, and with what results. An advantage of case studies is that, by limiting the study to relatively few research objects, the researcher can deal intensively with data collected in order to gain more comprehensive, 'rich' in-depth and complex results. The selected unit for analysis is not considered as being an interchangeable, unimportant part of a sample population, but is seen as being the relevant object of investigation for the interpretation of everyday life (Lamnek 1995). In order to derive results that can be transferred, or partially or broadly generalised, project case studies should reflect holistic and realistic pictures of EMA-related decision-making contexts including all relevant dimensions of the object of interest.

By making a research study of each individual case, the aim of every EMA case study is to analyse the concurrence of factors related to the application and implementation of an EMA tool or tools while focussing on the identification of characteristic processes in companies in South-East Asia. Accordingly, the units of analysis are the company's decision situations. These can differ substantially, depending on the management level (top management, middle management, supervisory management, etc.), department in charge (accounting, finance, production, environment, etc.), type of management activity (investment, operational production activity, ex-post assessment of a project, etc.), time frame, and risk attitude of managers.

One characteristic of emerging economy and newly industrialised countries is that they lack good quantitative data related to the generation and utilisation of environment-related information. For instance, information in the major life cycle databases is characterised by an almost complete absence of life cycle inventories from emerging economy countries (e.g. Ecoinvent Centre 2011). With little systematic prior work being available, case studies are especially useful for examining EMA in the four target countries in this research project. Moreover, the choice of case studies as the approach to research in this target area can be seen as a suitable way of examining complex social phenomena in such countries. Additional advantages of the case study approach are the triangulation of data collection over time, space, and people, investigator triangulation using multiple observers, the multiple analysis method, and the opportunity to obtain a picture of the nature of practice in the field (Yin 2003).

Several arguments against the use of case studies relate to problems associated with qualitative research in general, such as the presence of subjective preconceptions. Moreover, case studies are sometimes considered to produce theories that are too complex because of the variety of data collected for analysis (Eisenhardt 1989). One of the most important limitations of the case study approach is the expected or actual limitation for the generalisation of research findings (e.g. McClintock, Brannon, and Maynard-Moody 1979). Case studies do not produce empirical data about a sample that can be generalised to other populations (such as surveys using statistical generalisation). However, they rely on analytical generalisations through replications and verifications of certain findings in a second or more cases (Yin 2003), that is, the projected case studies may allow the generalisation of a particular set of results to some broader theory.

In the following section, the approach used for the EMA case studies in South-East Asia is explained.

Comparative case study on EMA in South-East Asia

The research design adopted is a comparative case study as a distinctive form of multiple or collective case studies (Yin 2003), comprising 12 exploratory case studies of small, medium-sized, and large enterprises in Indonesia, the Philippines, Thailand, and Vietnam. This specific research design has been chosen because, across cases, the studies aim to understand complex decision-making contexts and demonstrate why certain circumstances and incentives lead to certain results, whereas other cases create contrasting results. This case-orientated comparative approach tries to identify and highlight similarities and differences between the processes by which a decision was, or a set of decisions were, made (considering different sectors, organisational structures, and management levels). The case study analyses different types of environmental information that managers of different business functions may need when making decisions, depending on the decision-making context (Burritt *et al.* 2002). In order to identify generic sets of EMA tools and methods that may provide this specific information, the research design includes a set of multiple case studies for the purpose of cross-unit comparison. Results of the analysis of case studies will confirm or refute the usefulness of the framework adopted (Yin 2003) as well as address each research question. Conclusions from cross-case comparisons are to be derived when the researchers meet, present, and examine the 12 individual case reports (see also Larrinaga-González, Carrasco-Fenech, Caro-González, Correa-Ruiz, and Páez-Sandubete 2001), as happened in June and September 2010, in Lüneburg, Germany, and Nottingham, United Kingdom.

Based on the EMA framework (Burritt *et al.* 2002) the specific decision-making context of a company and its sub-units is analysed in order to choose the most suitable EMA tool(s). Instead of elaborating the usefulness of specific EMA methods for various businesses, the study approaches EMA from a different perspective by focussing on the needs and the specific decision situation of the company managers. This approach attempts to observe present practice, increase the benefit of EMA to management, and meet the reality of management accounting, in which internal decisions about varied and rather different issues have to be prepared, assessed, and made independently of pre-defined systems or standardised tools.

In order to cover a wide range of phenomena and to use the sources of data for cross-validation, several sources of evidence are required (data triangulation). The study draws from multiple data sources including:

- a large spectrum of contact persons (environmental, production, and financial managers, accountants, company owners/senior management, representatives from environmental and industry associations, for instance chambers of commerce);
- a variety of research methods (direct observation, documentation, archival records, interviews, and a questionnaire);
- different groupings of researchers (interviewing and observing in pairs); and
- different cases within and between sectors (e.g. electroplating, food, paper and pulp).

The 12 case studies (see Table 3.1) were conducted by analysing the data collected and developing conclusions and implications. Local resource persons were involved in most of the case studies. These were mainly environmental management and engineering experts who are both expected and able to multiply the EMA knowledge and experience they gained during the case studies in order to promote EMA in the South-East Asian region.

TABLE 3.1 EMA case studies examined in this book

Country	Company	Size	Number of employees[a]	Sector
Indonesia	PT Indah Jaya	Large	1600	Textile manufacturing
Indonesia	CV Bisma Jaya	Medium	50 (100)	Mechanical engineering and construction
Philippines	JBC Food Corporation	Large	400 (400)	Seed-based snacks manufacturing
Philippines	Oliver Enterprises I (Carbonisation)	Medium	28 (200)	Rice processing
Philippines	Oliver Enterprises II (Cogeneration)	Medium	28 (200)	Rice processing
Philippines	Well-Ever Electroplating Shop	Small	23	Electroplating
Thailand	Classic Crafts Corp. Ltd	Medium	300	Saa paper manufacturing
Thailand	Thai Cane Paper PLC	Large	402	Paper manufacturing
Vietnam	Tan Loc Food Co.	Small	70	Food products manufacturing
Vietnam	CTT Shrimp Farm	Small	8	Shrimp farming
Vietnam	Sai Gon Beer JV	Medium	200	Beverage manufacturing
Vietnam	Neumann Vietnam Ltd	Medium	80	Wholesale coffee

a   Number of full-time employees with number of part-time employees in brackets.

Interested companies were asked to apply for a case study by answering questions on their environmental situation and environmental management as well as their accounting system. The introductory questionnaire was kept simple to avoid creating a barrier to entering the research process. Based on this information the project partners chose several companies from different representative sectors (e.g. food, textiles, electroplating). Table 3.1 shows the range of company case studies discussed. To provide a good exploratory insight into the usefulness of the EMA framework, different industries and company sizes were chosen. The question of possible selection bias does not arise because the multiple cases are chosen to provide insight into specific EMA issues identified by the researchers and linked with the conceptual framework for EMA.

Conducting the case studies included a range of methods (site visits, interviews, document analysis, etc.) and took place over five years between 2004 and 2009. This raises the question of involvement by the researchers in the cases. Walsham (2006) views involvement as a spectrum with the outside researcher at one end and the fully involved researcher at the other, and different levels of involvement over time. The cases started with the researchers as outsiders trying to understand the specific situation of each company, drivers and motivation for using EMA, and the derivable EMA decision setting. Then the researchers got further involved and indeed influenced the implementation process simply by asking for specific information or by answering questions of company practitioners. Without doubt some of the companies would not have succeeded in actually implementing EMA without researcher involvement. Hence this part of the studies is interventionist following Malmi and Granlund (2009: 614): '[b]y acting as experts in real-life development projects, we can simultaneously produce research results that are both practically (practice relevance guaranteed) and theoretically interesting'.

In summary, the comparative case study research starts in an interpretative manner analysing the contexts of EMA application in each case, continues constructively by supporting the companies in applying EMA, and concludes in a positivistic spirit by trying to generalise and systematise the findings.

All participating companies, as well as additional companies informed by the intermediaries or the programme website, could signal their interest in becoming a research case by submitting a questionnaire. The questionnaire included general questions about industry, size, location, products, and perceived environmental issues. It also required the written approval of senior managers or owners to ensure commitment. Twenty-four submissions were received, of which four were unacceptable because of missing information or signatures. All companies were visited for initial discussions. About half of the companies visited did not become full case studies for a range of reasons. In some cases the initial visits revealed that the company was expecting sole engineering support or external funding for environmental technologies. For some companies the scope of the case study shifted away from EMA, for instance towards pure external accounting and fulfilling sustainability reporting requirements. Other companies ceased communication after a while, possibly to continue on their own or because of a lack of interest. Case studies were completed at 11 companies by means of site visits, informal interviews, inspection of accounting and other records, and remote communication by email and phone. In one company two separate case studies were conducted with different foci.

Overview of the EMA case study

The set of single case studies on EMA is introduced in Part II of this book. In this chapter, a brief description is provided outlining the purpose, scope, and outcome of the implementation of EMA tools identified with each case study. The embedded case studies are listed by country and finally placed within the EMA framework (Burritt *et al.* 2002; see Figure 3.1) corresponding to the

		Monetary EMA		Physical EMA	
		Short-term	Long-term	Short-term	Long-term
Past-oriented	Routinely generated	Indah Jaya (8)* JBC Food (10) Well-Ever (13) Classic Crafts (14) Sai Gon Beer (19) [1]	CTT Shrimp Farm (18) [2]	Indah Jaya (8) JBC Food (10) Well-Ever (13) Classic Crafts (14) Sai Gon Beer (19) [9]	CTT Shrimp Farm (18) [10]
	Ad hoc	Tan Loc Food (16) Neumann Coffee (17) [3]	Thai Cane Paper (15) Oliver Enterprises I (11) [4]	Bisma Jaya (9) Well-Ever (13) Thai Cane Paper (15) Tan Loc Food (16) Neumann Coffee (17) [11]	Thai Cane Paper (15) [12]
Future-oriented	Routinely generated	Bisma Jaya (9) Well-Ever (13) [5]	Thai Cane Paper (15) [6]	Thai Cane Paper (18) Bisma Jaya (9) [13]	Thai Cane Paper (15) [14]
	Ad hoc	Indah Jaya (8) Bisma Jaya (9) Classic Crafts (15) Tan Loc Food (16) [7]	Indah Jaya (9) Oliver Enterprises I+II (11,12) Classic Crafts (15) Tan Loc Food (16) Sai Gon Beer (19) Neumann Coffee (17) [8]	Indah Jaya (8) Well-Ever (13) Cane Paper (15) Tan Loc Food (16) [15]	Indah Jaya (8) Oliver Enterprises II (12) Thai Cane Paper (15) Sai Gon Beer (19) Neumann Coffee (17) [16]

FIGURE 3.1 Application of the EMA framework (Burritt *et al.* 2002) to the 12 case studies. Respective book chapters in round brackets; numbering of EMA boxes in square brackets.

various EMA settings covered. The following chapters (Chapters 4–15) present each embedded case study in detail.

All company-related information provided in the case studies has been disclosed by the companies involved and cross-checked by the authors. The information is simplified to ensure both confidentiality and understanding of the case. Currency conversion rates refer to the date of each case study's decision-making process.

Indonesia

Chapter 4: EMA for eco-efficiency in a towel production firm – Indah Jaya, Indonesia

The main focus of the Indah Jaya case is the linkage between environmental and business performance through the notion of eco-efficiency. Indah Jaya is an Indonesian textile manufacturer and exporter of towels to the world. Prior to the conduct of this case study, information was available to support an environmental management system in line with ISO 14001 and environmental measures of company performance. The Indah Jaya case study links this environmental management information to production and supply processes to examine its relevance for various decision settings, including monthly performance assessments, long- and mid-term eco-efficiency investments, and product pricing.

Chapter 5: Managing HSE in a mechanical engineering firm – Bisma Jaya, Indonesia

Bisma Jaya is a supply chain management-based case with a focus on responses to a health, safety, and environment (HSE) audit by a large oil and gas customer following an accident in a workshop. Bisma Jaya is an Indonesian engineering and offshore oil rig construction company. The customer audit system is used to rate Bisma Jaya in relation to risk assessment and control. Future supply contracts depend on the rating outcome. As a result of the ad hoc rating undertaken following the accident, a short-term, continuous improvement, monetary approach to addressing problems could be adopted in order to comply with suggestions for improved health, safety and environment performance. The case addresses improved relevant costing outcomes which can follow from strategic thinking beyond minimum compliance in the ratings improvement process.

The Philippines

Chapter 6: MFCA in a snack producer – JBC Food, the Philippines

This case study focuses on the application of EMA at JBC Food, a snack producer on the outskirts of the Philippine capital, Manila. It deals with the integration of environmental performance information with cost-accounting information using the concept of MFCA. The study reveals that a comprehensive consideration and cost valuation of waste flows leads to the identification and implementation of improvements in environmental and financial terms.

Chapter 7: EMA for cleaner rice processing – Oliver Enterprises I, the Philippines

Rice husk, the shell or outer covering of the rice seed, a residue from the rice milling process, tends to be deposited or burned in open fields in emerging economy countries. Based on a case study at Oliver Enterprises, a family-owned rice milling business in the northern Philippines, carbonisation of rice husk is analysed – a processing alternative to reduce environmental and social risks to improve the overall performance of the rice mill. The study examines EMA as a tool that supports environmental investment decision-making in the context of the emerging market for carbonised rice husk (CRH). Special emphasis is placed on the importance of ex-post appraisal as an ongoing check on the assumed costs and benefits of investment calculations in the environmental context.

Chapter 8: EMA for reducing greenhouse gas emissions in rice processing – Oliver Enterprises II, the Philippines

This case study is a follow-up to Oliver Enterprises I case study in which EMA support for a second rice husk-processing plant is examined. It elaborates on the use of physical and monetary environmental investment appraisal in husk processing to help generate electricity, thereby saving CO_2 emissions and obtaining additional revenues through the clean development mechanism (CDM), a topic of current major importance in South-East Asian countries such as the Philippines. The study reveals that husk-fired cogeneration is beneficial in terms of carbon emission reduction and additional monetary revenues for rice husk electricity generation to be used as a substitute for grid electricity. Further links between the CDM and environmental budgeting, material and energy flow accounting, and sustainability accounting are outlined.

Chapter 9: Environmental impact assessment, compliance monitoring and reporting in electroplating – Well-Ever, the Philippines

The study provides a classic example of the relationship between external demands for information, in this case from local government, and the need to gather such information for reporting purposes. In the Philippines, entities which cause considerable pollution such as electroplating companies are required to provide information to local environmental authorities concerning expected environmental impacts, planned improvement measures, and monitoring processes. In addition, actual measurements are needed to demonstrate compliance with environmental regulations on a regular basis. Using the example of a small-scale Philippine electroplating shop based in Manila, Well-Ever Electroplating Shop (Well-Ever), the case study deals with the identification, measurement, assessment, monitoring, and reporting of environmental impacts and, hence, reflects the 'outside-in' approach to EMA. The Well-Ever case also illustrates how supply chain pressure can influence the development of EMA to assist with environmental management and certification.

Thailand

Chapter 10: Relevant environmental costing and decision-making in a saa paper manufacturer – Classic Crafts, Thailand

The study of Classic Crafts Corporation Ltd (Classic Crafts) examines the application of EMA techniques in a medium-sized saa paper-manufacturing company in Thailand. The particular decisions addressed involve the potential for converting waste into a by-product and a related investment in relation to improving water quality. When the non-product costs of saa paper production are made apparent through relevant environmental costing, the decision to use low-quality wastepaper as input to the manufacturing process is questioned. Analysis is based initially on routinely generated environmental cost-accounting information from company job cost sheets, which in turn is founded on an assessment of the routine operating material and energy flows. An additional decision involves investments identified to improve water quality.

Chapter 11: Environmental risk assessment at a pulp and paper company – Thai Cane Paper, Thailand

The Thai Cane Paper case study emphasises risk analysis and assessment and long-term planning in relation to the management and use of scarce water in pulp and paper operations. Thai Cane Paper's main activity is the production of kraft paper in Thailand. EMA information is used to highlight the benefits from investment designed to meet environmental performance concerns of the company, as well as improved monetary performance associated with investment to address the water scarcity issue. The importance of physical EMA to reduce risk and secure a long-term continuous supply of water is demonstrated. The Thai Cane Paper case highlights the importance of a team-based approach to gathering EMA data, risk analysis and assessment, and planning to resolve the water scarcity issue for the long term.

Vietnam

Chapter 12: Decoupling economic growth from pollution – Tan Loc Food, Vietnam

This case study focuses on the application of EMA at Tan Loc Food, a small, family-run enterprise in Hue, the ancient capital of Vietnam. The case study reveals the environment-related decision situation at Tan Loc Food and subsequently elaborates upon a basic application of EMA. The implementation of EMA provides relevant information for increasing eco-efficiency at the current production site as well as at a planned new site. Several measures for improvement are described and assessed.

Chapter 13: Supply chain information and EMA in coffee exporting – Neumann Gruppe Vietnam, Vietnam

This case study focuses on the application of EMA at Neumann Gruppe Vietnam Ltd, a medium-sized coffee-refining and exporting enterprise in Southern Vietnam. It examines the use of material- and energy-related on-site information and highlights the relevance of environment-related supply chain information for corporate environmental and financial decision-making. In particular, the case study reveals possibilities for improving eco-efficiency within the supply chain and examines the means to achieve such improvements beyond company borders.

Chapter 14: Environmental and quality improvements as justification for higher capital expenditure and land use in shrimp farming – Chau Thanh Tam Shrimp Farm, Vietnam

Shrimp farming is a fast-growing industry in Vietnam, promising better income and employment to rural communities along the coastline. It is a potentially very profitable but risky business from a financial perspective and has severe ecological consequences. This case study assesses the financial and environmental performance of the Chau Thanh Tam Shrimp Farm through a retrospective comparison with neighbouring farms over a period of five years. The shrimp farm discussed has introduced a basic but effective measure to reduce environmental impacts and financial risks at the same time.

Chapter 15: Material and energy flow accounting in beer production – Sai Gon Beer, Vietnam

The Sai Gon Beer case study focuses on the application of EMA at a brewery located in central Vietnam. The company was alarmed by its rather weak performance in comparison with international benchmark figures for electricity and water consumption of beer brewing. The case study examines the relevance of material and energy flow accounting for environmental and production management and reveals options for improving eco-efficiency at the site level far beyond the company's former environmental objectives.

References

Ahrens, T. and Chapman, C.S. (2006) 'Doing qualitative field research in management accounting: positioning data to contribute to theory', *Accounting, Organizations and Society*, 31: 819–841.

Ansari, S. and Euske, K.J. (1987) 'Rational, rationalizing, and reifying uses of accounting data in organizations', *Accounting, Organizations and Society*, 12: 549–570.

Bartolomeo, M., Bennett, M., Bouma, J.J., Heydkamp, P., James, P., and Wolters, T. (2000) 'Environmental management accounting in Europe: current practice and future potential', *European Accounting Review*, 9: 31–52.

Burritt, R.L. (2004) 'Environmental management accounting: roadblocks on the way to the green and pleasant land', *Business Strategy and the Environment*, 13: 13–32.

Burritt, R.L. and Saka, C. (2006) 'Environmental management accounting applications and eco-efficiency: case studies from Japan', *Journal of Cleaner Production*, 14: 1262–1275.

Burritt, R., Hahn, T. and Schaltegger, S. (2002) 'Towards a comprehensive framework for environmental management accounting: links between business actors and environmental management accounting tools', *Australian Accounting Review*, 12: 39–50.

Ditz, D., Ranganathan, J., and Banks, R.D. (eds) (1995) *Green ledgers: case studies in corporate environmental accounting*, Baltimore, MD: World Resources Institute.

Ecoinvent Centre (2011) *Ecoinvent life cycle inventory database v2.2* [online – accessed on 1 July 2011]. Available from Internet: http://www.ecoinvent.org.

Eisenhardt, K.M. (1989) 'Building theories from case study research', *Academy of Management Review*, 14: 532–550.

Freeman, R.E. (1984) *Strategic management: a stakeholder approach*, Boston: Pitman.

Hill, W. (1991) 'Basisperspektiven der Managementforschung' [Basic perspectives of management research], *Die Unternehmung: Swiss Journal of Business Research and Practice*, 45: 2–15.

Ilinitch, A.Y. and Schaltegger, S.C. (1995) 'Developing a green business portfolio', *Long Range Planning*, 28: 29–38.

Jasch, C. (2009) *Environmental and material flow cost accounting: principles and procedures*, Vienna: Springer.

Kaplan, R.S. (1986) 'The role for empirical research in management accounting', *Accounting, Organizations and Society*, 11: 429–452.

Kloot, L. (1997) 'Organizational learning and management control systems: responding to environmental change', *Management Accounting Research*, 8: 47–73.

Kokubu, K., Campos, M.K.S., Furukawa, Y., and Tachikawa, H. (2009) 'Material flow cost accounting with ISO 14051', *ISO Management Systems*, January–February: 15–18.

Lamnek, S. (1995) *Qualitative Sozialforschung. Methoden und Techniken [Qualitative social research: methods and techniques]. Band 2*, Weinheim: Beltz.

Larrinaga-González, C., Carrasco-Fenech, F., Caro-González, F.J., Correa-Ruiz, C., and Páez-Sandubete, J.M. (2001) 'The role of environmental accounting in organizational change: an exploration of Spanish companies', *Accounting, Auditing & Accountability Journal*, 14: 213–239.

Letmathe, P. and Doost, R.K. (2000) 'Environmental cost accounting and auditing', *Managerial Auditing Journal*, 15: 424–431.

Malmi, T. and Granlund, M. (2009) 'In search of management accounting theory', *European Accounting Review*, 18: 597–620.

McClintock, C., Brannon, D., and Maynard-Moody, S. (1979) 'Applying the logic of sample surveys to qualitative case studies: the case cluster method', *Administrative Science Quarterly*, 24: 612–629.

Moon, J., Gond, J.-P., Grubnic, S., and Herzig, C. (2011) *Management control for sustainability strategy*, London: Chartered Institute of Management Accountants.

Parker, L. (1999) *Environmental costing: an exploratory examination*, Melbourne: Australian Society of Certified Practising Accountants.

Ryan, B., Scapens, R.W., and Theobald, M. (2002) *Research method and methodology in finance and accounting*, London: Thomson.

Saling, P., Kicherer, A., Dittrich-Krämer, B. Wittlinger, R., Zombik, W., Schmidt, I., Schrott, W., and Schmidt, S. (2002) 'Eco-efficiency analysis by BASF: the method', *International Journal of Life Cycle Assessment*, 7: 203–218.

Scapens, R.W. (1990) 'Researching management accounting practice: the role of case study methods', *British Accounting Review*, 22: 259–281.

Scavone, G.M. (2006) 'Challenges in internal environmental management reporting in Argentina', *Journal of Cleaner Production*, 14: 1276–1285.

Schaltegger, S. (1998) 'Accounting for eco-efficiency', in Nath, B., Hens, L., Compton, P., and Devuyst, D. (eds) *Environmental management in practice. Volume I: Instruments for environmental management*, London: Routledge, pp. 272–287.

Schaltegger, S. and Burritt, R.L. (2000) *Contemporary environmental accounting: issues, concepts and practice*, Sheffield: Greenleaf Publishing.

Schaltegger, S. and Dyllick, T. (2002) *Managing sustainability with the balanced scorecard*, Wiesbaden: Gabler.

Schaltegger, S. and Sturm, A. (1990) 'Ökologische Rationalität: Ansatzpunkte zur Ausgestaltung von ökologieorientierten Managementinstrumenten' [Ecological rationality: starting points for developing ecology-orientated management tools], *Die Unternehmung*, 4: 273–290.

Schaltegger, S. and Sturm, A. (1992) 'Erfolgskriterien ökologieorientierten Managements: die Notwendigkeit einer ökologischen Rechnungslegung' [Success factors of ecology-orientated management: the necessity of ecological accounting], *Zeitschrift für Umweltpolitik & Umweltrecht*, 2: 131–154.

Schaltegger, S. and Sturm, A. (1998) *Eco-efficiency by eco-controlling: theory and cases*, Zürich: vdf.

Schaltegger, S., Burritt, R., and Petersen, H. (2003) *An introduction to corporate environmental management: striving for sustainability*, Sheffield: Greenleaf Publishing.

Silverman, D. (1993) *Interpreting qualitative data*, London: Sage.

Walsham, G. (1995) 'Interpretive case studies in IS research: nature and method', *European Journal of Information Systems*, 4: 74–81.

Walsham, G. (2006) 'Doing interpretive research', *European Journal of Information Systems*, 15: 320–330.

Witzel, A. (1982) *Verfahren der qualitativen Sozialforschung: Überblick und Alternativen*, Frankfurt: Campus.

Yin, R.K. (2003) *Case study research*, Thousand Oaks, CA: Sage.

Part II
Case studies on EMA in South-East Asia

4

EMA FOR ECO-EFFICIENCY IN A TOWEL PRODUCTION FIRM

Indah Jaya, Indonesia

Introduction

The textile industry is of huge importance to South-East Asian economies but associated with large-scale negative environmental and social impacts. To reduce such impacts and avoid reputational risks, some international retail chains demand adherence to standards such as ISO 14001 or SA 8000.

This case study explores EMA at PT Indah Jaya Textile Industry (referred to as Indah Jaya), an Indonesian textile manufacturer and exporter of towels to the world. The company uses environmental management procedures and has a high reputation for its social performance including the provision of health care, sanitation, housing, and recreational facilities for its workers. Prior to this case study, information was available to support an environmental management system in line with ISO 14001 and environmental measures of company performance. This case study links environmental management information to production and supply processes to examine its relevance for various decision settings, including monthly performance assessments (Figure 4.1: Boxes 1 and 9), mid- and long-term eco-efficiency investments (Boxes 7, 8, 15, and 16), and product pricing (Box 7).

Decision setting

Indah Jaya is situated in Tangerang, Banten province, about 30 kilometres west of Jakarta. The privately owned company was founded in 1962 and produces various types of towels (pool, bath, hand, guest, face, and kitchen) and related textile products (washing gloves, bathmats, and bathrobes). Most of Indah Jaya's customers are large retail chains, such as Walmart (USA), Arcandor (former Karstadt Quelle) and Metro Real (both German), and Hayashi Co. Ltd

		Monetary EMA		Physical EMA	
		Short-term	Long-term	Short-term	Long-term
Past-orientated	Routinely generated	Environmental cost accounting including material flow cost accounting (MCFA) [1]	Environment-induced capital expenditure and revenue [2]	Material and energy flow accounting [9]	Environmental capital impact accounting [10]
Past-orientated	Ad hoc	Ex-post assessment of relevant environmental costing decisions [3]	Ex-post inventory assessment of projects [4]	Ex-post assessment of short-term environmental impacts [11]	Ex-post inventory appraisal of physical environmental investments [12]
Future-orientated	Routinely generated	Monetary environmental budgeting [5]	Environmental long-term financial planning [6]	Physical environmental budgeting [13]	Environmental long-term physical planning [14]
Future-orientated	Ad hoc	Relevant environmental costing [7]	Monetary environmental investment appraisal [8]	Tools designed to predict relevant enviromental impacts [15]	Physical environmental investment appraisal [16]

FIGURE 4.1 Application of the EMA framework (Burritt, Hahn, and Schaltegger 2002) to Indah Jaya.
Note: Dark (light) grey boxes represent the major (minor) EMA applications.

(Japan). Indah Jaya produces the chains' private brands and licensed designs on an order basis. With annual sales of €55 million and about 1,600 permanent employees Indah Jaya is a large enterprise.

The management structure of Indah Jaya can be characterised as hierarchical. The managing director is also one of the company's owners. He is the head of directors for the four main departments: human resources and general affairs, operations, finance, and marketing. The directors lead the managers, middle managers, department and section heads, and foremen (Figure 4.2). In addition to the four directors of main departments, a management representative exists to coordinate cross-functional tasks and assume charge of all management systems, particularly quality and environmental management systems. The management representative, Mr Suyanto, has shown an interest in EMA to improve the eco-efficiency of Indah Jaya.

Competitive and economic situation

High quality and compliance with environmental and social standards are competitive advantages for Indah Jaya's exports when compared with other textile companies in South-East Asia. Their markets are in industrialised countries, such as the European Union, Japan, and the United States. In the home markets of Indah Jaya, price is the decisive factor for buying textiles,

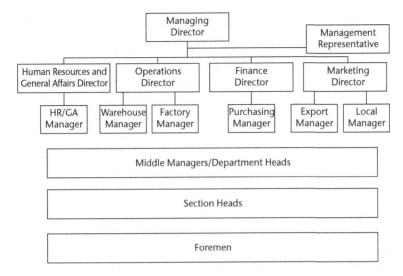

FIGURE 4.2 Organisational chart of Indah Jaya (source: Indah Jaya).

which leaves Indah Jaya uncompetitive in these markets. Newly industrialising countries, in particular China, produce towels much more cheaply and manage to increase the quality of their products annually. Thus, the quality gap between low-price-orientated competitors and Indah Jaya is getting smaller. In 2005, the Agreement on Textiles and Clothing, which included fixed quotas for textile-producing countries, was terminated (for the consequences of fixed quota termination see Nordås 2004). Since then, competition for Indah Jaya has increased.

Assuming that competitors from other Asian countries, such as India and Bangladesh, manage to close the quality gap and fulfil the social and environmental requirements of overseas customers in the next few years, Indah Jaya needs to be price-competitive, as well as continuing to be quality-competitive. The efficiency of Indah Jaya's operations has to be increased continuously if it is to prosper. Environmental costs are already a large part of the total textile production costs and are likely to increase. In textile companies in industrialising countries, costs of raw materials and energy are of even higher importance than in industrialised countries as they account for the biggest share of total production costs (see ITMF 2003 for a detailed analysis of the Indonesian textile industry; see also EKONID 2001). One main reason for the relative importance of materials and energy costs is comparatively low labour costs.

Environmental issues

Because of its proactive environmental and social management, Indah Jaya is not facing any current legal concerns. Stricter enforcement of environmental regulations would most likely increase Indah Jaya's competitive advantage in the Indonesian market.

Almost all Indah Jaya products are exported. Many of the company's overseas customers require compliance with environmental and social standards. In accordance with these requirements, Indah Jaya is ISO 9001, ISO 14001, Oeko-Tex (Eco-Tex), and SA 8000 certified. The certification processes helped Indah Jaya to improve environmental and social performance. The health and safety of employees has been improved, social facilities, such as housing for female workers, sports facilities, and new canteens, have been built, and wastewater treatment and proper handling of chemicals have been the focus of continuous improvement.

In addition to customer demand for environmentally and socially friendly products, Indah Jaya is also concerned about the water and wastewater situation at its Tangerang plant. To date, Indah Jaya uses groundwater in its production processes. The increasing demand for water in the area has consumed almost all groundwater stock. Seawater from the nearby Java Sea is flowing slowly into former freshwater sinks. In the future, instead of groundwater Indah Jaya may need to use low-quality river water, which will have to be treated using special facilities and chemicals.

Energy consumption is another important environmental issue for Indah Jaya. Currently the main source of energy is an on-site, coal-fired boiler producing heat for several production processes. Indonesia is heavily subsidising energy, in particular oil-based production of electricity. Oil price increases have led the government to raise subsidies. Oil subsidies amounted to US$12 billion in 2005, almost a third of total government spending (ADB 2005). Even though oil prices have improved since the global financial crisis, in the long-run it can be expected that energy costs for companies will rise again as the government begins to reduce subsidies.

It can be concluded that the environmental performance of Indah Jaya is very active compared with competitors producing in South-East Asia, meaning that the company abides by the law and is proactive in seeking options for environmental and social improvements.

Technological processes of towel production

Production at Indah Jaya covers a broad range of textile processes, starting with spinning and dyeing, as preparatory processes for the production of yarn. In the main stages of cloth production, yarn is transferred to weaving preparation and weaving, as well as wet processing. The cloth proceeds to cutting and sewing, embroidering and/or printing, and is prepared for sale in the final step of production. These main production steps are supported by auxiliary processes including steam production, compressed air, and wastewater treatment.

Company's motivation for using EMA

Indah Jaya established environmental and quality management systems to satisfy customer demand for environmentally friendly, high-quality products. In addition to this externally driven incentive for environmental management, Indah Jaya has faced higher costs for environmental resources and increasing competition in its markets. Hence, the management representative, Mr Suyanto, became interested in improving Indah Jaya's environmental performance. His intention was to link it to related financial issues and to find and assess options for eco-efficiency improvements. The decision situation before starting to implement EMA can be characterised as follows.

Environmental information concerning issues such as energy consumption, hazardous substances, and legal requirements was available to support the environmental management system based on ISO 14001. However, this information was not linked to production and supply processes. Environmental issues were treated separately from other business activities. Mr Suyanto intended to link environmental issues to production planning and control. In particular, he was interested in receiving regular reports on physical and related monetary aspects of production. This decision setting is located in Figure 4.1, Boxes 1 and 9.

Mr Suyanto developed ideas about how to improve the environmental performance of Indah Jaya but had not quantitatively assessed the options. He was eager to receive reliable and quantifiable information to support decision-making regarding whether to invest in such measures. This required future-orientated, long-term-focussed, ad hoc information in physical and monetary terms (Figure 4.1: Boxes 8 and 16).

Most of Indah Jaya's products are tailored according to the specific demands and requirements of overseas customers. A price has to be stated for each customer's order. Indah Jaya was interested to know the effect of environmental issues such as energy and water consumption on pricing, which can be characterised as short-term, future-orientated, ad hoc decision-making (Figure 4.1: Boxes 7 and 15).

EMA application

Mr Suyanto invited the authors of this case study for an initial visit to Indah Jaya's production facilities in September 2004. This was followed by two meetings during the following two years. An EMA team was established, which included Mr Suyanto and Mr Salim, an assistant of the director of finance, as well as other Indah Jaya managers, and an engineer who provided expertise and information on specific issues. The EMA team was initially supported by the authors and Mr Wirman, an environmental expert and consultant.

To provide adequate information for decision-making, the EMA team decided to focus on Indah Jaya's main production line, that is, towel production, and to apply several EMA tools in a sequential approach.

Material and energy flow accounting including costs

For a general overview of the towel production line and to provide a basis for further EMA tool selection and application, the EMA team created an accounting system for material and energy flows and associated costs. As a starting point, a list of the most relevant production and utility processes was developed (see Table 4.1).

The result of 11 major steps are depicted and numbered in Table 4.1. The processes have been simplified by aggregating several production steps. For each of these steps, Indah Jaya developed input–output tables to collect material and energy flows and additional information, including labour used in production. For each production step, the accounting department supplied unit cost information. Based on this information, the EMA team calculated the costs associated with materials and energy and allocated these costs to the desired output of each production step. The tracking and tracing of energy demand, material consumption, auxiliary use, and other physical and monetary items to single production steps stimulated discussion among the EMA team concerning the drivers of material and energy use and waste generation as well as possible measures for improvement. For instance, the input–output table related to the first production step, spinning (Table 4.2), confirmed the EMA team's assumption that increasing energy efficiency is the environmental and monetary hot-spot of that particular step. The monthly electric energy expense is IDR650 million or about €51,600, and accounts for 7.4 per cent of the operating cost of spinning, whereas labour accounts for 3.5 per cent of costs and all other auxiliaries and utility supplies are negligible.

The integrated representation of physical and monetary information aroused the attention of Indah Jaya's owners. The EMA team was asked to establish this type of accounting on a regular basis so that relevant information could be reported to the owners on a monthly basis. The material and energy flow accounting information was then used as a basis for additional EMA analyses.

Material flow cost accounting

At first glance, the input–output example in Table 4.2 supported the view that waste is not a particularly crucial issue in spinning. Only 1.6 per cent of the raw material input was waste and even this could be sold as a by-product, thereby creating a small amount of revenue. A further 1.2 per cent of raw material input is lost as dust. Applying the concept of material flow cost accounting

TABLE 4.1 Processes of Indah Jaya's towel production line

	Detailed process list	*Aggregated process list*
Production processes	Spinning	1: Spinning
	Winding	2: Yarn dyeing
	Yarn dyeing	
	Rewinding	
	Warping	3: Weaving preparation and weaving
	Sizing	
	Weaving	
	Shearing	4: Wet processing
	Piece dyeing and washing	
	Washing	
	Hydro extractor	
	Tumbler	
	Stenter	
	Reshearing	
	Long slitting	5: Cutting and sewing
	Long hemming and cutting	
	Cross cutting	
	Cross sewing	
	Embroidering	6: Embroidering
	Printing	7: Printing
	Sorting and packaging	8: Finalisation
	Manual rework	
Utility processes	Coal boiler	9: Steam production
	Gas boiler	
	Diesel boiler	
	Air compressor	10: Air compressor
	Wastewater treatment	11: Wastewater treatment

(MFCA), however, slightly changes this view. MFCA treats waste as material loss and assigns to it a portion of raw material and processing cost (Strobel and Redmann 2002; Kokubu, Campos, Furukawa, and Tachikawa 2009). Table 4.3 exhibits the results of applying MFCA for the spinning process. The monthly cost of generating a material loss of 14,000 kg is IDR228 million (€18,100), which equals a unit cost of IDR16,291/kg (€1.30/kg).

The EMA team applied MFCA to several production steps and types of

TABLE 4.2 Excerpt from the input–output table for spinning

Production step: 1 Spinning
Reference unit: 1 month (yearly average)

Input

Item	Amount	Unit	Unit cost (IDR/unit)	Cost (IDR '000)	Data quality and source
Cotton	490,000	kg	16,000	7,840	Calculated (records)
Electric energy	1,300,000	kWh	500	650	Measured (records)
Labour	352	Worker	864,500	304	Estimated (prod. manager)

Output

Item	Amount	Unit	Unit cost (IDR/unit)	Cost (IDR '000)	Data quality and source
Grey yarn	476,000	kg	18,442	8,778	Aggregated
Cotton waste (for sale)	8,000	kg	2,000	16	Calculated (records)
Dust	6,000	kg	–	–	Calculated (records)

TABLE 4.3 MFCA analysis for spinning

Material flows	Weight (kg)	Weight (%)
Product (grey yarn)	476,000	97.2
Material loss (dust and cotton waste)	14,000	2.8

Material flow costs	IDR '000	Unit cost (IDR/kg)
Production cost of spinning	8794	
Cost assigned to product	8543	17,947
Cost assigned to material loss	244	
less cotton waste revenues	–16	
Net cost of material loss	228	16,291

material loss. Analysis highlighted the financial relevance of material losses and changed the way managers appraised fabric and yarn rejects and leftovers. Indah Jaya could sell almost all rejects of fabric production as a second-grade product on local markets. MFCA analysis confirmed that the revenues from selling these rejects were less than one fifth of their production cost, thus making a net loss. MFCA analysis even questioned the production of so-called mambo towels. These towels were produced from excess yarn from customer orders, which was not possible to use for other orders. Revenues from the sale of mambo towels did not recover the full production cost of such towels. However, producing the mambo towels was still of greater benefit than simply disposing of the excess yarn.

Use of MFCA highlighted the importance of avoiding material losses and provided incentives for measures of efficiency improvement. In the following section, several examples of eco-efficiency measures and their appraisal are explained.

Assessment of eco-efficiency improvements

During conduct of the case study, several environmental improvements were discussed and assessed.

Steam supply

Indah Jaya operated several boilers to supply steam for its production processes, in particular yarn dyeing (Step 2, Table 4.1). For the continual production of heat, a coal-fired industrial furnace was used. The furnace consumed approximately 1,000 tonnes of coal at the cost of IDR250 million (€21,400) each month. The combustion of coal is associated with environmental impacts, most notably global warming. To increase eco-efficiency of the industrial furnace, Indah Jaya considered replacing it with an advanced coal-fired, fluid-bed furnace. Replacement would reduce down-time caused by maintenance and cleaning activities. Down-time is a driver of maintenance and diesel fuel costs, as Indah Jaya used a diesel-fuelled boiler as backup system. The new boiler would increase energy efficiency by reducing waste heat, that is, less heat is lost through thermal radiation. In addition, the amount of coal required could be substantially reduced by purchasing coal with a higher heating value (approximately 25 MJ/kg instead of 20 MJ/kg). To support this investment decision, the EMA team assessed potential financial and environmental benefits of a new industrial furnace focussing on reducing the global warming impact (Table 4.4).

A full capital investment appraisal was carried out by the financial department on the basis of the information provided in Table 4.5 using industry-specific discount rates. The environmental benefits were analysed using generic eco-inventory data for coal-fired industrial furnace processes. This data provides full life cycle inventories including details on air emissions and related environmental impacts for combustion processes (Dones, Bauer, Bolliger,

TABLE 4.4 Environmental and financial assessment of new industrial furnace

	Old furnace	New furnace	Difference
Unit cost of coal (IDR/kg)	270	350	+30%
Physical demand for coal (kg/h)	1,500	1,000	−33%
Total cost of coal (IDR/h)	405,000	350,000	−14%
Down-time cost (IDR/h)	50,000	22,000	−56%
Total operating cost (IDR/h)	456,500	373,000	−18%
Total annual operating cost (IDR/year – '000)	**3,703**	**3,026**	**−677 (−18%)**
Global warming potential (GWP) of direct emissions (tonnes CO_2eq/year)	**35,000**	**30,600**	**−4,400 (−12.5%)**

TABLE 4.5 Ecological investment appraisal (global warming potential) for new coal boiler

GWP caused by the investment (life cycle impacts of building and assembling the new boiler)	225 tonnes CO_2eq
GWP reduction potential	367 tonnes CO_2eq per month
Ecological payback	< 1 month
Ecological advantage ratio (benefits divided by impacts caused by investment; assumed life-span of 10 years)	200:1

Burger, Faist Emmenegger, Frischknecht, Heck, Jungbluth, and Röder 2007). Environmental impact was assessed using Intergovernmental Panel on Climate Change figures for global warming potential (GWP) (Solomon, Qin, Manning, Chen, Marquis, Averyt, Tignor, and Miller 2007). An ecological investment appraisal (Schaltegger and Burritt 2000: 306–313) was carried out using GWP as a main indicator for overall environmental impact (Table 4.5).

Both the financial investment and ecological investment appraisals confirmed the net benefits of the investment in both monetary (increased profitability) and physical (reduced environmental impact) terms. These benefits were realised after the case study concluded. From a purely environmental point of view, burning coal more efficiently (known as clean-coal production) is certainly not the most advantageous option. Other fossil fuels such as natural gas or renewable fuels such as biogas have lower environmental impacts. These options were not considered feasible because their financial costs were thought to be too high for the company to remain competitive.

Absorption chiller

To run spinning and weaving processes successfully, specific temperature and humidity levels are required. Indah Jaya consumes a huge amount of electricity for chilling units required in each of these production steps. At the same time, considerable energy is lost as heat when burning coal and other fuels. The EMA team researched ways to re-use available waste heat for chilling and discovered an absorption chiller to be the most feasible option. An investment appraisal for the absorption chiller confirmed its high environmental and financial profitability.[1] Absorption chillers use heat instead of mechanical compressors to provide cooling (for a detailed explanation of absorption chilling see Herold, Radermacher, and Klein 1996: 101–175). The specific type of chiller installed used the boiler's exhaust heat to run chilling units and completely replaced the previous electricity-driven chillers.

Water recycling

Indah Jaya is located in an area where water supplies are volatile. Indah Jaya relies on a constant, large, and high-quality supply of freshwater for its dyeing processes to ensure that the colours of final products match customer standards. To lower its freshwater consumption, Indah Jaya considered recycling the dyeing process water after wastewater treatment. To assess the profitability of water recycling the EMA team carried out a monetary investment appraisal (Table 4.6). Mr Suyanto and Indah Jaya's wastewater treatment and dyeing process engineers planned initially to recycle 20 per cent of wastewater and then to increase this percentage gradually without compromising the water quality for the dyeing units. They estimated that an investment of IDR291 million

TABLE 4.6 Investment appraisal for water recycling (million IDR)

	Years								
	0	*1*	*2*	*3*	*4*	*5*	*6*	*7*	*8*
Initial investment									
Reservoir tank	–210								
Piping	–26								
Pump	–25								
Construction incl. labour	–30								
Total	–291								
Annual cost savings (reduced freshwater)		79.2	79.2	79.2	79.2	79.2	79.2	79.2	79.2
Discounted cost savings (12%)		70.7	63.1	56.4	50.3	44.9	40.1	35.8	32.0
Sum of discounted net cash flows	393.4								
Net present value	**102.4**								
Profitability	**35%**								
Simple payback period	**3.7 years**								

(€23,100) was required to install additional equipment and tanks for wastewater recycling that would last at least eight years. Assuming the initial recycling rate of 20 per cent, Indah Jaya could save 440 m³ of freshwater per day at a cost of IDR500 per m³, that is, IDR79.2 million (€6,300) per year.

The results of the investment appraisal supported Mr Suyanto's idea to recycle water. From a purely financial point of view the investment was not considered excellent, but its profitability and its payback met the internal requirements. With the ecological advantages being the main incentive for the investment, Indah Jaya immediately installed the water-recycling equipment. At the time the case study was conducted, initial experience with the new system indicated that a recycling quota above 20 per cent seemed feasible without diminishing the quality of the dyeing processes.

Hot water pre-heating

The use of steam is a crucial issue for Indah Jaya from both environmental and financial points of view. Increasing eco-efficiency of the steam generation process is one option to improve Indah Jaya's performance; another option is the reduction of the overall demand for steam. The largest consumers of steam were the dyeing units for yarn and fabrics, which account for more than half of the total demand for steam. Dyeing requires steam to heat freshwater to a predetermined temperature depending on the type of yarn and chosen colour. After dyeing, the remaining water is discharged to Indah Jaya's wastewater treatment plant. The wastewater temperature of approximately 70°C made it necessary to cool the wastewater to a suitable temperature for bacteria and other organic compounds of the treatment process. Cooling was achieved by slowly sprinkling wastewater into the treatment facilities as shown in Figure 4.3. On one hand Indah Jaya had to heat up freshwater from approximately 25°C to temperatures of about 100°C, while in contrast wastewater from the process had to be cooled. The EMA team suggested installing a simple counter-current heat exchanger that pre-heats the freshwater by recovering the heat from wastewater. The actual implementation of a heat exchanger was included in the planning and implementation processes for water-recycling facilities and finished after the case study concluded.

FIGURE 4.3 Cooling of wastewater before treatment (source: author).

Job order costing at Indah Jaya

Indah Jaya's production was based on customer orders. Customers chose the type of yarn, size and shape of towels, type and quality of colours, number of different colours, and type of embroidery or print, as well as the number of towels needed. The sales department had to state a price for each customer order. Pricing decisions were based on various production cost drivers, such as the size of towels and number of colours, but also on other factors such as the importance and reliability of the customer. This pricing was based on a job-costing system as costs are separately assigned to each job. The counterpart of job costing is process costing, whereby costs are assigned to products on basis of costs averaged for the period under examination (for a comprehensive introduction to job costing see Bhimani, Horngren, Datar, and Foster 2008: 64–136).

Although in the case of Indah Jaya the system behind the company's approach to pricing was clearly job costing, the pricing system did include elements of process costing. For instance, energy use, waste generation, and water consumption were not considered in costing and pricing decisions on a job order basis. Instead, the same averaged figures per unit were used for each job. Material and energy flow-related cost information could help to improve the job costing by including information on energy and water consumption, amounts of excess yarn, and so forth. It supports identification of all relevant (environmentally induced) production costs for a customer order. Table 4.7 summarises the EMA team's results from the first analysis of material flows recorded in Indah Jaya's job order costing system.

Some of these cause-and-effect relationships, in particular those concerning type of yarn, packaging, and printing/embroidering, were well known to the decision-makers at Indah Jaya. Others appeared to be obvious and straightforward but the information had never been compiled this way. For instance, decision-makers were not fully aware that using dark colours in dyeing not only doubled the process time compared with light-colour dyeing, but also increased the per unit energy and chemical consumption in production and wastewater treatment. By identifying relevant material and energy flow aspects of pricing decisions, the EMA team supported profitable, environmentally benign decision-making by the sales department.

Discussion and conclusions

The implementation of EMA at Indah Jaya confirms that the systematic accounting for material and energy flows, and financial consequences, makes business sense in the setting examined. Indah Jaya's top management considered EMA to be a very useful concept for decision-making and, as a

TABLE 4.7 Impacts of customer orders on material and energy flows and costs

Driver	Material and energy flow aspects	Financial impacts	Environmental impacts
Size of towels	Higher number of rejects for bigger towels	Cost of material losses	Material loss-related resource use, energy use
	More cutting and sewing for small towels	Higher production costs in the cutting and sewing step	Higher energy consumption
Colour	Dark colours require longer dyeing processes, more cleaning water and more wastewater treatment	Higher price for dark dyestuffs, higher production costs for dyeing, higher costs for water and wastewater treatment	Water consumption, higher energy consumption in dyeing, more chemicals in wastewater treatment, more sludge from wastewater treatment
	Increased dyeing operating time for towels with several colours	Higher production costs for multi-colour towels, more rejects	Higher energy consumption, higher chemical consumption
Size of customer's order	Higher excess production for small orders, increased set-up times (in comparison with large orders)	Higher production costs per unit of product for small orders	Relatively more resource consumption for small orders, higher consumption of energy, chemicals, etc. during set-up
Type of yarn	–	Higher purchasing costs for certain types of yarn (e.g. organic)	–
Packaging	Piece-by-piece packaging vs. large bulk packaging	Higher cost for piece-by-piece packaging materials, higher labour cost, longer processing time per unit of product	Higher packaging material consumption, higher energy consumption
Printing/ embroidering	Additional production steps	Production cost for printing or embroidering including additional energy, water, and wastewater treatment cost	Environmental impacts of printing or embroidering

consequence of the EMA case study, requested monthly material and energy flow reports to support future decisions.

Implementation at Indah Jaya shows that EMA is not limited to one specific tool. Accounting for material and energy flows in the form of a flow chart led to the initial conclusions. In combination with financial information, improvements to production and supply processes could be achieved and options for further improvements assessed. In relation to products, a different perspective exists. Integration of material and energy flow aspects into job costing, as well as MFCA, helped to increase eco-efficiency through accurate product pricing and identification of the exact costs of unwanted products.

Not unexpectedly, the measurement of physical information turned out to be a major challenge for EMA implementation. In particular, precise measurement of energy and auxiliary consumption at the production and supply process levels were difficult and in several cases required the use of estimated values. The company's willingness to account for physical information and improve the measurements required, increased as some initial benefits from EMA became apparent. Although time for conducting the case study was restricted and did not allow a follow-up for all potential improvement measures, the implementation of EMA at Indah Jaya highlights the usefulness and benefits of continuously and systematically integrating environmental aspects into management decision-making.

Note

1 Exact figures of the appraisal cannot be provided because the information was considered confidential by the company for competitive reasons.

References

ADB (Asian Development Bank) (ed.) (2005) *Asian development outlook 2005*, Manila: ADB.

Bhimani, A., Horngren, C.T., Datar, S.M., and Foster, G. (2008) *Management and cost accounting*, 4th edition, Harlow: Pearson.

Burritt, R., Hahn, T. and Schaltegger, S. (2002) 'Towards a comprehensive framework for environmental management accounting: links between business actors and environmental management accounting tools', *Australian Accounting Review*, 12: 39–50.

Dones, R., Bauer, C., Bolliger, R., Burger, B., Faist Emmenegger, M., Frischknecht, R., Heck, T., Jungbluth, N., and Röder, A. (2007) *Life cycle inventories of energy systems: final report Ecoinvent data v2.0, No. 5*, Dübendorf: Swiss Centre for Life Cycle Inventories.

EKONID (German–Indonesian Chamber of Commerce and Industry) (2001) *Market survey of the Indonesian textile industry*, Bonn: GTZ.

Herold, K.E., Radermacher, R., and Klein, S.A. (1996) *Absorption chillers and heat pumps*, Boca Raton, FL: CRC Press.

ITMF (International Textile Manufacturers Federation) (ed.) (2003) *International production cost comparison: spinning/texturing/weaving/knitting*, Zurich: ITMF.

Kokubu, K., Campos, M.K.S., Furukawa, Y., and Tachikawa, H. (2009) 'Material flow cost accounting with ISO 14051', *ISO Management Systems* (January–February), 15–18.

Nordås, H.K. (2004) *The global textile and clothing industry post the agreement on textiles and clothing*, Geneva: WTO [online – accessed on 1 September 2009]. Available from Internet: http://www.wto.org/english/res_e/booksp_e/discussion_papers5_e.pdf.

Schaltegger, S. and Burritt, R.L. (2000) *Contemporary environmental accounting: issues, concepts and practice*, Sheffield: Greenleaf Publishing.

Solomon, S., Qin, D., Manning, M., Chen, Z. Marquis, M., Averyt, K.B., Tignor, M., and Miller, H.L. (eds) (2007) *Climate change 2007: the physical science basis. Contribution of working group I to the fourth assessment report of the intergovernmental panel on climate change*, Cambridge: Cambridge University Press.

Strobel, M. and Redmann, C. (2002) 'Flow cost accounting, an accounting based approach on the actual flows of materials', in Bennett, M., Bouma, J.J., and Wolters, T. (eds) *Environmental management accounting: informational and institutional developments*, Dordrecht: Kluwer, pp. 67–82.

5

MANAGING HSE IN A MECHANICAL ENGINEERING FIRM

Bisma Jaya, Indonesia

Introduction

In high-risk industrial sectors, health, safety, and environment (HSE) management systems play an important part in corporate responsibility management. Such importance has recently been reinforced with the oil-drilling platform and equipment problems of BP and the world's largest oil spill in the Gulf of Mexico (McNulty and Crooks 2010). HSE management systems support companies in at least minimising and at best eliminating adverse health effects, injuries, and environmental damages as well as complying with legislation, standards, and requirements of external stakeholders. Key elements in HSE management systems are risk assessment and risk control through implementation of preventative and protective measures, the preparation of emergency situations, and investigation of accidents as well as the integration of facilities into the surrounding environment (Rikhardsson 2006). HSE management systems have also become a common element of supply chain audits and management (Beske, Koplin, and Seuring 2008; Piplani, Pujawan, and Ray 2008). By increasing environmental and social transparency across the supply chain and gaining control over their contractors, companies aim to align compliance of suppliers with their corporate HSE goals and policy (NZBCSD 2003; BSCI 2009).

In this case study of CV Bisma Jaya (hereafter Bisma Jaya), an Indonesian company specialising in engineering and construction, the use of EMA as a response to an accident and subsequent HSE audits is discussed (for an overview of different approaches see Rikhardsson 2006). The audit under study has been carried out by one of its main customers from the oil and gas industry subsequent to an accident at one of Bisma Jaya's workshops. The audit ascertains failures with implementation of the HSE management system leading to a rating result that puts the collaboration between the two business partners at risk and could disqualify the company from participating in future tenders for supplies. The case study first explains how the results of an HSE audit and the measures taken by Bisma Jaya can flow into a non-monetary assessment (Figure 5.1: Box 11) and costing approach (Box 7) which support the company in meeting the requirements in the most cost-efficient way. Second, additional links to monetary and non-monetary HSE budgeting (Boxes 5 and 13) are outlined. Finally, a discussion of the benefits and limitations of the eco- and socio-efficient notion of strategic responses to regulatory systems such as rating systems and audits is presented, the result being that eco- and socio-efficiency are seen as only partially useful concepts which have to be complemented by effectiveness considerations on HSE performance.

Decision setting

Bisma Jaya, established in 1983, is a company specialising in engineering and construction for mechanical work. It is located in the oil city of Balikpapan, East Kalimantan (Borneo), Indonesia, and employs 132 people, of whom 50 are full-time employees. The core business is offshore construction and

		Monetary EMA		Physical EMA	
		Short-term	Long-term	Short-term	Long-term
Past-orientated	Routinely generated	Health, Safety, and Environment (HSE) cost accounting [1]	HSE-induced capital expenditure and revenue [2]	Physical accounting of HSE issues [9]	HSE capital impact accounting [10]
Past-orientated	Ad hoc	Ex-post assessment of relevant HSE costing decisions [3]	Monetary ex-post investment assessment of HSE projects [4]	Ex-post assessment of short-term HSE impacts [11]	Ex-post inventory appraisal of physical HSE investments [12]
Future-orientated	Routinely generated	Monetary HSE budgeting [5]	HSE long-term financial planning [6]	Physical HSE budgeting [13]	Long-term planning of HSE issues [14]
Future-orientated	Ad hoc	Relevant HSE costing [7]	Monetary HSE investment appraisal [8]	Tools designed to predict relevant HSE impacts [15]	Physical HSE investment appraisal [16]

FIGURE 5.1 Application of the EMA framework (Burritt, Hahn, and Schaltegger 2002) to Bisma Jaya.
Note: Dark (light) grey boxes represent the major (minor) EMA applications.

marine service. Starting its business with mechanical devices for the timber industry, Bisma Jaya has expanded in recent years to a larger region in East Kalimantan, including the oil, gas, and coal mining industries.

Technology

Bisma Jaya has three workshops on the coast or near rivers, all accessible by ship or car and available for construction activities such as building oil platforms. These three workshops are located in Balikpapan, Handil, and Senipah.

Like many engineering companies, Bisma Jaya works on a project basis and has carried out a large range of projects for its main customers in the oil and gas industry. These projects require mechanical engineering and construction work such as building pumping installations for a dredging system, revamping a network of fire water lines, protective coating and paintings, de-sanding installations, and fabrication of wellhead platforms and accessories.

Economic situation

Bisma Jaya is well situated financially. Its financial performance, however, is dependent on maintaining good relationships with its principal customer, a large Indonesian company engaged in onshore and offshore oil and gas exploration. The customer selects contractors carefully based on technical specifications and analysis of contractor risks, and supervises the contractor's worksites. The oil and gas company favours selection of its constructors on the basis of their ability to comply with its policy on quality and HSE. Thus Bisma Jaya undergoes regular external independent audits which involve the measurement of performance and compliance and require the formulation of action plans and the institutionalisation of suitable control procedures to ensure a safe workplace. In case of an accident at one of the workshops or on site, the company is audited on an ad hoc basis. Drawing on the findings from the management system audit, the contractor is rated using the customer's HSE rating system. A poor rating result can have a significant effect on future projects and the economic situation of the company. If the rating score does not meet the contracting company's expectations, Bisma Jaya cannot compete for a job that might be offered by the oil and gas company in the future, and even faces the possibility of losing ongoing projects.

Regulation of company performance

The audit and rating system applied in Bisma Jaya consists of two stages. Figure 5.2 shows that the first stage covers 10 primary factors such as HSE policy, emergency response procedures (ERPs), and the safety manual. These factors count for 70 per cent of the overall rating score. In the second stage,

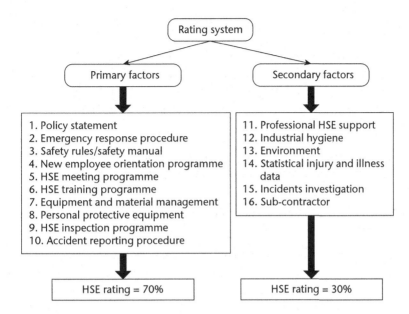

FIGURE 5.2 Rating system.

the remaining 30 per cent of the overall rating score is based on six secondary factors encompassing including professional HSE support, industrial hygiene, and the environment.

The rating is calculated as a sum of primary and secondary points. Each of the primary factors is rated out of 10, that is, a maximum of 100 rating points can be collected if all criteria are perfectly fulfilled by the organisation. Depending on their relevance, the secondary HSE factors are rated 10 (factor 14), 15 (factors 11, 15), or 20 (factors 12, 13, 16), adding up to a maximum total of 100 points. The primary points are given a weight of 70 per cent whereas the secondary factors are given a weight of 30 per cent of the overall rating. In total, all factors account for a maximum score of 100 weighted rating points.

Health, safety, and environment

Bisma Jaya has an HSE policy and an HSE committee headed by a HSE coordinator and supported by a manager for HSE personnel, equipment, and material. The HSE programme includes daily housekeeping, weekly safety talks, monthly meetings and inspections, an annual medical examination of all employees, and a check of personnel protective equipment.

The company's HSE management system is designed in line with the HSE rating system of its main client to meet supply chain management and assurance requirements. It coordinates and systematises Bisma Jaya's business activities with the aid of defined and documented steering and control mechanisms to protect people, equipment, material, and environment during project activities.

HSE performance reported for October 2005 was exceptionally poor. Table 5.1 shows the record of Bisma Jaya's HSE performance for October 2005. With one case of medical treatment per 132 employees, the medical treatment cases frequency is 0.76 and accident/near miss frequency 2.27 (three cases per 132 employees).

The incidents (see Table 5.1), which were considered to be too many and too severe by the main customer, provoked an additional assessment by the contracting company. Its results and implications are explained next.

Motivation for and application of HSE accounting approaches

As a consequence of the accident requiring medical treatment which occurred during one of Bisma Jaya's project activities in October 2005, the contracting company for which the activity had been carried out sent its auditors to evaluate Bisma Jaya's HSE management system. The aim of the assessment was to ensure employees' health and safety and secure environmentally sound practices at Bisma Jaya's workshops and facilities. Before the audit was conducted, an HSE clarification meeting between the customer and Bisma Jaya was held and an agreement was signed that, if the HSE audit indicated that performance was under the minimum requirement, the customer would withdraw the

TABLE 5.1 Health, safety and environment (HSE) performance of Bisma Jaya, October 2005

Man-hours	264,401
Fatality	0
Fatality frequency	–
Lost time injuries	0
Lost time injuries frequency	–
Restricted work day cases	0
Restricted work day cases frequency	–
Medical treatment cases	1
Medical treatment cases frequency	0.76
Accident/near miss	3
Accident/near miss frequency	2.27
Major environment damage	0
Major environment damage frequency	–

tender and Bisma Jaya would focus for six months on improvement of its HSE system. In the case of a further HSE incident or accident during the execution of the existing contract, the six-month period would recommence. With this agreement, HSE issues held the highest economic relevance for Bisma Jaya.

In the audit following the accident, Bisma Jaya received less than half of the maximum score (44 points). An improvement of at least six points was needed to meet the minimum requirement. Bisma Jaya wanted to achieve an immediate improvement to reach this goal and, taking a long view, aimed to achieve a significant increase in order to reduce the risk of falling below this benchmark in the future. This would require a more systematic and incremental approach that prioritises cost-efficient and cost-effective measures of HSE improvement.

In their general conclusions, the external auditors noticed that the HSE team had worked well to revise the HSE management system since the previous audit. However, a significant improvement of the HSE performance still could not be achieved. In particular, the two workshops at Handil and Senipah had not improved sufficiently since the last inspection. Apart from a stronger support and commitment from the management to improve HSE performance, several issues were raised by the auditors to improve the HSE implementation. These issues, and the range of possible measure for improvement and the costing of these options, are discussed in the next section.

HSE performance and system audit, action plan and costings

The discussion of the HSE audit results, the action plan, and the costing of different measures is organised in the following way: first, the underlying primary factors for the rating system are briefly introduced followed by consideration of secondary factors. Then, as a response to the external audit, findings from the audit are outlined and the measures from Bisma Jaya's action plan summarised in Table 5.2. The table also includes the cost calculations for the HSE measures with which Bisma Jaya responded to the findings of the audit.

Primary HSE rating factors

The primary HSE rating factors will be discussed one by one in the light of the audit results including the HSE policy, ERPs, safety rules, and the existence and contents of a safety manual, an information programme for new employees, an HSE meeting programme, an HSE training programme, the management of equipment and materials, personal protective equipment, the HSE inspection programme, and the accident reporting procedure.

TABLE 5.2 Costing of HSE measures addressing audit results

Measure	Explanation	One-off costs (IDR)	Annual costs (IDR)	Costs (€)
1. HSE policy				
1a. Make copy of all HSE policies and install in strategic areas		300,000	–	30
1b. Check that all personnel are familiar with HSE job description as part of their knowledge about HSE policy	12 teams, 0.5 h each, 10 persons per team, 1 trainer	375,000	–	38
2. Emergency response procedures (ERPs)				
2a. Drill for ERP	Monthly, Handil workshop		1,050,000	105
	Monthly, Senipah workshop		1,650,000	165
2b. Develop ERP for fire	Procedure development by HSE manager, discussion with two managers	250,000		25
2c. Develop ERP for hydrocarbon release	Procedure development by HSE manager, discussion with two managers	250,000		25
2d. Develop ERP for 'man overboard'	Procedure development by HSE manager, discussion with two managers	250,000		25
2e. Develop ERP for accident in site	Procedure development by HSE manager, discussion with two managers	250,000		25
2f. Develop ERP for workshop and install in strategic area	Procedure development by HSE manager, discussion with two managers	250,000		25
3. Safety rules and safety manual				
3a. Develop grinding procedure	Procedure development by HSE manager, discussion with two managers	250,000		25

Measure	Explanation	One-off costs (IDR)	Annual costs (IDR)	Costs (€)
3b. Develop welding and cutting procedure	Procedure development by HSE manager, discussion with two managers	250,000		25
3c. Develop lifting procedure	Procedure development by HSE manager, discussion with two managers	250,000		25

4. Information programme for new employees

4a. Orientation programme for new employees	2 per month		1,500,000	150
4b. Verification from employees that they have been given a safety briefing/safety talk	Same as above		1,500,000	150
4c. HSE refreshment programme for longer-term employees	Procedure development by HSE manager, discussion with two managers	250,000		25
	1.5 h briefing, 25 employees in total	137,500		14

5. HSE meeting programme

5a. Commit to a regular HSE meeting for all employees responsible for HSE	Monthly meeting, 20 persons, 2 h, snacks		1,500,000	150
5b. Develop focus agenda that is discussed in meetings, discuss current issues, review previous meeting	Guideline developed by HSE manager, 2 days	200,000		20

6. HSE training programme

6a. Develop matrix training for all employees in 2006	Matrix developed by HSE manager, 3 days	300,000		30
6b. Induction training to be implemented for workers from manpower supply	Internal: 15 people, 1 trainer, 9 topics, 0.5 h each	393,750		39
	External: 10 people, 1 trainer, 7 topics, 0.5 h each	306,250		31

TABLE 5.2 (continued)

Measure	Explanation	One-off costs (IDR)	Annual costs (IDR)	Costs (€)
6c. Training for first aid	22 people in-house training, external trainer, 2 days, accommodation (excl. labour costs)	20,000,000		2,000
	22 people in-house training, 2 days	220,000		22
6d. Training anomaly and incident reporting procedure for all employees	Internal training of supervisors (5 Senipah workshop, 3 Handii workshop) + site manager, 1 hr		52,500	5

7. Equipment and material management

7a. Verification of Bisma Jaya's equipment list	1 week per workshop	820,000		82
7b. Make inspection record and tagging for equipment	Developing of procedure by HSE manager, 1 day, 2 h discussion	250,000		25
	Record and tagging 1 day per month per workshop		2,400,000	240
7c. Make list and copy equipment certificates	External certification, every 6 months		100,000,000	10,000
7d. Coordination of relocation and maintenance of material/equipment and preservation area in the yard	2 days, crane, helpers, assisting operators	11,750,000		1,175
7e. First-aid kit boxes	15 kit boxes needed	1,500,000		150
	Medicaments refilled every 3 months		3,000,000	300
7f. Fire extinguisher	12 exist, 3 to buy	3,600,000		360

8. Personal protective equipment

8a. Develop record of personal protective equipment stock	1 day by HSE manager	100,000		10
8b. Make matrix personal protective equipment for all employees	Development of matrix 1 day by HSE manager, checking 1 week by HSE manager	600,000		60

Measure	Explanation	One-off costs (IDR)	Annual costs (IDR)	Costs (€)
8c. Monitoring personal protective equipment in yard	1 day per week by safety manager		4,800,000	480
9. HSE inspection programme				
9a. Regular inspection in the yard	Total for 9a, 9b, 9c: 1 day per month		1,200,000	120
9b. Develop follow-up matrix	See above			
9c. Bring to HSE committee meeting	See above			
10. Accident reporting procedure				
10a. Develop follow-up matrix for anomaly status	1 day HSE manager, per month		1,200,000	120
10b. Analyse all incidents and accidents	2 days by team (6 persons, inventory and analysis)	2,400,000		240
11. Professional HSE support				
11a. HSE organisation chart and job description	2 days per initial project chart by HSE manager, 1 day per further 4 projects	600,000		60
11b. Schedule of HSE committee meeting	–			
12. Industrial hygiene				
12a. Medical check-up/ medical certificate for all employees	Per person, per year	30,000,000		3,000
12b. Food and beverage procedure	Freezer, boxes, equipment, etc.	10,000,000		1,000
13. Environment				
13a. Schedule of environment inspection	3 days for revision	300,000		30
13b. Waste management area	Segregation of waste, good housekeeping, equipment, truck, fuel, driver		2,480,000	
13c. Relocation of waste near jetty in Handil (in December)	Crane 1 day, 4 employees	28,160,000		2,816

TABLE 5.2 (continued)

Measure	Explanation	One-off costs (IDR)	Annual costs (IDR)	Costs (€)
13d. Basin for oil tank		10,000,000		1,000
14. Statistical injury and illness data				
14a. Record monthly labour hours and other HSE factors	2 days collection and preparation (HSE manager)		200,000	20
14b. Analysis of HSE statistics	2 days by team (6 persons, inventory/ analysis)	2,400,000		240
14c. Guideline for causal analysis, 1 day by HSE manager			100,000	10
15. Investigation of incident				
15a. Adopt cause-and-effect tree analysis	–			
15b. Analysis of all incidents	2 days by team (6 persons, inventory and analysis)	2,400,000		240
15c. Training of team leaders in cause-and-effect tree analysis	–			
15d. Internal training for incident investigations	Included in 6d			
16. Sub-contractors				
16a. Review of procedures	2 days by HSE manager	200,000		20
16b. HSE audit for sub-contractor				
16c. Monitoring of sub-contractor on HSE matters				

HSE policy

This first HSE rating item aims to ensure that the company has a written policy which is aligned with and supports the realisation of government regulations. It has to be signed by senior and line management. HSE structures and job descriptions, as well as the revision process for the HSE policy, are also addressed. The establishment of the HSE policy requires strategic consideration, safety briefings before starting a project, and the introduction of safety meetings and talks. The HSE policy has to be included in the 'pocket book' of the company which each employee receives.

The audit revealed that the policy statement was issued in both English and Bahasa Indonesia, but that the HSE policies posted on the walls of the personnel changing rooms were different at both workshops, Senipah and Handil. The same was true for the HSE on-site issues in the job description issued for line management and key personnel.

Emergency response procedures

According to the customer's HSE rating scheme ERPs must be suitable for work areas as well as all projects. This means that all staff must be aware of the emergency numbers for key personnel, the nearest doctors, and hospital, as well as emergency services. An official agreement with the clinics or hospitals to accept injured employees is also required. Specific ERPs are needed for accidents, fire, 'man overboard', and specific HSE site issues. In addition, Bisma Jaya must show that regular training is conducted for all ERPs with its employees.

The auditors made the remark that a flow chart of the processes was missing and therefore needed to be drawn up and communicated to all parties and that training must also be conducted and registered. In addition, the auditors criticised the observation that some certified first-aid boxes were invalid and that a suitably certified first-aid box had to be provided per five employees working at a remote area.

Safety rules and safety manual

Safety rules are defined on the basis of the work procedures for welding, cutting, lifting, hydro-testing, painting, and blasting, and should be specified according to the scope of work. In the manual, a reference is needed to the operating procedures for the equipment used in the project. The audit revealed that some of the main safety procedures relating to the contract, such as cutting, grinding, and lifting procedures, were still missing.

Information programme for new employees

New employees have to be informed about the HSE procedures, rules, documents, and responsible staff. Key issues for the auditors were (i) the existence of a New Employee Information Programme, (ii) the clear definition of a procedure, and (iii) whether the programme is implemented and training recorded. The procedure must cover all information about the HSE policy, work procedures and personal protective equipment (i.e. helmet, shoes, goggles, and clothing), and the 'pocket book' containing specific HSE information must be handed out and explained to employees. The auditors emphasised the necessity to provide refreshment possibilities for employees and guidance for employees of sub-contractors.

HSE meeting programme

Systematic HSE management, and, in this case, the HSE rating system, asks for a HSE committee meeting programme which defines the frequency of committee meetings, requires minutes, secures coherency between the meetings over time, and ensures that the results of the meetings are reviewed.

Bisma Jaya has always conducted monthly meetings and safety talks and minutes were kept. However, the monthly safety meeting had not been reviewed and not all HSE issues had been followed up. The audit results had not been followed up in the monthly meeting and the auditors mentioned that involvement of management in the meetings could be improved. Additional measures include the writing of minutes for HSE meetings and follow-up review of all HSE matters. Because the salaries of the staff involved were already covered, these activities were not calculated separately. From this perspective these measures were not seen to create additional costs.

HSE training programme

To organise HSE training for all employees, an annual programme has to be developed. Further relevant aspects which have to be included in the training documentation are (i) the recording of the training which has taken place, (ii) copies of certificates received, (iii) lists of all employees who attended the trainings, (iv) a list of organisations which offer HSE training, and (v) information on internal HSE training. The audit revealed that a training matrix has been issued; however, the matrix needed to cover all employees, permanent as well as contracted employees. Some first-aid certificates were out of date and therefore not valid.

Bisma Jaya took up the recommendations and defined various measures to improve the HSE training programme. The cost of listing and copying employee certificates was not calculated specifically because this was seen as an activity the current administrator could cover without additional cost.

Equipment and material management

The management of materials and equipment plays a crucial role in HSE. Issues addressed under this category are the existence of a comprehensive list of certified equipment and tools, a copy of all equipment certificates, the inspection and tagging procedure, the inspection form for all pieces of equipment, and a list of all inspection tags. The audit showed that not all equipment lists were completed to cover the whole range of electrical equipment and tools. Moreover, it was pointed out that no records existed about the inspection of tools. Certificates did exist but were not documented in a single list and follow-up inspections had to be improved and documented. No calculation was made for the cost of distributing the minutes and results of equipment inspections to the responsible staff as this was completed in meetings already scheduled as part of ordinary working procedure.

Personal protective equipment

The existence of a procedure to distribute and check the functionality of personal protective equipment is a substantial element of HSE management. This includes the recording by employees as part of their normal working procedures. Stocks of personal protective equipment are also required for each site. The external auditors confirmed a sufficient supply of personal protective equipment. However, they observed that no stock of equipment existed at the workshops and that enforcement of the procedures for checking stock levels would need to be more stringent.

HSE inspection programme

The HSE inspection programme defines a procedure and time schedule for inspections, including a list with the status of the inspections which have taken place (time, by whom, and when the next inspection is planned). It also includes a follow-up improvement programme on the basis of the results of the inspections. The inspection results should be discussed at the HSE committee meeting, and minutes including the correction plans have to be kept. Furthermore, a record of the corrective actions is required. The audit revealed that the HSE inspection programme had been carried out and guidelines were made available. However, the inspection forms did not mention follow-ups to check the effect of corrective actions, and the management did not seem to be aware of the status of HSE inspections.

Accident reporting procedure

The accident reporting procedure was rated very positively in the external audit. It requires the existence of (i) a written document explaining the procedure for the reporting of accidents and anomalies, (ii) a list of the current status of incidents and corrective actions taken, (iii) a form to characterise and report accidents and anomalies, and (iv) training for all employees how to behave in such cases. Improvement was seen with follow-up procedures and their recording and reporting. The total cost of activities to improve the primary HSE rating factors include developing the HSE policy, ERPs, safety rules and safety manual, an information programme for new employees, an HSE meeting programme, a HSE training programme, the management of equipment and materials, personal protective equipment, the HSE inspection programme, and the accident reporting procedure.

Secondary HSE rating factors

Professional HSE support

Professional HSE support encompasses, for example, an HSE committee organisational chart, a job desk for the HSE committee, the curricula vitae and certificates of the HSE committee members, a list of employees who contribute to the project, including certificates, and a record of all HSE committee meetings. The audit findings indicated that an HSE organisational chart was missing and the training of HSE staff needed to be implemented. Bisma Jaya responded to these audit findings by designing the HSE organisational chart and scheduling HSE committee meetings.

Industrial hygiene

Industrial hygiene requires medical certificates for all employees, a table summarising all employee medical checkups, agreements with a hospital to accept staff in case of illnesses or injuries, a procedure to ensure safe catering or food, and a first-aid kit box with standard medical remedies. Furthermore, employees trained in first-aid are needed with one first-aid trained employee per five people.

The audit shows that medical certificates are available for personnel working on site. For office employees, the certificates exist only for staff, not for management. Supply of food and beverages has not been checked during multi-day trips and staying overnight on long boats. The audit findings were taken up by Bisma Jaya by acquiring medical certificates for all employees and by introducing food and beverage procedures.

Environment

The environmental audit assesses whether the company has implemented an environment management system which refers to or is certified in line with ISO 14001. The waste management is of interest, in particular whether a waste management system exists and a separation of waste and scrap occurs. General housekeeping and environment inspections conducted by the owners are in the scope of the audit. The audit results showed that the underlying procedures of the systems were not well implemented on site. The inspection found many oil spills in both the Senipah and the Handil yard. In addition, scrap metal pieces were scattered about the yards. Moreover, insufficient waste management seemed to be the reason why the waste and scrap accumulated in the Handil yard.

As a response to the audit findings the company planned to (i) schedule environmental inspections, (ii) develop a waste dumping area, (iii) relocate waste in the jetty of the Handil yard, and (iv) improve employees' familiarity with the results of environment inspections and show the results of the analysis on the notice board of the main changing rooms and offices in the yard.

Statistical injury and illness data

A procedure for collecting, storing, and communicating statistical data is required by the rating system. This includes the display of statistical information about man-hours, fatality, anomalies, incidents and accidents, frequency and severity of these incidents, analyses of statistical factors, recommendations for improvement, action plans, and the communication and implementation of recommendations.

The auditors recognised an improvement in the analysis of man-hours per accident/incident. However, the statistical system started by Bisma Jaya did not allow for long-term comparisons.

Investigation of incident

This category includes the necessity for a procedure to track and investigate incidents, to create an incident reporting form, ensure data collection about incidents, and analyse the chronology of incidents. In addition, at its meetings the HSE committee should develop tree analyses and a recommendation programme to prevent incidents and accidents.

The existing procedure did not allow for the identification of a basic cause of all accidents. Thus, the auditors recommended using 'cause-and-effect tree' analysis. As a response Bisma Jaya took four actions: developing a cause-and-effect tree analysis, analysing all former incidents, training team leaders in cause-and-effect tree analysis, and implementing internal training in accident analyses.

Sub-contractors

Managing sub-contractors requires a procedure for training and qualification, including HSE inspections and audits, HSE ratings, and the proper use of HSE documents by the sub-contractors. The rating system reviews how the HSE programme is implemented by sub-contractors. The external auditors analysed Bisma Jaya's management of HSE issues in its relationship with sub-contractors and asked for an improved implementation and a review of the procedures.

Other audit factors

Three other factors are part of the overall audit but not explicitly included in the rating score: safety campaign, housekeeping, and electrical issues. Corresponding measures, such as display of HSE posters and installation of electrical panels, have been implemented by Bisma Jaya in order to meet the HSE requirements of the contracting company in the three areas (not listed individually in Table 5.2), at a cost of IDR3,700,000.

Efficiency

The decision situation at Bisma Jaya is characterised by a mix of past-orientated HSE information and future-orientated monetary information. Table 5.3 provides an overview of the auditing results and the cost implications relating to the improvement measures necessary if re-contracting is to be secured. The table provides an ex-post assessment of the past short-term non-monetary impacts (i.e. HSE deficiencies, see Figure 5.1: Box 11) and combines the information collected with a future-orientated ad hoc monetary assessment (Figure 5.1: Box 7) of the necessary measures to improve the rating. A close inspection of Table 5.3 shows the costs of each measure, the costs to improve for one rating point, the rating for each rating item, the next rating step and the current score. From a purely economic point of view Bisma Jaya can optimise its efforts to improve its rating by addressing the cheapest improvements per rating point (i.e. professional HSE support for IDR30,000 per rating point, then the writing of a safety rules manual for IDR131,259 per rating point, then the development of a policy statement for IDR157,000 per rating point, etc.). Depending on the risk Bisma Jaya wishes to accept, the measures can be implemented until the minimum necessary rating has been achieved. However, this will lead Bisma Jaya to a position where even small accidents and incidents will curtail future bidding activity as insufficient rating results. Therefore, even from a financial point of view, it is to be recommended that management continues to improve the overall HSE measures incrementally.

Further use of EMA

The costing of HSE measures is helpful for assessing the economic consequences of the measures taken. However, the HSE costings can also be used for future-orientated decision-making as they build a basis for subsequent budget settings. Periodic target-setting and budget control of HSE measures can help Bisma Jaya to ensure an ongoing comparison between actual results

TABLE 5.3 Overview of HSE measures

Factor/rating item	Costs	Costs/rating point	Rating				Score (28/11/05)	Next step
			D	C	B	A		
1. Policy statement	675,000	157,500	0	3	7	10	7	10
2. Emergency response procedure	3,950,000	691,250	0	3	7	10	3	7
3. Safety rules / safety manuals	750,000	131,250	0	3	7	10	3	7
4. New employee orientation programme	3,387,500	790,417	0	3	7	10	7	10
5. HSE meeting programme	1,700,000	297,500	0	3	7	10	3	7
6. HSE training programme	21,272,500	3,722,688	0	3	7	10	3	7
7. Equipment and material management	129,320,000	22,631,000	0	3	7	10	3	7
8. Personal protective equipment	22,300,000	7,433,333	0	3	7	10	7	10
9. HSE inspection programme	1,200,000	210,000	0	3	7	10	3	7
10. Accident reporting procedure	3,600,000	840,000	0	3	7	10	7	10
Weighted Score HSE Primary Factors = (SUM relevant score/SUM relevant maximum)[a] 0.7							32	

TABLE 5.3 (continued)

Factor/rating item	Costs	Costs/rating point	Rating				Score (28/11/05)	Next step
			D	C	B	A		
11. Professional HSE support	600,000	30,000	0	5	11	15	5	11
12. Industrial hygiene	40,000,000	1,500,000	0	6	14	20	6	14
13. Environment	40,940,000	1,535,250	0	6	14	20	6	14
14. Statistical injury and illness data	2,700,000	270,000	0	3	7	10	7	10
15. Incident investigation	2,400,000	180,000	0	5	11	15	11	15
16. Sub-contractor[a]			0	6	14	20	6	20
Other HSE measures[b]	3,700,000							
Weighted Score HSE Secondary Factors = (SUM relevant score/SUM relevant maximum)[a] 0.3							**12**	
Overall HSE Score = (Primary Score + Secondary Score)							**44**	

Notes
a Costs for improvement measures regarding sub-contractor (rating item 16) are not considered here.
b Other HSE measures do not have impacts on the rating score.

and budgeted estimates and to implement corrective plans for the future, if considered necessary. Such a future-orientated cost management approach has been under development to improve both the HSE performance and cost performance. Moreover, short-term costing and budgeting can serve account-ability processes and thus give credence to Bisma Jaya's efforts for continuous improvement of its HSE performance in the future.

Concluding discussion

In many places in Indonesia, and specifically in more remote areas where many of the engineering and mechanical activities of Bisma Jaya take place, regulations often cannot be checked or supervised in the same way as in urban areas of industrialised countries. Therefore, regulation, such as rating systems and audits by customers and self-control by management, becomes more important and plays a crucial role in the design and implementation of HSE measures. In Bisma Jaya's case, regulation in the form of process standards (Gunningham and Sinclair 1999) exists through the HSE rating system of the main client.

As with a large number of small suppliers in many industries, Bisma Jaya is influenced by a large customer with a closely observed image which sets high HSE standards for its suppliers. Bisma Jaya can survive as a supplier only if it performs and demonstrates its HSE performance in non-monetary terms. Environmental and social accounting provides tools to track this performance and is audited regularly by the main customer. If Bisma Jaya does not apply HSE accounting methods in a more systematic manner and does not conduct internal audits on a regular basis, it will always face the risk of failing with the professional audits of the internationally orientated customer. Thus, physical, HSE management accounting has significant economic relevance for Bisma Jaya, even if the physical data collected are not directly related to internal mon-etary data of the company or if the improvement in physical environmental terms does not pay off with a cost reduction in operations. Failure to meet the required environmental performance can endanger the relationship with the core customer and lead to a total loss of the main business and terminate the existence of the company as a whole.

Given that the HSE performance must be improved, documented, audited, and verified, however, HSE accounting provides also tools to optimise the most cost-efficient achievement of the required minimal standards. This cost-ing approach represents a pragmatic but systematic way of addressing failures of the current HSE management system.

This case study shows one particular limitation of the eco- and socio-effi-cient concept if applied too narrowly. Calculating the eco- and socio-efficiency of different measures would not necessarily lead to the HSE performance result which is required by the main, international customer. Given the weak political incentives under which the company operates, a reduction of some HSE impacts is not linked with sufficient cost reductions to justify eco- and socio-efficiency-orientated operational points of view (e.g. Schaltegger 1998). However, if the eco- and socio-efficiency notions are interpreted in a broader sense, acknowledging the potential loss of the main customer as an unlimited high economic risk, many improvements of HSE performance become compelling in terms of eco- and socio-efficiency and otherwise. As a consequence, calculating operational eco- and socio-efficiency is only a partially useful concept when rating systems and audits have a strong influence on customer loyalty in general. In such cases the eco- and socio-efficiency calculations have to be complemented by effectiveness considerations on HSE performance. In a narrow view, eco- and socio-efficiency considerations can focus on the objective of how to reach an improved performance measured in rating scores and include a safety margin (e.g. 60 points) with the lowest cost possible. Such a narrow interpretation of applying the eco- and socio-efficiency approach would suggest doing just enough to avoid trouble and could involve the risk of not meeting the minimum standards when unforeseen events occur.

It would not be fair to reduce the activities of the company and the possibilities and benefits of enhancing accounting procedures to just meet minimal standards. The tracking, assessment, and costing approach discussed allows the company to achieve the highest HSE benefit over time by entering a systematic process of improving its HSE performance in the least costly way possible. With increasing routine and experience many measures discussed may be achieved with lower costs than estimated. Further, some measures build on other measures and the self-regulation costs for their implementation may also decrease with a higher general standard. Even if Bisma Jaya aimed at achieving the highest score possible, it would make sense to start with implementation of the least costly actions and gradually to improve through more sophisticated actions over time. Furthermore, the company can also develop an annual budget for rating improvements and achieve the highest HSE improvement for this budget by following the recommendations suggested.

References

Beske, P., Koplin, J., and Seuring, S. (2008) 'The use of environmental and social standards by German first-tier suppliers of the Volkswagen AG', *Corporate Social Responsibility and Environmental Management*, 15: 63–75.

BSCI (2009) *Business social compliance initiative* [online – accessed 11 July 2009]. Available from Internet: http://www.bsci-eu.com.

Burritt, R., Hahn, T., and Schaltegger, S. (2002) 'Towards a comprehensive framework for environmental management accounting: links between business actors and environmental management accounting tools', *Australian Accounting Review*, 12: 39–50.

Gunningham, N. and Sinclair, D. (1999) 'Regulatory pluralism: designing policy mixes for environmental protection', *Law & Policy*, 21: 49–76.

McNulty, S. and Crooks, E. (2010) 'BP oil spill: a spreading stain', *Financial Times*, 6 May.

NZBCSD (New Zealand Business Council for Sustainable Development) (2003) *Business guide to a sustainable supply chain: a practical guide*, Auckland: NZBCSD.

Piplani, R., Pujawan, N., and Ray, S. (2008) 'Sustainable supply chain management', *International Journal Production Economics*, 111: 193–194.

Rikhardsson, P. (2006) 'Accounting for health and safety costs: review and comparison of selected methods', in Schaltegger, S., Bennett, M., and Burritt, R. (eds), *Sustainability accounting and reporting*, Dordrecht: Springer, pp. 129–152.

Schaltegger, S. (1998) 'Accounting for eco-efficiency', in Nath, B., Hens, L., Compton, P., and Devuyst, D. (eds), *Environmental management in practice, Volume I: Instruments for environmental management*, London: Routledge, pp. 272–287.

6

MATERIAL FLOW COST ACCOUNTING IN A SNACK PRODUCER

JBC Food, the Philippines

Introduction

This case study explores the application of EMA at JBC Food Corporation, a snack producer on the outskirts of the Philippine capital Manila. Prior to the case study, a group of managers and engineers was constantly working on measures to improve the company's environmental performance. This happened without a systematic linkage to monetary figures and performance outcomes; this lack hampered the process of getting top management approval and appreciation for such measures. The case study demonstrates the importance of integrating environmental and financial information for corporate decision-making. The study focuses on the application of material flow cost accounting (MFCA) as an important step towards this integration. MFCA supports JBC Food in tracking and costing material use and material losses to support material efficiency improvements and the vision of zero waste (Figure 6.1: Boxes 9 and 1). MFCA became an international standard (ISO 14051) in late 2011. The case study describes outcomes and limitations of this approach.

Decision setting

JBC Food Corporation (called JBC) was founded in 1988 and is located in Caloocan City within the Metro Manila region. The company is a subsidiary of the family-owned Republic Biscuit Corporation (Rebisco) Group, which incorporates several Philippine food-producing companies.

		Monetary EMA		Physical EMA	
		Short-term	Long-term	Short-term	Long-term
Past-orientated	Routinely generated	Environmental cost accounting [1]	Environment-induced capital expenditure and revenue [2]	Material and energy flow accounting [9]	Environmental capital impact accounting [10]
Past-orientated	Adhoc	Ex-post assessment of relevant environmental costing decisions [3]	Ex-post inventory assessment of projects [4]	Ex-post assessment of short-term environmental impacts [11]	Ex-post inventory appraisal of physical environmental investments [12]
Future-orientated	Routinely generated	Monetary environmental budgeting [5]	Environmental long-term financial planning [6]	Physical environmental budgeting [13]	Environmental long-term physical planning [14]
Future-orientated	Adhoc	Relevant environmental costing [7]	Monetary environmental investment appraisal [8]	Tools designed to predict relevant environmental impacts [15]	Physical environmental investment appraisal [16]

FIGURE 6.1 Application of the EMA framework (Burritt, Hahn, and Schaltegger 2002) to JBC Food.
Note: Dark (light) grey boxes represent the major (minor) EMA applications.

Economic performance, products and production technology

Since its foundation, JBC has grown steadily and aims at becoming the largest, best-known snack producer in the Philippines. With 400 full-time employees and another 400 occasional workers, the company generates an annual sales turnover of PHP560 million (Philippine pesos, around €8 million). According to JBC its business performance is about average for the Philippine food industry allowing for continuous growth.

The main ingredients of JBC's snack products are peanuts, peas, and watermelon seeds. These ingredients are processed in various ways to generate a variety of brands and products including for instance HAPPY Peanuts (peanuts in flavours such as barbecue or chilli), DINGDONG Mixed Nuts (a mix of peanuts, nuts, maize bits, green peas, and fava beans), Chikito (coated peanuts in several flavours), Barnuts (chocolate-peanut bars), MAGIC Peanut Butter, and Captain Sid (roasted watermelon seeds).

HAPPY Peanuts is the best selling product of JBC and the most popular peanut snack brand in the Philippines, JBC's main market. A smaller proportion of its products is exported to North America and Saudi Arabia. Customers of JBC products are wholesalers and supermarkets, but also small-scale intermediaries such as kiosks. All seed- and nut-based products are wrapped in plastic foil and sold in two different sizes: small packs around 10 grams for immediate consumption and large packs around 100 grams.

In terms of production technology, snack producing is a straightforward business which does not require high-technology equipment (a comprehensive overview of food processing and technology is provided in Brennan 2006 and Fellows 2009). In comparison with food producing in highly industrialised countries, JBC employs a large number of workers because of relatively low labour costs. For example, sorting and selecting of peanuts is carried out manually (see Figure 6.2). Typical production processes at JBC are boiling, frying, seasoning, coating, and wrapping, for which standard food-processing equipment is used. How to create taste and flavours is the real trade secret of JBC and is managed by the research and development department, which operates a laboratory to create and test new flavours and products.

Environmental and social issues and performance

The direct and indirect environmental impacts of food production are manifold, including deforestation, destruction of ecosystems, salination, and global warming. Therefore, the 'food industry is facing increasing pressure to improve environmental performance, both from consumers and regulators responding to consumer pressures' (Mattsson and Sonesson 2003: 1).

FIGURE 6.2 Sorting of peanuts at one production line (source: author).

JBC is a food processor, transforming agricultural raw materials such as peanuts and peas into food products, snacks in particular. In general, the processing of food is associated with two major environmental issues: waste management, especially packaging waste, and energy use. Upstream environmental impacts, such as from agriculture, are assigned to the food processors' products and require a comprehensive approach to environmental management and improvement (Mattsson and Sonesson 2003; Klemes, Smith, and Kim 2008; for a general overview of food production and the environment see Dalzell 2000).

Remarkably for a medium-sized company in the Philippine food industry, JBC has a relatively long history of environmental management dating back to the mid-1990s when first wastewater treatment measures were implemented. As part of an international capacity development project on green productivity, JBC implemented a software-based environmental performance indicator (EPI) system that monitors a large number of indicators concerning production processes, utility supplies (i.e. electricity) and waste and wastewater treatment. JBC has established an EPI taskforce that includes environmental staff but also the head of research and development, the plant manager, and the quality control manager. With the commitment of top management, the taskforce stated ambitious environmental targets including a 10 per cent efficiency increase in water use and electric energy consumption in 2003 (JBC Food Corporation 2003). A number of measures were used to help achieve these targets as well as other goals related to environmental performance and productivity in general.

- JBC replaced imported rubber bushings damaged in vibrating machines and required frequent exchange. Rubber bushings are fitted into machines to reduce vibration and absorb shock. Instead of imported rubber bushings, JBC uses recycled rubber bushings from scrap aeroplane tires. This reduces machine downtime and purchasing costs. The measure is beneficial from an environmental point of view as no new rubber bushing has to be produced and scrap aeroplane tires are recycled rather than dumped.
- JBC introduced waste segregation (biodegradable, recyclable non-biodegradable, and non-recyclable non-biodegradable). The segregation led to waste disposal cost reduction and revenues from selling recyclable waste.
- By purchasing new blowers, JBC improved its ventilation system. This improved the working conditions significantly and increased productivity. The number of skin diseases, headaches, and other illnesses caused by high temperatures in the confectionary area decreased dramatically.
- JBC installed an automatic moisture expeller in the air compressor to avoid product contamination (Opierzynski and Müller 2005; IFF and JBC n.d.).

According to Opierzynski and Müller (2005), the annual savings related to the EPI measures amount to PHP6.6 million (€94,300), that is 1 per cent of total sales turnover. Encouraged by these improvements and savings, the EPI taskforce started to involve JBC's workers in the environmental improvement processes. They established training programmes on basic environmental awareness, preventative maintenance, and several safety-related issues. A newsletter is published regularly to inform all employees on the progress of environmental performance, product quality, and safety and productivity in general. Employees are encouraged to provide suggestions for technical, quality, and environmental improvements and receive awards for the best ideas.

Food processing follows high quality and safety standards as contaminated final products can severely affect human health. Bovine spongiform encephalopathy (BSE), dioxins in olive oil, and deaths from food poisoning are familiar examples of failed food quality and safety monitoring. This has led to a steady increase in regulation and involvement of advisory bodies in hygiene in the food industry (see Cocker 2003; also a general introduction to food hygiene is provided in Lelieveld, Mostert, Holah, and White 2003). At the time of conducting the case study, JBC was in the process of establishing a hazard analysis and critical control point (HACCP) system. Originally, HACCP was a voluntary, process-orientated system to ensure food safety and hygiene, but it has developed to become a widely accepted food safety standard that acts like an international trade standard (Caswell and Hooker 1996). This is the case for JBC, as its international customers demand the implementation of HACCP.

During conduct of the case study, the EPI taskforce emphasised the need for an integrated view of product quality and safety, environmental performance, working conditions, and productivity. Ideally, their EPIs lead to improvements in one or several of the dimensions without compromising others. Thus, JBC's EPI taskforce is actually going beyond pure environmental management measures. It clearly addresses the integration challenges of sustainability management as defined by Schaltegger, Herzig, Kleiber, and Müller (2002). However, the taskforce is limited to examining improvements of the production system and shows an operational rather than a strategic focus. Therefore, strategic aspects and external, societal effects of JBC's products and processes were not considered.

An important societal aspect is that many of JBC's customers belong to the lowest socio-economic group. JBC sells its major brands in small 10-gram packets. This enables resellers to offer the small bags for PHP1 (less than €0.02), an affordable price for people with very low incomes. In this way, JBC is actually conducting profitable business with the poorer members of society. Whether and how to do business with this group and the implications for poverty reduction are subject to ongoing discussion in business research (see Hammond and Prahalad 2004; Prahalad 2004; Karnani 2007; Seelos and Mair

2007). JBC's business rationale in making products affordable to the poor is driven not by poverty alleviation strategy, but by market opportunity. However, selling the snacks in small bags requires more packaging material per gram of wrapped product. This increases the amount of waste at the consumption stage and means that the proportion of packaging cost of total product cost is higher than for larger bags. As a consequence, purchasers of small bags pay more per gram of snack and generate more waste. JBC, being located in a rather poor neighbourhood, also sells used oil from frying peanuts and other raw materials to local residents, which they use for cooking as they cannot afford to buy oil elsewhere. The use of this waste oil is likely to affect the health of the poor as it contains high levels of saturated fats and impurities such as burned leftovers of peanuts. Therefore, the environmental manager suggested converting the used oil to biodiesel as a more sustainable option and was carrying out further research on this at the end of this case study conduct.

Company's motivation for using EMA

JBC's decision to establish the EPI project led to various environmental and social improvements and financial savings. Despite this, the EPI taskforce often found it difficult to convince the company's senior management about the value of introducing additional measures to enhance social and environmental performance. For instance, extending a series of environmental awareness training seminars for JBC's employees was not approved since the expected monetary results were unquantifiable; the EPI taskforce was unable to demonstrate any financial benefits from the planned training. The taskforce was convinced that these, and other EPI measures, improve environmental performance and thereby cut costs. The EPI system in place provides physical information about such measures. Referring to the EMA framework of Burritt and colleagues (2002) (see Figure 6.1), the EPI system can be linked to Box 9 of the framework: on a regular basis, routinely generated, physical EPIs were measured and monitored weekly and monthly (past-orientated, short-term).

Before this case study, the EPI system was used as a source of inspiration for environmental improvement measures. Suggestions for new measures were assessed by predicting their effect on the EPIs and in some cases also by estimating financial consequences on an ad hoc basis. Thus, JBC's main interest in applying EMA was to link corporate environmental performance to monetary aspects in a systematic way. The EPI taskforce expected to identify further areas for improvement, to demonstrate the benefits of past environmental measures, and to assess the value of new environmental measures. Linking the existing EPI system to business performance is related to Box 1 of the EMA framework: the routinely generated, short-term, past-orientated physical EPIs (Box 9) need to be linked to their monetary consequences and requires the establishment of environmental cost accounting.

EMA application

In food processing, waste, product rejects, and energy are important general environmental issues. JBC's production processes feature a flow perspective, that is, raw materials are processed through several production steps to form the final products. Hence, environmental cost accounting at JBC should ideally take on a flow-orientated perspective with attention to energy and waste issues. MFCA is a specific environmental cost-accounting approach that meets these requirements. The importance of material costs is highlighted by the fact that, according to JBC, labour costs account for less than 2 per cent of total production costs whereas material costs including packaging, water, and energy account for the majority of the remaining 98 per cent. Capital costs, including for instance the depreciation of equipment, are low compared with raw material cost and are not included in the direct production costs.

MCFA implementation at JBC

Monetary quantification and visualisation of material losses is the overall objective of MFCA. The approach aims to reduce waste-induced inefficiencies in business decision-making. The crucial difference from conventional cost accounting is that material and other costs of processes are first allocated to products and then also allocated to product-related waste based on physical activity-based drivers. MFCA implies a linear relationship between inputs and outputs: a reduction of product-related waste leads to a reduction of input flows. MFCA is a widely used methodology, especially in Japan, and known by different names such as resource efficiency accounting, flow cost accounting, or material-flow orientated activity-based costing (Schaltegger and Burritt 2000; Strobel and Redmann 2002; Wagner and Enzler 2006; METI 2007). MFCA became an environmental management standard (ISO 14051) in late 2011 (see also Kokubu, Campos, Furukawa, and Tachikawa 2009).

Physical flows and material losses

JBC's EPI taskforce decided to first focus the application of MFCA to peanut production line No. 1, which accounts for the largest portion of production costs. Figure 6.3 depicts a Sankey diagram of activity for that production line for an average month. After delivery, raw peanuts are stored in a warehouse, boiled, peeled, dried, fried, seasoned, cooled, and finally selected before they are wrapped. This requires the intake of energy (electricity and liquefied petroleum gas [LPG]), water, and other food ingredients (palm oil and seasoning). The diagram is based on more detailed information provided by the company's EPI system.

Figure 6.3 includes the graphical representation of material losses. Four types of material losses can be distinguished: peanut skin, used oil, seasoning, and other.

- Peanut skin: Naturally, peanuts have a very thin skin (not to be confused with the outer and thicker shell). The skin needs to be removed before peanuts are further processed and it accounts for 7–8 per cent of the initial peanut weight. The peanut skin could be considered as an unavoidable material loss that leads to a small disposal fee. However, it is possible to purchase skinless peanuts, which means that the supplier removes the skin before delivery.
- Used oil: Used oil is left over from frying. Most of the palm oil used in frying is soaked up by the peanuts, but roughly 6 per cent remains and may be sold to poor people for cooking purposes.
- Seasoning: 'Food soil' is the term used for the small portion of seasoning (about 3 per cent) that does not adhere to the peanuts and is wasted.
- Other: All other material losses are peanuts that do not fulfil quality requirements. The amount of rotten and broken peanuts depends on the workers' skills and knowledge of the process, for instance, stopping the boiling process at exactly the right moment.

Material losses from used oil, seasoning, and other provides a performance indicator that had been monitored by JBC's EPI system before applying MFCA. The target set for this waste to product output ratio was 5 per cent, that is, any rate below 5 per cent was acceptable and did not require further action. The ratio for the month under surveillance kept within the target (4.7 per cent), that is, the sum of all non-product output percentages except peanut skin.

Linking physical flows to costs

To link physical data from the EPI system to cost information, input–output tables were derived for each production step and cost information was added. Table 6.1 depicts an extract of the input–output table for seasoning. Data have been changed slightly for confidentiality reasons.

With support from the accounting department, the EPI taskforce stated the unit price and resulting cost for each input. For seasoning, only two outputs occur. 'Food soil' is a material loss that can be sold at a low price. 'Seasoned peanuts' is the desired outcome from the process. The cost of seasoned

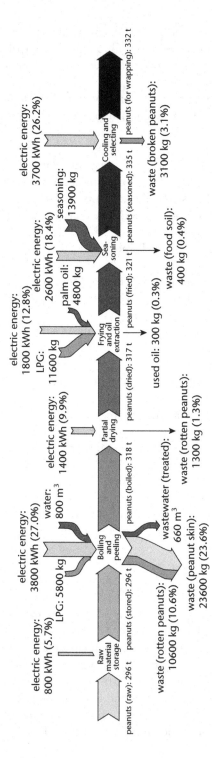

FIGURE 6.3 Monthly physical flows in peanut line 1 (source: author, based on JBC data). Notes: percentage of waste in relation to final output; percentage of electric energy in relation to total electric energy; peanut flows (tonnes) are not proportional to all other mass flows (kg).

TABLE 6.1 Excerpt from monthly seasoning input–output table including costs

In	Data quality	Volume per month	Unit	Unit price	Cost (PHP)	Out	Data quality	Volume per month	Unit	Unit price	Cost (PHP)
Fried-oil extracted peanuts	E	433,064	kg	Internal (from previous step)		Seasoned peanuts	E	446,901	kg	Left blank for confidentiality	833,054
Labour (seasoning operator)	C	3	h	263	29,559	Food soil (accumulated flavour in mixer)	E	433	kg	5	(2,295)
Electricity (seasoning tumbler and fluorescent)	C	526	kWh	6	3,107						
Seasoning in plastic bags (garlic powder – 10 g)	C	781	kg	83	65,024						
Labour (garlic powder – 10 g)	C	40	h	33	1,316						
Seasoning in plastic bags (salt and anti-oxidants – 10 g)	C	1,874	kg	6	10,973						
Labour (salt and anti-oxidants – 10 g)	C	74	h	33	2,445						
Seasoning in plastic bags (fresh garlic – 10 g)	C	2,603	kg	31	79,854						

TABLE 6.1 (continued)

Seasoning in plastic bags (garlic powder – 120 g)	C	49	kg	83	4,074
Labour (garlic powder – 120 g)	C	1	h	33	34
Seasoning in plastic bags (salt and anti-oxidants – 120 g)	C	49	kg	6	286
Labour (salt and anti-oxidants – 120 g)	C	2	h	33	64
Seasoning in plastic bags (fried garlic – 120 g)	C	130	kg	88	11,437
Labour (fried garlic 120 g)	C	11	h	33	372
Seasoning in plastic bags (garlic oleo – 120 g)	C	15	kg	3,681	55,040

. . . continued (30 items to follow)

Note: modified to preserve confidentiality
Source: JBC.

peanuts of PHP833,054 (€11,900) is the sum of all process input costs less revenues for the by-product 'food soil' without considering production costs of the intermediate product 'fried oil extracted peanuts'.

Depiction of the costs of all production steps including the internal costs of intermediates is shown in Table 6.2. For simplicity, the separate production steps 'raw material storage' and 'boiling and peeling' (see Figure 6.3) are combined in one process; the same applies to 'partial drying' and 'frying and oil extraction'. Several smaller cost items, including coconut oil, liquid soap, and 'system costs', are aggregated into 'other material costs', that is, other process-related costs affected by material flows such as direct labour costs. Revenues from waste that can be sold are depicted as flows leaving the processes; costs are depicted as flows entering the processes. The resulting flows for the main outputs, that is, peanuts in the various stages of processing, comprise the accumulated costs and revenues for each step.

According to Table 6.2, total monthly production costs of peanut line 1 equal PHP14,339,000 (€204,843), implying that all material flow- and process-related production costs are assigned to the final product. In comparison with these total production costs, material loss-related costs (waste costs and waste revenues) appear to be almost negligible. MFCA challenges this perception of material loss-related costs by identifying material loss-induced production costs in a more precise manner. The result of the MFCA calculation for peanut line No. 1 are depicted in Figure 6.4 and explained for each production step as follows:

TABLE 6.2 Conventional view of material flow-related costs in peanut line 1

Conventional production cost assignment	Boiling and peeling	Frying and oil extraction	Seasoning	Cooling and selecting	Total
Peanuts (raw)	12,796				**12,796**
Palm oil		146			**146**
Seasoning			690		**690**
Other material costs	34		66	139	**239**
Electric energy	32	22	18	26	**98**
LPG	179	36			**215**
Water	4				**4**
System costs	72	26	46	52	**196**
Waste costs (peanut skin)	24				**24**
Waste revenues (various)	–43	–12	–1	–13	**–69**
Total	**13,098**	**218**	**819**	**204**	**14,339**

Source: based on simplified JBC data.

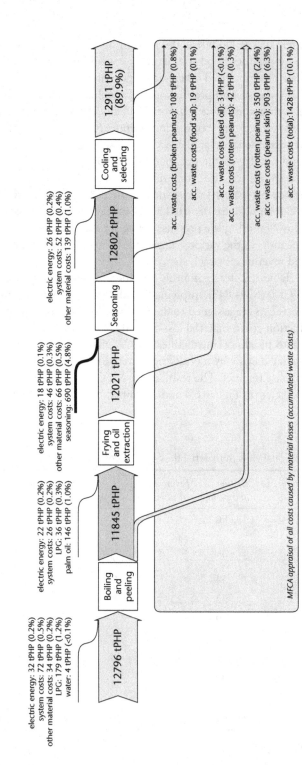

FIGURE 6.4 MFCA view of material flow costs in peanut line 1 (source: author, based on simplified JBC data and MFCA computation).

- Boiling and peeling: Total production costs of boiling and peeling are allocated to the desired output (boiled and peeled peanuts) and material losses (rotten peanuts and peanut skin) based on the relative output weight ratio. Then the revenue from selling rotten peanuts is subtracted and the disposal cost of peanut skin is added (Table 6.3).

    The total accumulated cost of material losses in this production step equals PHP1,253,000 (€17,900) or PHP36.6/kg (€0.52/kg) of material loss in comparison with PHP11,845,000 (€169,200) or PHP37.2/kg (€0.53/kg) of product-related cost.

- Frying and oil extraction: Material loss from used oil is related to the intake of palm oil, not to peanut throughput, therefore the costs of used oil have been computed using the ratio of used oil to palm oil intake (6.25 per cent). If JBC reduced the amount of used oil to zero, that is, all palm oil were taken up as part of finished product, the company could save PHP3,000 (€43): PHP9,000 (€129) is 6.25 per cent of the palm oil purchase cost less the used oil revenue of PHP6,000 (€86). Other cost reductions (e.g. less energy use if less palm oil is required) are minor and thus ignored. The accumulated cost of rotten peanuts is computed in a similar way to Table 6.3.[1]

- Seasoning: Similar to the used oil in frying and oil extraction, the material loss 'food soil' is related not to peanut throughput, but to the amount of seasoning that is used in the process. Roughly 3 per cent of the seasoning purchase cost, less the food soil revenue, could be reduced if no food soil were generated, equal to a potential saving of PHP19,000 (€270).

- Cooling and selecting: The material loss from broken peanuts is directly related to peanut throughput. If no peanuts were broken, about 1 per cent of the process's total production costs could be saved, that is PHP123,000 (€1,750).

The MFCA approach reveals that about 10 per cent of total production costs are caused by material losses. Peanut skin (6.3 per cent) and rotten peanuts (2.4 per cent) in boiling and peeling contribute most to these avoidable costs, followed by broken peanuts (0.8 per cent) in cooling and selecting (Figure 6.4).

TABLE 6.3 MFCA cost allocation for boiling and peeling

Material loss	Weight total (kg)	Weight ratio (%)	Production cost (PHP)	Specific cost or revenues (PHP)	Accumulated cost (PHP)
Rotten peanuts	10,600	3.0	393,000	–43,000	350,000
Peanut skin	23,600	6.7	879,000	24,000	903,000
Boiled and peeled peanuts	318,000	90.3	11,845,000	0	11,845,000
Total	352,200	100.0	13,117,000	–19,000	13,098,000

Results from MFCA application

The implementation of MFCA for peanut line No. 1 provides relevant information for several decision-making situations and leads to new ideas for improving JBC's environmental and business performance. Boiling and peeling, which features the highest portion of energy cost and the highest amount of material loss-induced cost, is clearly the focal point for further improvements, but other processes and material flows also show improvement potential.

The precise figure for the accumulated cost of peanut skin in boiling and peeling supports the purchasing manager's decisions about whether to buy skinless peanuts from suppliers. For one month's production output, JBC requires 272.4 tonnes of skinless peanuts instead of 296 tonnes of peanuts with skin (the difference derives from the weight of peanut skin). Relating the accumulated peanut skin cost of PHP903,000 (€12,900) to the required input of skinless peanuts shows that JBC could pay a premium of 7.6 per cent per kilogram for skinless raw peanuts without diminishing its profits, that is, PHP46.5 (€0.664) per kilogram of skinless peanuts instead of PHP43.2 (€0.617) per kilogram of peanuts with skin.

MFCA information on boiling and peeling strengthened JBC's attempts to replace the old technology for this production step by a steaming device for peeling the peanuts with greater energy efficiency: the snack producer has started to look for more efficient technologies, such as systems that use steam in a semi-closed system to boil and peel the peanuts rather than using a constant flow of hot water. This measure had been discussed before the case study was conducted, but the finding that boiling and peeling accounts for 67 per cent of total energy and water costs, that is, PHP15,000 (€3,070), strengthened efforts to find better solutions. The EPI taskforce estimated that using steam instead of boiling would reduce the energy demand by more than 50 per cent. This equals an annual saving potential of at least PHP1,290,000 (€18,420) and supports the appraisal of several investment options for this production step after the case study was completed.

The high value of the peanut skin also provides an incentive to seek more profitable ways to re-use or recycle skin rather than to dispose of it as waste. Selling peanut skin as admixture to animal feed and using it as fuel in biogas combustion are possible solutions (see Chapter 8, Oliver Enterprises II case, and Chapter 12, Tan Loc Food case, in this book). A sophisticated and probably more profitable solution is use of the skin as a food ingredient. According to recent research, peanut skin 'was found to contain potent antioxidants and could provide an inexpensive source of antioxidants for use as functional ingredients in foods or dietary supplements' (Yu, Ahmedna, Goktepe, and Dai 2006: 1).

Greater attention is paid to the reduction of material losses in general. The accumulated costs of material losses strongly support the decision of the

EPI taskforce to facilitate employee training in relation to waste reduction and to establish a suggestion scheme that includes awards and bonuses for employee ideas about further improvement. For instance, each kilogram of rotten or broken peanuts in cooling and selecting incurs a loss of PHP34.8 (€0.50). If training of workers in this production step leads to an awareness to reduce waste and result in waste reduction of just 10 per cent, JBC would save PHP129,600 (€1,850) each year. The MFCA analysis shows that all peanut oil- and palm oil-related material wastes also cause large financial losses, which are not compensated for by the revenues gained at local markets. The accumulated cost of rotten and broken peanuts and used oil amounts to PHP522,000 (€7,460) and is 7.5 times higher than the revenues of PHP69,000 (€990). From a purely financial point of view, the selling of these peanut and palm oil material wastes on local markets still makes sense as long as no options for reducing the wastes have been implemented.

Another important reason to reduce material waste losses lies in the social aspects of wasted peanuts and used oil. Contaminated broken or rotten peanuts sold to people with low incomes could have severe effects on consumer health and badly affect JBC's reputation. Hence, material losses do not only lead to production costs and 'waste money'; they also lead to bigger risks in terms of corporate reputation or liabilities deriving from problems caused by such losses. An extreme example is the nuclear industry, where material losses could well find their way into nuclear arms production and the impact on society could be very significant (Prasad, Booth, Hu, and Deligonul 1995; Prasad and Calis 1999).

Even the physical flow chart (Figure 6.3), developed as a basis for the MFCA analysis, led to some ideas for energy savings. The taskforce was surprised that 1,400 kWh or 10 per cent of overall electric energy consumption came from partial drying and causes monthly expenses of PHP10,000 (€143). Partial drying ensures that the moisture content of peanuts is appropriate for frying. Test runs without partial drying show no reduction in peanut quality, with the result that partial drying is no longer applied in general. It can still be used if the production manager or workers responsible for the frying step detect that the moisture content is too high. This measure reduces the energy costs for partial drying almost to zero.

Outlook

The MFCA application, based on the EPI system, has been beneficial for JBC and supports both the continuous environmental improvement process and assessment of related financial benefits. At the time of the case study, JBC's environmental taskforce planned to implement MFCA in other production lines and processes. They also decided to widen the scope of MFCA application, to assess the financial consequences of machine downtime caused by lack of maintenance and inappropriate handling of machines, and to benchmark JBC's products in terms of the specific costs for energy, raw materials, auxiliaries, utilities, and packaging.

JBC's environmental officer has started to use the MFCA approach for integrating environmental and financial performance for his work at other companies as well. For instance, his colleagues and he have established a wastewater minimisation programme at two of JBC's sister companies instead of just implementing the pollution control programme required by the Philippines Government. The wastewater minimisation programme included training and workshops with managers and key employees. These workshops led to suggestions for dry-cleaning methods to lower the biological oxygen demand to capture oil and grease at source and to recover further materials that would otherwise have been wasted. Thereby, the two companies have achieved annual savings of approximately PHP2 million (€28,600).

Discussion and conclusions

The JBC case study highlights the importance of linking environmental information and environmental management measures to financial figures. MFCA helps identify focal points for environmental and eco-efficiency improvements and helps to quantify and justify such measures for top management. Through MFCA, JBC has changed its perception about the value of assessing material losses. Rather than perceiving material losses as a minor quality management issue as long as the losses are below a given percentage, material losses are now considered as an important determinant of production profits and losses. JBC's environmental management activities and also its general management decisions have benefited from applying MFCA, for instance through the provision of relevant figures on purchasing raw peanuts versus purchasing peeled peanuts.

The success of JBC's MFCA application was facilitated by the availability of an environmental taskforce and the EPI system implemented. To measure and gather the requisite physical information in order to establish the EPI system required considerable expertise and manpower prior to the MFCA application.

Burritt (2004) elaborates upon the limitations of conventional management accounting in an environmental context and derives challenges for EMA. This case study reveals that MFCA overcomes some of these limitations, in particular the perception that environmental costs are not significant. The case study also reveals that some key problems remain. As with conventional management accounting, MFCA primarily focuses on short-term, manufacturing-orientated win–win solutions. Neither supply chain or life cycle aspects and the handling of externalities nor strategic considerations are yet included in the core of MFCA.

Given the multitude of ideas available for environmental improvements and environmental information, the case study research had to be limited to the EPI taskforce's main concern, which was the linkage between environmental and financial performance for the peanut production line. Other issues, for instance the environmental and social aspects of selling snack products to the poor, remain a subject for future research.

One of the challenges for EMA research that Burritt (2004: 23) identifies is the question of whether pure physical information is environmental management accounting information. The case of JBC shows that pure environmental information is useful to identify options for improvement but, when corporate decision-makers need to be convinced, linking environmental information to its financial consequences is essential.

Note

1 The 6.25 per cent portion of palm oil that is allocated to the material loss of used oil should not be included in the computation of the accumulated cost of rotten peanuts and of fried peanuts.

References

Brennan, J.G. (ed.) (2006) *Food processing handbook*, Weinheim: Wiley-VCH.

Burritt, R.L. (2004) 'Environmental management accounting: roadblocks on the way to the green and pleasant land', *Business Strategy and the Environment*, 13: 13–32.

Burritt R., Hahn, T., and Schaltegger, S. (2002) 'Towards a comprehensive framework for environmental management accounting: links between business actors and environmental management accounting tools', *Australian Accounting Review*, 12: 39–50.

Caswell, J.A. and Hooker, N.H. (1996) 'HACCP as an international trade standard', *American Journal of Agricultural Economics*, 78: 775–779.

Cocker, R. (2003) 'The regulation of hygiene in food processing: an introduction', in Lelieveld, H.L.M., Mostert, M.A., Holah, J., and White, B. (eds) *Hygiene in food processing*, Boca Raton: CRC Press, pp. 5–21.

Dalzell, J.M. (ed.) (2000) *Food industry and the environment in the European Union: practical issues and cost implications*, Gaithersburg, MD: Aspen.

Fellows, P.J. (ed.) (2009) *Food processing technology: principles and practice*, Boca Raton, LA: CRC Press.

Hammond, A.L. and Prahalad, C.K. (2004) 'Selling to the poor', *Foreign Policy*, 142: 30–37.

IFF and JBC (Fraunhofer Institute IFF and JBC Food Corporation) (n.d.) *Impact of the EPI pilot project to JBC Food Corporation*, company-internal document.

JBC Food Corporation (2003) *EPI system targets*, company-internal document.

Karnani, A. (2007) 'The mirage of marketing to the bottom of the pyramid: how the private sector can help alleviate poverty', *California Management Review*, 49: 90–113.

Klemes, J., Smith, R., and Kim, J.-K. (eds) (2008) *Handbook of water and energy management in food processing*, Boca Raton, LA: CRC Press.

Kokubu, K., Campos, M.K.S., Furukawa, Y., and Tachikawa, H. (2009) 'Material flow cost accounting with ISO 14051', *ISO Management Systems*, January–February: 15–18.

Lelieveld, H.L.M., Mostert, M.A., Holah, J., and White, B. (eds) (2003) *Hygiene in food processing*, Boca Raton, LA: CRC Press.

Mattsson, B. and Sonesson, U. (eds) (2003) *Environmentally-friendly food processing*, Boca Raton, LA: CRC Press.

METI (Japanese Ministry of Economy, Trade, and Industry) (2007) *Guide for material flow cost accounting*, Tokyo: METI.

Opierzynski, R. and Müller, F. (2005) 'Using sustainability management applications to improve business performance: practical experiences and success stories in Asia', paper presented at the International Symposium on Corporate Sustainability Management. Approaches and Applications, Bangkok, Thailand, 24–25 November.

Prahalad, C.K. (2004) *The fortune at the bottom of the pyramid: eradicating poverty through profits*, Upper Saddle River, NJ: Wharton School Publishing.

Prasad, S. and Calis, A. (1999) 'Capability indices for material balance accounting', *European Journal of Operational Research*, 114: 93–104.

Prasad, S., Booth, D., Hu, M.Y., and Deligonul, S. (1995) 'Detection of nuclear losses', *Decision Sciences*, 26: 265–281.

Schaltegger, S. and Burritt, R. (2000) *Contemporary environmental accounting: issues, concepts and practice*, Sheffield: Greenleaf.

Schaltegger, S., Herzig, C., Kleiber, O., and Müller, J. (2002) *Sustainability management in business enterprises: concepts and instruments for sustainable organisation development*, Bonn: Federal Ministry for the Environment, Nature Conservation, and Nuclear Safety.

Seelos, C. and Mair, J. (2007) 'Profitable business models and market creation in the context of deep poverty: a strategic view', *Academy of Management Perspectives*, 21: 49–63.

Strobel, M. and Redmann, C. (2002) 'Flow cost accounting, an accounting approach based on the actual flows of materials', in Bennett, M., Bouma, J.J., and Wolters, T. (eds) *Environmental management accounting: informational and institutional developments*, Dordrecht: Springer, pp. 67–82.

Wagner, B. and Enzler, S. (eds) (2006) *Material flow management: improving cost efficiency and environmental performance*, Heidelberg: Physica.

Yu, J.M., Ahmedna, M., Goktepe, I., and Dai, J.A. (2006) 'Peanut skin procyanidins: composition and antioxidant activities as affected by processing', *Journal of Food Composition and Analysis*, 19: 364–371.

7

EMA FOR CLEANER RICE PROCESSING

Oliver Enterprises I, the Philippines

Introduction

This case study explores the potential of environmental management accounting (EMA) in the context of cleaner production measures in the rice-milling industry of the Philippines. It examines whether EMA can provide useful information to decision-makers concerned with the environmental and social impacts of rice husk as waste from the milling process. To achieve this, it explores changes to the current mode of production through the mechanism of technology transfer via an automated carbonisation system (ACS) that is widely used in Japan.

The main question is whether EMA provides a useful way to show whether investment in the ACS technology is justifiable (Figure 7.1: Box 8). Associated with this question is whether an ex-post review of the decision reached confirms it to have been correct (Box 4). To answer these questions information was gathered at Oliver Enterprises, a rice miller in the Philippines. Longitudinal assessment of the development and installation of cleaner production technologies and issues arising at Oliver Enterprises took place over a 2.5-year period (2004–2007; see also the follow-up case study in Chapter 8 of the book).

The next section examines the decision-making context related to the introduction of a possible new closed loop system and discusses key diagnostic information about the company. The following section explains the company's motivation for using EMA. The case continues in the fourth section with an illustration of the results of monetary environmental investment appraisal for the automated carbonisation of rice husk, with conclusions being drawn in the context of an ex-post assessment of the costs and savings observed in the initial phase of the pilot investment in ACS. Following a discussion, the final section outlines implications of the analysis for corporate decision-makers.

		Monetary EMA		Physical EMA	
		Short-term	Long-term	Short-term	Long-term
Past-orientated	Routinely generated	Environmental cost accounting [1]	Environment-induced capital expenditure and revenue [2]	Material and energy flow accounting [9]	Environmental capital impact accounting [10]
Past-orientated	Ad hoc	Ex-post assessment of relevant environmental costing decisions [3]	Ex-post inventory assessment of projects [4]	Ex-post assessment of short-term environmental impacts [11]	Ex-post inventory appraisal of physical environmental investments [12]
Future-orientated	Routinely generated	Monetary environmental budgeting [5]	Environmental long-term financial planning [6]	Physical environmental budgeting [13]	Environmental long-term physical planning [14]
Future-orientated	Ad hoc	Relevant environmental costing [7]	Monetary environmental investment appraisal [8]	Tools designed to predict relevant environmental impacts [15]	Physical environmental investment appraisal [16]

FIGURE 7.1 Application of the EMA framework (Burritt, Hahn, and Schaltegger 2002) to Oliver Enterprises I.

Note: Dark (light) grey boxes represent the major (minor) EMA applications.

Decision setting

Oliver Enterprises is a family-owned rice mill located at Talavera in the Nueva Ecija region of the Philippines. The family has been running the business since 1985 and the company employs 28 full-time workers and has about 200 part-time workers. The core business of the company is rice milling, although it has a variety of related business interests such as poultry, piggery, game farming, cockfighting, and aquaculture.

The basic steps involved in transforming paddy rice into white rice are cleaning, hulling, milling, polishing, grading, sorting, and packaging. The concern here is with disposal of rice husk, the shell or outer covering of rice seeds. Rice husk is a waste stream produced when the outer covering of each grain of rice is removed. In 2004, when the study commenced, the Oliver Enterprises rice mill produced about 400 tonnes of rice husk a day. Disposal was by transportation to two dumping fields (5 and 10 hectares in size) by trucks owned by the company. Until recently, the conventional waste treatment by Oliver Enterprises had been through regular burning of the rice husk, depending on prevailing weather conditions and the amount of accumulated rice husk. As the following section describes, the owner identified the problems associated with rice husk disposal as a key consideration for investing in rice husk-processing technology.

Environmental and social issues

What then were the main problems with rice husk disposal? First, the owners of the rice mill were concerned about the environmental and social impacts of dumping and burning of rice husk in open fields. Open field burning is difficult to control because of unexpected high winds in the Philippines and is conspicuous because it emits black smoke. In the past few years, people have settled near to the two dump sites owned by the rice miller. Skin, nose, and eye irritation caused by the smoke and by particulate matter created from the open burning, as well as decreased lung function and disease caused by asbestos-like silica fibres that are released through the burning process, posed potentially serious health and safety risks. Furthermore, as husk ashes can be deceivingly cold on the surface of the burning dump but red hot inside, children playing nearby and passers-by sometimes badly burned themselves while looking for rice in the rice husk heaps. Three specific incidents causing up to third-degree burns in 2004 were mentioned by the owners. The rice mill operators spent about PHP30,000 (PHP100 = €1.34) for the hospitalisation and medication of the victims. Other incidents also occurred but could not be identified by the owners because no regular recording of incidents took place.

Second, the company had growing concerns about reduced productivity of the land, caused through rice husk dumping and burning. Burning rice husk in open fields kills beneficial micro-organisms located in the topsoil. The overcarbonised rice husk or the ash hinders the growth of rice planted in the burn-off area, and holds and prevents water from reaching plant roots, thereby decreasing productivity. From time to time the rice husk, blown away during a typhoon, also blocked the nearby river and flooded the land, reducing productivity of the surrounding land to zero. White ash could be blown up to 25 kilometres during a typhoon. Finally, considered in a separate study is the fact that dumping and burning of rice husk contributes to global warming by releasing methane emissions (see Chapter 8).

The method Oliver Enterprises used to process rice husk is similar to the situation in many other emerging economy countries (World Bank 2001). Dumping followed by burning in open fields is the main method of husk disposal applied by almost 9,500 rice mills dispersed across the Philippines (National Food Authority 2007). Growth in concern about the related environmental and social impacts led to the Philippine government passing new environmental regulations and initiating new programmes. These regulations and programmes are examined next.

Regulations and governmental programs/strategies

By 2006, with increasing national production of paddy rice, the amount of husk waste rose to over 3 million tonnes per annum (Philippine Biomass

Energy Laboratory 2000; Bureau of Agricultural Statistics 2006; IGES 2006). To reduce the environmental and social impacts caused by dumping and burning of rice husk, 'command and control' environmental regulations have recently been introduced, outlawing dumping and burning (Republic of the Philippines 1999, 2000). Also cleaner production has been made state policy in the Philippines, thereby encouraging investment in new technologies (Environmental Management Bureau 2003). In particular, the Ecological Solid Waste Management Act of 2000 (Republic of the Philippines 2000) affects the method of husk processing by prohibiting open dumps for solid waste and declaring open burning of solid waste to be a criminal offence. However, it was evident at the time of the case study that command and control regulation was not yet working effectively, as the following shows. The new Act required the conversion from open to controlled dumping to be completed by February 2004 and the closure of converted dumpsites by February 2006 (Republic of the Philippines 2000). However, in February 2006, 309 dump sites and nine sanitary landfills controlled by the government were made available for dumping (National Solid Waste Management Commission 2006a,b) but 707 open dumpsites for burning rice husk were still operating (National Solid Waste Management Commission 2006c).

A complementary government approach to improving husk processing and to promoting investment in cleaner production technologies is the provision of assistance to small and medium-sized rice mill operators through research and development. Several national and regional research and development institutions are based in Nueva Ecija, which enjoys the support of many government programs as the agro-industrialised province moves towards becoming one of the major food bowls in the country (Nueva Ecija Provincial Government 2006). One of these is the government-owned Philippine Rice Research Institute (PhilRice), which develops and promotes new environment-friendly and sustainable rice-based technologies, practices, and related services.

In 2003–2004, Oliver Enterprises conducted a pilot project on innovative methods of processing husk in cooperation with PhilRice. In an attempt to guide the company away from its end-of-pipe dumping and burning method for husk disposal and to solve related environmental and social problems, the company decided to install technology that would eliminate waste. In spite of the current lack of enforcement, the rice mill expected the importance of husk-processing technology to increase considerably with more stringent enforcement of the regulations in the future. By deciding to invest in an alternative method of processing husk in 2004, the Oliver Enterprises rice mill tried to anticipate the future consequences of dumping and open burning of solid waste. Initiated through a Filipino and Japanese joint venture, the pilot project on husk-processing alternatives aimed to adapt and implement

Japanese automated carbonisation of rice husk technology to the local conditions. The technology is now outlined.

Technological issues

Carbonisation represents a method of processing rice husk. In the carbonisation process, which involves an incomplete or partial combustion of rice husk, the size of organic molecules is reduced without damage. The residual material is called carbonised rice husk (CRH). CRH contains an increased volume of nutrient salts such as phosphorus, potassium, calcium, and magnesium. CRH has many uses in agriculture and other industries, for example, as an input to fertiliser production, a soil enhancer, soils for seed-beds and flower pots, inoculants in food for farm animals, and heat insulation or oil adsorbent (Kumagai, Noguchi, Kurimoto, and Takeda 2005; Tadeo, Constancio, Corales, and Cordero 2005).

Simple, small-scale types of carbonisers are available for farmers to produce CRH. An upscale technology, the ACS, is the investment analysed in this study. An ACS consists of the following processes. Rice husk from the mill (on site or delivered from other rice mills) is stored before it is used in the carboniser. In the carboniser, the rice husk is heated to between 600 and 800°C. The chemical process is termed pyrolysis. In carbonisation no extra heat source is needed; the heat required for the carbonisation process is obtained by burning the gases and pyrolysis vapours. This makes the process energy independent (except in the initial start-up phase). After carbonisation, the CRH is cooled in an extinguisher before being packed and stored. It is possible that heat from the carbonisation process can be used by a waste heat boiler and a turbine generator to produce electric power.

In principle the ACS can operate for 24 hours a day. One ACS unit can process about 1,000 kg of husk per hour, with a theoretical maximum capacity of 24,000 kg of carbonated husk per day. In Japan, where the technology is well established, the system is usually operated for about eight to nine hours per day and the practical capacity per machine is about 8,500 kg per day. As conditions such as temperature, climate, variety of rice, production and handling, and physical properties differ from country to country, these generate variability in relation to output from carbonisation.

Economic issues

Against the background of falling rice prices and an intensification of competition for markets (Bureau of Agricultural Statistics 2006), the development of alternative income streams and cost reduction were seen as being increasingly important to the company. If the ACS investment is successful, the husk-processing alternative was viewed as holding potential for contributing to the elimination of environmental and social impacts caused by rice husk dumping and burning and providing a promising opportunity to generate income for Oliver Enterprises. In 2004, energy supply was widely subsidised in the Philippines and the pressure for securing non-fossil supplies of energy was not prioritised; hence investment in CRH technology, rather than the need to reduce energy costs, took centre stage in decision-making. Why then did the company wish to consider the possible contribution of EMA towards helping with its husk carbonisation decision?

Company's motivation for using EMA

A simple method of appraisal widely used by smaller companies, the investment payback ratio, was used by the joint venture partners for deciding whether to move forward with the investment. The penchant for Japanese companies to favour payback over discounted cash flow techniques also helps explain the use of this technique (Blayney and Yokoyama 1991; Drury and Tayles 1997; Shinoda 2010). The projected payback ratio of less than two years for recovery of the initial investment was considered acceptable to the joint venture partners, and Oliver Enterprises considered moving ahead with the project. However, the company wished to assess the profitability of the proposed ACS in a more systematic and comprehensive way and so monetary environmental investment appraisal was undertaken by the researchers using discounted cash flow analysis (see next section) and the identification of previously unspecified environmental costs and cost savings (Figure 7.1: Box 8). During the pilot study there were teething problems with implementing the ACS, and it did not reach full production capacity. After operating the ACS for six months, the company thus wanted to know whether the investment decision could be reconfirmed (Figure 7.1: Box 4). The revised monetary environmental investment appraisal based on an ex-post assessment of actual costs is illustrated below.

EMA application

Monetary environmental investment appraisal

The first EMA appraisal at Oliver Enterprises commenced in 2004 and aimed to assess ex-ante the implementation of the ACS. The basic notion of environmental project appraisal is to determine the expected financial benefits that can be gained from the ACS investment based on a given set of assumptions about predicted costs and revenues and placing special focus on environmental costs and cost savings (Schaltegger and Burritt 2000). Assumptions relating to capital and operating considerations, as used in the monetary environmental investment appraisal, are briefly discussed below.

Capital expenditures

Information was gathered about Oliver Enterprises' plan to purchase three ACS units with the intention of operating 16 hours per day, in parallel with the two eight-hour shifts being worked in the rice mill, leading to a maximum capacity of 16,000 kg of CRH per day. Capital expenditure of PHP21 million was required for each of the three ACS units, to be contributed equally by Oliver Enterprises and the Japanese joint venturer. Additional capital expenditures relating to construction of the CRH building, an organic fertiliser building, and machinery associated with processing the CRH products were the responsibility of Oliver Enterprises.

Operating revenues

Opportunities for cost savings and revenue generation were identified in relation to the operation of the ACS. The processed husk could be either sold as CRH on the local or international market or mixed with manure to produce organic fertiliser. The local market price for CRH was about PHP30 per 10-kg bag. In the medium term, Oliver Enterprises intended to enter the international market, where higher prices for CRH could be generated (up to PHP50 per 10 kg). Operating revenues were expected to be achieved by mixing the CRH with bio-organic materials, such as farm manure, and selling the by-product as organic fertiliser to the local market at a price of PHP150–170 per 50-kg bag.

As transport of the husk to the dump is eliminated through the investment, environmental cost savings results are expected from reduced diesel fuel usage. Oliver Enterprises maintained its trucks and dump sites until the ACS was operational. The opportunity cost of fuel savings was included to cover this situation. Existing trucks were needed on standby in case the carbonisation system did not work as expected and husk dumping was reinstated. However, as the drivers could be used for other duties, there was an expected labour saving attributable to the ACS project. A final expected benefit was out-of-pocket cost savings associated with the elimination of hospital and medical costs related to accidental burns to members of the local community.

Operating expenses

A major part of the operating costs is related to the production of organic fertiliser. Other expenses caused by the production and the sale of organic fertiliser are for marketing and labour associated with moving bags of organic fertiliser from the store to the gate of the rice mill. In addition, operation of ACS consumes energy. The consumption per ACS unit is 14 kWh, ignoring a small amount of kerosene needed to ignite the furnace. Labour costs are related to husk storage, the bagging and storage of CRH, and supervision of the ACS control panel. Information obtained indicated that maintenance costs account for 1 per cent of the total operating costs.

Table 7.1 illustrates the results of the monetary environmental investment appraisal undertaken to evaluate viability in the lead-up to the pilot trial. Two calculations are presented based on possible market conditions. The first calculation is made on the assumption that half of the CRH is mixed with manure to produce organic fertiliser and the remainder is sold as CRH on the open market. The assumed selling price of CRH is based on local market prices as no international market existed. The second computation is based on the assumption that 100 per cent of the CRH is converted into organic fertiliser. The investment appears acceptable based on all criteria whichever product mix is assumed. Conversion to organic fertiliser appeared to be the most attractive alternative.

On the information available the joint venturers decided to proceed with the investment. After operating the ACS for six months, problems with implementation were evident. In particular, the ACS did not reach full production capacity, and the company wanted to know whether the decision to invest was correct. The next section shows the results of the second EMA application, the re-assessment of the ACS technology.

Ex-post assessment of the environmental investment

Based on the needs of the joint venture parties, an ex-post assessment was undertaken providing a revised monetary calculation in relation to material and energy flow costs based on the actual costs incurred in the initial phase of the pilot project (Schaltegger, Burritt, and Petersen 2003). In addition, a sensitivity analysis was undertaken on relevant parameters, the main environmental aim being to replace the process of burning and dumping husks and remove its related impacts on the environment and society. Physical data on the material and energy flows related to the carbonisation of rice husk were gathered by the research team to calculate related costs and conduct the revised monetary environmental investment appraisal of the ACS.

Additional experiments with production of organic fertiliser by-products

TABLE 7.1 Initial ACS investment results using various indicators

Indicator	50% CRH, 50% organic fertiliser	100% organic fertiliser
Payback period	1.5 years	1.1 years
Internal rate of return	58%	84%
Net present value	PHP49 million	PHP81 million
Profitability index	2.3	3.2

led the owners temporarily to stop production of CRH in 2006 pending re-assessment of the financial results. The ACS was tested several times between April and December 2005, and close interaction was maintained between the owners, researchers, and PhilRice. Data gathered during the testing and operation of the ACS units was used in the reappraisal of the initial investment decision. Site visits and interviews with Oliver Enterprises to obtain a detailed picture of actual operations were conducted for the revised assessment.

The results of initial testing revealed the conversion rate of rice husk to CRH at 33 per cent, lower than expected (the initial investment estimate had been 40 per cent), but, given prevailing weather conditions at the plant, it appeared that the best CRH quality could be achieved at the lower rate. Hence, total costs for producing one kilogram of CRH were higher than expected.

The pilot showed that a carbonisation machine could be operated in practice continuously for 72 hours (with a maximum of 96 hours) before residual ash at the chimney base had to be cleared and the system restarted. Modification to lengthen the operation time to six days without interruption would have cost about PHP2 million. The result of the test also indicated that two operators and four assistants were needed to operate one ACS unit for 24 hours (over two shifts), including storage of husk and bagging of CRH.

Finally, an important finding from operating the ACS for six months was that the potential for selling CRH and organic fertiliser had been overestimated. Oliver Enterprises was able to sell only a portion of the CRH and organic fertiliser produced during the test period. There were two reasons for this. First, the demand for organic fertiliser made from CRH was slow to grow; much of the reluctance to use organic fertiliser stems from the belief of users that its quality is not high enough and that it imposes additional costs over those of conventional farming. To commercialise the organic fertiliser product, the owners plan to register and certify it. Second, Oliver Enterprises is engaged in trying to develop the international market to increase revenues by selling CRH at a higher price to countries and regions such as Australia, Japan, Taiwan, the Middle East, and Europe.

To refocus on meeting the limited demand for CRH products while keeping labour costs controlled, the ACS units' projected running time was reduced (see Figure 7.2). Operation was projected to restart in July 2006. In the first year Unit 3 was planned for periods of 72 hours' continuous use, Unit 2 for 48 hours, and Unit 1 was to be treated as a back-up unit. The entire system could be operated by one operator and two assistants. From the second year onwards, it was expected that, given projected demand for the CRH products, two units could be operated simultaneously for 72 hours and one unit for 48 hours, requiring two operators and five assistants (see Figure 7.2).

Revised monetary environmental investment appraisal results are presented in Table 7.2. A longer payback period and lower profitability are evident. All discounted cash flow indicators show the investment to be worthwhile but

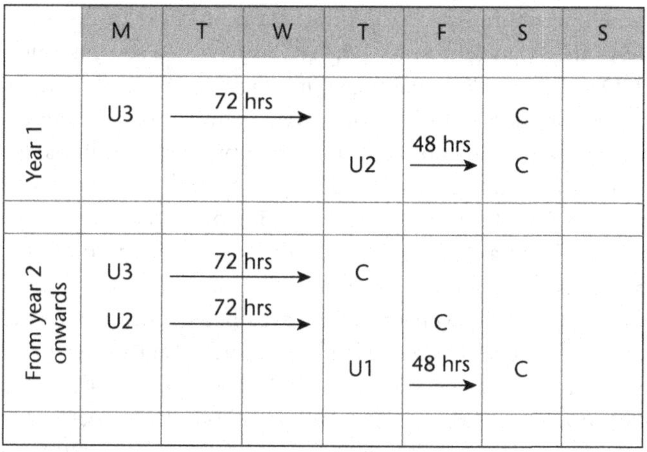

	M	T	W	T	F	S	S
Year 1	U3	72 hrs →		U2 48 hrs →	C C		
From year 2 onwards	U3 U2	72 hrs → 72 hrs →	C	C U1 48 hrs →	C C		

U1–U3: three ACS units. C: cleaning of ACS unit.

FIGURE 7.2 Projected ACS running times.

TABLE 7.2 Revised appraisal of the ACS investment

Indicator	50% CRH, 50% organic fertiliser	100% organic fertiliser
Payback period	3.0 years	2.4 years
Internal rate of return	20%	32%
Net present value	PHP8 million	PHP21 million
Profitability index	1.2	1.6

Note: Indicators are based on actual observations from the trial period and projected running times.

that the payback period was worse, thereby making the joint venturers less satisfied with the investment. The option of producing 100 per cent organic fertiliser again dominates, provided that the market size can be increased.

In order to assess the impact of the changes in the financial results, sensitivity analysis was carried out on the CRH selling price and organic fertiliser selling price parameters (see Figure 7.3). The most sensitive parameter affecting financial results and the associated benefits to the environment and social impacts of carting and burning avoided is the market price of organic fertiliser.

Discussion

Evidence is provided about the development and installation of automated carbonisation technology for processing rice husk in order to reduce environmental and social problems for a rice miller in the Philippines. The study initially identified carbonisation of rice husk as a promising alternative to

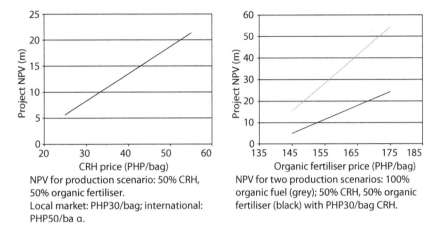

NPV for production scenario: 50% CRH, 50% organic fertiliser.
Local market: PHP30/bag; international: PHP50/ba g.

NPV for two production scenarios: 100% organic fuel (grey); 50% CRH, 50% organic fertiliser (black) with PHP30/bag CRH.

FIGURE 7.3 ACS project sensitivity to market prices.

replace the dumping and burning of rice husk in open fields currently in use and to eliminate related environmental and social impacts. An ex-ante investment appraisal indicated that the project would be a financial success. However, because of differences between expected ideal and practical capacity of production in the first six months of the project, an ex-post audit revealed that the physical rice husk and CRH flows and financial benefits were less than expected and that the payback period had become more marginal. Although the financial results remained positive, the full environmental benefits were not achieved because the market capacity for CRH products and organic fertiliser was lower than expected. This discouraged the owners of Oliver Enterprises from production of further CRH. The company expressed its keen interest in expanding market demand.

Given the revised target operating times for the ACS units, Oliver Enterprises was not able to process all husk emanating from the mill as originally intended. As an interim arrangement, surplus rice husk was dumped on site next to the rice mill, where a friend of the owners collected it for use in a paper mill company about 140 kilometres away. In addition, the supply–demand gap for rice husk became wider as rice volumes continued to increase, requiring the owners to operate their rice mill 24 hours during peak periods. As a result, a further rice mill unit was added to production. As a consequence, environmental and social impacts of rice husk as waste from the milling process continue to exist, preventing the owners from achieving their environmental and social objectives. However, the owners remain resolute in their determination to find a long-term alternative for disposal or elimination of the surplus husk. Initiatives to develop the market for CRH and CRH-based organic fertiliser product acceptance by consumers are described above. An alternative which emerged during the pilot ACS project is energy recovery from the remaining biomass. EMA support for rice husk-processing through cogeneration is examined in a follow-up case study (Chapter 8).

The research has implications for government policy. Findings of the study substantiate the usefulness of responsive regulation in cleaner production-related areas and encourage policy-makers to design a balanced policy mix for environmental protection in the rice-milling industry using the promotion of an EMA-based information strategy as a complement to command-and-control regulation (Burritt, Herzig, and Tadeo 2009).

Outcomes from the case study highlighted several important issues. First, as revealed by the EMA analysis, for rice husk pollution issues to be resolved, regulatory bodies should focus on developing the organic fertiliser and CRH markets. This could provide an important impetus for the introduction and use of ACS in the Philippines. If the market can be built up and the ACS investment is viewed as successful, the technology could be rolled out in the Philippines.

A caveat about using a single case study as the basis for general policy is appropriate; however, the pilot project is being used specifically by PhilRice, the government research body, with this aim in mind: specifically examining the practical problems of implementation so that others can learn from this experience, and markets in CRH and organic fertiliser can be developed.

Second, the joint-venture party encouraged Oliver Enterprises with a 50 per cent capital subsidy for the purchase of technology. In this case EMA provides guidance about the sensitivity of results to the level of subsidy provided and gives guidance for determining the most effective rate of subsidy to encourage take-up of ACS by other millers. A generic investment appraisal based on practical capacity of the ACS shows that a capital subsidy from the Japanese firm or the national government in the Philippines is unnecessary for environmental, social, and monetary gains to accrue.

Conclusions

An important premise behind this study is the perceived need to help managers and policy-makers to reduce the environmental and social impacts associated with the dumping and burning of rice husk. The findings suggest that EMA can help with the voluntary adoption of cleaner production technology by rice mill owners and managers. By observing the processes and outcomes of a cleaner production investment in a capital project that improve the environment, this case study highlights how EMA supports long-run decision-making. This is achieved by promoting awareness of environmental and social issues through the identification, collection, analysis, and use of physical and monetary environmental information.

Two conceptual contributions emerge. First, the importance of ex-post appraisal is highlighted as an ongoing check on the assumed costs and benefits of investment calculations in the environmental context (Brealey and Myers 1984). Second, most previous EMA research has focussed on the identification, recording, and tracing of past and current environmental costs to promote cleaner production, through short-term tools such as mass-balance and flow cost accounting (e.g. Parker 2005; Gale 2006; Jasch 2006). In contrast, this study highlights the importance of future and long-term physical and monetary information in environmental management and investment appraisal.

Finally, the study has a number of limitations. The scope of the study is limited to the application of EMA in the operation of a pilot investment by Oliver Enterprises, a Philippine rice mill. Further, the rice-milling industry is highly competitive and so the process of obtaining sensitive data was lengthy, involving the development of trust between the parties involved: the government rice agency, rice miller, and researchers. To ensure confidentiality, some numbers have been slightly changed, generalised, and/or aggregated without affecting the nature or direction of conclusions reached. Finally, in recent times shortages have increased the price of milled rice, energy supplies have been subject to the shock from increased oil prices, and cogeneration appeals to the need for non-fossil sources of power. Hence, the focus has shifted towards energy generation from rice husk and this is examined in a separate study (see Chapter 8).

References

Blayney, P. and Yokoyama, I. (1991) *Comparative analysis of Japanese and Australian cost accounting and management practices*, working paper, The University of Sydney, Sydney.

Brealey, R. and Myers, S.C. (1984) *Principles of corporate finance*, New York: McGraw-Hill.

Bureau of Agricultural Statistics (2006) *Rice and corn situation and outlook*, Quezon City: Republic of the Philippines, Department of Agriculture, Bureau of Agricultural Statistics.

Burritt R., Hahn, T., and Schaltegger, S. (2002) 'Towards a comprehensive framework for environmental management accounting: links between business actors and environmental management accounting tools', *Australian Accounting Review*, 12: 39–50.

Burritt, R.L., Herzig, C., and Tadeo, B.D. (2009) 'Environmental management accounting for cleaner production: the case of a Philippine rice mill', *Journal of Cleaner Production*, 17: 431–439.

Drury, C. and Tayles, M. (1997) 'The misapplication of capital investment appraisal techniques', *Management Decision*, 35: 86–93.

Environmental Management Bureau (2003) *Guidebook on Environmental Management System, Pollution Prevention/Cleaner Production and Environmental Cost Accounting*, Quezon City: Environmental Management Bureau.

Gale, R. (2006) 'Environmental management accounting as a reflexive modernization strategy in cleaner production', *Journal of Cleaner Production*, 14: 1228–1236.

IGES (Institute for Global Environmental Strategies) (2006) *CDM country guide for the Philippines*, Kanagawa: IGES.

Jasch, C. (2006) 'How to perform an environmental management cost assessment in one day', *Journal of Cleaner Production*, 14: 1194–1213.

Kumagai, S., Noguchi, Y., Kurimoto, Y., and Takeda K. (2005) 'Oil adsorbent produced by the carbonization of rice husks', *Waste Management*, 27: 554–561.

National Food Authority (2007) *Grains business statistics (preliminary report) January to December 2006* [online – accessed on 8 April 2008]. Available from Internet: http://www.nfa.gov.ph/nfa22.html.

National Solid Waste Management Commission (2006a) *List of controlled dumpsites: 3rd quarter updates 2006* [online – accessed on 21 February 2007]. Available from Internet: http://www.denr.gov.ph/nswmc/6.php.

National Solid Waste Management Commission (2006b) *List of sanitary landfill sites: 3rd quarter updates 2006* [online – accessed on 21 February 2007]. Available from Internet: http://www.denr.gov.ph/nswmc/6.php.

National Solid Waste Management Commission (2006c) *List of open dumpsites: 3rd quarter updates 2006* [online – accessed on 21 February 2007]. Available from Internet: http://www.denr.gov.ph/nswmc/6.php.

Nueva Ecija Provincial Government (2006) *Province of Nueva Ecija* [online – accessed on 8 April 2008]. Available from Internet: http://www.nuevaecija.gov.ph.

Parker, L. (2005) 'Social and environmental accountability research: a view from the commentary box', *Accounting, Auditing and Accountability Journal*, 18: 842–860.

Philippine Biomass Energy Laboratory (2000) *Resource assessment study of biomass potential for major agricultural and forestry resources in the Philippines*, Laguna: Los Banos College.

Republic of the Philippines (1999) *Philippine Clean Air Act.*.

Republic of the Philippines (2000) *Ecological Solid Waste Management Act*.

Schaltegger, S. and Burritt, R. (2000) *Contemporary environmental accounting, issues, concepts and practice*, London: Greenleaf.

Schaltegger, S., Burritt, R.L., and Petersen, H. (2003) *An introduction to corporate environmental management: striving for sustainability*, Sheffield: Greenleaf.

Shinoda, T. (2010) 'A focus on the use of capital budgeting methods: capital budgeting management practices in Japan', *Economic Journal of Hokkaido University*, 39: 39–50.

Tadeo, B.D., Constancio, A.A., Corales, R.G., and Cordero, J.C. (2005) *Carbonized rice hull: rice technology bulletin*, Maligaya: PhilRice.

World Bank (2001) *Philippines environment monitor 2001*, Washington, DC: World Bank.

8

EMA FOR REDUCING GREENHOUSE GAS EMISSIONS IN RICE PROCESSING

Oliver Enterprises II, the Philippines

Introduction

In the context of the need for reduction of carbon dioxide (CO_2) or carbon dioxide equivalent (CO_2eq) emissions by business, a number of new approaches have been introduced which highlight benefits from linking climate change and corporate opportunities. One of the approaches is the clean development mechanism (CDM), which holds considerable promise to help reduce the impacts of global warming while bringing income to businesses. The design of a CDM project involves the survey, analysis, and supply of site-specific information to meet registration, monitoring, and reporting requirements. Most of these issues have already been explored in the context of environmental management accounting (EMA) (Burritt, Hahn, and Schaltegger 2002); however, as yet EMA has not been referred to in the discussion of CDM projects. Links between CDM and EMA are explored here through a Philippine case study. The study illustrates how EMA helps companies to secure carbon credits by means of biomass energy production through environmental and financial assessment of potential investment in a CDM project.

This case study complements the study by Burritt, Herzig, and Tadeo (2009) in which Oliver Enterprises, a Philippine rice mill operator, identified carbonisation of rice husk as a promising investment alternative to its rice husk dumping and burning in open fields – a major environmental problem in many emerging countries (Chapter 7). In spite of the financial and environmental benefits of the carbonisation technology revealed over a 2.5-year longitudinal study, a set of teething problems with implementation and unexpected low market demand discouraged the rice mill owner from the production of carbonised rice husk (CRH). In these circumstances a second processing alternative, husk-fired cogeneration, emerged as a possibility, when combined with the potential benefits of the CDM as implemented through a joint arrangement with foreign companies. The cogeneration process in which the owners of Oliver Enterprises could use waste rice husk as an alternative source of fuel to produce electricity and/or heat is the subject of this case study.

In the study two EMA techniques (Figure 8.1) are used to address two principal CDM issues: (i) the calculation of expected emissions reductions and (ii) the calculation of expected additional revenues from selling certified emission reductions (CERs) certificates. Physical environmental investment appraisal is used to calculate CO_2 emission reductions (Figure 8.1: Box 16). Monetary environmental investment appraisal aims to assess the additional revenues gained from the reduction of greenhouse gas emissions through the CDM in the appraisal of a cogeneration power plant (Figure 8.1: Box 8). Additional links to EMA tools such as environmental budgeting and material and energy flow accounting (Figure 8.1: Boxes 5, 13, 9) as well as the broader concept of sustainability accounting are outlined.

The remainder of this chapter is structured as follows. In the next section, key company diagnostic information is provided and the decision-making context of the rice mill established. The motivation for the company's involvement with EMA is examined in the following section. Findings from the application of physical and monetary environmental investment appraisal and further potential benefits of EMA in the context of CDM are elaborated after

		Monetary EMA		Physical EMA	
		Short-term	Long-term	Short-term	Long-term
Past-orientated	Routinely generated	Environmental cost accounting [1]	Environment-induced capital expenditure and revenue [2]	Material and energy flow accounting [9]	Environmental capital impact accounting [10]
	Ad hoc	Ex-post assessment of relevant environmental costing decisions [3]	Ex-post inventory assessment of projects [4]	Ex-post assessment of short-term environmental impacts [11]	Ex-post inventory appraisal of physical environmental investments [12]
Future-orientated	Routinely generated	Monetary environmental budgeting [5]	Environmental long-term financial planning [6]	Physical environmental budgeting [13]	Environmental long-term physical planning [14]
	Ad hoc	Relevant environmental costing [7]	Monetary environmental investment appraisal [8]	Tools designed to predict relevant environmental impacts [15]	Physical environmental investment appraisal [16]

FIGURE 8.1 Application of the EMA framework (Burritt *et al.* 2002) to Oliver Enterprises II.
Note: Dark (light) grey boxes represent the major (minor) EMA applications.

that. Discussion of the findings is presented before the chapter draws conclusions and outlines limitations of the case study in the final section.

Decision setting

Oliver Enterprises operates its rice milling business in the northern Philippines. The owners of the private, family-owned company have been expanding their rice mill operation during the last few years, aided by representatives from PhilRice, a government research and development body. Rice milling is in heavy demand locally, and during peak periods the rice mill operates 24 hours a day. To help cope with the inflow of rice and extra demand, an additional rice mill has recently been added. One waste product from the rice milling process is rice husk. With greater production of milled rice comes increasing amounts of husk. An attempt to convert husk to a by-product through automated carbonisation failed to cope with the quantity of husk being produced and alternative uses were considered by the mill owners. One alternative is to use the husk as a fuel for cogeneration of electricity for the rice mills. The renewable energy produced could then substitute for (i) electricity drawn from the grid which is produced with fossil fuels such as coal and oil and (ii) electricity cogenerated by company-owned diesel generators. The decision to introduce cogeneration, which would help to address global warming, also depends on potential sources of income associated with a new market in CERs offered through the CDM scheme introduced under the Kyoto Protocol (UN 1997). The context of the decision to consider cogeneration is further considered below.

Environmental, social, and regulatory issues

Environmental and social risks are associated with husk dumping and burning in open fields: smoke hazard, particulates which affect local residents, burns associated with children and adults foraging for rice in the burning husk dumps, and so forth (see Chapter 7). Solid waste management plans were developed by many local government units in the Philippines (e.g. Philippine Government 2005; DENR and DILG 2006). However, lack of commitment to enforcement of existing environmental regulations meant the environmental and social problems of husk disposal persist. Hence, husk-processing alternatives grew in importance as the pressure on local government units to comply with the law increased (PIA 2006).

Given the excess of husk waste and a failure to solve the initial environmental and social problems by investing in the carbonisation technology to reduce waste and produce a by-product (see Chapter 7), a second investment option – husk-fired cogeneration – emerged from discussions with PhilRice. The mill operators decided to examine the possibility that cogeneration would enable the company to achieve energy self-sufficiency for the rice mills, with initial spare capacity being available to accommodate expected increases in rice milling and associated husk residue. In addition, potential CDM-based revenues were seen as a way to enhance the profitability of cogeneration. Financial considerations of the CDM mechanism are examined in the next sub-section, followed by an outline of the investment options for the cogeneration technology.

Economic and market issues

Energy recovery from rice husk biomass is a processing alternative which did not seem attractive to Oliver Enterprises when the initial automated carbonisation project commenced (see Chapter 7). However, ongoing daily power outages, fluctuating electricity energy supply, and increasing energy costs encouraged the assessment of acquiring a self-managed power plant that makes use of Oliver Enterprises husk waste as a local renewable energy source. In addition to the reduction in dependency on imported fossil fuels and fossil-based power plants, a strong motivation for investigation of the viability of a power plant is growing awareness of the financial benefits from the CDM scheme related to the reduction of greenhouse gas emissions.

The CDM scheme was suggested under the Kyoto Protocol in 1997 and was adopted when the Protocol entered into force in 2005. The Protocol allows industrialised countries [called Annex B countries (UN 1997)] to reduce a proportion of their greenhouse gas emissions by investing in emissions reduction projects in emerging countries (Annex A countries). Such investments by companies located in Annex A countries tend to be cheaper because of the low levels of investment in basic emissions reduction in emerging countries in the past. However, these investments rely on the incentive provided by giving CER credits, or carbon credits, to companies in Annex A countries to offset against their CO_2 or CO_2eq emissions. Companies located in emerging countries, which do not have emission reduction targets, benefit from investments under the CDM scheme and the financial support of investors. From the perspective of Oliver Enterprises, which wishes to carry out a clean energy project activity, CDM offers potential as a basis for enhancing project profitability by gaining additional revenues from selling CERs. To invest in such a clean energy project, two alternatives for cogeneration are available. These alternatives are explained next.

Technological issues

The first alternative for cogeneration was to invest in a power plant which was integrated with the automated carbonisation system (ACS) units installed. This integrated alternative to the husk problem was the original idea of the

Filipino and Japanese joint venture (see Chapter 7) and was rejected at the initial decision point. The second alternative was to invest in a separate power plant.

Option 1: integrated power plant

The first option involves a 0.5-MW power plant for each ACS unit and requires continuous operation of the system. The integration of cogeneration technology raises a number of considerations for the design of the ACS project, which failed to cope with the quantity of husk waste being produced. Some of the most important considerations are: (i) the need to modify the ACS units for continuous operation, (ii) high purchase cost of the power plant because the technology can be installed under the joint venture agreement with the Japanese company owning it, and (iii) the limit of the total power supply to about 1.5 MW in aggregate (if all three ACS units are fully operated). A further issue is related to the amount of processed husk and the generation of husk and related products. Even if full technical operation of the ACS units installed were reached, the husk processing could not cope with the total volume of husk produced by the company and would not produce sufficient electricity to meet the company's average power demand, and uncertainty about market demand for husk products would remain.

Option 2: separate power plant

Oliver Enterprises sought EMA information about investment in a separate power plant with sufficient spare capacity to cope with increases in husk generation. A plant designed for a gross 2.5-MW generating capacity would enable the company to achieve energy self-sufficiency and completely remove surplus rice husk from fields in the local community and the associated social and environmental impacts. Data revealed that a condensing steam turbine generator could produce up to 2.5 MW at 11 kV. A small amount of the electricity generated could be used for internal plant consumption (the parasitic load) while net electricity, amounting to around 2.25 MW, would be used, in part, for meeting the energy consumption of the rice mill as well as exported to the transmission grid. The plant could operate for at least 7,500 hours per year and consume 4.8 tonnes of husk per hour when at maximum capacity. The figures revealed that additional husk from other rice mills would be needed to operate at full capacity, thereby helping to reduce social and environmental problems more broadly. The boiler using husk would generate super-heated steam of about 18.3 tonnes per hour at 25 bar pressure and 300°C. Installation of a programmable logic controller for the boiler system would provide fully automatic monitoring, process control, safety control, and alarm feedback when necessary.

With the technology readily available, the question then arose whether the owners would be motivated to invest, thereby (i) solving the local environmental and social problems, (ii) providing a signal to government that policy to stop dumping and burning could be successful, and (iii) showing that existing government policy to support the dissemination and use of EMA tools in the Philippines could be seen as a useful change. The motivation of the rice mill operators to proceed is considered next.

Company's motivation for using EMA

The first alternative, integrated cogeneration, was rejected because of its limited capacity to process husk (given the low demand for carbonised husk products) and generate electricity as well as the high costs of modifying the existing ACS units and Japanese cogeneration technology. This left option 2, a stand-alone cogeneration system. The company was aware that greenhouse gas emissions avoided through a clean energy project in the form of sellable CER certificates could be sold under the CDM scheme, thereby producing both income and environmental benefits. Without taking potential CDM revenues into account, the cogeneration technology could have been a less attractive proposal than maintaining the status quo with no investment. EMA information was used to show what the potential environmental and monetary benefits might be.

One essential condition in a CDM project activity application, and in verifying CERs, is the calculation and documentation of emissions reductions expected to occur when implementing the new clean energy technology. For validation purposes, calculations need to show how much the investment reduces greenhouse gas emissions relative to a business-as-usual scenario. Such information is provided by physical environmental investment appraisal, one of the EMA tools, with a focus on long-term decision-making, planning, and control (Figure 8.1: Box 16).

In the next section, first, the physical appraisal provides information to enable the rice mill operators to make transparent the potential greenhouse gas mitigation from the power plant investment. Second, the physical environmental information also provides the basis for assessing potential revenues gained through the CDM scheme from the reduction in CO_2eq emissions. Third, a simple monetary environmental investment appraisal outlines the financial implications of selling CERs (Figure 8.1: Box 8). A final sub-section elaborates on further potential benefits of using EMA for the planned CDM project activity.

EMA application

Physical environmental investment appraisal

The basic notion of a physical environmental investment appraisal is to provide information that helps to assess the ecological effectiveness of a planned project or to facilitate an environmental comparison between investment alternatives. Such assessment determines whether or not the investment project can reduce environmental impacts and, if so, by how much. The scope of the assessment can vary. It can be limited to specific environmental impact categories (e.g. the impact on water quality, air quality, biodiversity, or greenhouse gas emissions) or be set wider, aggregating all environmental interventions under one impact category (e.g. environmental impact added) (Schaltegger and Burritt 2000). In this study, ecological investment appraisal is limited to greenhouse gas emissions – the main concern in the CDM scheme. To calculate the net environmental effect of the power plant investment, baseline emissions from the disposal of the husk treated in the power plant are compared with the project emissions resulting from the operation of the husk-fired power plant. The difference shows the emissions benefit from the new investment.

Step 1: calculation of baseline emissions

The baseline (BE_y) is the level of greenhouse gas emissions prior to introducing the proposed CDM project activity. To determine the baseline, and the emissions that would occur in the absence of the planned investment, methodologies are available from the United Nations (UNFCCC 2008a), or new methodologies have to be proposed to and accepted by the CDM Executive Board. Two sources of greenhouse gas emissions are seen as relevant for the business-as-usual scenario at Oliver Enterprises: emissions related to the current disposal of husk and emissions related to the previous method of power generation.

$$BE_y = BE_{piling, y} + BE_{electricity, y} \qquad (8.1)$$

where:

$BE_{piling, y}$ = baseline emissions for methane avoidance in the year 'y'

$BE_{electricity, y}$ = baseline emissions for power generation in the year 'y'

Calculation of the baseline emissions is carried out in accordance with two corresponding baseline methodologies for small-scale project activities approved by the CDM Executive Board (UNFCCC 2006a,b).

(a) Baseline emissions for methane avoidance $(BE_{piling, y})$

The investment in a controlled combustion of husk reduces the greenhouse gas emissions as it prevents the anaerobic decay of husk. Emissions from the previous method of husk processing, that is, the potential methane from the decay of biomass content of husk treated in the power plant $(BE_{piling, y})$, amounts to more than 730 tonnes of methane for the first seven-year period, or more than 15,000 tonnes of CO_2eq, based on use of 21 as the conversion factor required to calculate the global warming potential of methane, as used for the first commitment period of the Kyoto Protocol 2008–2012 (IPCC 2001). According to the United Nations Framework Convention on Climate Change (UNFCCC 2006b), methane that would be destroyed or removed for safety or legal regulation $(MD_{y, reg})$ would need to be subtracted from the methane generation potential. However, there are no effective regulations requiring the destruction or removal of methane emission and so the issue is not relevant to the Oliver Enterprises cogeneration project.

$$BE_{piling, y} = (MB_y - MD_{y, reg}) \star GWP\_CH_4 \qquad (8.2)$$

where:

MB_y = methane generation potential in the year 'y' (tonnes of methane)

$MD_{y, reg}$ = methane that would be destroyed or removed in the year 'y' for safety or legal regulation

GWP_CH_4 = global warming potential of methane

(b) Baseline emissions for power generation $(BE_{electricity, y})$

The baseline emissions for power generation $(BE_{electricity, y})$ are the amount of greenhouse gas emissions from the displacement of energy. The net quantity of the electricity displaced (EG_y) accounts for 2.25 MWh. Of this, 0.95 MWh could be sold to the grid while the remaining 1.3 MWh could be used by Oliver Enterprises to cover the energy demand of the rice mill operations and replace energy generated by company-owned diesel generators. The consumption of energy from the grid (the weighted average emissions of the current generation mix in kg CO_2eq/kWh is about 0.5) and generated by company-owned diesel generators [emissions factor for diesel generator in kg/CO_2eq is 0.9 (URC 2005)] would be reduced. Considering the CO_2 emissions intensities of the electricity displaced $(CEF_{electricity, y})$ the kWh produced by the husk-fired power plant over a seven-year period would result in a potential saving of about 78,000 tonnes of CO_2.

$$BE_{electricity, y} = EG_y \star CEF_{electricity, y} \qquad (8.3)$$

where:

EG_y = net quantity of the electricity displaced during year 'y'

$CEF_{electricity, y}$ = CO_2 emissions intensity of the electricity displaced during year 'y'

Step 2: calculation of project emissions (PE)

Emissions from the previously described baseline scenario are to be compared with the expected project emissions of the planned investment. According to the United Nations Framework Convention on Climate Change (UNFCCC 2006a) three categories of direct emissions from project activity need to be considered: project emissions through combustion of non-biomass carbon ($PE_{comb, y}$), incremental transportation ($PE_{transp, y}$), and electricity or diesel consumption ($PE_{power, y}$).[1]

$$PE_y = PE_{comb, y} + PE_{transp, y} + PE_{power, y} \qquad (8.4)$$

where:

$PE_{comb, y}$ = project emissions through combustion of non-biomass carbon in the year 'y'

$PE_{transp, y}$ = project emissions through incremental transportation in the year 'y'

$PE_{power, y}$ = project emissions through electricity or diesel consumption in the year 'y'

Under the category 'project emissions through combustion of non-biomass carbon' all carbon dioxide emissions related to the combustion of non-biomass carbon content of the waste such as plastics, rubber, and fossil-derived carbon and auxiliary fuels used in the combustion facility are listed. Since husk is the only material that will be used as fuel in the boiler of the steam thermal power generation system, project emissions through combustion of non-biomass carbon are zero. Moreover, there are only minor emissions through incremental transportation, that is, emissions from collection activities, as husk is generated at the power plant site. The only source of considerable greenhouse gas emissions is the transportation of husk from the rice mill units to the power plant (direct on-site emissions) as well as the transportation of husk ash to a disposal site (direct off-site emissions). These emissions are not taken into account here as the emissions for the transportation of husk to a disposal site have also been excluded in the calculation of the baseline emissions. The only emissions which are attributable to the project activity are caused by the energy consumption of the power plant investment. These emissions account for approximately 6,500 tonnes of CO_2eq.

Step 3: calculation of net emission reductions

In total, the investment results in emission reductions of 86,500 tonnes of CO_2eq or on average about 12,350 tonnes of CO_2eq per year.

Monetary environmental investment appraisal

When potential revenues from selling CERs are considered, the power plant investment becomes more attractive to the owners of the rice mill. Taking the CDM revenues into consideration, a net present value of between PHP111 million and PHP123 million over a seven-year horizon could be achieved, compared with PHP83 million without CDM. The payback period fell to maximum 3.48 years or minimum 3.39 (compared with 3.73 years). To produce an upper and lower estimate of the net present value the following figures were derived for the project:

- *Upper limit.* The maximum calculation is based on €10 (PHP681) per tonne of CO_2eq. At this upper end of the range, total project costs: PHP310 million; annual revenues: PHP124 million with CDM (PHP115 million without CDM), that is, additional PHP9 million from selling CERs; annual costs: PHP32 million; NPV: PHP123 million with CDM (PHP83 million without CDM); payback period: 3.39 years with CDM (3.73 years without CDM).
- *Lower limit.* A floor price for CO_2eq was about €7 in 2006. Using €7 per tonne (PHP477) the figures above change as follows: annual revenues: PHP121 million; that is, additional revenues from CDM, PHP6 million; NPV, PHP111 million; payback period, 3.48 years. The other figures remain the same.

The range of €7–10 adopted for CERs above may be wider (Springer and Varilek 2004), but it serves to illustrate the potential impact on the investment. The range adopted makes the project more acceptable for Oliver Enterprises in terms of the improved discounted cash flows (see also discussion of discount rates in UNFCC 2007; World Bank 2007). Based on the information above, the owners needed to reflect further on the net changes revealed by the physical and financial analyses.

Additional benefits of EMA

There was considerable potential for additional aspects of support from the EMA in the planned CDM project activity of Oliver Enterprises. However, these opportunities, which are briefly outlined below, were not taken up as they are relevant for managing the CDM project activity only after it is validated and officially registered (except for the contribution to sustainability development evaluation). Environmental budgeting (Figure 8.1: Boxes 5 and 13), monitoring of emissions (Figure 8.1: Box 9), and demonstration of the contribution to sustainable development are all available for consideration. These potential benefits are briefly described below.

Environmental budgeting

Based on the approved CDM project activity documents, the future green-house gas emission reductions can be forecast. Short-term budgeting of expected greenhouse gas emission reductions can serve planning, control, and accountability purposes (Burritt and Schaltegger 2001; ICLEI 2003). Periodic target-setting, control, and reporting would have enabled Oliver Enterprises to ensure an ongoing comparison of actual results with budgeted estimates, and implement corrective plans if considered necessary. The budgeting process is not limited to greenhouse gas emission reduction measures and could include other expected material and energy flow reductions and related environmental cost budgets (Burritt and Schaltegger 2001).

Monitoring of emissions

For the CDM documentation, Oliver Enterprises would need to specify how it monitors emission reductions during the implementation and operation of the project. Monitoring of and reporting on the periodic calculation of greenhouse gas mitigation is a condition for regular verification, certification, and issuance of carbon credits (UNFCCC 2007). The gathering of physical environmental information on a regular basis, including material and energy amounts relating to the past for control purposes, is addressed by material and energy flow accounting, an important sub-component of EMA (IFAC 2005; Wagner and Enzler 2006; Jasch 2009).

Contribution to sustainable development evaluation

In a broader sense, EMA could also contribute to accounting for the project activity to assist in achieving sustainable development in the Philippines. In contrast to the assessment of the greenhouse gas emission reductions, the pro-ject's contribution to sustainable development is assessed by the Designated

National Authority of the Philippines (USAID Asia 2007) and addressed by the Designated Operational Agency only if sustainability issues are included in the monitoring protocols. The assessment is based on a list of economic, social, and environmental criteria. To meet the requirements of the Designated National Authority approval process, Oliver Enterprises would need to describe the sustainable development benefits of the planned cogeneration investment project (IGES 2008). Expected benefits would include (i) providing economic opportunities in the community by contracting local companies for the construction of the power plant, (ii) promoting local participation in the project through integration with the community, and (iii) improving local environmental quality and complying with environmental policies and standards (Republic of the Philippines 1999, 2000) by eliminating open field burning (for further information on the Designated National Authority approval criteria see IGES 2008).

These three potential contributions of EMA to the CDM process have not eventuated, as Oliver Enterprises remains in the process of deciding whether to take the stand-alone cogeneration opportunity further.

Discussion

The results of the study revealed that the planned cogeneration power plant would be beneficial in terms of carbon emission reduction and additional discounted cash flow financial revenues for rice husk to be used as a substitute for grid electricity. In addition, the findings from the physical environmental investment appraisal revealed that cogeneration would be beneficial in terms of carbon emission reduction and achieving energy self-sufficiency.

The CDM case study and its links with EMA address a current topic of major importance, business carbon emissions, and provide an example that encourages companies to consider the use of EMA in calculating the carbon emissions of a company's activity (WRI and WBCSD 2003, 2007). Business carbon emissions reduction or reduction in the carbon footprint can be defined as the total set of greenhouse gas emissions caused directly and indirectly by the organisation (Wiedmann, Minx, Barrett, and Wackernagel 2006; EPLCA 2007; BSI 2008). In the Oliver Enterprises CDM case study, EMA reveals that carbon footprint reduction could be achieved by (i) substituting combustion for fossil fuel consumption, (ii) replacing electricity from the grid and company-owned diesel generators, (iii) exporting electricity to the grid and replacing 'dirty' electricity, and (iv) eliminating the dumping of husk in open fields with its related methane emissions. However, the case study also shows that the sole focus on physical flows is not sufficient to bring about investment actions to reduce business carbon footprints, even when these can be clearly demonstrated.

In other words, the findings suggest that cogeneration could help Oliver Enterprises to generate additional revenues with husk-fuelled electricity generation to be used as a substitute for grid electricity. Gaining additional revenues from selling the CERs could enhance the attractiveness of the cleaner production investment. The information made evident by EMA is one crucial element of a CDM project validation, namely the independent evaluation against the requirements of the CDM – carried out by an independent third party, the Designated Operational Entity.

In sum, the study reveals that applying physical and monetary environmental investment could help Oliver Enterprises in the process of identifying a voluntary market-based opportunity for improved and profitable management and use of husk. Problems with calculating incorrect baseline and project emissions as well as the establishment of false credits can be avoided by appropriate application of EMA. Potential benefits of EMA in this context include the measuring, assessing, monitoring, and control of greenhouse gas emissions and other related material and energy flows and costs on a regular operational planning and control basis. From a broader perspective, an environmental/sustainability management accounting system could also enhance transparency where external monitoring and audit of the project activity's contribution to sustainable development is concerned.

There is ongoing discussion about the problems associated with the contribution of CDM projects to sustainable development; for instance, whether CDM host countries should set strong sustainable development criteria, thereby lowering the country's attractiveness for investors, or set weak requirements and attract larger volumes of foreign capital (Cosbey, Parry, Browne, Babu, Bhandari, Drexhage, and Murphy 2005; van Asselt and Gupta 2009). An environmental (or sustainability) management accounting system cannot solve all sustainability evaluation problems associated with the CDM scheme, but a more holistic view and balanced accounting for economic, ecological, and social impacts of a CDM project activity through environmental/sustainability management accounting methods would help operationalise the sustainability goal of the CDM scheme for all parties involved in the CDM process. It could also help with the handling of trade-offs between the sustainability dimensions of project activity impacts – a topic which has to date received little attention in current CDM and sustainability management discussions (Schaltegger and Burritt 2005; Schaltegger, Bennett, Burritt, and Jasch 2008; Hahn, Figge, Pinkse, and Preuss 2010).

Conclusions

Use of the CDM is a challenging process and the rice husk cogeneration proposal examined in this case study is yet to be submitted to the inventory of 2,600 projects currently awaiting assessment (UNFCC 2009). However, environmental management accounting can help companies improve the credibility of information being used in the CDM application process, help demonstrate environmental and social advantages of projects, and demonstrate where improvements to the financial bottom line occur.

The study offers initial insights into conceptual linkages between EMA and CDM. It illustrates how EMA enables companies and organisations to streamline the development of their CDM projects. CDM requires standardised supply and monitoring of site-specific information. Future research could further analyse the potential role of EMA in advancing the gathering, monitoring, and reporting of environment-related information needed for the approved consolidated methodologies of the CDM scheme and crucial to the effective verification and issuance of CERs from CDM projects.

The case study on its own has limitations in regard to the need to avoid generalisation from a single case. A further limitation is that the study considered only the two methods of husk processing which were seen as relevant by the owners of the company – integrated and separate cogeneration. The EMA framework can also be applied to other cleaner production technologies. For example, a separate study examined the use of EMA to assess an ACS (Burritt *et al.* 2009). The next logical step would be to analyse an integrated approach to husk processing, whereby both cleaner production investments are combined, something which was not practical in the present study as the potential of cogeneration appeared more attractive only after the CDM was developed. Oliver Enterprises rejected the idea of a subsequent investment to integrate power plants into each ACS unit because this would have required an overly expensive modification for permanent continuous operation and the installation of additional units to ensure sufficient energy supply for the mill. Finally, problems associated with the additionality criterion of the CDM (UNFCCC 2008b) have not been addressed. The basic idea of additionality is that those project activities that would occur without the CDM, in other words, that represent investments which would be made through business as usual, should not be certified under the CDM.

Note

1 The calculation of project activity emissions is made in accordance with Type III.E./version 9 of the simplified baseline and monitoring methodologies for selected small-scale CDM project activity categories. This category comprises:

> measures that avoid the production of methane from biomass or other organic matter that would have otherwise been left to decay anaerobically in a solid waste disposal site without methane recovery. Due to the project activity, decay is prevented through controlled combustion. The project activity does not recover or combust methane (unlike III G). Measures shall both reduce

anthropogenic emissions by sources, and directly emit less than 15 kilotonnes of carbon dioxide equivalent annually (UNFCCC 2006a).

Moreover, this category is eligible for investments which result in emission reductions below 25,000 tonnes CO_2eq per year.

References

BSI (British Standards Institution) (2008) *Specification for the assessment of the life cycle greenhouse gas emissions of goods and services, Publicly Available Specification PAS 2050:2008*, London: BSI.

Burritt, R. and Schaltegger, S. (2001) 'On the interrelationship between eco-efficiency and operational budgeting', *Environmental Management and Health*, 2: 158–174.

Burritt, R., Hahn, T., and Schaltegger, S. (2002) 'Towards a comprehensive framework for environmental management accounting: links between business actors and environmental management accounting tools', *Australian Accounting Review*, 12: 39–50.

Burritt, R.L., Herzig, C., and Tadeo, B.D. (2009) 'Environmental management accounting for cleaner production: the case of a Philippine rice mill', *Journal of Cleaner Production*, 17: 431–439.

Cosbey, A., Parry, J-E., Browne, J., Babu, Y.D., Bhandari, P., Drexhage. J., and Murphy, D. (2005) *Realizing the development dividend: making the CDM work for emerging countries – Phase 1 report*, Winnipeg: International Institute for Sustainable Development.

DENR and DILG (Department of Environment and Natural Resources and Department of the Interior and Local Government) (2006) *Joint memorandum circular: nationwide search for model barangay for eco-waste management system 2006–2007*, Quezon: DENR and DILG.

EPLCA (European Platform on Life Cycle Assessment) (2007) *Carbon footprint: what it is and how to measure*, Ispra: European Commission.

Hahn, T., Figge, F., Pinkse, J., and Preuss, L. (2010) 'Trade-offs in corporate sustainability: you can't have your cake and eat it', *Business Strategy and the Environment*, 19: 217–229.

ICLEI (International Council for Local Environmental Initiatives) (2003) *eco-Budget: a model of environmental budgeting* [online – accessed on 3 June 2008]. Available from Internet: http://www.iclei.org/europe.

IFAC (International Federation of Accountants) (2005) *International guidance document of EMA*, New York: IFAC.

IGES (Institute for Global Environmental Strategies) (2008) *CDM country guide for the Philippines*, Kanagawa: IGES.

IPCC (Intergovernmental Panel on Climate Change) (2001) *Technical Summary – climate change 2001: mitigation – a report of Working Group III of the IPCC*, Cambridge: Cambridge University Press.

Jasch, C. (2009) *Environmental and material flow cost accounting: principles and procedures*, Dordrecht: Springer.

PIA (Philippine Information Agency) (2006) *DENR urges LGUs to follow RA 9003 PIA press releases 2006/05/25* [online – accessed on 27 December 2006]. Available from internet: http://www.pia. gov.ph.

Philippine Government (2005) 'Department of Environment and Natural Resources (DENR), Pampanga Sign agreement on solid waste management', *Philippine Government News*, 22 February.

Republic of the Philippines (1999) *Philippine Clean Air Act (RA 8749)*.

Republic of the Philippines (2000) *Ecological solid waste management Act (RA 9003)*.

Schaltegger, S. and Burritt, R. (2000) *Contemporary environmental accounting, issues, concepts and practice*, London: Greenleaf.

Schaltegger, S. and Burritt R. (2005) 'Corporate sustainability', in Folmer, H. and Tietenberg, T. (eds) *The international yearbook of environmental and resource economics 2005/2006: a survey of current issues*, Cheltenham: Edward Elgar, pp. 185–222.

Schaltegger, S., Bennett, M., Burritt, R.L., and Jasch, C. (2008) *Environmental management accounting for cleaner production*, Dordrecht: Springer.

Springer, U. and Varilek, M. (2004) 'Estimating the price of tradable permits for greenhouse gas emissions in 2008–2012', *Energy Policy*, 32: 611–621.

UN (United Nations) (1997) *Kyoto protocol to the UN framework convention on climate change*, New York: United Nations.

UNFCCC (United Nations Framework Convention on Climate Change) (2006a) *AMS-I.D.: grid connected renewable electricity generation, version 8* [online – accessed on 8 April 2008]. Available from Internet: http://cdm.unfccc.int/methodologies/SSCmethodologies/approved.html.

UNFCCC (2006b) *AMS-III.E.: avoidance of methane production from biomass decay through controlled combustion, version 9* [online – accessed on 8 April 2008]. Available from Internet: http://cdm.unfccc.int/methodologies/SSCmethodologies/approved.html.

UNFCCC (2007) *Project 1258: Quezon City controlled disposal facility biogas emission reduction project: project design document form* [online – accessed on 8 April 2008]. Available from Internet: http://cdm.unfccc.int/Projects/DB/DNV-CUK1185342160. 98/view.

UNFCCC (2008a) *Baseline and monitoring methodologies* [online – accessed on 8 April 2008]. Available from Internet: http://cdm.unfccc.int/methodologies/index.html.

UNFCCC (2008b) *Methodological tool: tool for the demonstration and assessment of additionality, version 5* [online – accessed on 3 June 2008]. Available from Internet: http://cdm.unfccc.int/methodologies/PAmethodologies/AdditionalityTools/Additionality_tool.pdf.

UNFCCC (2009) *Registered CDM project activities* [online – accessed on 31 January 2009]. Available from Internet: http://cdm.unfccc.int/Projects/registered.html.

USAID Asia (United States Agency for International Development) (2007) *Philippines country report: from ideas to action: clean energy solutions for Asia to address climate change – Annex 4*, Bangkok: USAID Asia.

URC (UNEP Risoe Centre on Energy, Climate and Sustainable Development) (2005) *Baseline methodologies for clean development mechanism projects: a guidebook*, Roskilde: URC.

van Asselt, H. and Gupta, J. (2009) 'Stretching too far? Developing countries and the role of flexibility mechanisms beyond Kyoto', *Stanford Environment Law Journal*, 289: 311–376.

Wagner, B. and Enzler, S. (2006) *Material flow management: improving cost efficiency and environmental performance*, Berlin: Springer.

Wiedmann, T., Minx, J., Barrett, J., and Wackernagel, M. (2006) 'Allocating ecological footprints to final consumption categories with input–output analysis', *Ecological Economics*, 56: 28–48.

World Bank (2007) *State and trends of the carbon market 2007*, Washington, DC: World Bank.

WRI and WBCSD (World Resources Institute and World Business Council for Sustainable Development) (eds) (2003) *The greenhouse gas protocol: protocol for project accounting*, Washington, DC: WRI and WBCSD.

WRI and WBCSD (eds) (2007) *Guidelines for quantifying GHG reductions from grid-connected electricity projects*, Washington, DC: WRI and WBCSD.

9

ENVIRONMENTAL IMPACT ASSESSMENT, COMPLIANCE MONITORING AND REPORTING IN ELECTROPLATING

Well-Ever, the Philippines

Introduction

The electroplating industry has significant public exposure because of its significant health, safety and environmental impacts (US EPA 1997). Among the most important impacts are the use of hazardous inputs and the generation of hazardous wastewater (Bashkin 2003). In the Philippines, entities which cause considerable pollution, such as electroplating companies, are required to provide information to local environmental authorities concerning expected environmental impacts, planned improvement measures, and monitoring processes (Figure 9.1: Box 15). In addition, actual measurements are needed on a regular basis to demonstrate compliance with environmental regulations (Boxes 9, 11) (DENR 2003a,b).

This case study deals with identifying, measuring, assessing, and monitoring environmental impacts in a small-scale Philippine electroplating company based in Manila, Well-Ever Electroplating Shop (Well-Ever). The study provides a classic example of the relationship between external demands for information, in this case from local government, and the need to gather such information for reporting purposes. Hence, Well-Ever reflects the outside-in approach to environmental management accounting (EMA) (Schaltegger and Wagner 2006). An important consideration for the development of EMA is that environmental regulations in emerging economies are often not well enforced and this removes some of the external pressure for environmental accounting and reporting (Reinhardt, Stavins, and Vietor 2008), thereby raising institutional barriers to the acceptance and development of EMA tools (Desai 1998; Shi, Peng, Liu and Zhong 2008). Second, the Well-Ever case illustrates how supply chain pressure can influence the development of EMA to assist with environmental management and certification (Croom, Romano,

		Monetary EMA		Physical EMA	
		Short-term	Long-term	Short-term	Long-term
Past-orientated	Routinely generated	Environmental cost accounting [1]	Environment-induced capital expenditure and revenue [2]	Material and energy flow accounting [9]	Environmental capital impact accounting [10]
	Ad hoc	Ex-post assessment of relevant environmental costing decisions [3]	Ex-post inventory assessment of projects [4]	Ex-post assessment of short-term environmental impacts [11]	Ex-post inventory appraisal of physical environmental investments [12]
Future-orientated	Routinely generated	Monetary environmental budgeting [5]	Environmental long-term financial planning [6]	Physical environmental budgeting [13]	Environmental long-term physical planning [14]
	Ad hoc	Relevant environmental costing [7]	Monetary environmental investment appraisal [8]	Tools designed to predict relevant environmental impacts [15]	Physical environmental investment appraisal [16]

FIGURE 9.1 Application of the EMA framework (Burritt, Hahn, and Schaltegger 2002) to the Well-Ever Electroplating Shop.
Note: Dark (light) grey boxes represent the major (minor) EMA applications.

and Giannakis 2000; NZBCSD 2003; Seuring and Müller 2008). Suppliers can also be considered an external party reinforcing the outside-in perspective which brings pressure on management to gather and supply relevant environmental information in order to gain a competitive advantage.

Decision setting

Well-Ever is a small-scale business involved in electroplating assorted metal parts. It is located in the northern part of the Manila metropolitan area and has 23 regular employees. The company specialises in copper-, nickel-, and chrome-plating of metal parts and accessories which are used in a wide variety of machines and appliances such as cars, motorcycles, sewing machines, furniture, fixtures, plumbing, and musical instruments.

Well-Ever started as a backyard business in Caloocan City in 1961. In August 2003 the company was required to move its electroplating shop because of land ownership problems. A private lot was leased in the northern part of metropolitan Manila on the assumption that the company could work towards gaining a certificate from local government to conduct industrial activities. The business gradually built up its presence and by 2005 the location was graded for industrial purposes according to the Manila's land-use plan, which included plating and other chemical-related businesses. The decision situation involved the gathering of environmental information as the basis for acquiring a compliance certificate from the government in order to gain a licence to operate in the new location.

Technological situation

The basic steps in the production process at Well-Ever can be described as follows (see Figure 9.2). Upon arrival from suppliers, raw materials are inspected for defects and sorted according to use before being pre-treated by de-rusting and rinsing. To remove oil and grease adhering to the raw materials, the de-rusted materials are de-greased with an alkali solution. After de-greasing, the raw materials are buffed to smooth rough surfaces. Next, the materials are pre-treated for the electroplating process by soak-cleaning with alkali and acid solutions, followed by rinsing with water. The first step of the electroplating process is the copper strike treatment. The pre-treated materials are dipped in cyanide solutions and rinsed with water. To achieve desired copper brightness, the materials are dipped in a copper solution and rinsed in water. The next steps are nickel treatment, rinsing, and chrome treatment until the desired colour is achieved. After the final rinsing and drying with rags, the finished products are inspected for quality and packed for delivery.

Total production capacity of the plant is about 900,000 pieces of assorted plated metal parts and accessories per year. In 2005, the company operated six days per week and eight hours per day. The production process is well established but there is scope for minor improvements and changes to layout where efficiency can be gained or productivity improved.

Regulatory situation

Under *Presidential Decree 1586* (PD 1586 1978), which established the Philippine environmental impact system, any government or private-owned project or undertaking which has significant environmental impacts, whether commercial, industrial, or institutional in operation, may not undertake or operate its activities without first securing an environmental compliance certificate

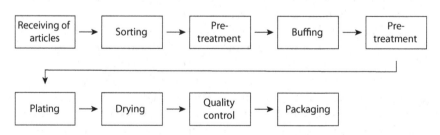

FIGURE 9.2 Plating process flow at the Well-Ever Electroplating Shop.

(ECC). An environmental compliance certificate indicates that the proponent has undertaken an environmental impact assessment and complies with all legal requirements (PD 1586 1978). Application for an ECC requires an environmental performance report and management plan to be submitted to the Department of Environment and Natural Resources (DENR). The purpose of the plan is to identify, predict, and evaluate potential environmental impacts associated with the activities inherent to the operation of the project. This type of report is needed for two purposes. First, it is needed for operating projects with existing ECCs, where the owners are planning or applying for clearance to modify, expand, or restart operations. Second, as with Well-Ever, the report is required for projects that currently operate without an ECC but where the business owners wish to apply in order to demonstrate compliance with existing regulations. Substantive elements of the environmental performance report and management plan include (i) an initial environmental examination of the business and documents such as an environmental management plan, (ii) an environmental monitoring plan, and (iii) an institutional plan.

After securing an ECC, Well-Ever would need to submit compliance reports to the Environmental Management Bureau of the DENR on a regular basis. Implications for the implementation of EMA are examined here with regard to two compliance reports: (i) a semi-annual compliance monitoring report required by *DAO 2003–30* (DENR 2003a,b), which is required to demonstrate Well-Ever's compliance with the conditions or restrictions stated in the ECC and (ii) a quarterly self-monitoring report that demonstrates compliance with environmental regulations which are compulsory for companies listed in Annexes A and B of *DAO 92–26* and which require the services of a pollution control officer (DENR 1992). Hence, the focus of Well-Ever EMA tends towards meeting the need for compliance with regulations relating to the establishment and operation of its business.

Economic situation

Relocating the business led to problems arising from the mixed-zone declaration and affected the economic performance of the company. In 2004, the company had a total loss of over PHP430,000 (Philippine pesos, €7,360). In 2005, total income improved by more than PHP300,000 (€5,135). However, net income remained negative at about –PHP130,000 (–€2,225).

Declaration of the company's site as an industrial zone by the Manila council made the application for an ECC the highest priority of the company. From an economic point of view, the aim was officially to restart the business and rebuild towards operating at full capacity. Compliance would provide a sound foundation for improved financial performance of the company.

Another strong financial motive for environmental data collection lies in increased supply chain pressure, particularly from one of Well-Ever's largest clients in Japan. In order to become more attractive to customers and better serve customers' needs, Well-Ever strives to become certified under ISO 14001. One requirement for becoming a company with its environmental management system certified under ISO 14001 is the issuing of an ECC, which requires compliance with a country's environmental regulations on national, regional, and local government levels. Hence, there are two inter-related external pressures on the business for environmental management information and an accounting system which will provide the necessary data.

Initial, and ongoing, collection of environmental data necessary to secure the ECC and ISO 14001 certification was expected to also help reduce material and energy consumption and related costs.

Environmental situation

With the intention of becoming an ISO 14001-certified company, a specific environmental management system had been implemented by Well-Ever a few years earlier. This system helps Well-Ever to ensure the safety of employees in the factory environment, which includes exposure to chemicals and emissions in daily operations. The system also helps provide a better understanding of improvement in the management of environmental impacts. Stated environmental objectives of Well-Ever are presented in Table 9.1.

The electroplating industry has particularly high levels of hazardous inputs such as toxic electrolytes which are potentially dangerous to employees and the local community (US EPA 1997; Haveman and Foecke 1998; Rao, O'Castillo, Intal, and Sajid 2006). As required by *DAO 92–26* (DENR 1992), Well-Ever has an environmental officer responsible for management and planning of

TABLE 9.1 Environmental objectives of Well-Ever

1	Minimise water consumption
2	Minimise water pollution
3	Optimise chemical usage
4	Comply with government laws and regulation
5	Minimise energy usage
6	Improve product service and quality
7	Improve profitability and productivity
8	Implement green productivity programme
9	Safeguard workers' health and safety
10	Value formation training program among workers
11	Improve competitiveness
12	Formulate economic and environmental long-term plan

environment-related issues and concerns. Education and training of the environmental officer was implemented through seminar attendance. She was then in a position to (i) initiate improvement measures including the establishment of improved plating tanks for operations, (ii) implement additional tanks for the treatment of wastewater, and (iii) introduce a ventilated buffing area to help avoid noxious fumes, which had created a problem for employees at the previous site.

Company's motivation for using EMA

As is evident from the above discussion of certification, the application of EMA at Well-Ever is mostly driven by regulatory requirements and supply chain pressures. Although Well-Ever's interest in accounting for its environmental impacts also aims to provide a basis for continuous identification of cost reduction potential (e.g. by reducing material and disposal costs), systematic identification, evaluation, and monitoring of potential impacts about the environment in which it operates serves to meet regulatory requirements and achieve environmental compliance. Acquisition of the ECC is a precondition for obtaining a government licence to operate. Disclosure of environmental information is needed for obtaining the ECC and for the compliance and self-monitoring reports. The information required is determined by government. In addition, environmental information and compliance certification assist with meeting supply chain expectations. Close examination indicates that three EMA tools lend support to the certification, reporting, and planning process: (i) ex-ante environmental impact assessment to predict and evaluate environmental impacts, (ii) ex-post assessment of environmental impacts as part of the overall environmental impact assessment study, and (iii) basic material and energy flow accounting supporting the control and monitoring of actual environmental impacts. These are explained in the next section.

Well-Ever undertook an environmental study for the required assessment of the existing electroplating shop. Potential environmental impacts were identified by analysing the production process and evaluating it against known potential impacts identified by source for electroplating operations (e.g. Rau and Wooten 1980; World Bank 1991; ADB 1993). Past information was also gathered as it is useful for predicting future impacts of business as usual. The analysis included an ex-post assessment of environmental impacts. Based on the information derived, environmental management and monitoring plans were developed to describe planned environmental measures and demonstrate how the company would handle and monitor the potential environmental impacts identified. These ex-ante measures (and associated ex-post data) as well as their relationship with the development of the initial environmental performance report and management plan are described below. The sub-section on compliance monitoring reveals further links between environmental management accounting and reporting to external stakeholders: it describes the regular measuring and compliance monitoring processes which take place after publishing the environmental performance report and management plan and securing the ECC. Finally, further uses of monetary EMA information are described.

EMA application

Physical EMA, required by regulation, provides the foundation for reporting and use of accounting information at Well-Ever. Information about the initial environmental impact assessment and material and energy flows is considered next.

Environmental impact assessment

An environmental impact assessment involves the prediction and evaluation of impacts on the biophysical and human environment that are likely to occur during construction, commission, operation, and abandonment of operations (DENR 2007). The review and evaluation of environment-related concerns, investigated in the following sub-section, focusses on determining the impacts caused by the operation of the existing Well-Ever electroplating shop. Although information about socio-economic and socio-political spheres of influence is part of the overall assessment, only impacts on the natural environment impacts are addressed here.

Integration of environmental concerns in the planning and management decision-making process of the company also requires designing appropriate preventative, mitigating, and enhancing measures. Accordingly, successive sub-sections introduce the environmental management and environmental monitoring plans which illustrate the managerial and control consequences of an environmental impact assessment, and then describe the links between accounting measures and management plans to identify, evaluate, and monitor environmental impacts and the use of the information gathered for external reporting and environmental compliance certification.

Identification, prediction, and evaluation of environmental impacts

The initial ex-ante analysis of environmental impacts was undertaken by evaluating the business's operations against the known list of potential impacts identified by sources relevant for this type of project (Rau and Wooten 1980; World Bank 1991; ADB 1993). Assessment results presented are partly based on past knowledge about corporate impacts on the natural environment (measured in physical terms) caused by the operation of the electroplating shop.

Ex-post information is used to predict expected impacts. The ex-post impacts embodied in current operations at Well-Ever (Figure 9.1: Box 11) provide a better understanding of long-term environmental impacts (Figure 9.1: Box 15). The aim of environmental impact assessment is to assess the effectiveness of the business by considering environmental improvements of new or improved technology and production processes. The following impacts were identified and assessed at Well-Ever: environmental hazards, water demand, wastewater generation, waste, and air emissions.

Environmental hazards

In operating its electroplating unit, chemicals are used that are hazardous. The hazardous chemicals are mixed with water during electroplating and this contaminated wastewater needs to be captured and treated, rather than expelled into nearby waterways or sewerage. The probability of an impact is considered minimal as Well-Ever has its own wastewater treatment facility to treat its effluents. Another potential impact can be caused by materials that are being used in the operation and maintenance of the plant, for instance petrochemical products such as lubricants, and oils or grease. The waste coming from the use of these hazardous materials needs to be carefully stored for hauling and treatment by an Environmental Management Bureau-certified environmental service provider to avoid water and soil pollution. In addition, the company needs to register as a hazardous waste generator with the Environmental Management Bureau.

Water demand

The water requirement of the plant is estimated to be about 90 m^3 per month (i.e. 3.5 m^3 per day for 26 operating days per month). Most water is used for domestic purposes, with about 1 m^3 per month needed in the electroplating process. The plant employs recycling and water conservation in the electroplating process to minimise water consumption.

Wastewater generation

Wastewater can be classified into its domestic and industrial components. Domestic wastewater, generated from lavatories, comfort rooms, and washing area for employees, is about 3 m^3 per day. The water is accommodated by the plant's multichamber septic tank (compliance with Philippine effluent standards was not verified in this study). The small amount of water used for the weekly cleaning of the equipment and facilities is discharged to the drains. Industrial wastewater generated from the electroplating operation and washings is treated and neutralised at the wastewater treatment facility prior to discharge to the plant drains, as it may contain traces of organic and inorganic solvents. The sludge recovered is temporarily stored in sealed containers and collected for treatment by a third-party DENR-accredited treater of waste. However, the amount of sludge (on a dry basis) that has been generated since 2004 is very small.

Analysis of the project's effluent quality was conducted to determine the effectiveness of the shop's wastewater treatment process. One effluent sample was taken from the outflow of electroplating shop on September 2005 and submitted to an accredited laboratory for analysis of hexavalent chromium and total cyanide content. These are two specific deleterious pollutants in the electroplating industry that have to be monitored for compliance with effluent standards. The ex-post assessment (Figure 9.1: Box 11) revealed that one parameter (total cyanide) was high in comparison with the prescribed effluent standard set by the DENR. After reviewing the wastewater treatment process system, modification on the treatment procedure was carried out to reduce the level of total cyanide content in wastewater. A second sampling in October 2005 showed that the result was well within the prescribed DENR effluent standard. The wastewater effluent produced by the company's operation revealed favourable results; it conformed to the DENR effluent standards.

Waste

Domestic and production solid waste generated by the company are segregated according to type. Ordinary office refuse, the major part of the company's waste, is collected by a collector on a regular basis and dumped in a designated landfill. There are no toxic or environmentally harmful materials. Solid waste from production is either recycled or sold to scrap buyers and includes lona (canvas/cloth), copper wire, sawdust, cartons, paper, plastic bags, and rags.

Air emissions

The main source of in-house air emissions is acid fumes from the use of hydrochloric acid. Although only three gallons per month of hydrochloric acid is being used in the electroplating area, and generation of acid fumes can be considered to be comparably low, gas masks are provided to the workers for protection. Another possible source of air pollution is the buffing area. Employees in the buffing area are likewise required to wear dust masks to protect them from suspended particulates dispersion and dust. Noise pollution from the operation of the manufacturing equipment is minimal.

The results of the ex-post environmental impact assessment are summarised in Table 9.2. For each impact area, its nature and magnitude is illustrated. The probabilities of the occurrence of impacts and their permanence are described. The study reveals that, during the operation phase and electroplating processes,

TABLE 9.2 Results of the environmental impact assessment

Potential impact	Nature	Magnitude	Probability of occurrence	Permanence
Environmental hazards	Negative	Moderate to minimal	High	Permanent
Wastewater generation	Negative	Moderate to minimal	High	Permanent
Water demand	Negative	Minimal	High	Permanent
Waste generation	Negative	Minimal	High	Permanent
Air emissions	Negative	Minimal to nil	High	Permanent

the generation of wastewater and environmental hazards are the main source of potential environmental impacts and risks. Most of the other impacts are not seen as being relevant.

In the next sub-section plans for environmental impact mitigation and monitoring are presented.

Formulation of environmental management and monitoring plans

Based on the impacts identified, Well-Ever formulated environmental management and monitoring plans for improvement and control of environmental impacts. These plans describe the mitigation measures and monitoring strategies for operations. Implementation of these plans is to reduce the adverse environmental impacts of the project and proposed actions.

Table 9.3 shows the environmental management plan and corresponding costs and benefits of handling the potential impacts identified and discussed above. The activities summarised in the table occur in the entire plant. Institutional support and commitment is ensured through appointment of the pollution control officer (PCO), who is officially accredited by DENR. The PCO is responsible for planning and managing all environment-related issues that may arise during operation of the business, including coordination with DENR and other agencies, monitoring and reporting environmental compliance, and all activities concerning the ECC (DENR 2004). On the basis of management by exception, project activities and mitigation measures with minimal or insignificant impacts are not addressed in the plan. Measures for handling safety issues or socio-economic concerns have been excluded from the table.

The environmental monitoring plan (Table 9.4) presents major environment-related operational activities and monitoring measures including the relevant parameters, procedure, location, frequency of data gathering, and related costs. The environmental monitoring plan describes (i) the procedure

TABLE 9.3 Environmental management plan

Activity	Impact description	Mitigation program	Cost in PHP per annum
Control the source of pollution	Improper handling and/or disposal of hazardous or toxic chemicals/ materials may cause contamination of nearby surface water, soil, and groundwater	In compliance with *RA 6969*, registration of toxic and hazardous materials to Environmental Management Bureau Cyanide-containing chemicals are required, following prescriptions under the chemical control order Observe proper handling and storage of hazardous chemicals All chemicals to be properly labelled Hazardous materials to be kept in a storage room with secondary containment and hard stands Consumption of all chemicals to be logged in a special log book to determine their usage so that overstock of unnecessary volume of chemicals will be avoided Chemical inventory as to usage to be regularly undertaken	> 25,000 (€425)
Solid waste management plan	Aesthetics and pollution because of disposal to the environment	Implement preventative maintenance program, waste minimisation practice, material segregation, recycling and re-use, good housekeeping and efficient inventory management, strict quality controls, and process monitoring Industrial solid wastes to be sold to scrap buyers or any interested buyers	> 10,000 savings (€170)
		Domestic solid wastes to be collected by the local government unit's solid waste collection services	> 10,000 (€170)
Industrial wastewater management plan	Disposal of untreated industrial wastewater to the existing drainage system will lead to the contamination of groundwater and nearby river water	Eliminate heavy metals in the wastewater stream through waste treatment facilities before discharging it to drainage	> 50,000 (€850)
		Compliance with the effluent standards prescribed by DENR	> 50,000 (€850)
		Engage the services of DENR-accredited treaters for the treatment and disposal of sludge from waste treatment facilities	> 10,000 (€170)

Activity	Impact description	Mitigation program	Cost in PHP per annum
Domestic wastewater management plan	Disposal of untreated domestic wastewater to the drains will lead to the contamination of nearby river water	Water-sealed multi-chamber septic tank for domestic wastewater	> 10,000 (€170)
		Periodic de-sludging of septic tanks every five years	> 5,000 (€85)
		Engage the services of DENR-accredited treaters for the treatment and disposal of sludge from septic tanks	> 10,000 (€170)
Air pollution control	Dust emission from buffing process could be harmful to health of workers; acid fumes (minimal only) from electroplating process	Adherence to the Department of Labour and Employment's Occupational Safety and Health Standard Personal protective equipment which specifies the use and type of eye and face protection, respiratory protection, hand and arm protection, safety belts life lines and safety nets, and safety shoes Implementation of good house-keeping practices for dust control	> 10,000 (€170)

RA 6969 – Toxic substances and hazardous and nuclear wastes control act (Republic of the Philippines 1990).

to assess the environmental performance of the company against the conditions set in the ECC and (ii) assess its compliance with existing environmental regulations and environmental best practices (DENR 2007). The environmental monitoring plan also aims to ensure the effectiveness of environmental measures in preventing or mitigating actual environmental impacts, compared with predicted impacts, and provides a base for continuous review of the environmental management plan by responding to actual project operations and impacts.

Both Tables 9.3 and 9.4 include monetary environmental budget allocations (Figure 9.1: Box 5). In most cases annual costs are attributed to the various environmental improvement measures and monitoring activities. One-off costs and cost savings are exceptions.

Environmental performance report and management plan

The results of the environmental impact assessment and managing and monitoring plans discussed above constituted substantive elements of Well-Ever's environmental performance report and management plan. In 2006,

TABLE 9.4 Environmental monitoring plan

Activity	Parameter	Procedure	Location	Frequency	Cost in PHP per annum
Control of source of pollution	Proper handling and storage of hazardous chemicals in compliance with RA 6969; chemical inventory	Visual observation; statistical data of stored chemicals and incidental chemical spills	Within the vicinity of the project site	Daily	> 10,000 (€170)
Wastewater management	Effluent water to be tested for conventional parameters (BOD, COD, TDS, TSS, pH, colour, alkalinity, cyanide, and hexavalent chromium) based on class C water	Wastewater sampling and laboratory analysis	Outfall	Quarterly	> 10,000 (€170)
Sludge collection	Volume of sludge	Statistical data on sludge volume	Wastewater treatment tanks	Every time after wastewater treatment	> 5,000 (€85)
Solid waste management	Volume of solid wastes; checking of the proper disposal and collection of solid wastes; proper waste minimisation practice (material segregation, recycling, and re-use)	Statistical data on solid wastes	Within the vicinity of the project site	Daily	> 5,000 (€85)
Air pollution control	Air quality parameters for dust emissions	Statistical data using the Staplex high-volume sampler	Vicinity of the project site	Quarterly	> 10,000 (€170)

RA 6969 – Toxic substances and hazardous and nuclear wastes control act (Republic of the Philippines 1990).
BOD, biological oxygen demand; COD, chemical oxygen demand; pH, potential of hydrogen; TDS, total dissolved solids; TSS, total suspended solids.

the environmental performance report and management plan was sent to the Environmental Management Bureau to apply for an ECC. The report is one of seven major types of environmental impact assessment reports in the Philippines.[1] The typical structure of an environmental impact assessment report is outlined below (DENR 2007: 8):

- *project description*: location, scale and duration, rationale, alternatives, phases and components, resource requirements, manpower complement, estimate of waste generation from the most critical project activities and environmental aspects, project costs;
- *baseline environmental description* (of land, water, air and people): focussed on the sectors and resources most significantly affected by the proposed action;
- *impact assessment*: focussed on significant environmental impacts (in relation to pre-construction, construction/development, operation, and decommissioning stages), taking into account cumulative, unavoidable, and residual impacts;
- *environmental management plan*: specifying the impact mitigation plan, areas of public information, education, and communication, social development programme proposal, environmental monitoring plans (with multi-sector public participation for environmental impact system-based projects) and the corresponding institutional and financial requirements/arrangements.

As shown, further information disclosed in the report addresses the project description and institutional arrangements for the plan as well as present environmental conditions at the production site and its surroundings (physical, biological, socio-cultural, economic, and political).

The ECC was issued based on the submission of Well-Ever's environmental performance report and management plan and a subsequent on-site visit. After securing the ECC, Well-Ever had to apply for the discharge permit for hazardous waste. Disclosure requirements by the DENR also include a quarterly hazardous waste generators report. Further implications of required disclosures for accounting and reporting measures are described next.

Compliance monitoring

Monitoring compliance is one of the most important elements to implement (DENR 2003b) and ensure the establishment of sound environmental management within a company and its areas of operation (DENR 2007). The conceptual framework for compliance monitoring by the DENR (2003b) favours three sources of compliance information over periodic inspections: self-monitoring, record-keeping, and self-reporting. These approaches are recognised as providing more extensive information on compliance than can be obtained with periodic inspections, increasing the level of management attention devoted to compliance, and potentially encouraging management to improve production efficiency and prevent pollution. Apart from educating the regulated entity about the requirements of compliance, self-monitoring, in particular, is seen as a cost-effective way for enforcement programs that shifts the economic burden more to the regulated entity.

In this regulatory context, Well-Ever is responsible for measuring and monitoring environmental impacts and performance parameters, maintaining its own records, and providing regulatory bodies with self-monitoring and recordkeeping data upon request and at specified periods. In the following discussion, first the development of a measurement and monitoring system at Well-Ever is described and then two self-reporting requirements of the legal environmental framework are presented through which Well-Ever will report its compliance performance. In effect, a regulatory mix is being used whereby reporting companies are being trusted to self-report, based on prior experience with the company, otherwise they are being required (mandated) to report (Ayres and Braithwaite 1992).

Measuring and monitoring actual environmental impacts

In 2004, anticipating the monitoring and reporting requirements needed after the issuance of the ECC, Well-Ever started to measure and monitor corporate environmental performance by accounting for basic material and energy flows, aiming to improve the quality of data collection in subsequent years (Figure 9.1: Box 9). The initial measurement of material and energy flows can be seen as rather a simple and reactive approach to data collection for anticipated reporting requirements. The control of source of pollution requires the proper handling and storage of hazardous chemicals in compliance with *RA 6969*, and a chemical inventory. Statistical data about stored chemicals is presented in Table 9.5 and reveals the monthly variation in quantities used through the year. Monitoring is undertaken by an in-house environmental team headed by the designated PCO, based on the internal reporting system.

Going beyond a simple, checklist-based monitoring process, in 2005 the PCO began to look at the explicit inputs and outputs of its electroplating processes. Anticipating the monitoring requirements resulting from certification led to an increased interest in material and energy flow accounting information. As a first step, the company recorded chemical consumption in the plating process (actual preparation, see Table 9.6). This tracking enabled the company to better control of the actual use of chemicals in the electroplating process and provided a basis for measures of future improvement.

The accurate accounting of material flows led to an improvement in information quality. Table 9.7 displays the results from measuring solid waste in 2004 and 2005. The increase in liquid waste by more than 400 per cent is

TABLE 9.5 Excerpt of chemical inventory 2004 and 2005

Item	Jan 2004	Feb 2004	Mar 2004	Apr 2004	...	Total 2004	Total 2005
Activated carbon (kg)	0	0	0	0	...	8	1
Ammonia water (l)	0.24	0.12	0.24	0.12	...	3.36	8.92
Boric acid (kg)	9.5	0	5	0	...	32.5	23
Caustic soda (kg)	0	3	0	0	...	15	23
Chrome acid (kg)	10	0	0	3	...	135	66

TABLE 9.6 Excerpt of plating chemical consumption 2005

Process step	Jan 2005	Feb 2005	Mar 2005	Apr 2005	...	Total 2005
Pre-treatment						
Hydrochloric acid (gallons)	7.5	6.5	8.0	6.0	...	218.75
De-greaser						
Alkali base (kg)	0	0	0	0	...	0
Plating						
Copper cyanide (kg)	0	0	0	0	...	0
Sodium cyanide (kg)	10	10	10	10	...	106.00
Caustic soda (kg)	0	0	0	0	...	0
Copper anode (kg)	12.1	18.2	4.55	0	...	1168.17

considerable and not matched by the parallel increase in production; quite the contrary, it was the improved measurement of the total amount of waste generated through the plating process which led to these results and stimulated the need for management to look closely at control. As the PCO stated: 'consumption for liquid waste for the year 2005 is much higher than 2004 because everything now is recorded and treated'.

In contrast to these periodic measurements and monitoring procedures that take place on a daily basis, the ex-post analysis of plating solutions undertaken by a third party – commencing with the issuance of the ECC – will need to be reported every three months (Figure 9.1: Box 11). Results of ex-post assessments in December 2005 were satisfactory. In some instances the use of additives (such as copper pyrophosphate) was recommended by an external laboratory in order for there to be compliance with environmental standards.

The relevance of this information gathered by physical EMA for environmental disclosure statements in monitoring reports is illustrated next.

TABLE 9.7 Excerpt of waste management year end reports 2004 and 2005

Type of waste	Jan 2004	Feb 2004	Mar 2004	Apr 2004	...	Total 2004	Total 2005
Solid waste							
Lona (canvas) (pieces)	18.0	21.0	31.0	24.0	...	249.0	176.0
Copper wire (kg)	1.5	2.0	1.6	3.75	...	26.7	30.2
Rag (kg)	2.0	1.0	2.0	2.5	...	20.5	21.5
Paper (kg)	4.0	3.0	2.0	2.0	...	25.5	24.0
Cartons (kg)	1.0	2.0	1.0	2.0	...	17.0	15.0
Sawdust (kg)	3.0	2.0	2.0	2.0	...	26.5	16.0
Plastic (kg)	1.0	2.0	1.0	2.0	...	16.5	31.0
Total solid waste (kg)[a]						**132.7**	**106.7**
Liquid waste							
Chrome (l)	40.0	60.0	60.0	40.0	...	520.0	8120.0
Cyanide (l)	400.0	200.0	200.0	0.0	...	2240.0	3954.0
HCl (l)	16.0	16.0	8.0	4.0	...	104.0	50.0
Nickel (l)	0.0	0.0	0.0	0.0	...	0.0	650.0
Total (liquid waste)						**2864.0**	**12774.0**

a Excludes canvas.

Monitoring reports

For industries that require a PCO as described in *DAO 2003–27* (DENR 2003a,b), there are two main types of monitoring reports that are required to be submitted to the Environmental Management Bureau: (i) a self-monitoring report and (ii) a ECC compliance monitoring report. The self-monitoring report is required by *DAO 2003–27* (DENR 2003a,b), whereas *DAO 2003–30* (DENR 2007) requires the submission of an ECC compliance monitoring report. The two reports differ in the type of information contained the report and the frequency of reporting. The self-monitoring report covers all environmental aspects of a company's operations such as hazardous waste generation, water pollution, air pollution, solid waste generation, and environmental training. The ECC compliance monitoring report focuses only on the compliance of a company with the conditions of the ECC. A discussion of the two types of reports is presented in the following sub-sections.

Self-monitoring report

Monitoring is essential to (i) detect and correct violations, (ii) provide evidence to support enforcement actions, and (iii) evaluate enforcement progress by establishing compliance status (DENR 2003b). However, monitoring by the environmental agencies (i.e. Environmental Management Bureau) is limited by the logistical and resource requirements for monitoring industry regulatory compliance. Thus, the Environmental Management Bureau requires companies to monitor its compliance and submit results of self-monitoring on a quarterly basis for review and evaluation.

In self-monitoring, facilities measure practices and operations which affect their environmental performance, such as raw material consumption, solid and hazard waste generation, emissions, and wastewater discharge. A standard report format is prescribed by the Environmental Management Bureau (DENR 2003b). The self-monitoring report is composed of seven modules (see Table 9.8).

TABLE 9.8 Modules of the self-monitoring report (DENR 2003a,b)

No.	Module title	Module description
0	General information sheet	Provides basic information about the company (such as type of industry, service and/or products). This module shall only be prepared once
1	General information	Provides background information about the company particularly changes or modifications in module 0
2	RA 6969	Provides information on compliance with the requirements of RA 6969 (Toxic Substances and Hazardous and Nuclear Wastes Control Act). This module is composed of three sub-modules: (a) compliance with Chemical Control Order-related requirements, (b) for hazardous wastes treater and recycler, and (c) for hazardous wastes generator
3	PD 984	Provides information on compliance with the requirements of PD 984 (Water Pollution)
4	RA 8749	Provides information on compliance with the requirements of RA 8749 (Air Pollution)
5	PD 1586	Provides information on compliance with the requirements of PD 1586 (Environmental impact system requirement, e.g. ECC conditions). This is left blank in lieu of the ECC compliance monitoring report, the second type of reporting, which will be explained in the next section
6	Others	Provides additional information that is not exclusive to any of the other modules such as accidents, emergencies and environmental training

Well-Ever is required to submit all the modules of the self-monitoring report. The following relevant information should be provided in the company's quarterly self-monitoring reports:

- kinds of permits and registrations and their corresponding issuance and expiration dates (i.e. permit-to-operate air pollution source installations, water discharge permit, ECC, hazardous waste generator registration);
- operating hours (per day and per week);
- average production rates (per day and per reporting quarter);
- water and electricity requirements (per reporting quarter);
- chemicals with chemical control orders such as cyanide use (quantity purchased, source, quantity used);
- other hazardous wastes generated, including information about storage, transport, treatment, and disposal (e.g. broken fluorescent bulbs, used oil, plating wastewater);
- wastewater generation (quantity and flow rates, characterisation or pollutant concentration, location of discharge, e.g., city drain, and cost for treatment such as chemicals, manpower, equipment purchase, utilities, laboratory testing, and overhead costs);
- air emissions data (type of equipment, raw material usage, e.g. quantity of fuel used, operational hours, emissions testing results, and cost of treatment such as chemicals, manpower, equipment purchase, utilities, laboratory testing, and overhead costs);
- accidents and emergency records (if any); and
- training records (if any).

ECC compliance monitoring report

Although Module 5 contains information about a company's compliance with its ECC conditions, by virtue of *DAO 2003–30* the Environmental Management Bureau requires a separate report to be submitted every January and July, covering the operating months of July–December and January–June respectively (DENR 2007). Thus, the ECC compliance monitoring report replaces Module 5 of the self-monitoring report.

The objective of the ECC compliance monitoring report is to ensure the following (DENR 2007):

- project compliance with the conditions set in the ECC;
- project compliance with the environmental management plan;
- effectiveness of environmental measures on prevention or mitigation of actual project impacts vis-à-vis the predicted impacts used as basis for the environmental management plan design; and
- continual updating.

To date, the implementation of the use of the ECC compliance monitoring report is not yet widespread and is used only by selected regional offices on account of its complexity compared with former Module 5 format of the self-monitoring report. The ECC compliance monitoring report contains five sections, which contain the information listed in Table 9.9.

In the following sub-section, further use of EMA in the context of Well-Ever's electroplating operations is briefly discussed.

TABLE 9.9 Sections of the compliance monitoring report (DENR 2007)

No.	Section title	Section description
1	Basic project information and updates	Provides the following information: • ECC number • project title • project type • location • project coordinates • current project stage/phase: (i.e. construction; commissioning, etc.) • contact person • changes in project design (if any)
2	Executive summary	Provides a summary of findings on the following items for the covered monitoring period: • compliance with ECC conditions • compliance with environmental management plan • implementation of appropriate and effective environmental impact remedial actions in case of exceedances • complaints management (if any)
3	Results and discussion	Provides the results and discussions on the following items: • compliance to ECC conditions (with explanation on non-compliance) • impact monitoring (presenting the summary of previous monitoring and detailing the results of the current monitoring activities based on the environmental monitoring plan)
4	Conclusions and recommendations	Provides a summary of compliance to the following: • ECC conditions • environmental management and monitoring plans
5	Attachments	Contains supporting documents such as laboratory results and updates on environmental management and monitoring plans

Further use of EMA information

Material and energy flow accounting information generated was also used by Well-Ever to analyse further areas not covered by the environmental monitoring and reporting requirements described above because of their relatively low environmental importance (such as electricity and water consumption). However, actual analysis of material and energy flow-related costs (Figure 9.1: Box 1) revealed that electricity and chemical consumption constitute an important cost. They amounted to over 10 per cent of the total cost of operations in 2005. To reduce the costs of electricity and chemical consumption, Well-Ever decided to return to the old process of using kerosene as way of cleaning items before plating instead of using the electro-cleaner process. Detailed cost–benefit analyses has not yet been undertaken but the example indicates the necessity of further exploring potential for improvement not only in environmental but also in monetary terms using the data gathered by EMA techniques. Considerable improvements can be expected by also calculating and analysing the material purchase value of wastes as shown in a US EPA (1997) study in the electroplating industry (see also Gale 2006). Uncovered wasted material costs in electroplating operations include coating materials, process chemistry, addition agents, cleaners, and water. Of particular interest are hidden costs caused by the difference between the amount of coating materials purchased and the amount of metal that actually is distributed in parts, and the amount that is actually needed to meet production requirements (US EPA 1997).

Discussion

Well-Ever involves a type of exposure to EMA which is likely to be fairly common: a business is seeking to comply with environmental regulations so that it can obtain its licence to operate. It also faces competitive pressures which demand that a business has an ECC which confirms good environmental management practices and procedures are in place. From these foundations, a fuller EMA system may develop, but the initial impetus and catalyst is compliance.

Within this context, the Well-Ever case study illustrates the particular relevance of physical EMA tools caused by a government regulator requiring information which must be obtained if the company is to survive. The information could be gathered by an external adviser to the company if records are not kept; it could be collected by environmental management staff who would provide regular information for existing ex-post gathering of data about chemical spills and clean-ups, wastewater quality testing on a regular basis, and testing of air quality for workers. The information is unlikely to be gathered by management accountants, with their focus on costs and revenues or income improvement. In the case of Well-Ever, one of the owners, who is responsible for the environmental management system, developed and maintained the information records under tightly controlled circumstances. She attended seminars on environmental management systems and EMA and became the PCO.

A second source of demand for physical EMA tools at Well-Ever is the growing supply chain pressure on small suppliers based in emerging economy countries (Rao 2002). Although formal preparation of an application for ISO 14001 certification is somewhat distant, the intention to apply is surprising given the small-scale business of Well-Ever. However, there is increasing pressure from key customers as larger, often multinational, purchasers wish to reduce any potential liability associated with environmental risks from the supply chain. In this context it is notable that the trend towards increased certification is growing in the Philippines, with the relatively low number of certified organisations growing by over 50 per cent between 2005 and 2007 (ISO 2008).

The link between external reporting to government for corporate environmental impact assessment purposes and EMA tools provides another key aspect of the Well-Ever case. First, the link between previously gathered information and its use in predicting or estimating environmental impacts is brought out in the study. Hence, the decision-making interrelationship between, say, Boxes 11 and 15 (Figure 9.1) for short-term assessment of ad hoc environmental impacts is clarified through this illustration. The link between EMA information that is gathered on an ad hoc basis to meet the demands of a one-off report, such as the environmental performance report and management plan (Figure 9.1: Box 11), as well as EMA information that supports continuous disclosure of environmental information (Box 9), is contrasted.

The case study further develops links between the environmental impact assessment system and EMA framework: Well-Ever plans to use the environmental performance report and management plan, related to the environmental impact assessment, for its internal management purposes, as a guide in planning and improving the environmental practices of the company. This illustrates how external accounting requirements can potentially influence internal management and accounting for environmental issues. As Adams (2004) finds, attempts to integrate internal management systems and external reporting processes can assist in optimising environmental performance outcomes, as in this case with Well-Ever.

Conclusions

The period of the Well-Ever case study coincided with a time when the company was re-establishing itself in a new planning zone in Manila. In the restart phase it is to be expected that a focus would be on receiving licences from governments to operate and that the government would be interested in making sure that the environmental impacts of this electroplating company did not introduce environmental problems to the local community. It is also expected that a business which provides its output to manufacturing industries, many with significant local and international influence, would seek to gain market approval, as well as regulatory approval, for operations that are certified green as part of supply chain management initiatives. However, green certification does not emerge in a vacuum. It requires appropriate information that can be used by managers or owners of small businesses to substantiate claims of greenness in operations.

First is the EMA information behind the need for claims to be made to gain a certificate to legitimise operations. Use of a physical environmental impact assessment was needed to substantiate a claim which required predictions of the impacts of the business under a business-as-usual scenario. Where certain activities related to business as usual would not lead to compliance and certification, the EMA tools are used to appraise long-term investments and short-term material and energy flows, which lead to innovations and changes that move the business into future compliance and the awarding of an ECC.

Second is the need for certificates in order to legitimise the ability to contract with purchasers seeking green-based products with no liability surprises and no downside environmental risk. Gathering information for environmental management system certification is entirely voluntary, if the company wishes to be a market participant sometimes in very competitive circumstances. EMA information to support environmental management system procedures tends to be regular and supportive of continual improvement (or innovation) through a plan–do–check–act cycle. The information can also be based on past activities, but is used in planning processes to predict impacts and how they might be ameliorated.

Well-Ever has many tangential EMA possibilities related to investing in greener materials inputs, process improvement based on information from environmental cost accounting and budgeting, and product labelling. The fundamental first step of promoting EMA development in this small company was the pressure of government regulation ameliorated by the lack of resources available to enforce legislated regulations.

Note

1 See DENR (2007) for further information on the different types of environmental impact assessment reports and preparation and application procedures.

References

Adams, C.A. (2004) 'The ethical, social and environmental reporting–performance portrayal gap', *Accounting, Auditing and Accountability Journal*, 17: 731–757.

ADB (Asian Development Bank) (1993) *Environmental guidelines for selected infrastructure project*, Metro Manila: Office of the Environment.

Ayres, I. and Braithwaite, J. (1992) *Responsive regulation: transcending the deregulation debate*, Oxford: Oxford University Press.

Bashkin, V.N. (2003) *Environmental chemistry: Asian lessons*, Heidelberg: Springer.

Burritt, R., Hahn, T., and Schaltegger, S. (2002) 'Towards a comprehensive framework for environmental management accounting: links between business actors and environmental management accounting tools', *Australian Accounting Review*, 12: 39–50.

Croom, S., Romano, P., and Giannakis, M. (2000) 'Supply chain management: a literature review and taxonomy', *European Journal of Purchasing and Supply Management*, 6: 67–83.

Desai, U. (ed.) (1998) *Ecological policy and politics in developing countries: economic growth, democracy, and environment*, New York: State University of New York Press.

DENR (Department of Environment and Natural Resources) (1992) *DENR Administrative Order No. 29, Series 1992: implementing rules and regulations of Republic Act 6969*, Quezon City: Republic of the Philippines Department of Environment and Natural Resources.

DENR (2003a) *DENR Administrative Order No. 2003-27 (Series of 2003): amending DAO 26, DAO 29 and DAO 2001–81 among others on the preparation and submission of self-monitoring report (SMR)*, Quezon City: Republic of the Philippines Department of Environment and Natural Resources.

DENR (2003b) *Procedural and reference manual for DAO 2003–27: self-monitoring report (SMR) system*, Quezon City: Republic of the Philippines Department of Environment and Natural Resources.

DENR (2004) *DENR Administrative Order No. 36, series of 2004: procedural manual title III of DAO 92-29 hazardous waste management*, Quezon City: Republic of the Philippines Department of Environment and Natural Resources.

DENR (2007) *Revised procedural manual for DENR Administrative Order No. 30 Series of 2003 (DAO 03–30): implementing rules and regulations of Presidential Decree No. 1586, Establishing the Philippine environmental impact statement system*, Quezon City: Republic of the Philippines Department of Environment and Natural Resources.

Gale, R. (2006) 'Environmental management accounting as a reflexive modernization strategy in cleaner production', *Journal of Cleaner Production*, 14: 1228–1236.

Haveman, M. and Foecke, T. (1998) 'Applying environmental accounting to electroplating operations: an in-depth analysis', in Bennett, M., and James, P. (eds) *The green bottom line: current practice and future trends*, Sheffield: Greenleaf, pp. 212–235.

ISO (International Organization for Standardization) (2008) *The ISO Survey of Certifications*, Genève: ISO.

NZBCSD (New Zealand Business Council for Sustainable Development) (2003) *Business guide to a sustainable supply chain: a practical guide*, Auckland: NZBCSD.

PD 1586 (1978) Presidential Decree No. 1586: establishing an environmental impact statement system including other environmental management related measures and for other purposes.

Rao, P. (2002) 'Greening the supply chain: a new initiative in South East Asia', *International Journal of Operations and Production Management*, 22: 632–55.

Rao, P., O'Castillo, O.L., Intal, P.S. Jr, and Sajid, A. (2006) 'Environmental indicators for small and medium enterprises in the Philippines: an empirical research', *Journal of Cleaner Production*, 14: 505–515.

Rau, J.G. and Wooten, D.C. (1980) *Environmental impact analysis handbook*, New York: McGraw-Hill.

Reinhardt, F.L., Stavins, R.N., and Vietor, R.H.K. (2008) 'Corporate social responsibility through an economic lens', *Review of Environmental Economics and Policy*, 2: 219–239.

Republic of the Philippines (1990) Toxic Substances and Hazardous and Nuclear Wastes Control Act of 1990, Republic Act No. 6969 (RA 6969), Senate and House of Representatives of the Philippines in Congress.

Schaltegger, S. and Wagner, M. (2006) 'Integrative management of sustainability performance, measurement and reporting', *International Journal of Accounting, Auditing and Performance Evaluation*, 3: 1–19.

Seuring, S. and Müller, M. (2008) 'From a literature review to a conceptual framework for sustainable supply chain management', *Journal of Cleaner Production*, 16: 1699–1710.

Shi, H., Peng, S.Z., Liu, Y., and Zhong, P. (2008) 'Barriers to the implementation of cleaner production in Chinese SMEs: government, industry and expert stakeholders' perspectives', *Journal of Cleaner Production*, 16: 842–852.

US EPA (United States Environmental Protection Agency) (1997) *Applying environmental accounting to electroplating operations: an in-depth analysis.* [online – last accessed 14 November 2008]. Available from Internet: http://www.epa.gov/oppt/library/pubs/archive/acct-archive/pubs/indepth.pdf.

World Bank (1991) *Environmental assessment sourcebook volume III: guidelines for an environmental assessment of energy and industry projects*, Washington, DC: World Bank.

10

RELEVANT ENVIRONMENTAL COSTING AND DECISION-MAKING IN A SAA PAPER MANUFACTURER

Classic Crafts, Thailand

Introduction

Classic Crafts Corporation Ltd (hereafter Classic Crafts) examines the application of environmental management accounting (EMA) techniques in a medium-sized saa paper-manufacturing company in Thailand. The particular decisions addressed involve the potential for converting waste into a by-product and a related investment to improve water quality. Once the non-product costs of saa paper production are made apparent through environmental costing (Figure 10.1: Box 7), the decision to use low-quality wastepaper as an input to the manufacturing process is questioned. Analysis reveals that an attractive alternative is to sell this low-quality paper as a by-product and buy cheaper material as input to the high-quality paper. The analysis is initially based on routinely generated environmental cost accounting information (Figure 10.1: Box 1) from the company's job cost sheets, which is founded on an assessment of the routine operating material and energy flows (Box 9). These sheets link job costs with units of output and, once costs are corrected, indicate a strong incentive to improve eco-efficiency levels as the high costs of waste materials is revealed. An additional decision involves investments identified to improve water quality (Figure 10.1: Box 8).

In the Classic Crafts case study, first a general discussion of the decision situation of the target company is presented. Second, material and energy flows are outlined and relevant costing is used to show the importance of environmental cost savings to the decision about the fate of low-grade paper output. Third, analysis of an investment decision to reduce water and chemical consumption as well as wastewater is undertaken. Finally, implications from the analysis are drawn in the context of Figure 10.1 and these indicate that relevant environmental costing and monetary environmental investment

		Monetary EMA		Physical EMA	
		Short-term	Long-term	Short-term	Long-term
Past-orientated	Routinely generated	Environmental cost accounting [1]	Environment-induced capital expenditure and revenue [2]	Material and energy flow accounting [9]	Environmental capital impact accounting [10]
	Ad hoc	Ex-post assessment of relevant environmental costing decisions [3]	Ex-post inventory assessment of projects [4]	Ex-post assessment of short-term environmental impacts [11]	Ex-post inventory appraisal of physical environmental investments [12]
Future-orientated	Routinely generated	Monetary environmental budgeting [5]	Environmental long-term financial planning [6]	Physical environmental budgeting [13]	Environmental long-term physical planning [14]
	Ad hoc	Relevant environmental costing [7]	Monetary environmental investment appraisal [8]	Tools designed to predict relevant environmental impacts [15]	Physical environmental investment appraisal [16]

FIGURE 10.1 Application of the EMA framework (Burritt, Hahn, and Schaltegger 2002) to Classic Crafts.
Note: Dark (light) grey boxes represent the major (minor) EMA applications.

appraisal, used in combination, lead to a reversal of decisions about, first, whether to sell low-quality paper on the market or use it as input in future batches of production and, second, whether an investment in new galvanised pipes is worth undertaking.

Decision setting

Classic Crafts is a family-owned manufacturer and exporter of saa papers and related finished products. Saa paper is a natural paper made from the bark of the mulberry tree, which grows in most soils in the northern region of Thailand (Udomchoke, Mongkolsook, Anapanurak, Thanasombat, and Kasjinda 2001). Saa is the local Thai name for the mulberry tree. The long saa fibre products have a unique texture and can be used for making high-quality paper (Oka and Ohyama 1989). Classic Crafts produces a wide range of saa paper products such as writing and decorative papers (e.g. notebooks, greeting cards, letter-sets, and paper for gift wrapping), handicrafts (e.g. umbrellas, flowers, boxes, and bags), and specialist products (e.g. book restoration paper) (see a full range of products for saa paper at GTZ and DEQP 2007).

The company employs about 300 people, mainly at its factory, which is located in the Nan province of Thailand on the border with Myanmar, one of the main regions of the saa paper industry. Classic Crafts' sales office is based in Bangkok. Despite increasing economic and environmental pressure, the environmental improvement measures suggested by the production manager are not considered relevant by the owner. The production manager uses the ideas but not the terminology associated with eco-efficiency. Eco-efficiency is concerned with adding economic value while reducing the overall environmental impact of operations (Schaltegger 1998). The following section describes the company's saa paper production processes, its economic situation, and relevant government, regulatory, and environmental issues.

Technology

Classic Crafts' saa paper production can be divided into hand-made and machine-made production. The hand-made production consists of a simple series of processes that have not changed over the centuries (Arunotai, Gordon, Jarubenja, Katleeradapan, Petchprasert, and Pongsapich 2007). All stages of production are labour-intensive, using natural fibres; for example, wood, water, flower petals, and leaves. Classic Crafts is one of a very few companies in Thailand applying a fully integrated manufacturing process to the production of high-quality natural fine-fibre saa paper products (Forsen, Larsson, and Samuelsson 2001; GTZ and DEQP 2005a). The machine-made production process of Classic Crafts using two standard machine processes is the subject of this case study.

The production process is linear and proceeds in several stages (see Figure 10.2). First is colouring, mixing, and beating. Stirred and beaten fibre is used in the paper production machine and combined with pulp and other inputs. Raw materials, in particular bark, are bought mainly from within Thailand. However, product demand is so high that the company needs to import raw bark from neighbouring Laos – one of the key supplier countries for mulberry bark (GTZ and DEQP 2007). In the next step of production, the paper is rolled and cut into sheets. Before packaging, the sheets are subject to quality control. Packed sheets are transferred to inventory before being sold or recycled as input if unsold after a period of time. The production process produces

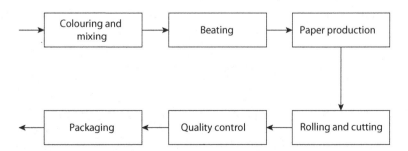

FIGURE 10.2 Saa paper machine production stages at Classic Crafts.

three main paper outputs: Grade A, Grade B, which the company predominantly treats as waste, and wastepaper (non-product output) associated with the beginning and end of rolls. Grade A paper has the highest contribution margin, but when unsalable can be recycled as material input, when there is overproduction. Grade B paper can be sold at a lower contribution margin or used as recycled input. Wastepaper has no contribution margin but can be fed back into production as recycled paper.

Economic situation

The 'Saa Thai' brand was launched about 20 years ago. The large range of Classic Crafts' products and its long experience with saa paper production allow a strong presence in major segments of the home decoration market. Most products are exported, mainly to Italy, Germany, and North America (see Teeravanich, Jarivejvattana, Sareerat, Teeravanich, Sangwipark, Rakveeradhum, and Njuttikul 2001; GTZ and DEQP 2007; Ribeiro and Darnhofer 2007). Exports amount to 80–90 per cent of total sales, which is at the upper end of the sector average (GTZ and DEQP 2005a).

With high pressure on its margins and a relatively stagnant price for saa paper for many years, Classic Crafts is concerned about the profitability of the business. The management regards the main reasons for unsatisfactory profitability as being the lack of skilled employees and their low motivation. The uncertain labour supply situation is difficult to manage because of high employee turnover. Many employees come from neighbouring countries and after going home for a visit may not return at all. A continual improvement programme has recently been conducted by management, but has not led to the economic success expected. Subsequent to this, management sought efficiencies through cost reduction, and EMA tools appeared to offer an opportunity.

Regulatory and governmental programme

Despite a strong legal framework for environmental regulation, monitoring and inspection of industrial plants is rather limited in Thailand (Angel and Rock 2005). The weak regime of regulatory inspection and environmental law enforcement, as well as the absence of taxes or other incentives which could enhance eco-efficient production (GTZ and DEQP 2005a), make the introduction of voluntary initiatives at firm level, such as environmental management techniques, relevant for strengthening environmental performance (Angel and Rock 2005). In this context, strong efforts have been made by the Department of Environmental Quality Promotion (DEQP) and the Thai Ministry of Natural Resources and Environment to increase competitiveness of the saa paper industry through advanced production technologies and improved knowledge dissemination (GTZ and DEQP 2005b).

Moreover, the company's business benefits from the One Tambon One Product (OTOP) programme of the Thai government (Royal Thai Government 2007), which was based on the 'One Village One Product Concept' in Japan. A *tambon* is an administrative unit, a sub-district in English. The purpose of the OTOP programme is to promote local industries that reflect an ancient heritage, local inspiration, and applied ingenuity, through mass media, training, and product development. The government has provided tambons with technical assistance to enable more efficient production of goods and has assisted in marketing products throughout the country and around the world. In terms of social dimensions, this project helps prevent rural migration into major cities, such as Bangkok and Chiang Mai, in search of jobs. It has generated income and employment in each locality (Thai Government Public Relations Department 2005). As a result it strengthens the linkages between livelihood strategies, poverty alleviation, and the environment (Neefjes 2000; Redclift 2000; Chifos 2006). The saa paper industry, mainly located in the provinces of Chiang Mai, Chiang Rai, and Nan, is a long-established handicraft tradition in Thailand. However, associated with the natural and environmentally sound image of the product, customer-driven concerns about the need for environmentally sound production methods are gaining significance (GTZ and DEQP 2005a, 2007).

Environment

Paper manufacturing is conventionally associated with environmental problems caused by waste which affects the environment (Hua, Bian, and Liang 2007; Tewari, Batra, and Balakrishnan 2009). Attempts to overcome the problem can be made in one of two ways: (i) through minimisation of waste (non-product output) and (ii) by the reduction of inputs required for production to occur (Vencheh, Matin, and Kajani 2005; Thant and Charmondusit 2009). Hua and colleagues (2007) recognise that reduction of non-product output and of critical inputs need to be addressed simultaneously as both can influence, either favourably or unfavourably, the monetary and environmental performance of the business being evaluated. In this case study of Classic Crafts both of these issues are examined as ways of improving eco-efficiency. Input reduction considers reduction of the water and chemicals being used in paper production, whereas the improvement of water quality reduces non-product output.

The increasing importance of environmental factors in customer demands on products for import to their countries (GTZ and DEQP 2005a, 2007) makes uncontrolled environmental impacts a high-consequence business risk. Chemicals, including chlorine, hydroxide, and dyes, used in the production process make wastewater one of the main environmental issues in the production of saa paper (Ali and Sreekrishnan 2001; GTZ and DEQP 2005b). The existence of a wastewater treatment plant at the factory is designed to safeguard the environment as well as promote a greener image down the supply chain to the export consumer.

To improve water quality for the machine-made production process and the quality of the paper produced, the production manager has suggested measures for improvement to the owner of the company (see Table 10.1). For example, with replacement of a galvanised pipe in the paper production machine the manager expects to reduce water and chemicals usage and improve the quality of paper, and thus lead to less Grade B paper. Another investment opportunity would be water filters that improve the quality of water used in the paper production, mixing and beating machines, and for the office and an associated residence. The total possible investments are estimated to cost THB280,000 (Thai baht, €5,703).

As yet, the proposed investment options are not given top priority because management sees greater potential for increased profit through improving the qualifications, motivation, and control of employees. Furthermore, the invest-ments appear to represent a cost only, with expected cost savings to justify the expense not being calculated.

Company's motivation for using EMA

Ongoing concerns about the profitability of the production site have led the owner of the company to fly more frequently from the office in Bangkok to the factory in Mae Sai to analyse and monitor production processes. Although the owner considers human resources as the main reason for the unsatisfactory profitability, the necessity of identifying ways of reducing costs whilst simul-taneously improving environmental quality raised her interest in the potential of EMA.

TABLE 10.1 Overview of investment options to improve water quality for the machine-made production process

No.	Investment	Process addressed	THB	€
1	Water filter 100 cm × 150 cm	Clean water for paper production machine	60,000	1,222
2	Water filter 100 cm × 150 cm	Clean water for mixing and beating machine	60,000	1,222
3	Water filter 100 cm × 150 cm	Clean water for production process (hand-made and machine-made), office and residency	60,000	1,222
4.	Replacement of galvanised pipe	For machine-made production only	100,000	2,037
Total			280,000	5,703

Initial contact with the Environmental Management Accounting – South-East Asia project was established through an ongoing eco-efficiency project in Thailand (GTZ and DEQP 2005a,b). At the first meeting with the researchers in February 2005, the owner acknowledged the potential importance to the company of its material and energy flows, their associated costs, and their impact on profits. The researchers were made aware that the investment options proposed by the production manager seemed unattractive and were not seen as a high priority by the owner.

Investigation of the potential of EMA over the course of about 1.5 years took the following path. It was agreed that the first step in the EMA application would be to obtain a clear understanding of machine-based production of saa paper and identify processes within the organisation that use resources which have an environmental impact. Next, based on the initial analysis of material and energy flows and observation of the production process, the team decided to study the job-costing system of Classic Crafts whereby costs were linked with products for pricing and for inventory purposes. Following the identification of an understatement of the costs of non-product output and a revised environmental investment appraisal, the view about the relevance of environmental improvement measures changed.

EMA application

Initial analysis of the material and energy flows

Figure 10.3 shows the basic material and energy flow chart for Classic Crafts' production process. The colouring, mixing, and beating steps consume electricity, groundwater, steam, and chemicals. Whereas saa paper is the main output, the main non-product output is wastewater. The main input consists of different pulps and, occasionally, wastepaper from previous production jobs, depending on the match of colours of wastepaper and job order. Further inputs are electricity, oil, water, and direct labour. Rolling of the paper takes place before it is cut by a machine. Rolling and cutting consumes electricity and direct labour. Unwanted outputs incurred in paper production and rolling and cutting are wastepaper and wastewater.

Intensive cleaning of machinery using water and chemicals (a supportive process, see Figure 10.3) takes place once a week. A further, shorter, cleaning process occurs on an as-needs basis, for example when changing from dark- to light-coloured paper. The wastewater from the preparation of the colours and machine cleaning is treated in a separate wastewater treatment plant by adding chemicals and using electricity (a supportive process). Treated wastewater is discharged into a pond.

When observing the quality control process it was noticed that a great many job cost sheets do not conform to product quality standards in particular

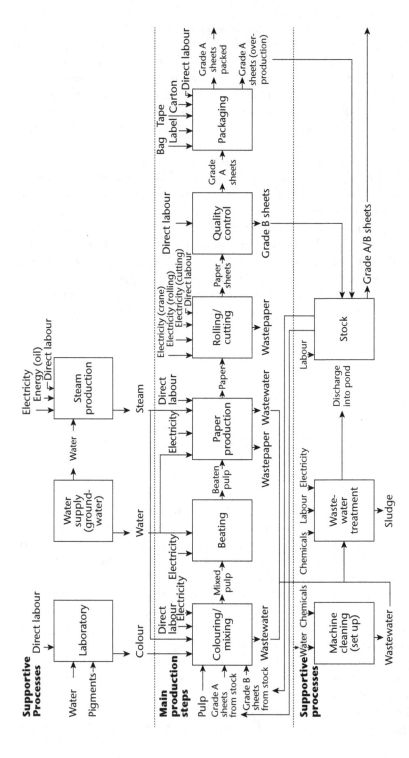

FIGURE 10.3 Material and energy flow chart for Classic Crafts' production process.

required for export quality products (GTZ and DEQP 2005a, 2007) and are rejected as Grade A paper. Ten to twenty-five per cent of sheets are deemed Grade B paper following internal inspection. Grade B paper is generally regarded as waste rather than a saleable by-product because of its low resale value. Batches of such paper are usually stored and re-used in production to substitute for, or supplement, raw material in later batches of production. Grade A sheets from overproduction that are stored and not saleable are occasionally re-used in the production process as raw material too. The storage area has numerous piles of saa paper sheets but, although the management is unhappy about the relatively high rejection rate, by re-using the sheets the company avoids excessive accumulation of stored paper sheets and saves working capital costs.

Reduction in the rejection rate of saa paper sheets through the production of fewer imperfections by adding economic and environmental value at the same time appeared to be a key to improving the eco-efficiency of production (Dyllick and Hockerts 2002). With possible eco-efficiency improvement in mind, the EMA team considered examining how environmental costs were currently accounted for as the next step towards establishing the link between reducing environmental impacts and improving economic performance. The job-costing system, the main formal cost-accounting system at Classic Crafts, became the focus in the context of revealing relevant costs for decision-making about the product mix.

Analysing the job costs of Classic Crafts through relevant costing

To assign costs to products and services, Classic Crafts uses a job-costing system (Horngren, Bhimani, Datar, and Foster 2005). Job costing is one of the most common cost-accounting techniques in small- and medium-sized enterprises (Fayek and Eng 2001; Cassia, Paleari, and Redondi 2005). The products are custom-made and expenses incurred are tracked against the budgeted or estimated costs for each job. Direct and indirect costs are assigned to distinct product units, batches, or lots of saa paper (see Moustafa 1978 for a view of why indirect costs should not be added to the process of export products by emerging countries). Tracking such data allows Classic Crafts to build a profile of its jobs and improve its estimates of the cost of work involved.

All costs assigned to a specific job are recorded and accumulated in separate job cost sheets, which represent the key source document in a job costing system. As shown in Figure 10.4, each sheet accumulates direct material and energy costs for such items as steam, electricity, raw materials, and chemicals; direct labour costs for mixing, beating, paper production, rolling, cutting, and packaging; and overhead (indirect) costs allocated as the job moves through different production steps. It can be seen in Figure 10.4 that raw materials

Summary of production data of machine-made paper	22 January 2005

Customer: J.S. Dreamworld	Order Number: COC-109/05	Code: Dark purple	Size: 70* 100 cm	Weight: 100 g

Mixing	Quantity		Price/pc	Total (Baht)
Steam	840	min	1.15	966.00
Labour (2 persons)	10	min	10.00	100.00
Total mixing cost				1,066.00

Beating	Quantity		Price/pc	Total (Baht)
Electricity (crane)	30	min	0.12	3.60
Electricity (beater)	70	min	0.15	10.50
Labour (2 persons)	100	min	0.56	56.00
Total beating costs				70.10

Producing Paper	Quantity		Price/pc	Total (Baht)
Electricity (testing colour)	40	min	0.80	32.00
Electricity	130	min	1.64	213.20
Fuel	130	min	1.53	198.90
Labour	170	min	6.01	1,021.70
Total producing costs				1,465.80

Roll-cut-check- count-pack	Quantity		Price/pc	Total (Baht)
Electricity (crane)	3	min	0.12	0.36
Electricity (rolling machine)	10	min	0.09	0.90
Electricity (cutting machine)	50	min	0.29	14.50
Labour (roll-cut)	120	min	0.40	48.00
Labour (check- count-pack)	600	min	0.26	156.00
Cardboard-tape- label	4	Pack	6.61	26.44
Total roll-cut-check-count-pack costs				246.20

Raw material	Quantity		Price/pc	Total (Baht)
Pulp saa	300	kg	29.00	8,700.00
Pulp pine	10	kg	28.00	280.00
Wastepaper	100	kg	18.00	1,800.00
RFR (colour)	2,205	g	0.22	485.10
R4BS (colour)	155	g	0.26	40.30
B4BL (colour)	690	g	0.55	379.50
Salt	40	kg	4.50	180.00
Pum	400	ml	0.00008	0.03
Pum/white water	400	ml	0.00008	0.03
Poly ethylene oxide (PEO)	400	ml	0.00014	0.06
PEO/white water	400	ml	0.00014	0.06
Total raw material costs				11,865.08

Summary	Total (Baht)
Total material costs	11,891.52
Total labour costs	1,381.70
Electricity costs of production process	275.06
Fuel costs of production process	1,164.90
Total production cost	14,713.18
Less beginning and ending part of the paper on roll 8 kg	144.00
Less Grade B paper 300 sheets (25 kg), 1.5 Baht/sheet of paper	450.00
Total final costs	14,119.18
Overhead costs 18% of final costs	2,541.45
Production costs of Grade A 2,280 paper sheets	16,660.63
Production costs/sheet of paper	7.31

FIGURE 10.4 Example of a Classic Crafts job cost sheet.

account for about 80 per cent of the total production cost. Hence, any possibilities for reducing material costs can lead to substantial improvement in profits.

The general job cost sheet provides information not about non-product output, but only about good output. The Classic Crafts job cost sheet shows the costs of Grades A and B paper as well as wastepaper produced and later taken into production as raw material. Grade B paper is recycled into production in later batches. Hence, by inference, the cost of this non-product output is revealed at THB450 (€9.14) for job COC-109/05 (see Figure 10.4). When the summarisation and aggregation of these production costs was discussed among the members of the EMA team, the amount of the non-product output caught their attention. Before subtracting overhead costs, the costs of waste-paper and Grade B paper are subtracted from the production costs. However, the costs of these unwanted outputs are understated. Figure 10.4 shows that the costs of one sheet of Grade B paper amounts to THB1.5 (€0.03) whereas production costs of one sheet of Grade A paper are THB7.31 (€0.15). In fact, the cost of Grade B paper does not correspond to the actual costs related to total material, energy flows, and labour used in its production. Apart from the last production step, packaging, Grade B paper passes through the same production process as Grade A paper; in other words they both lead to almost the same material and energy flows and related costs. Addressing the issue of understatement of costs, the production manager explained that Grade B paper could not be sold except at a lower price. It is in effect a by-product – a secondary or incidental product made during the production of a primary product. The manager was told by the marketing department in Bangkok to use the costs of about THB1.5 per kilogram of Grade B paper, as this is the corresponding price for low-quality saa paper which can be obtained on the local market.

The understatement of the by-product costs in the existing job-costing system makes environmental measures, which are aiming to improve the production process and reduce the non-product output, unattractive to the management because the potential savings appear low. Although the low grade paper is an unwanted side-effect of Classic Crafts' production, the management did not address the problem in terms of costs relevant to the decision at hand. Moreover, understatement of the cost of what is treated as non-product output leads the production manager to consider the production and then recycling of Grade B paper as being acceptable. The low cost of Grade B paper, based on information from the marketing department, results in a relatively cost-effective use as wastepaper input to the production process. Figure 10.4 shows that one kilogram of wastepaper has a lower cost in the cost sheet than one kilogram of raw material, although wastepaper has previously passed through the whole production process, as well as being processed through the addition of various kinds of material and energy, and probably has a cost of at least the same amount as Grade A paper: THB7.31 per sheet. This means that part of the overall material and energy costs associated with the Grade B paper output has not been added to the job costs. Material, labour, and overhead need to be added to the product which ends up as Grade B paper. Hence, incentives for generating and using Grade B paper in production work against the aim of reducing non-product output because the low cost makes the paper appear attractive for recycling into future production.

Improvement in monetary investment decision-making

The improvement measures proposed by the production manager were re-examined on the basis of the estimated cost of Grade B paper. Using investment option 4 in Table 10.1, replacement of the galvanised pipe in the production machine, illustrates how the job-costing analysis influences the evaluation of investment options (Table 10.2).

Management considers the current state of the galvanised pipe as contributing to a low quality of product output (high amount of Grade B paper) and undesirable cleaning costs. Chemical cleaning is necessary because of colour residue in the pipe, which, if untreated, results in unwanted colour spots on the sheets of paper and consequently in higher output of Grade B paper. The poor condition of the pipe calls for excessive chemical treatment, as cleaning the pipe with water alone is insufficient, especially when subsequent to production of dark-coloured sheets of paper. Chemical, labour, and water costs related to cleaning the pipe amount to a total of more than THB57,000 (€1,157.10) per year. Replacing the pipe with a new one is expected to facilitate the cleaning process, leading to a significant reduction in the consumption of chemicals, water, and labour hours. For the assessment of the environmental investment, a conservative estimate of cost reduction is used (50 per cent).

TABLE 10.2 Environmental investment appraisal: replacement of galvanised pipe

	Year 0	Year 1	Year 2	Year 3	Year 4	Year 5
Initial investment	−100,000					
Reduced chemical usage		25,920	25,920	25,920	25,920	25,920
Reduced labour costs		3,300	3,300	3,300	3,300	3,300
Additional benefit of improving Grade B paper to Grade A quality		94,805	94,805	94,805	94,805	94,805
Reduced water costs		32	32	32	32	32
Annual reduction of costs		124,057	124,057	124,057	124,057	124,057
Net cost savings		124,057	124,057	124,057	124,057	124,057
Discounted cost savings (r = 12.5%)		110,274	98,021	87,130	77,449	68,843
Sum of discounted cost savings	441,716					
Net present value	341,716					

Note: values in baht. THB100 equals €2.03.

Initially, the owner took a negative view of the cash flows associated with the environmental investment. Without consideration of the real costs of Grade B paper, potential cost savings have been underestimated. However, once the additional benefits from improving Grade B paper to Grade A quality have been added to the computation and net present value placed in front of the owner, the substantial benefits from cash savings became obvious. Table 10.2 shows that the proposed investment is highly profitable in net present value terms. According to the production manager, the new pipe leads not only to chemical and water savings but to a reduction of about 2–4 per cent of non-product output. On the basis of a conservative estimate of a 2 per cent reduction of non-product output, the additional savings amount to almost THB95,000 (€1,928.50) per year. This is almost equal to the initial investment cost of replacing the galvanised pipe (simple payback period: 0.8 years). Taking the discount rate to be 12.5 per cent, as used by the company for similar investments, the investment has a net present value of THB341,716 (€6,922.30) over the expected five year life-span of the investment. The owner's view of the environmental investment thus changed once the EMA technique was demonstrated.

Discussion

Two types of implications can be drawn from the saa paper case study: those for management and those for researchers. There appear to be three implications for management.

First, the use of EMA information improves decision-making by helping managers to identify, track, and monitor environmental costs while improving quality of the products and processes. Making transparent the additional costs of the by-product Grade B paper, which is predominantly treated as non-product output and recycled as waste, raises the owner's awareness of the importance of reducing non-product outputs by correctly costing and pricing by-products. These costs per sheet include a portion of the original material costs, labour, and overheads incurred when producing a sheet of good-output Grade A paper. Opportunity costs associated with working capital requirements have been ignored, as they would be similar for Grade A and Grade B paper. The EMA information led to the managers changing their attitude and decisions as they could see the cost of Grade B paper was similar to that of Grade A paper and that they were better-off producing Grade A paper in the first place. Relevant costing shows that the lowest cost of materials for batch production is the cost of new raw materials rather than the use of recycled Grade B paper. As a result, investment options to improve the proportion of Grade A paper, which had been proposed and in most cases rejected, gained higher priority.

Second, the job-costing system can be revised to add the costs of non-product output, thereby increasing transparency and accuracy in relation to higher-cost jobs while adding support to decision-making which improves eco-efficiency. Price competition is strong in the saa paper industry (Teeravanich *et al.* 2001) and Classic Crafts is a price-taker and cannot increase the price per sheet of paper because of a lack of market power. However, it can either reduce costs or improve the efficiency of production by reducing waste, or non-product output. Information about cost savings provides a further incentive to invest in environmental improvement measures to help realise these savings and reduce job costs. The evaluation of the waste pipe investment indicates potential savings that can be advantageous in a highly competitive market.

Third, the EMA system provides a useful information base about three key areas of concern to business in the saa paper industry: water and chemical reduction as well as energy use.

Likewise, there are three implications for research. First, the rationale behind EMA support for environmental investments in the saa paper-manufacturing plant is clarified through relevant costing and investment appraisal. Eco-efficiency initiatives, research, and capacity-building projects are evident in the Thai saa paper industry (Kasetsart University Research and Development Institute *et al.* 2001; Mungcharoen and Papong 2001; GTZ and DEQP 2005a,b). Voluntary corporate measures in the paper industry aiming to reduce environmental impacts and increase economic performance have been studied for many years (Parthasarathy and Krishnagopalan 1999; Barla 2007; Tewari *et al.* 2009; Thant and Charmondusit 2009). These previous company- and/or sector-related case studies have concentrated on promoting cleaner technologies and cost–benefit analyses. In contrast, this study approaches eco-efficiency improvements in the saa paper industry from a different perspective: it examines the specific company decision-making context and related accounting practice.

Second, in the case of Classic Crafts those costs which change when two different short-term options are apparent (sell or recycle), and where the existing costs of selling the product are seen to exceed the benefits, do not induce management to take action to improve the situation through technological development. However, the use of relevant environmental costing and investment appraisal methods changes this perspective. The case elaborates on factors which hamper the realisation of eco-efficiency improvements and which influence the generation of higher-quality environmental information.

Third, relatively few attempts have been made to research social and environmental accounting in non-Western, and especially Asian, contexts (Kuasirikun 2005). The Classic Crafts study provides further evidence about environmental accounting in Thailand. Institutionalisation of environmental and social accounting by the professional accounting bodies in Thailand is moving at a relatively slow pace (Kuasirikun 2005), as are non-financial external reporting (Kuasirikun and Sherer 2004) and environmental management accounting (Setthasakko 2010). A potential reason worthy of further research might be the lack of legal enforcement of regulations designed to encourage improved actions on the environment by business (Kuasirikun and Sherer 2004). Another could be the lack of strong stakeholder pressure on corporations in emerging countries (Coulter 2001; Belal and Owen 2007). A third reason could be the low strength of the accountancy and auditing professions in emerging economies, combined with a lack of accounting personnel resources and training, especially in environmental auditing (Watson and Emery 2004). Finally, there is the benefit from making the owner aware of cost savings associated with the reduction of environmental impacts through relevant costing, which encourages the removal of non-product output and use of investment appraisal; this can convert the owner's view of environmental issues as a cost, to environmental issues as a benefit.

Conclusions

The Classic Crafts case study leads to two main conclusions. First, EMA tools can be used to provide information about the net benefits from applying short-term relevant cost analysis (Figure 10.1: Box 7) as well as the application of long-term investment appraisal (Box 8).

Relevant costing illustrates that the exclusion of certain environmental costs related to wastewater means that inappropriate short-term decisions are made in relation to the use of a by-product, Grade B paper, as a non-product output (i.e. waste). Grade B paper is seen by the production manager as worth producing as a cheaper input to future production batches because it is cheaper than the current cost of materials. Appropriate costing, to show whether it is worth selling Grade B paper, brings environmental cost savings into the analysis, and revised figures reveal that it is attractive to sell Grade B paper instead of recycling the paper as input.

Investment appraisal, using discounted cash flows adjusted for environmental cost savings, shows that the net advantage from the replacement of galvanised piping is an increased output of Grade A paper and reduced use of chemicals, labour, and water in production.

Second, the use of EMA brings to the fore the interrelated aspects of short- and long-term decision-making about the profitable reduction of environmental impacts of the business (Figure 10.1: Boxes 7 and 8). In essence, appropriate costing demonstrates that, in the short run, once costs previously hidden from analysis are made visible, they change the decision, from producing and using Grade B paper as waste input for future production, towards the sale of Grade B paper on the market. As a result, the production manager moves to reduce the production of Grade B paper because when sold as a by-product, as relevant costing suggests is desirable, it has a lower contribution margin than Grade A paper. To encourage greater production of Grade A paper from each batch produced and, hence, a greater contribution margin, it is necessary to consider various investment options.

One of the options, the replacement of galvanised pipe, is illustrated. Without considering the cost savings and additional contribution margin generated by changing the product mix towards greater quantities of Grade A paper, investment in galvanised piping appears unattractive. The business faces an immediate capital expenditure on piping of THB100,000 (€2,037). However, once the cost savings are addressed, because the need to increase Grade A paper produced in each batch is recognised, the net present value makes it an attractive proposal. Figure 10.1 shows how these two ad hoc, future-orientated monetary tools applied through EMA work together to help develop long-term thinking and a competitive business strategy for cost reduction.

References

Ali, M. and Sreekrishnan, T.R. (2001) 'Aquatic toxicity from pulp and paper mill effluents: a review', *Advances in Environmental Research*, 5: 175–196.

Angel, D.P. and Rock, M.T. (2005) 'Global standards and the environmental performance of industry', *Environment and Planning A*, 37: 1903–1918.

Arunotai, N., Gordon, N., Jarubenja, R., Katleeradapan, N., Petchprasert, N., and Pongsapich, A. (2007) 'Subcontracted homework in Thailand', in Mehrotra, S. and Biggeri, M. (eds) *Asian informal workers: global risk, local protection*, London: Routledge, pp. 322–358.

Barla, P. (2007) 'ISO 14001 certification and environmental performance in Quebec's pulp and paper industry', *Journal of Environmental Economics and Management*, 53: 291–306.

Belal, A.R. and Owen, D. (2007) 'The views of corporate managers on the current state of, and future prospects for, social reporting in Bangladesh: an engagement based study', *Accounting, Auditing and Accountability Journal*, 20: 472–494

Burritt, R., Hahn, T., and Schaltegger, S. (2002) 'Towards a comprehensive framework for environmental management accounting: links between business actors and environmental management accounting tools', *Australian Accounting Review*, 12: 39–50.

Cassia, L., Paleari, S., and Redondi, R. (2005) 'Management accounting systems and organisational structure', *Small Business Economics*, 25: 373–391.

Chifos, C. (2006) 'Culture, environment and livelihood: potential for crafting sustainable consumptions in Chiang Mai', *International Journal of Environment and Sustainable Development*, 5: 315–332.

Coulter, C. (2001) *Corporate social responsibility monitor 2001: global public opinion on the changing role of companies*, Glen Allen, VA: Environics Foundation International.

Dyllick, T. and Hockerts, K. (2002) 'Corporate sustainability: beyond the business case', *Business Strategy and the Environment*, 11: 130–141.

Fayek, A.R. and Eng, P. (2001) 'Activity-based job costing for integrating estimating, scheduling, and cost control', *Cost Engineering*, 43: 23–32.

Forsen, M., Larsson, J., and Samuelsson, S. (2001) *Paper mulberry cultivation in the Luang Prabang Province, Lao PDR: production, marketing and socio-economic aspects – minor field study, No. 140*, Uppsala: Uppsala University.

GTZ and DEQP (German Technical Cooperation and Department of Environmental Quality Promotion) (eds) (2005a) *Export market for Thai saa paper (mulberry paper): analysis and recommendations*, Bangkok: GTZ.

GTZ and DEQP (eds) (2005b) *Facilities for enhancing competitiveness of the Thai saa paper industry*, Bangkok: GTZ.

GTZ and DEQP (eds) (2007) *Market survey for saa paper: European market potential for environmentally-friendly saa paper, Thai–German programme for enterprise competitiveness*, Bangkok: GTZ.

Horngren, C.T., Bhimani, A., Datar, S.M., and Foster, G. (2005) *Management and cost accounting* (3rd edn), Harlow, UK: Prentice Hall/Financial Times.

Hua, Z., Bian, Y., and Liang, L. (2007) 'Eco-efficiency analysis of paper mills along the Huai River: an extended DEA approach', *Omega*, 35: 578–587.

Kasetsart University Research and Development Institute, Kasetsart Agricultural and Agro-Industrial Product Improvement Institute and Japan International Co-operation Agency (eds) (2001) *Final report of the research project for higher utilization of forestry and agricultural plant materials in Thailand (HUFA) 1996-2001*, Bangkok: Kasetsart University.

Kuasirikun, N. (2005) 'Attitudes to the development and implementation of social and environmental accounting in Thailand', *Critical Perspectives on Accounting*, 16: 1035–1057.

Kuasirikun, N. and Sherer, M. (2004) 'Corporate social accounting disclosure in Thailand', *Accounting, Accountability and Auditing Journal*, 17: 629–660.

Moustafa, M.E. (1978) 'Pricing strategy for export activity in developing nations', *Journal of International Business Studies*, 9: 91–102.

Mungcharoen, T. and Papong, S. (2001) 'Cleaner technology: application to paper mulberry pulp and paper industry', in Kasetsart University Research and Development Institute, Kasetsart Agricultural and Agro-Industrial Product Improvement Institute, and Japan International Co-operation Agency (eds), *Final report of the research project for higher utilization of forestry and agricultural plant materials in Thailand (HUFA) 1996-2001*, Bangkok: Kasetsart University, pp. 741–750.

Neefjes, K. (2000) *Environments and livelihoods: strategies for sustainability*, London: Oxfam Publishing.

Oka, S. and Ohyama, K. (1989) 'Paper mulberry', in Bajaj, Y.P.S. (ed.) *Biotechnology in agriculture and forestry: Volume 5, Trees II*, Berlin: Springer, pp. 402–411.

Parthasarathy, G. and Krishnagopalan, G. (1999) 'Effluent reduction and control of non-process elements towards a cleaner Kraft pulp mill', *Clean Products and Processes*, 1: 264–277.

Redclift, M. (ed.) (2000) *Sustainability: life chances and livelihoods*, London: Routledge.

Ribeiro, N.N. and Darnhofer, I. (2007) *Understanding the supply chain of paper mulberry bark in Lao PDF using causal mapping*, Vienna: University of Natural Resources and Applied Life Sciences.

Royal Thai Government (2007) *Highlight Thailand: OTOP* [online – last accessed 28 March 2007]. Available from Internet: http://www.thaigov.go.th/en/highlight-thailand/listnews.aspx?M_CODE=30.

Schaltegger, S. (1998) 'Accounting for eco-efficiency', in Nath, B., Hens, L., Compton, P., and Devuyst, D. (eds) *Environmental management in practice: volume I*, London: Routledge, pp. 272–287.

Setthasakko, W. (2010) 'Barriers to the development of environmental management accounting: an exploratory study of pulp and paper companies in Thailand', *EuroMed Journal of Business*, 5: 315–331.

Teeravanich, A., Jarivejvattana, K., Sareerat, S., Teeravanich, R., Sangwipark, A., Rakveeradhum, J., and Njuttikul, N. (2001) 'Marketing and value-added of paper mulberry product', in Kasetsart University Research and Development Institute, Kasetsart Agricultural and Agro-Industrial Product Improvement Institute, and Japan International Co-operation Agency (eds) *Final report of the research project for higher utilization of forestry and agricultural plant materials in Thailand (HUFA) 1996– 2001*, Bangkok: Kasetsart University, pp. 372–377.

Tewari, P.K., Batra, V.S., and Balakrishnan, M. (2009) 'Efficient water use in industries: cases from the Indian agro-based pulp and paper mills', *Journal of Environmental Management*, 90: 265–273.

Thai Government Public Relations Department (2005) *Poverty eradication: inside Thailand review*, Bangkok: Foreign Office.

Thant, M.M. and Charmondusit, K. (2009) 'Eco-efficient assessment of pulp and paper industry in Myanmar', *Clean Technologies and Environmental Policy*, 12: 427–439.

Udomchoke, V., Mongkolsook, Y., Anapanurak, W., Thanasombat, M. and Kasjinda, K. (2001) 'The environmental conditions for natural distribution of paper mulberry in Thailand', in Kasetsart University Research and Development Institute, Kasetsart Agricultural and Agro-Industrial Product Improvement Institute, and Japan International Co-operation Agency (eds) *Final report of the research project for higher utilization of forestry and agricultural plant materials in Thailand (HUFA) 1996–2001*, Bangkok: Kasetsart University, pp. 4–13

Vencheh, A.H., Matin, R.K., and Kajani, M.T. (2005) 'Undesirable factors in efficiency measurement', *Applied Mathematics and Computation*, 163: 547–552.

Watson, M. and Emery, A.R.T. (2004) 'Environmental management and auditing systems the reality of environmental self-regulation', *Managerial Auditing Journal*, 19: 916–928.

11

ENVIRONMENTAL RISK ASSESSMENT AT A PULP AND PAPER COMPANY

Thai Cane Paper, Thailand

Introduction

The pulp and paper industry, both in Thailand and worldwide, is associated with high levels of pollution and intensive consumption of resources (Parthasarathy and Krishnagopalan 1999; Lang 2002). In spite of its positive association with local community development through job creation in rural areas (ICFPA 2006), the industry has been under continual pressure to improve its practices. Pulp and paper production is considered a major source of environmental pollution and associated with a high consumption of energy and water (Thant and Charmondusit 2009). Specific techniques to help the pulp and paper industry reduce the toxicity of effluents and other environmental impacts and environmental strategies, such as reduction of energy use and use of different energy sources to improve eco-efficiency of production and related processes, have been studied at length in previous research (Servos, Munkittrick, Carey, and Kraak 1996; Parthasarathy and Krishnagopalan 1999; Ali and Sreekrishnan 2001; Barla 2007; Thant and Charmondusit 2009). In this context, environmental management accounting (EMA) tools, such as material and energy flow accounting, environmental cost accounting, and environmental investment appraisal, have been applied (Servos *et al.* 1996; Parthasarathy and Krishnagopalan 1999; Thant and Charmondusit 2009). This case study extends previous research by exploring the use of EMA for risk analysis and assessment, and for long-term planning including investment appraisal in the context of water management issues. Research addressing the relationship between EMA and risk management is in general in short supply (Burritt 2005).

Thai Cane Paper Public Company Limited (hereafter Thai Cane Paper), is a company engaged in pulp and paper production and distribution in Thailand.

The EMA practices observed at Thai Cane Paper support the company in long-term decision-making to improve management of environmental risks associated with growing water scarcity.

First, a general discussion of the decision situation at Thai Cane Paper is presented. The initial use of EMA information is outlined with a particular focus on an ex-post analysis of two investments introduced to reduce water use in production: the double doctor blade project and a dissolved oxygen content (DOC) online monitoring project. Regular water supply is of such importance to the company that the risk of shortage, which has been growing, needs to be assessed on a regular basis. EMA tools help the company (i) identify, analyse, and assess the risks associated with water shortage and (ii) respond to this situation through the development of a regular environmental long-term plan. Investment scenarios are developed for addressing the identified risks. Finally, implications from the analysis are drawn in the context of the conceptual framework (see Figure 11.1) and an outlook provided.

Decision setting

Thai Cane Paper was established in 1987. Its main activities are the production and distribution of kraft paper for use in corrugated paper packaging. The company is a member of the Siam Cement Group, the biggest kraft paper

		Monetary EMA		Physical EMA	
		Short-term	Long-term	Short-term	Long-term
Past-orientated	Routinely generated	Environmental cost accounting [1]	Environment-induced capital expenditure and revenue [2]	Material and energy flow accounting [9]	Environmental capital impact accounting [10]
Past-orientated	Ad hoc	Ex-post assessment of relevant environmental costing decisions [3]	Ex-post inventory assessment of projects [4]	Ex-post assessment of short-term environmental impacts [11]	Ex-post inventory appraisal of physical environmental investments [12]
Future-orientated	Routinely generated	Monetary environmental budgeting [5]	Environmental long-term financial planning [6]	Physical environmental budgeting [13]	Environmental long-term physical planning [14]
Future-orientated	Ad hoc	Relevant environmental costing [7]	Monetary environmental investment appraisal [8]	Tools designed to predict relevant environmental impacts [15]	Physical environmental investment appraisal [16]

FIGURE 11.1 Application of the EMA framework (Burritt, Hahn, and Schaltegger 2002) to Thai Cane Paper.
Note: Dark (light) grey boxes represent the major (minor) EMA applications.

producer in Thailand, manufacturing about 805,000 tonnes of paper bags per year to hold its cement. Thai Cane Paper ranks at number 3 in production capacity, with about 275,000 tonnes per year. Product lines are categorised into two principal groups: kraft liner board used in packaging surfaces and kraft paper for corrugated medium. Several grades of products are offered to meet the needs of the local and international market.

Thai Cane Paper operates two main production facilities. The first is a paper mill established in 1990 and located in Tamuang District, Kanchanaburi Province. The facility has an annual production capacity of 100,000 tonnes and employs about 175 people. The second paper mill was built in 1998 and is located in Kabinburi District, Prachinburi Province. The second mill is one of the most technologically advanced mills in Asia with a production capacity of 175,000 tonnes per year. It is located about 180 kilometres north-east of Bangkok and has 169 employees. With 58 people working in the Bangkok office, Thai Cane Paper employs 402 people in three sites.

This case study centres on the use of EMA at the second mill in Prachinburi. The mill is a rich subject for analysis because accounting for environmental information at Thai Cane Paper is advanced and is supported by a recently installed system application programme (SAP) information system. Climate changes and related water scarcity represent a major challenge at the Prachinburi site. The focus is on EMA development in response to the water scarcity using environmental risk analysis, long-term planning, and investment appraisal.

Technology

At present Thai Cane Paper is the only company in Thailand to produce four-ply kraft paper using modern high technology imported from Metso, a Finnish company, and electricity consumption controlled by Siemens. The highly advanced machine is only the second of its type in Asia and provides a greater potential for output than other paper mills, which can often produce only two- and three-ply kraft paper. The company operates a strict quality control system which covers every stage of production to ensure that the paper meets the highest standards.

The manufacturing process occurs in two main steps: preparation of paper pulp and production of paper. First, the production of corrugated board begins with used scrap paper, which is pulverised to separate out the fibres in a pulp solution. At this stage, input that cannot be pulverised, such as wire and string, is removed from the process. The liquid pulp is then sent through a separator to extract all minute, light-weight objects, such as staples, plastic, and foam. After these solid objects have been eliminated, the liquid pulp requires further cleaning, and passes through a machine to remove other contaminants, such as ink and asphalt, by means of heat-induced molecular displacement. The resulting clean pulp is then stored in a pulp tank and controlled for density, pressure, temperature, and acid-based content. Various chemicals are introduced at this point to prepare the pulp for conveyance to head boxes.

Second, the liner board surfaces require different kraft paper, for which the proportion of long and short fibres differs. Production of liner board begins with pulverisation of both kinds of fibres until they separate into a solution. This process is closely controlled to ensure the highest possible strength and firmness of the finished product. The pulp is then stored in another tank, which is also controlled for density, pressure, and temperature. Finally, chemicals are mixed in to prepare the pulp for delivery to its own head boxes for production of surface-quality kraft paper.

Raw materials required for the production of kraft paper are:

- scrap paper, which accounts for approximately 82 per cent of total raw materials and is received both from within Thailand and from abroad;
- long- and short-fibre pulp, providing 15 per cent of materials, with long-fibre pulp improving strength of the paper and short-fibre pulp improving smoothness; and
- various chemicals, providing about 3 per cent of materials, which are added to provide waterproofing.

Economic situation

For success, Thai Cane Paper depends on its technology, the growth of the corrugated paper-manufacturing industry, local economic stability, and the export market for its products. After a small decrease in sales revenues in 2004 (–0.09 per cent), the company increased these by 11.31 per cent in 2005, leading to total sales revenues of THB3,805 million (€78,358,300). Slower economic growth and expansion in production capacity from both local and regional paper manufacturers caused intense price-based competition. In 2006 this led sales revenues to fall by THB35 million (€737,529) (–0.92 per cent).

The use of a large quantity of recycled of corrugated cardboard scraps as input raw material in the technologically advanced production process provides a major competitive advantage for Thai Cane Paper in terms of financial and environmental benefits (see next sub-section).

The company aims at achieving continuous cost reductions and profitability improvements. As part of the existing management accounting system, environmental cost reduction targets are set and measured. These measures are important because total costs of production have increased on the back of rising oil and energy prices and large fluctuations in the price of wastepaper and pulp.

Environment

The company's efforts towards environmental protection stem from the senior management's establishment of an environmental policy, which is dedicated to the prevention and reduction of pollution, minimisation of waste, and optimisation of energy consumption. One section of the policy relates to monitoring to ensure legal compliance with wastewater standards, monthly monitoring to reveal water consumption, and process improvement to reduce water usage, increase the amount of recycled water, and provide continuous improvement in wastewater treatment. Meeting high international environmental management system standards is part of the management philosophy at Thai Cane Paper. The Prachinburi mill was the company's first to obtain ISO 14001 environmental management system certification in 2003, followed by the Kanchanaburi mill in late 2006. The environmental management system is applied throughout the organisation. Control of environmental performance is supported by an environmental performance indicator system consisting of more than 35 indicators in the areas of water, energy, raw material use, re-use and recycling of material, wastewater, waste, and air emissions.

Significant environmental impacts of the organisation were initially identified as being:

- wastewater;
- waste;
- air emissions;
- sludge from the wastewater plant; and
- rejects from the wastepaper-making process.

In 2004, attention was first drawn to waste management as being the key environmental concern of Thai Cane Paper's management. In fact, the recycling of industrial waste has long been seen as an important part of environmental control and protection at Thai Cane Paper. The extensive use of recycled paper in the production process is an example of the company's involvement in waste recycling initiatives. An area of high priority for the company is the use of a large volume of water and treatment of the liquid waste products to obtain reusable waste in the paper-manufacturing process. To ensure the company's treatment and recovery system meets the highest environmental standards, Thai Cane Paper uses an activated sludge process for wastewater treatment, designed by a leading company from Finland specialising in wastewater treatment. Although energy reduction was regarded as a key issue for the company, the demand for, and supply of, water and the necessity to recycle and re-use water are of equal significance. Water demand is rising because of the installation of a new power plant to replace the bunker oil-fired boiler with a coal-fired system (Moore and Rittof 2005). In addition, the company has increasingly been threatened by a decline in water supply as the rainfall in the Prachinburi province has declined in recent years. Hence, a long-term goal of the company is to introduce a closed-loop system which uses the sludge from wastewater treatment as a fuel source in the new boiler.

The focus here is on the assessment of risks related to water scarcity and the use of EMA tools to help provide information to assess this problem. Two of the risks relate to (i) overuse of water (as steam) in papermaking when water is in short supply and (ii) the risk of releasing wastewater into a public flow when the river is not in an appropriate condition (i.e. not having enough water) and presents a risk to aquatic life.

One investment considered below is the introduction of a double doctor blade system to improve productivity and reduce steam and water use. Doctor blades were developed to address a number of papermaking needs. Some peel the sheet from the paper roll at start-up or after a break; others clean rolls, redirect the sheet, direct the flow of water, regulate coatings, perform crêping functions, or condition rolls. In many applications, a vacuum is created between the circumference of the roll and the underside of the doctor blade. This causes fibre and fillers to be pulled to the underside of the blade, accumulate, and break away, causing holes in the sheet and sheet breaks. In this situation, it helps to provide more than one doctoring function on a single roll. However, on most modern paper machines, there is simply not enough space to mount two separate doctor assemblies, but where it can be installed efficiencies arise in relation to cleaner rolls, improved roll life, fewer sheet breaks, better-quality sheets, and longer blade life, as well as the steam and water gains already mentioned.

A second investment relates to an instrument for measurement of DOC of water, necessary for assessing the ability of wastewater to support aquatic life. A high-cost DOC online monitoring system was purchased. Costs associated with online monitoring include (i) capital costs (instrumentation purchase and installation), such as water treatment plant upgrades, facilities to house online monitors, and system upgrades, and (ii) operating costs including consumables (reagents, bulbs, probes), factory calibration and maintenance, internal maintenance staff, training, instrument replacement and upgrades, communication charges, and laboratory costs. The company is clearly proactive in its approach to investing in up-to-date technology to address environmental issues.

Regulation

The Thai paper industry operates within a strong legal framework for environmental regulation because impacts on the natural environment and people in surrounding areas are high (Sonnenfeld 1998a). Therefore, systematic control of environmental performance and regular compliance monitoring, for example in wastewater and air pollution, represent substantial components of Thai Cane Paper's environmental policy and management system.

To minimise the pollution of the river water to which the treated wastewater from Thai Cane Paper's production is discharged, government regulation requires that wastewater discharge into the river is allowed only in six months of the year. Despite having an onsite wastewater treatment facility, the risk of overpolluting river water is too high in the other half of the year because of cyclical low rainfall and low water levels. Pollution of the river would also raise dissent in the community as the local population depends on the river as a water source. The role of rural communities and social movements is considered to be important by the company, whose reputation may suffer when public and government attention is raised about particular firms and industry issues (Sonnenfeld 1998a,b). Movement towards a closed-loop system would reduce this constraint on operations. Therefore, Thai Cane Paper is exploring new ways to recycle and re-use the water in its production processes. In these circumstances, there is strong motivation for using EMA information to assess options for reducing the water and to recycle water.

Company's motivation for using EMA

The case study covers the use of EMA techniques over a period of 1.5 years. In September 2004, a meeting with Thai Cane Paper's executive vice president, the managing director, the production manager, the environmental manager, and the accountant focussed attention on the Pranchinburi mill and its environmental problems. The review team consisted of the production manager, environmental management staff (who had environmental engineering experience), and the accountant.

Environmental accounting information has been collected by the company since the environmental management system was installed in 2003 and has been supported by the SAP system since early 2004. A selection of environmental performance and eco-efficiency measures were provided by the environmental manager at the first meeting. A strong motivation for the generation of environmental information has been the monitoring of environmental performance and exploration of ways to improve the profitability of production and reduce risks from environmental impacts. Institutional factors seem to have had a bearing on the engagement of Thai Cane Paper with EMA. For example, the parent company, Siam Cement, provided instructions to Thai Cane Paper to invest in measures which reduced wastewater. Involvement by the parent company meant information was needed for the assessment of environmental capital investments. Progress and outcomes of the various environmental investment projects are described in the next section (Figure 11.1: Box 4).

At the end of 2005, ad hoc analysis of annual rainfall and days of rain over a period of six years (2000–2005) (Figure 11.1: Box 12) alerted the company to potential risks from shortages in river water supply in the near future. Based on the data analysis, a long-term environmental planning system (Figure 11.1: Box 14) which would forecast and address these risks was installed, enabling the company to examine possible environmental investment options and secure future water supplies (Figure 11.1: Box 16). The various uses of EMA in this context are described next (Figure 11.1: Boxes 4, 6, 11, 12, 13, 14, 15, 16).

EMA application

Ex-post assessment of environmental investment appraisals

Ex-post assessments of two environmental investments (Figure 11.1: Box 4) in September 2005 revealed the financial and environmental benefits.

The anticipated environmental and financial improvements of the double doctor blade investment project were realised. The double doctor blade project has been completed, and the technology installed has led to cost savings from steam reduction at THB11 (€0.22) per tonne of paper produced. Initial investment costs of THB1,132,061 (€22,615) were recouped within 7.1 months (see Table 11.1). This took slightly longer than the expected 6.4 months because, on average, only about 13,500 tonnes of paper was actually processed compared with the expected figure of 15,000 tonnes used in the initial investment appraisal.

The DOC online monitoring project was implemented but only one month of data was available at the time of the project because of teething problems with the implementation of one of the aerators, which forced the company to delay completion of the project for over six months. The one-month trial run, however, indicated favourable results with a 9 per cent decrease in power consumption equivalent to 2.4 kW per tonne of paper and cost reductions of THB6 per tonne of paper.

No significant progress had been made in the attempt to advance the recycling of wastewater. Increasing pressure from the parent company and government regulations reinforced Thai Cane Paper's efforts to search for investments that would enable the company to re-use a larger portion of water. The company decided to set up a project team in December 2005, commissioned to elaborate upon the possibilities for water recycling and develop a feasibility study. The initial aim of the Recycle Water Initiative was to decrease water consumption by 5,000 m³/day or 45 per cent of the water currently discharged.

This initiative was accompanied by another initiative which evolved from changes in local environmental conditions. Declines in rainfall over recent years had resulted in a shortage of river water, forcing the company to examine the use and re-use of water at the Prachinburi site in broader ways as described in the following section.

TABLE 11.1 Investment in the double doctor blade system, illustrating the break-even point

Month	Jul 05	Aug 05	Sep 05	Oct 05	Nov 05	Dec 05	Jan 06	Feb 06	Mar 06	Apr 06	May 06	Jun 06	Jul 06	Aug 06	Sep 06
Actual production per month (tonnes)	10,507	12,540	13,626	14,696	13,750	14,038	15,008	13,571	14,829	14,406	14,509	13,535	15,107	14,924	10,041
Cost savings (THB/month)	124,720	148,851	161,736	174,440	163,208	166,625	178,147	161,084	176,019	171,005	172,225	160,663	179,322	177,145	119,183
Initial investment – cost savings	1,007,341	858,490	696,755	522,315	359,107	192,482	14,335	–146,749	(Payback in Feb 2006)						

1. Production plan = 175,511 tonnes/year (production budget for the year 2004)

2. Steam consumption = 2.36 tonnes steam/tonne paper (bunker oil consumption = 145 litres/tonne paper); unit consumption for year 2003

3. Calculation steam savings 1.0%

   Steam reduction 1% of 2.36 = 0.0236 tonne steam/tonne paper
   1 tonne steam = 61.35 litres of bunker oil
   0.0236 × 61.35 = 1.448 litres/tonne paper
   1.448 × 8.2 baht/litres = THB11.87/tonne paper

   Cost savings 11.87 × 13,500 tonnes/month = THB160,245/month

4. Investment cost THB1,132,061

5. Payback 1,132,061/160,245 = 7.1 months

Environmental risk assessment and environmental long-term planning

Environmental risk assessment

Although the company does not use any formal environmental risk assessment systems, such as the internationally accepted risk assessment standard *AS/NZS ISO 31000* (e.g. ISO 2009a), the water management situation draws upon issues raised by such a standard. However, in this EMA analysis no attempt was made to consult with different stakeholders on the issue; instead, the starting point was recognition by management that water shortages are of growing concern. Figures 11.2 and 11.3 indicate the noticeable decrease in rainfall and number of rainy days in the area during the period 2000–2005. This raised the matter of long-term and regular planning to address this important emerging risk. The impact of the reduced rainfall is to lower water supplies in the river which feeds into the Pranchinburi site and production process, thereby making alternative water sources important for longer than usual each year. The main

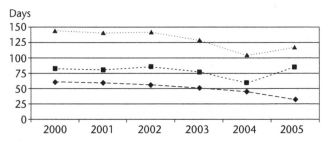

Top line (▲): total; middle line (■): second half of the year;
bottom line (♦): first half of the year.

FIGURE 11.2 Days of rain per year in Prachinburi Province (2000–2005).

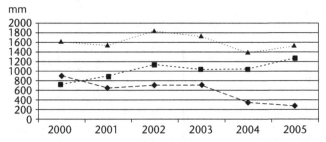

Top line (▲): total; middle line (■): second half of the year;
bottom line (♦): first half of the year.

FIGURE 11.3 Annual rainfall in Prachinburi Province (2000–2005).

alternative source of water is the company's ponds. Production levels are yet to be affected but additional demand for water caused by the installation of a new power plant in August 2006 increased the probability that water will be unavailable at some future time and production will have to be stopped.

Environmental risk assessment is a tool which provides a systematic analysis of the types of risk faced, likelihood of occurrence, and consequences, as a basis for stimulating action to accept, reduce, or remove potential risks. The consequences of a water shortage can be classified as severe, but the probability of water running out varies from month to month, depending on the accessible supply, usage, and an acceptable safety stock. Environmental risk assessment provides a formal mechanism for assessing the risk. Hence, the use of physical information about predicted water flows based on evidence is essential information. The purpose of gathering past information and predicting possible water shortages is to ensure that production can continue. Lost production means lost contribution. Monetary information about the income associated with lost production made environmental risk analysis of the developments in water supply at the Prachinburi mill of additional significance. This drives the need for long-term environmental planning expressed in physical and monetary terms and operated on a routine basis. The following sections provide greater detail about the analysis of changes in local environmental conditions (Figure 11.1: Box 12) through statistical data provided by the government and an analysis of changes of water flows (Boxes 11 and 15) caused by the installation of the new power plant. Based on this information, changes in water supply and usage are predicted for the next two years (Box 16) and conclusions drawn from risk analysis and assessment.

Ex-post analysis of change in environmental conditions

Evidence indicates that the total number of rainy days per annum is decreasing (see Figure 11.2 and Table 11.2). The ex-post analysis (Figure 11.1: Box 12) illustrates how the decline is largely attributable to a decrease in rainy days in the first half of the year, a reduction of 50 per cent between 2000 and 2005. Yet in 2005 there is a larger number of rainy days in the second half of the year than in 2000. Hence, a shift in rain patterns means that for six months of each year there is almost no rain. Rainfall in the first half of the year has decreased from about 900 mm in 2000 to 275 mm in 2005 (see Figure 11.3 and Table 11.2). The management predicts that the period without rain will increase from six to eight months, presenting a significant risk to business operations. If this trend continues, water supply for production at Prachinburi mill is going to be threatened during the first half of each year.

However, the mill secures its water supply for use in the dry season through two ponds located on site with a total capacity of 830,000 m³. If the change in

TABLE 11.2 Days of rain and rainfall in first and second half of the years in Prachinburi province (2000–2005)

Year	Period	Days of rain	Rainfall (mm)
2000	1st half	61	894
	2nd half	83	729
2001	1st half	60	651
	2nd half	81	902
2002	1st half	56	711
	2nd half	86	1,138
2003	1st half	52	708
	2nd half	77	1,035
2004	1st half	45	339
	2nd half	59	1,053
2005	1st half	32	276
	2nd half	85	1,273

rainfall pattern persists over time, the available volume may not be enough to support ongoing operations. As two other pulp and paper companies in the surrounding area also use the river's water, demand from the production of all three companies will most likely exceed the available supply of water.

Analysis of change of water flows and use

The analysis of change of water flows caused by the installation of the new power plant is based on a comparison of water flows at present with the predicted situation from August 2006 (Figure 11.1: Boxes 11 and 15). Water enters the mill water plant from the ponds and is distributed to the paper mill and the bunker oil boiler, with certain proportions being released through evaporation and steam (see Figure 11.4). The analysis of water flows and use (Figure 11.1: Box 11) shows that the remaining water used in the pulp and paper mill process is then treated as wastewater, with some being recycled back into production and the remainder passing on to the polishing pond for future use in the mill or into the river at an acceptable quality level once treated. With investment in the new power plant from August 2006, the volume of water required increased (see Figure 11.5). The analysis of predicted water flows (Figure 11.1: Box 15) shows that the new power plant consumes an additional 2,500 m^3 of water per day with 960 m^3 per day of additional wastewater being created.

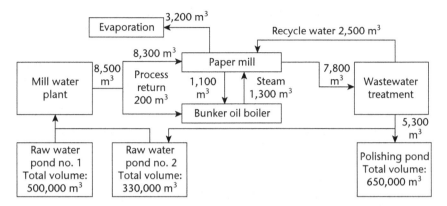

FIGURE 11.4 Flow diagram water use in 2005 (present situation). Note: m³ for ponds total volume; otherwise daily flow.

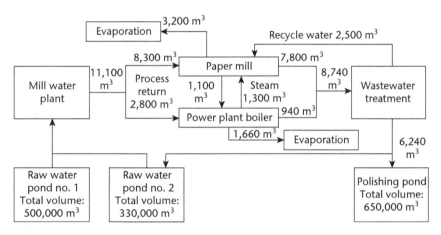

FIGURE 11.5 Flow diagram of future water use from August 2006 onwards (situation with new power plant).
Note: m³ for ponds total volume; otherwise daily flow.

Predicted long-term changes in water supply and usage

Given the context outlined above with supplies of water in decline and demand increasing, risk analysis can be used to provide information about how these risks should be managed. In short, risk treatment involves identifying the range of options for managing risks in the circumstances identified, assessing the available options, and implementing risk management plans to accept, control, or implement investment and/or actions to prevent unacceptable risks occurring (ISO 2009b). From late 2005 into early 2006, a detailed analysis of expected water supply and demand was undertaken as the basis for any risk management decision by Thai Cane Paper. The importance of EMA comes to the fore in that it provides a tool necessary for addressing perceived risky situations.

The prediction of water supply and demand at the Prachinburi site on an ad hoc basis for the years 2006 and 2007 (Figure 11.1: Box 16) revealed significant changes from the current situation. Table 11.3 shows the amount of water available with storage in the two existing ponds (row 1) and the pond water used for the production facilities and other facilities at the Prachinburi site (row 3). The predicted water demand takes the start-up of the new power plant in August 2006 into account (an increase from 255,000 to 330,000 m³). The amount of water which is pumped from the river to the ponds (row 2) is limited to 160,000 m³ per month in the dry season (first half of the year), whereas ponds can be refilled to the maximum of pond capacity during wet season thanks to quasi-unlimited river water availability (maximum capacity of pumps 803,500 m³). In this period of the year, water supply capacity at the Prachinburi site is usually between three and four months, in other words production could last for three to four months without further water supply from the river. In the other half of the year, this capacity decreases continuously because water usage for pulp and paper production exceeds the amount of water that can be taken from the river. However, water supply capacity is never below one month.

In the past, the ponds used to be refilled in June and July every year. The predicted expansion of the period without rain from six to eight months entails that in the years 2006 and 2007 ponds can be refilled only in September. As a result, the water supply capacity in 2006 drops below one month in July and, accompanied by the start-up of the new power plant, water shortage is caused in August of the same year. From 2007 onwards, in every dry season the increased water demand, caused by the new power plant, will be exceeding by more than twofold the amount of water that can be pumped from the river to the ponds. The extended dry season along with the increased water demand cause water shortages in four months in 2007 (May–August) and a decline in production by half between the months June and August.

The analysis indicates several risks for Thai Cane Paper. First, water supply for pulp and paper production is most likely to be at risk during certain periods, leading to a decline in production for up to four months. A production stop of one month would cost Thai Cane Paper THB60 million (€1,198,600). The financial risks from a 50 per cent decline in production over a period of three months in 2007, as predicted above, would equal about THB90 million (€1,797,900). Similar figures can be extrapolated to future years.

Second, discharge of wastewater can become more difficult if there is less river water, which makes wastewater discharge more obvious and dangerous for the aquatic life because of higher concentration of pollutants. The government might extend the six-month period of wastewater discharge prohibition

TABLE 11.3 Predicted changes in water supply and usage for 2006 and 2007

	Jan	Feb	Mar	Apr	May	Jun	Jul	Aug	Sep	Oct	Nov	Dec
2005												
Water in pond (m³)	830,000	539,400	447,000	368,000	313,600	246,000	820,800	830,000	830,000	830,000	830,000	830,000
River water pumped to pond (m³)	0	160,000	160,000	160,000	160,000	803,500	263,500	244,000	204,000	227,000	244,000	261,000
Water used from pond (m³)	290,600	252,400	239,000	214,400	227,600	228,700	254,300	244,000	204,000	227,000	244,000	244,000
Balance at end of month (m³)	539,400	447,000	368,000	313,600	246,000	820,800	830,000	830,000	830,000	830,000	830,000	847,000
Water supply capacity (months)	1.9	1.8	1.5	1.5	1.1	3.6	3.3	3.4	4.1	3.7	3.4	3.5
2006												
Water in pond (m³)	830,000	735,000	640,000	545,000	450,000	355,000	260,000	165,000	0	470,500	830,000	830,000
River water pumped to pond (m³)	160,000	160,000	160,000	160,000	160,000	160,000	160,000	160,000	803,500	692,500	333,000	333,000
Water used from pond (m³)	255,000	255,000	255,000	255,000	255,000	255,000	255,000	333,000	333,000	333,000	333,000	333,000
Balance at end of month (m³)	735,000	640,000	545,000	450,000	355,000	260,000	165,000	(8,000)	470,500	830,000	830,000	830,000
Water supply capacity (months)	2.9	2.5	2.1	1.8	1.4	1.0	0.6	(0.0)	1.4	2.5	2.5	2.5
2007												
Water in pond (m³)	830,000	657,000	484,000	311,000	138,000	0	0	0	0	470,500	830,000	830,000
River water pumped to pond (m³)	160,000	160,000	160,000	160,000	160,000	160,000	160,000	160,000	803,500	692,500	333,000	333,000
Water used from pond (m³)	333,000	333,000	333,000	333,000	333,000	333,000	333,000	333,000	333,000	333,000	333,000	333,000
Balance at end of month (m³)	657,000	484,000	311,000	138,000	(35,000)	(173,000)	(173,000)	(173,000)	470,500	830,000	830,000	830,000
Water supply capacity (months)	2.0	1.5	0.9	0.4	(0.1)	(0.5)	(0.5)	(0.5)	1.4	2.5	2.5	2.5

as a response to reduced rainfall at certain times of the year. In addition, social movements in the surrounding area and communities that complain about the water pollution add to the external pressure on the company and, in turn, might again affect the regulatory situation. With decreasing rainfall in Prachinburi province and communities which depend on water from the same river as the three companies use for their pulp and paper production, industry will be under particular surveillance. In this context, carelessness can be seen as a big threat to reputation.

Finally, the consequence of the water shortage trend continuing would be very severe if production were required to cease as a result. No safety stocks have been included in the analysis but they add to the riskiness of the situation. In order to avoid shortages in water supply at the Prachinburi site and to reduce environmental, social, and financial risks, the company decided to monitor changes in environmental conditions and build a long-term environmental planning system. This included a long-term prediction of water demand from production and other facilities and a prediction of water supply conditions. In January 2006, with the total water capacity of the existing ponds at 830,000 m^3, the question from a long-term perspective was whether an investment in additional pond capacity would make sense, working on the assumption that larger volumes of water are to be stored pending their use in future drier periods and/or whether water demand can be reduced by investing in closed-loop and water-recycling technologies. No assessment of the likelihood of current trends continuing was available and so several possible scenarios were developed. The next sub-section describes the environmental long-term planning system and possible scenarios.

Environmental long-term planning and related tools

There are important implications for water management at Thai Cane Paper flowing from the risk analysis. Investments to reduce any predicted shortages in water supply need to be identified and assessed through, for example, the use of ad hoc scenario analysis (Figure 11.1: Box 16). The immediate issue is for such investment scenarios to be considered and implemented by August 2006 to avoid restrictions in production and power generation.

The various scenarios for water supply and demand at Thai Cane Paper can be drawn into three situations: two extreme possible outcomes and a most-likely situation. If a company is risk averse it will tend towards investments which reduce risk to a minimum acceptable level. Hence, when examining how future water supply can be secured to meet expected demand in order to avoid financial, environmental, and social risks from water scarcity, the first possibility is to expand the inventory of water controlled on site through the build-up of additional pond storage capacity. A second possibility is for recycling technologies to be introduced. Finally, a third possibility is to invest in a combination of these two types of investment with additional storage capacity and recycling being introduced. These three scenarios are examined below.

Scenario 1: investment in new pond, no further investments

Given available land on site, investment in a new third pond would expand the capacity to store water by a maximum additional amount of 500,000 m³, increasing the total to 1,330,000 m³ (see Figure 11.6 and Table 11.4). The result of constructing and using such a pond is that water would still be in short supply during August. The water stocks and flows from this physical investment would not be sufficient to completely remove the risks from supply fluctuations.

Scenario 2: investment in new water-recycling technology, no further investments

In contrast with Scenario 1, investment in new water-recycling technology would reduce demand for pond water by 90,000 m³ per month, a reduction of 3,000 m³ per day (see Figure 11.6 and Table 11.5). The initial aim of the company's Recycle Water Initiative was to recycle an additional amount of 5,000 m³ per day and this target would not be met. However, no shortages would be expected in any month during the planning period (see Table 11.5) but water supply capacity remains low at 0.7 of a month in August 2007.

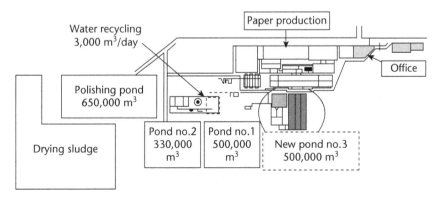

FIGURE 11.6 New pond and water recycling at Prachinburi mill.

TABLE 11.4 Long-term planning of water supply and use for 2006 and 2007, Scenario I (with investment in new pond with 500,000 m³ capacity a total of 1,330,000 m³)

	Jan	Feb	Mar	Apr	May	Jun	Jul	Aug	Sep	Oct	Nov	Dec
2006												
Water in pond (m³)	1,330,000	1,157,000	984,000	811,000	638,000	465,000	292,000	165,000	0	470,500	941,000	1330000
River water pumped to pond (m³)	160,000	160,000	160,000	160,000	160,000	160,000	160,000	160,000	803,500	803,500	722,000	243,000
Water used from pond (m³)	333,000	333,000	333,000	333,000	333,000	333,000	333,000	333,000	333,000	333,000	333,000	333,000
Balance at end of month (m³)	1,157,000	984,000	811,000	638,000	465,000	292,000	119,000	(8,000)	470,500	941,000	1,330,000	1,240,000
Water supply capacity (months)	3.5	3.0	2.4	1.9	1.4	0.9	0.4	(0.0)	1.4	2.8	4.0	4.0
2007												
Water in pond (m³)	1,330,000	1,157,000	984,000	811,000	638,000	465,000	292,000	119,000	–	470,500	941,000	1,330,000
River water pumped to pond (m³)	160,000	160,000	160,000	160,000	160,000	160,000	160,000	160,000	803,500	803,500	722,000	333,000
Water used from pond (m³)	333,000	333,000	333,000	333,000	333,000	333,000	333,000	333,000	333,000	333,000	333,000	333,000
Balance at end of month (m³)	1,157,000	984,000	811,000	638,000	465,000	292,000	119,000	(54,000)	470,500	941,000	1,330,000	1,330,000
Water supply capacity (months)	3.5	3.0	2.4	1.9	1.4	0.9	0.4	(0.2)	1.4	2.8	4.0	4.0

TABLE 11.5 Long-term planning of water supply and use for 2006 and 2007, Scenario II (with investment in water recycling; reduce demand for pond water by 90,000 m³/month)

	Jan	Feb	Mar	Apr	May	Jun	Jul	Aug	Sep	Oct	Nov	Dec
2006												
Water in pond (m³)								165,000	82,000	642,500	830,000	830,000
River water pumped to pond (m³)								160,000	803,500	430,500	243,000	243,000
Water used from pond (m³)								243,000	243,000	243,000	243,000	243,000
Balance at end of month (m³)								82,000	642,500	830,000	830,000	830,000
Water supply capacity (months)								0.3	2.6	3.4	3.4	3.4
2007												
Water in pond (m³)	830,000	747,000	664,000	581,000	498,000	415,000	332,000	249,000	166,000	726,500	830,000	830,000
River water pumped to pond (m³)	160,000	160,000	160,000	160,000	160,000	160,000	160,000	160,000	803,500	346,500	243,000	243,000
Water used from pond (m³)	243,000	243,000	243,000	243,000	243,000	243,000	243,000	243,000	243,000	243,000	243,000	243,000
Balance at end of month (m³)	747,000	664,000	581,000	498,000	415,000	332,000	249,000	166,000	726,500	830,000	830,000	830,000
Water supply capacity (months)	3.1	2.7	2.4	2.0	1.7	1.4	1.0	0.7	3.0	3.4	3.4	3.4

Scenario 3: investment in both projects

The capacity of the new pond varies from 100,000 to 500,000 m³ (see Tables 11.6a–11.6e). With investment(s) in water-recycling technology combined with the building of additional pond capacity, the possibility of future water shortages is reduced to the optimal level. Figures in Table 11.6 illustrate the results from investment in recycling and different levels of additional storage pond capacity. The stock of water on hand is thereby increased from a low amount of 1.1 months (100,000 m³) to 2.7 months in August 2007 (500,000 m³). Any decision by the management about the level of pond capacity to be developed will depend on expected rises in production, the conviction that rainfall patterns will continue to get worse rather than revert to normal (average) levels, and other speculative matters. However, the EMA information from the potential environmental flows in the long term, based on current expectations for demand and supply, provides support for the decision made. For example, in this case it indicates that the Recycle Water Initiative was slightly overoptimistic in the target set for recycling. However, setting a challenging target may be what was required to at least reduce water consumption through recycling by the amount of 3,000 m³ per day. The gap between a technical resolution of the water shortage problem, requiring a reduction of about 3,000 m³ per day, and the higher, more difficult to achieve targets needed to bring this technical solution into being should not be ignored (Hansen and Van der Stede 2004).

Based on the different scenarios outlined above and the management attitude towards accepting the risk of water shortage, Thai Cane Paper decided to invest in both projects (total investment costs calculated at THB27 million = €539,369), by increasing the recycling of water by 3,000 m³ per day, taking the total to 5,500 m³ per day, as well as increasing pond capacity by 500,000 m³ to a total of 1,330,000 m³ (see Figure 11.7). The new position provided a maximum capacity of water in the three ponds of 5.5 months (see Table 11.6e).

Short- and long-term planning of future water flows is of critical importance if future production is to continue uninterrupted. In particular, physical stock and flow information will be needed on a regular basis to assess changes in environmental conditions in order to avoid the negative impacts of water shortage (e.g. monthly, twice a year, annually) (Figure 11.1: Boxes 13 and 14). The integration of short-term with long-term planning is important and will involve feedback about the success of the investments undertaken to rectify predicted long-term water shortages (Figure 11.1: Box 12).

Discussion

Water supply is a critical issue for pulp and paper organisations and has a high potential to create significant environmental problems for local communities

TABLE 11.6 Long-term planning of water supply and use for 2006 and 2007, Scenario II (with investment in water recycling and new pond)

(a) Water recycling and new pond 100,000 m³

	Jan	Feb	Mar	Apr	May	Jun	Jul	Aug	Sep	Oct	Nov	Dec
2006												
Water in pond (m³)	930,000	847,000	764,000	681,000	598,000	515,000	432,000	165,000	82,000	642,500	930,000	930,000
River water pumped to pond (m³)	160,000	160,000	160,000	160,000	160,000	160,000	160,000	160,000	803,500	530,500	243,000	243,000
Water used from pond (m³)	243,000	243,000	243,000	243,000	243,000	243,000	243,000	243,000	243,000	243,000	243,000	243,000
Balance at end of month (m³)	847,000	764,000	681,000	598,000	515,000	432,000	349,000	82,000	642,500	930,000	930,000	930,000
Water supply capacity (months)	3.5	3.1	2.8	2.5	2.1	1.8	1.4	0.3	2.6	3.8	3.8	3.8
2007												
Water in pond (m³)	930,000	847,000	764,000	681,000	598,000	515,000	432,000	349,000	266,000	826,500	930,000	930,000
River water pumped to pond (m³)	160,000	160,000	160,000	160,000	160,000	160,000	160,000	160,000	803,500	346,500	243,000	243,000
Water used from pond (m³)	243,000	243,000	243,000	243,000	243,000	243,000	243,000	243,000	243,000	243,000	243,000	243,000
Balance at end of month (m³)	847,000	764,000	681,000	598,000	515,000	432,000	349,000	266,000	826,500	930,000	930,000	930,000
Water supply capacity (months)	3.5	3.1	2.8	2.5	2.1	1.8	1.4	1.1	3.4	3.8	3.8	3.8

TABLE 11.6 (continued)

(b) Water recycling and new pond 200,000 m³

	Jan	Feb	Mar	Apr	May	Jun	Jul	Aug	Sep	Oct	Nov	Dec
2006												
Water in pond (m³)								165,000	82,000	642,500	1,030,000	1,030,000
River water pumped to pond (m³)								160,000	803,500	630,500	243,000	243,000
Water used from pond (m³)								243,000	243,000	243,000	243,000	243,000
Balance at end of month (m³)								82,000	642,500	1,030,000	1,030,000	1,030,000
Water supply capacity (months)								0.3	2.6	4.2	4.2	4.2
2007												
Water in pond (m³)	1,030,000	947,000	864,000	781,000	698,000	615,000	532,000	449,000	366,000	926,500	1,030,000	1,030,000
River water pumped to pond (m³)	160,000	160,000	160,000	160,000	160,000	160,000	160,000	160,000	803,500	346,500	243,000	243,000
Water used from pond (m³)	243,000	243,000	243,000	243,000	243,000	243,000	243,000	243,000	243,000	243,000	243,000	243,000
Balance at end of month (m³)	947,000	864,000	781,000	698,000	615,000	532,000	449,000	366,000	926,500	1,030,000	1,030,000	1,030,000
Water supply capacity (months)	3.9	3.6	3.2	2.9	2.5	2.2	1.8	1.5	3.8	4.2	4.2	4.2

(c) Water recycling and new pond 300,000 m^3

	Jan	Feb	Mar	Apr	May	Jun	Jul	Aug	Sep	Oct	Nov	Dec
2006												
Water in pond (m^3)								165,000	82,000	642,500	1,130,000	1,130,000
River water pumped to pond (m^3)								160,000	803,500	730,500	243,000	243,000
Water used from pond (m^3)								243,000	243,000	243,000	243,000	243,000
Balance at end of month (m^3)								82,000	642,500	1,130,000	1,130,000	1,130,000
Water supply capacity (months)								0.3	2.6	4.7	4.7	4.7
2007												
Water in pond (m^3)	1,130,000	1,047,000	964,000	881,000	798,000	715,000	632,000	549,000	466,000	1,026,500	1,130,000	1,130,000
River water pumped to pond (m^3)	160,000	160,000	160,000	160,000	160,000	160,000	160,000	160,000	803,500	346,500	243,000	243,000
Water used from pond (m^3)	243,000	243,000	243,000	243,000	243,000	243,000	243,000	243,000	243,000	243,000	243,000	243,000
Balance at end of month (m^3)	1,047,000	964,000	881,000	798,000	715,000	632,000	549,000	466,000	1,026,500	1,130,000	1,130,000	1,130,000
Water supply capacity (months)	4.3	4.0	3.6	3.3	2.9	2.6	2.3	1.9	4.2	4.7	4.7	4.7

TABLE 11.6 (continued)

(d) Water recycling and new pond 400,000 m³

	Jan	Feb	Mar	Apr	May	Jun	Jul	Aug	Sep	Oct	Nov	Dec
2006												
Water in pond (m³)								165,000	82,000	642,500	1,203,000	1,230,000
River water pumped to pond (m³)								160,000	803,500	803,500	270,000	243,000
Water used from pond (m³)								243,000	243,000	243,000	243,000	243,000
Balance at end of month (m³)								82,000	642,500	1,203,000	1,230,000	1,230,000
Water supply capacity (months)								0.3	2.6	5.0	5.1	5.1
2007												
Water in pond (m³)	1,230,000	1,147,000	1,064,000	981,000	898,000	815,000	732,000	649,000	566,000	1,126,500	1,230,000	1,230,000
River water pumped to pond (m³)	160,000	160,000	160,000	160,000	160,000	160,000	160,000	160,000	803,500	346,500	243,000	243,000
Water used from pond (m³)	243,000	243,000	243,000	243,000	243,000	243,000	243,000	243,000	243,000	243,000	243,000	243,000
Balance at end of month (m³)	1,147,000	1,064,000	981,000	898,000	815,000	732,000	649,000	566,000	1,126,500	1,230,000	1,230,000	1,230,000
Water supply capacity (months)	4.7	4.4	4.0	3.7	3.4	3.0	2.7	2.3	4.6	5.1	5.1	5.1

(e) Water recycling and new pond 500,000 m³

	Jan	Feb	Mar	Apr	May	Jun	Jul	Aug	Sep	Oct	Nov	Dec
2006												
Water in pond (m³)								165,000	82,000	642,500	1,203,000	1,330,000
River water pumped to pond (m³)								160,000	803,500	803,500	370,000	243,000
Water used from pond (m³)								243,000	243,000	243,000	243,000	243,000
Balance at end of month (m³)								82,000	642,500	1,203,000	1,330,000	1,330,000
Water supply capacity (months)								0.3	2.6	5.0	5.5	5.5
2007												
Water in pond (m³)	1,330,000	1,247,000	1,164,000	1,081,000	998,000	915,000	832,000	749,000	666,000	1,226,500	1,330,000	1,330,000
River water pumped to pond (m³)	160,000	160,000	160,000	160,000	160,000	160,000	160,000	160,000	803,500	346,500	243,000	243,000
Water used from pond (m³)	243,000	243,000	243,000	243,000	243,000	243,000	243,000	243,000	243,000	243,000	243,000	243,000
Balance at end of month (m³)	1,247,000	1,164,000	1,081,000	998,000	915,000	832,000	749,000	666,000	1,226,500	1,330,000	1,330,000	1,330,000
Water supply capacity (months)	5.1	4.8	4.4	4.1	3.8	3.4	3.1	2.7	5.0	5.5	5.5	5.5

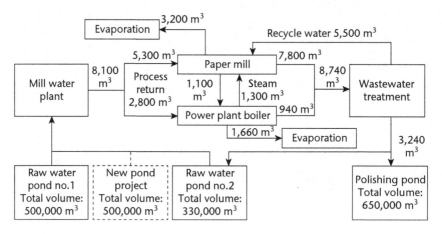

FIGURE 11.7 New flow diagram.
Note: m³ for ponds total volume; otherwise daily flow.

as well as production problems for firms. Water has long been regarded as a free good by many organisations in the pulp and paper industry. The threat of water shortage leads these organisations to commence the gathering of physical information about water stocks and flows through EMA, to ensure that production does not cease, employees are not laid off for short periods, water supply is not reduced, and contribution margin continues to flow into the companies.

Disposal of wastewater is equally significant as a concern for firms in the industry and local communities, with the government restricting the disposal of wastewater into the river for six months of the year. Water shortage risks were perceived as important during the period of the case study. Two investments were made, in new water- and steam-reducing technology and monitoring systems, and ex-post assessment confirmed their merits in financial and environmental terms.

In the case examined, demand for water increases as production throughput increases. It also increases as other uses arise, such as for the new coal-fired boiler. Likewise, variable weather patterns lead to changes in the supply of water and encourage analysis of the associated business risk. EMA provides clear support to this dimension of water management.

Although this was significant to management, and planning processes were implemented, water issues were never seen as being of sufficient importance to report to shareholders in the annual financial report. For example, in the 2008 annual report risks facing the business specify only management equity stake in the business, credit risk, interest rate and foreign currency risks, fair value risk, and raw material price variation risk (Thai Cane Paper 2008a). However, formal risk indicators and levels of tolerance are set by the Management Committee in accordance with expectations of the Audit Committee (Thai Cane Paper 2008a: 275). Water management issues and associated risk analysis remained an operating and investment concern for management to grapple with, rather than an issue to be disclosed to investors. Internal EMA was used to confirm the need for changes in water storage and recycling practices and these were viewed as a possible technical constraint on the continuity of operations in the dry season.

Somewhat in contrast, Thai Cane Paper's energy reduction plans have also been successful. A cogeneration plant to produce steam and electricity was installed and started in the fourth quarter of 2006. Coal and plastic waste (as well as other scrap mixed with paper waste, which was the major raw material, including fibre sludge drained from manufacturing process through the wastewater treatment system) replaced bunker oil to fuel the plant in 2007. The investment enabled the company to save approximately THB1 million (€22,635) per day in energy costs (Thai Cane Paper 2008b: 9). Hence, wastewater treatment has become an integral part of the integrated solution to energy and water management at Thai Cane Paper, as has the regular provision of information from the EMA system in order to support regular planning of water supply and demand.

In the future, global warming could mean further changes in the seasonal supplies of water and where shortage is anticipated this could lead to the introduction of pricing of water supplies (Rogers, de Silva, and Bhatia 2002). In these circumstances EMA as a support for water management is likely only to grow in significance.

Conclusion

The aim of the Thai Cane Paper case was to explore possibilities for operations management resulting from the use of EMA tools to cope with increased environmental interest and related change. The case study explored the manifold use of EMA for operations management in the pulp and paper industry. Using a case study of a company in Thailand, the chapter first demonstrated the importance of ex-post appraisal as an ongoing check on the assumed costs and benefits of investment calculations in the environmental context. Based on the analysis of historical environmental data, it then explored the support of EMA in assessing short- and long-term environmental impacts and how environmental risks can be taken into account as one of the parameters in production planning and control.

Production planning under environmental constraints presents a new and increasingly important challenge for industry. The information that a project team can obtain from the use of EMA tools is of considerable value in this context. For instance, in our case study, gathering past information and predicting possible water shortages ensured continued production and avoided lost contribution. This drove the need for long-term environmental planning expressed in monetary and physical terms. Previous studies into environmental management and operations management have hardly looked at the assessment and management of long-term risks associated with the use of environmental resources and implications for production plans. The exploration of the usefulness of the EMA framework, within the case study setting of a Thai paper and pulp company, may help to increase the awareness of the importance of this area of operations management and encourage further consideration and integration of environmental risk in production planning and control at other companies.

Finally, a collaborative approach between the production manager, environmental management staff with environmental engineering experience, and the accountant was necessary for success. It is useful to adopt such an interdisciplinary approach in order to generate information that supports risk analysis, assessment, and long-term planning in the context of environmental management issues.

References

Ali, M. and Sreekrishnan, T.R. (2001) 'Aquatic toxicity from pulp and paper mill effluents: a review', *Advances in Environmental Research*, 5: 175–196.

Barla, P. (2007) 'ISO 14001 certification and environmental performance in Quebec's pulp and paper industry', *Journal of Environmental Economics and Management*, 53: 291–306.

Burritt, R.L. (2005) 'Environmental risk management and environmental management accounting: developing linkages', in Rikhardsson, P., Bennett, M., Bouma, J.J., and Schaltegger, S. (eds) *Implementing environmental management accounting: status and challenges*, Dordrecht: Kluwer Academic Publishers, pp. 123–141.

Burritt, R.L., Hahn, T., and Schaltegger, S. (2002) 'Towards a comprehensive framework for environmental management accounting: links between business actors and environmental management accounting tools', *Australian Accounting Review*, 12: 39–50.

Hansen, S.C. and Van der Stede, W.A. (2004) 'Multiple facets of budgeting: an exploratory analysis', *Management Accounting Research*, 15: 415–439.

ICFPA (International Council of Forest and Paper Associations) (2006) *Sustainability: the forest and paper industry – on its way to sustainability* [online – accessed on 27 June 2011]. Available from Internet: http://www.icfpa.org/_documents/ICFPAStatement1.pdf.

ISO (International Organization for Standardization) (2009a) *ISO 31000 Risk management: guidelines and principles*, Geneva: ISO.

ISO (2009b) *ISO 31000 Environmental Management Risk Standard*, Geneva: ISO.

Lang, C. (2002) *The pulp invasion: the international pulp and paper industry in the Mekong region*, Montevideo: World Rainforest Movement.

Moore, W.E. and Rittof, T.J. (2005) *Matching water treatment options to power plant requirements, Part I* [online – accessed on 27 June 2011]. Available from Internet: http://www.waterworld.com.

Parthasarathy, G. and Krishnagopalan, G. (1999) 'Effluent reduction and control of non-process elements towards a cleaner Kraft pulp mill', *Clean Products and Processes*, 1: 264–277.

Rogers, P., de Silva, R., and Bhatia, R. (2002) 'Water is an economic good: how to use price to promote equity, efficiency and sustainability', *Water Policy*, 4: 1–17.

Servos, M.R., Munkittrick, K.R., Carey J.H., and Kraak, G.J. (1996) *Environmental fate and effects of paper and pulp mill effluents*, Delray Beach, FL: St. Lucie Press.

Sonnenfeld, D.A. (1998a) 'Social movements, environment, and technology in Indonesia's pulp and paper industry', *Asia Pacific Viewpoint*, 39: 95–110.

Sonnenfeld, D.A. (1998b) 'From brown to green? Late industrialization, social conflict, and adoption of environmental technologies in Thailand's pulp industry', *Organization & Environment*, 11: 59–87.

Thai Cane Paper (2008a) *Annual report 2008*, Bangkok: Thai Cane Paper.

Thai Cane Paper (2008b) *Minutes of the ordinary general meeting of shareholders for the year 2008 (attachment 1)*, Bangkok: Thai Cane Paper.

Thant, M.M. and Charmondusit, K. (2009) 'Eco-efficient assessment of pulp and paper industry in Myanmar', *Clean Technologies and Environmental Policy*, 12: 427–439.

12

DECOUPLING ECONOMIC GROWTH FROM POLLUTION

Tan Loc Food, Vietnam

Introduction

This case study focuses on the application of environmental management accounting (EMA) at Tan Loc Food Processing Co. (referred to as Tan Loc), a small, family-run enterprise in Hue, the ancient capital in the centre of Vietnam. The company manually produces local food specialities and does not possess specialised production equipment. Nevertheless, environmental issues such as odour, organic waste, and wastewater treatment are of importance. Prior to the case study no environmental management or environmental accounting was in place. Hence, the implementation of EMA aimed at providing basic information for increasing eco-efficiency at the current production site as well as for a planned new site.

The case highlights the applicability of EMA even in very small companies and reveals that a simple, ad hoc approach is required in the beginning, starting with the collection and analysis of the company's environmental and related financial performance at present (Figure 12.1: Boxes 3 and 11), followed by the identification and assesment of measures to reduce environmental impacts, and increase environment-related financial performance (Boxes 7 and 15). To anticipate developments, some improvement measures concerning the new plant were discussed and broadly assessed (Box 8).

Decision setting

Tan Loc is a family-run business in Hue City, Hue Province. The company is managed by Mrs and Mr Phuc, who own the company and make all important decisions. They employ about 70 workers, mostly women. Tan Loc produces various local food specialities, such as shrimp sauce, fish paste, pickled aubergines, and soy sauce. The company sells its products to retailers and shops

		Monetary EMA		Physical EMA	
		Short-term	Long-term	Short-term	Long-term
Past-orientated	Routinely generated	Environmental cost accounting [1]	Environment-induced capital expenditure and revenue [2]	Material and energy flow accounting [9]	Environmental capital impact accounting [10]
	Ad hoc	Ex-post assessment of relevant environmental costing decisions [3]	Ex-post inventory assessment of projects [4]	Ex-post assessment of short-term environmental impacts [11]	Ex-post inventory appraisal of physical environmental investments [12]
Future-orientated	Routinely generated	Monetary environmental budgeting [5]	Environmental long-term financial planning [6]	Physical environmental budgeting [13]	Environmental long-term physical planning [14]
	Ad hoc	Relevant environmental costing [7]	Monetary environmental investment appraisal [8]	Tools designed to predict relevant environmental impacts [15]	Physical environmental investment appraisal [16]

FIGURE 12.1 Application of the EMA framework (Burritt, Hahn, and Schaltegger 2002) to Tan Loc Food.
Note: Dark (light) grey boxes represent the major (minor) EMA applications.

in central Vietnam, mainly in the Hue region (see Figure 12.2). Tan Loc's employees prepare the food products in the traditional way with much manual labour involved. The quality and special taste of Tan Loc's products have won several high-ranked Vietnamese quality awards, among them the Vietnamese Gold Star 2004.

Economic situation

The business performance of Tan Loc is excellent for Vietnamese small- to medium-sized enterprises (SMEs). The company has been able to increase production year by year. However, Tan Loc's rapid growth has also lead to capacity problems. The company is situated in two adjacent houses in a residential neighbourhood in Hue and one house on the outskirts of Hue, where fish paste is produced. These production facilities are unsuitable for an enlargement of the business. As Tan Loc intends to expand its production threefold in the next five years, access to new production facilities is vital. The company plans to move to a newly established industrial estate outside Hue. When the case study was conducted the owners had developed the first draft of a construction plan in collaboration with local authorities. The company started to design the set-up of new technical equipment. It planned to automate those parts of production which do not affect the taste and quality of the products.

FIGURE 12.2 Tan Loc Food products at Hue railway station.

Environmental situation

Tan Loc's current production does not cause particularly harmful environmental impacts. The company consumes electricity and generates small amounts of solid waste and wastewater. It also causes some emissions because of truck-based transportation of goods to local retailers. Until now the only distinctive environmental issue has been malodorous smells, mainly caused by fish preparation. To avoid any trouble with the local community, Tan Loc removed fish paste production to a house in the outskirts of Hue two years ago. Other environmental issues are not perceived as critical. In consequence, Tan Loc has not adopted an environmental management system or other environmental measures.

Production processes

Tan Loc products are well known for their taste, which originates from the family's inherited recipes. Production facilities and devices to produce these specialties are relatively basic. Processes to produce the different products include:

- washing and chopping of raw materials (cleaning fish and vegetables, removing shrimp heads, chopping vegetables, etc.);
- salting and storing of raw materials (pickled materials are stored for a few days to two months);
- preparation of flavours (mixing sauces by cooking chilli, sugar and further additives depending on the type of product);
- mixing and mashing of raw materials, flavourings, and further ingredients;
- bottling, labelling, and packaging of products; and
- delivering products to shops and distributors.

Various processes and activities are illustrated in Figure 12.3 in chronological order starting from the top left and going to the bottom right corner: slicing of vegetables, chopping of mushrooms, salting of shrimps, pickling of shrimps, mixing and cooking of flavouring sauces, mashing of food sauce ingredients, bottling, sealing, and delivery.

Company's motivation for using EMA

The owners of Tan Loc plan to remove their business to a new industrial site outside Hue to enlarge their production capacity. At the new site, Tan Loc will be charged for the discharge of wastewater. Thus, the owners decided to take environmental issues, particularly those with financial consequences, into account. They were interested in finding and assessing options to improve the eco-efficiency of current and future production at the new site. In other words, the overall target was to decouple the company's economic growth from the pollution it causes. The authors of this study visited Tan Loc in September 2004 to support the company in achieving their target.

Tan Loc had a rudimentary type of accounting in place, which mainly records the purchases of materials and sales of products. Environment-related information was present only in the form of electricity bills.

The decision-making situation is characterised by an almost complete absence of environmental information and of environment-related financial information, and by the desire of Tan Loc's owners to find a set of practical measures to improve their eco-efficiency in the future.

Identification and assessment of relevant environmental issues and their financial consequences for Tan Loc is a precondition for further EMA applications. As no (reliable) environmental accounting information was on hand, the first step of applying EMA was to collect and analyse information on the company's environmental and related financial performance on an ad hoc basis (Figure 12.1: Boxes 3 and 11). In the next step, measures to reduce environmental impacts and increase environment-related financial performance of typical daily operations were identified and assessed (Boxes 7 and

FIGURE 12.3 Tan Loc Food production processes.

15). Eventually, some improvement measures concerning the new plant were discussed with the owners. For one of these measures, potential cost savings were appraised and linked to investment costs (Box 8).

EMA application

Based on the decision situation outlined above, EMA was implemented to provide relevant information to increase eco-efficiency at the current as well as at the planned new site production site. Several improvement measures are described and assessed in the following discussion.

Important environmental issues

To understand the environmental performance better and identify relevant material and energy flows, production process flow charts were developed (an example for fish paste production is given in Figure 12.4). The main material and energy inputs and outputs of each production step were identified and analysed using input–output tables (Table 12.1).

Input–output tables developed to track water consumption, wastewater and waste treatment, energy consumption, and odour at Tan Loc made it possible to identify all relevant environmental issues (for an overview of generally important environmental issues in Vietnam see UNEP RRC.AP 2001).

- *Water consumption.* Tan Loc consumes about 3 m³ of water each day. Most of the water is used to clean the production facilities. A small portion is required as product ingredient. The city of Hue is situated in central Vietnam, where precipitation is high compared with other parts of the country. In the dry season, water can be scarce. More importantly, pollution of the water supply has become a serious problem in most of

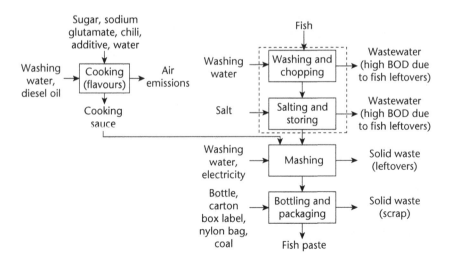

FIGURE 12.4 Fish paste production flow chart.
BOD: biological oxygen demand.

TABLE 12.1 Input–output table of production step 'fish paste mashing' (October 2004)

Input					Output				
Item	Amount	Unit	Time period	Data quality	Item	Amount	Unit	Time period	Data quality
Salted fish	1050	kg	1 month	Calculated	Fish paste	1200	kg	1 month	Calculated
Sauce	200	kg	1 month	Calculated	Solid waste (leftovers)	50	kg	1 month	Calculated
Electricity	42	kWh	1 month	Estimated	Wastewater	0.1	m³	1 month	Estimated
Washing water	0.1	m³	1 month	Estimated					

Vietnam's urban settlements (Thanh Nien News 2006). Reducing the consumption of water is therefore a useful measure to improve Tan Loc's environmental performance.

* *Wastewater.* Most of Tan Loc's wastewater consists of used cleaning water. If the company manages to reduce water consumption, wastewater from cleaning will be reduced as well. A small portion of wastewater contains the leftovers of food ingredients (shrimp heads, fish leftovers, skin of vegetables, etc.). This portion is salty and high in biological oxygen demand (BOD). Tan Loc does not separate or treat the two kinds of wastewater. From an environmental perspective, proper treatment of the organic wastewater is crucial.

* *Solid waste.* Tan Loc generates a small amount of solid waste. The company's main components are plastic bags used for storing food ingredients (shrimp, fish) after salting, leftovers of food ingredients, and other scrap. There is no separation or pre-treatment of solid waste.

* *Energy.* Diesel oil, coal, natural gas, and electricity provide Tan Loc's energy sources. Cooking processes consume the most energy. Burning of different types of fuel generates air emissions which are not treated. The total amount of energy consumed is rather low. From an environmental point of view substitution of coal is desirable to increase efficiency and to reduce emissions from the heating processes.

* *Odour.* Odour from fish paste production is the strongest environmental impact. Although the odour is not a health hazard, it is a permanent burden to the neighbourhood and to employees. Currently fish paste is produced at a separate house away from Hue's town centre. However, at the new site all production facilities are located at the same place, so that odour needs to be considered.

Present environmental costs

Input–output balances also help Tan Loc to trace environmental costs. Material and energy costs of processes and products can be assessed by multiplying physical inputs and outputs and related unit costs. Furthermore, it is possible to estimate the financial consequences of material losses in production. An example of the tracing environmental costs is given in Table 12.2. It shows sales, direct production costs (including costs for waste, labour costs, and operating profits of two Tan Loc products).

Energy and water costs account for only 1 per cent of the direct production costs. Packaging and storing materials and wasted raw materials are more important from an environmental cost-accounting point of view.

* *Waste.* The organic leftovers of food, both in wastewater as well as solid waste, account for the biggest portion of raw materials waste. It is

TABLE 12.2 Profit computation (VND) for Tan Loc chilli sauce and shrimp paste

	Chilli sauce	Shrimp paste
Sales	31,500,000	21,760,000
Direct production costs	17,560,000	8,260,000
Energy	*160,000*	*60,000*
Water	*20,000*	*20,000*
Wasted raw materials	*420,000*	*1,420,000*
Raw materials in product	*13,360,000*	*4,440,000*
Packaging and storing materials	*3,600,000*	*2,320,000*
Labour	8,400,000	6,300,000
Operating profit	5,560,000	7,200,000

impossible to avoid this waste completely. The waste contains peelings of vegetables, fish bones, heads and tails of shrimp, etc. Nevertheless, the figure indicates the potential benefit of reducing wasted raw materials as much as possible.

- *Packaging.* Most of Tan Loc's products are bottled. The bottles are labelled, sealed, and packed into cardboard boxes without generating much waste. Tan Loc uses thick plastic bags for storing salted raw materials for periods from a few days up to a month. These bags have to be disposed of after usage. However, the cost of buying these bags is negligible.

This initial analysis of important environmental issues and costs helps to identify some hot spots for improvement. Tan Loc could transfer the results of this ad hoc approach into periodic material and energy flow-based cost accounting. Changing prices of raw materials, energy, and water affect the company's financial performance in general. Moreover, regular environmental cost accounting helps Tan Loc assess the monetary value of environmental improvement measures, in particular those focussing on wasted raw materials.

Measures to increase eco-efficiency at present

The basic analysis of Tan Loc's initial situation revealed several possibilities for increasing eco-efficiency. Reduction of organic waste and its related costs has been identified as the first priority. Based on the following assessment, Tan Loc decided to introduce two measures which affect day-to-day operations (for a comprehensive overview of environmental measures in the food industry see, for example, Mattsson and Sonesson 2003).

- *Building concrete storage tanks to replace the plastic bags.* This measure has reduced the amount of non-organic waste from storing salted raw

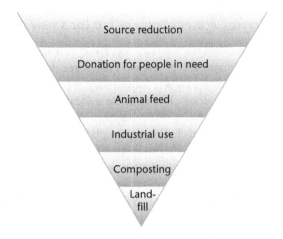

FIGURE 12.5 Food waste recovery hierarchy (source: US EPA 2006: 2).

materials nearly to zero and thus improved Tan Loc's environmental performance. The financial dimension of this measure is very low. Tan Loc spent €60 to purchase the storage tanks and saves about €30 per year on plastic bags. Economic feasibility (a two-year payback) and environmental improvements made this operational measure a favourable option.

- *Improved treatment of organic waste.* The best option for organic waste is to prevent it occurring. Most of the organic matter in wastewater and solid waste, however, is not avoidable as it contains leftovers such as shrimp heads or vegetable peelings. According to the US EPA's food waste recovery hierarchy, which prioritises measures to recover food waste according to their societal and environmental benefits, the use of food waste as feed would be the next best option (see Figure 12.5; also US EPA 1996). Mr Phuc, the owner of Tan Loc, investigated the utilisation of food production leftovers as animal feed. His employees separate and collect the solid organic waste as well as portions of wastewater which are high in organic matter. These by-products can be sold to farmers, which results in additional revenues of approximately VND45 million (€2,250) per year. This measure paid off in no time and led to a reduction of solid food waste of almost 100 per cent and a reduction of organic content in wastewater of roughly 40 per cent.

Both measures increased the eco-efficiency of Tan Loc and are applicable at the new site. While conducting the case study, further eco-efficiency improvements which could be realised at the current production site were discussed. Tan Loc's owners decided to consider these options for the planning of the new site.

Measures to increase eco-efficiency at Tan Loc's new site

Tan Loc's current production facilities were not suitable to cope with the rapidly increasing demand for products. Therefore, the owners decided to remove all operations to a new site where they intend to increase production threefold within five years. The new site is located in an industrial estate outside Hue. At the time the case study was being completed, Tan Loc was still waiting for official approval to build its new plant. Nevertheless, the owners developed plans for the outlay on production facilities. On this basis, several options for eco-efficiency improvements were assessed, but no final decisions were made. For the owners, a major reason to apply EMA, and to attend to environmental issues in general, has been the wastewater fee at the new site (see below). Therefore, improvement options regarding the use of water and treatment of wastewater are described in detail. Further improvement options are then outlined.

At the new industrial site, wastewater fees will be collected based on the volume of water consumed and the wastewater pollutant load. Table 12.3 provides an example of a future wastewater fee computation at Tan Loc, given the current amount and quality of wastewater. Total pollution is computed by multiplying freshwater consumption and measured pollution concentration (see Viet Nam Government 2003). Considering the water input, rather than the wastewater output, is common in Vietnam but is subject to criticism as incentives to reduce the amount of wastewater remain low (see Thong and Ngoc 2004). Assuming an annual consumption of freshwater of 3,000 m³ and a pollution concentration in wastewater typical for the food industry (see Hansen 2003), the annual wastewater fee is VND3,820,000 (€191).

There are two ways for Tan Loc to reduce its wastewater fees: (i) reducing pollution concentration and (ii) reducing freshwater consumption. One option, to reduce the pollution concentration, has been realised at the current

TABLE 12.3 Example of wastewater fee calculation

Freshwater consumption		Pollution indicator	Pollution concentration (mg/litre)	Total pollution (kg)	Pollution fee per unit (VND/kg)	Pollution fee (VND)
m³	litres					
3,000	3,000,000	Chemical oxygen demand (COD)	2,500	7,500	280	2,100,000
		Total suspended solids (TSS)	1,750	5,250	320	1,720.000
						3,820,000

site by selling organic waste to farmers. It requires the separation of wastewater with high organic matter contents from less polluted water. The average organic pollution of wastewater is lower than before.

An option to reduce freshwater consumption is to use rainwater for cleaning the production facilities. This would not only reduce the potential wastewater fees but also leave Tan Loc less vulnerable to rapidly increasing water prices. In Ho Chi Minh City, for instance, authorities increased water prices by 60 per cent in one year because of ever-increasing water provision costs and rising demand for clean water (Viet Nam News 2004). In Hue, precipitation in the wet season (August–February) is very high. Table 12.4 shows a preliminary appraisal of rainwater usage at Tan Loc. Rainwater could be used as cleaning water for several purposes. The target is to completely substitute cleaning water in the wet season, which equals a total reduction of public freshwater consumption by 25 per cent. The annual cost saving potential is about VND8,400,000 (€420), without considering future increases in water prices or wastewater fees. To collect the required amount of rainwater, Tan Loc needs a surface area of 375 m², ideally the roof of the new plant, and a water tank or other container of 50 m³. From the financial point of view, the investment is feasible if it recoups the initial expenses within a given period of time. For instance, if the owners of Tan Loc expect a payback within three years, the costs to build the tank and to install the equipment to channel water from the roof to the tank may not exceed VND24,000,000 (€1,200).

The fact that water consumption not only incorporates purchasing costs but also affects the wastewater fee is likely to lead to further measures to reduce consumption.

Another important area for eco-efficiency improvements at the new site is energy consumption.

TABLE 12.4 Rainwater utilisation at Tan Loc

Annual freshwater demand (predicted)	3,000 m³
Cleaning water (50% of total demand)	1,500 m³
Reduction target (50% equals the wet season's demand)	750 m³
Cost savings potential (freshwater purchases and wastewater fee)	11,200 VND/m³
Annual cost saving potential	8,400,000 VND
Average annual rainfall in Hue	3,000 mm/m²
Usable (estimation; high amounts of rainfall in the wet season will exceed the tank capacity)	2,000 mm/m²
Required surface area to meet cleaning water demand during the wet season	375 m²
Required tank size to store cleaning water for two weeks	50 m³

- *Cooking.* A certain increase of energy efficiency at the new site compared with the old site will be realised by the purchase of new production equipment. From an environmental point of view, the replacement of diesel-fuelled cooking devices with gas fire or steam heat is an important step, which is also highly profitable (see, for example, GTZ 1999). Eco-efficiency could be increased further by using solar power, for instance by pre-heating cooking water in a black, heat-absorbing hose.
- *Electricity.* To reduce the cost of electricity and related environmental impacts, Tan Loc intends to make use of natural lighting at the new site, for example by integrating translucent elements into the plant's roof. This will reduce the need for electric energy and at the same time reduce electricity costs for Tan Loc.

Conclusion

The case study confirms the findings of Dieu (2006: 229), who analyses Vietnamese food processing industries and concludes that more emphasis should be put on efforts to 'overcome urgent pollution problems with ways to prevent wastes from being generated or to re-use their valuable material' instead of focussing on the conventional end-of-pipe approach that 'only deals with treating the symptoms'.

The Tan Loc case shows that EMA can help to identify and realise beneficial measures for eco-efficiency improvements even for small, family-run businesses. At first, neither the environmental nor the financial improvements seemed to be important in comparison with the benefits for big enterprises. However, the vast majority of Vietnamese businesses are small and family-run. Furthermore, additional annual sales of VND45,000,000 (€2,250) from selling food leftovers to farmers increases in importance if compared, for example, with the Vietnamese gross national income per capita of US620 (€460) in 2005 (World Bank 2006).

The realised and projected measures to improve eco-efficiency are conventional measures of environmental management concepts such as cleaner production (for the further use of EMA for cleaner production see, for example, Schaltegger, Bennett, Burritt, and Jasch 2008; Burritt, Herzig, and Tadeo 2009) or good housekeeping. An additional benefit from EMA is the systematic assessment of the current and future situation in physical and monetary terms. This enabled the owners of Tan Loc to prioritise measures and to aim to achieve the most eco-efficient first. Selling food leftovers as by-products, replacing plastic bags by reusable tanks, using rainwater for cleaning, and increasing energy efficiency are important steps towards decoupling the economic growth of Tan Loc from its pollution. In the long run, Tan Loc could systemise and prioritise the various improvement options and convert them into a strategic planning process for further development of the company (this corresponds to Boxes 6 and 14 in Figure 12.1). It should be mentioned that the EMA application at Tan Loc would barely have been possible without the support of external EMA resource persons. However, further SMEs can adapt the results of this case study for their production processes and circumstances.

In future, rising prices for energy, water and raw materials as well as increasing wastewater fees and other environmental treatment costs are likely to provide further financial incentives to increase eco-efficiency. The implementation of EMA allows Tan Loc to anticipate such changes at an early stage.

References

Burritt, R.L., Hahn, T., and Schaltegger, S. (2002) 'Towards a comprehensive framework for environmental management accounting: links between business actors and environmental management accounting tools', *Australian Accounting Review*, 12: 39–50.

Burritt, R.L., Herzig, C., and Tadeo, B.D. (2009) 'Environmental management accounting for cleaner production: the case of a Philippine rice mill', *Journal of Cleaner Production*, 17: 431–439.

Dieu, T. (2006) 'Greening food processing industries in Vietnam: constraints and opportunities', *Environment, Development and Sustainability*, 8: 229–249.

GTZ (German Technical Cooperation) (ed.) (1999) *Application of PREMA tools in food processing*, Bonn: GTZ.

Hansen, C.L. (2003) 'Waste treatment', in Mattsson, B. and Sonesson, U. (eds) *Environmentally-friendly food processing*, Cambridge: Woodhead Publishing, pp. 218–240.

Mattsson, B. and Sonesson, U. (eds) (2003) *Environmentally-friendly food processing*, Cambridge: Woodhead Publishing.

Schaltegger, S., Bennett, M., Burritt, R.L., and Jasch, C. (2008) *Environmental management accounting for cleaner production*, Dordrecht: Springer.

Thanh Nien News (2006) 'Water shortage and pollution a major issue in Vietnam', *Thanh Nien News*, 21 March [online – accessed on 2 April 2007]. Available from Internet: http://www.thanhniennews.com/features/?catid=10andnewsid=13719.

Thong, L.Q. and Ngoc, N.A. (2004) *Incentives for wastewater management in industrial estates in Vietnam: economy and environment program for Southeast Asia research report*, Singapore: EEPSEA.

US EPA (United States Environmental Protection Agency) (1996) *Managing food scraps as animal feed*, Washington, DC: US EPA.

UNEP RRC.AP (United Nations Environment Programme Regional Resource Centre for Asia and the Pacific) (ed.) (2001) *State of the environment in Vietnam 2001*, Bangkok: UNEP RRC.AP.

Viet Nam Government (2003) Decree No. 67/2003/ND-CP of June 13, 2003 on Environmental Protection Charges for Wastewater.

Viet Nam News (2004) 'City's water prices increase by whopping 60% in March', *Vietnam News Online Edition*, 7 January [online – accessed on 2 April 2007]. Available from Internet: http://vietnamnews.vnanet.vn/2004–01/06/Stories/10.htm.

World Bank (2006) *World development indicators database* [online – accessed on 2 April 2007]. Available from Internet: http://siteresources.worldbank.org/DATASTATISTICS/Resources/GNIPC.pdf.

13

SUPPLY CHAIN INFORMATION AND EMA IN COFFEE EXPORTING

Neumann Vietnam, Vietnam

Introduction

This case study focusses on the application of environmental management accounting (EMA) at Neumann Gruppe Vietnam Ltd, a medium-sized coffee refining and exporting enterprise in southern Vietnam. It examines the relevance of environment-related supply chain information for corporate environmental and financial decision-making and reveals possibilities to improve eco-efficiency at the site level and for its supply chain.

Neumann Gruppe Vietnam Ltd (called Neumann Vietnam in the following) refines and exports coffee. Eighty employees work at its plant in Binh Doung Province, near to Ho Chi Minh City. The annual volume of sales is €12 million, which correlates to the high value of the raw material; about 95 per cent of the sales value comprises raw material purchasing costs. Considering the low volume of production costs excluding raw materials, and the number of employees, the company can be classified as medium-sized. Neumann Vietnam is a subsidiary of the German Neumann Gruppe GmbH, one of the largest coffee trading companies.

The case study starts with analysing the relevance of environmental aspects on the production costs (Figure 13.1: Boxes 3 and 11). Refining and exporting coffee is a small part of the international coffee supply chain, in terms of both environmental and financial importance. Therefore, attention is paid to the company's performance in relation to the system of dependences in which it operates. In particular the environmental and environment-related financial importance of the supply chain and the life cycle of coffee are explored (Figure 13.1: Boxes 8 and 16).

		Monetary EMA		Physical EMA	
		Short-term	Long-term	Short-term	Long-term
Past-orientated	Routinely generated	Environmental cost accounting [1]	Environment-induced capital expenditure and revenue [2]	Material and energy flow accounting [9]	Environmental capital impact accounting [10]
	Ad hoc	Ex-post assessment of relevant environmental costing decisions [3]	Ex-post inventory assessment of projects [4]	Ex-post assessment of short-term environmental impacts [11]	Ex-post inventory appraisal of physical environmental investments [12]
Future-orientated	Routinely generated	Monetary environmental budgeting [5]	Environmental long-term financial planning [6]	Physical environmental budgeting [13]	Environmental long-term physical planning [14]
	Ad hoc	Relevant environmental costing [7]	Monetary environmental investment appraisal [8]	Tools designed to predict relevant environmental impacts [15]	Physical environmental investment appraisal [16]

FIGURE 13.1 Application of the EMA framework (Burritt, Hahn, and Schaltegger 2002) to Neumann Vietnam.
Note: Dark (light) grey boxes represent the major (minor) EMA applications.

Decision setting

Neumann Vietnam is situated at the interface of smallholders and local companies on one side and multinationals and global competition for commodities on the other. Neumann's sales follow the demand and rules of international markets, whereas its procurement depends on the availability and quality of the local supply. The same appears for environmental and social issues: international requirements for more sustainable coffee production meet the local, not necessarily congruent, perception of environmental importance. In the following, the economic and environmental situation of Neumann Vietnam and the Vietnamese coffee supply chain are elaborated further.

Low quality, low price: the economic situation of the Vietnamese coffee supply chain

Coffee is one of the most valuable traded commodities in the world. Until the late 1990s it was the most valuable commodity after oil (Ponte 2004). Vietnam is a newcomer on the international coffee market and has experienced a rapid growth of coffee farming for the last two decades. This rise has not only made Vietnam the second biggest coffee exporter of the world after Brazil, but also contributed to shrinking prices and ever-increasing competition in the world market. Since 1970 the average annual price decline has been 3 per cent for arabica and 5 per cent for robusta coffees (Lewin, Giovannucci, and Varangis 2004).

Globally, the declining prices are associated with rising unemployment and poverty in some of the coffee-exporting countries. At the same time, the profits made in the coffee-importing countries have remained stable or even increased with the introduction of new brands and blends and other value-adding activities (Lewin *et al.* 2004). Thus Ponte (2004) characterises the coffee supply chain as a buyer-driven or more specifically roaster-driven one.

Vietnam is a mass producer of coffee, not a quality leader. Robusta, the main type of coffee produced in the country, is considered less valuable than arabica, which is the main type of coffee produced in most other countries. Robusta achieves lower prices in the world market and is mostly used as admixture in down-market coffee products. Most consumers prefer the taste of arabica except for certain types of espresso. Hence, Vietnam's current competitive situation is a purely price-driven one: it needs to produce a cheap type of coffee for the mass market at lowest possible costs. It should be noted, though, that there are initiatives to change this situation; for instance the Vietnamese Ministry of Agriculture is planning to increase the production of arabica coffee, to improve the quality of coffee processing and to participate more actively in international coffee trading (*People's Daily Online* 2006). This may lead to the development of higher-quality grades in the future, which are less dependent on the fluctuating world market prices. At the time of writing, the world market prices were picking up, which is relieving news for Vietnamese coffee production (Flexnews 2007).

Economic situation and refinement process at Neumann Vietnam

Neumann Vietnam purchases and refines coffee to export it to overseas roasters. Their customers expect a coffee quality which is above average and pay premiums for certain quality grades. Competitors of Neumann Vietnam are various Vietnam-based international, private, and state-owned coffee exporters. The company is not aiming at a huge market share; rather it is focussing on higher qualities.

Neumann Vietnam exports coffee beans of different quality grades. To produce these grades, the coffee beans are processed once or twice through the following refinement steps.

- *Coffee cleaning.* This basic cleaning step produces the lowest exportable quality grade of robusta coffee beans. The step ensures that no foreign matter which could harm the customers' roasting devices is included in exported products.

- *Gravity sorting.* Neumann Vietnam's customers pay a premium for deliveries of homogeneous coffee beans. This step allows Neumann to produce export coffee beans within a determined range of sizes.
- *Colour sorting.* Further value is added to the coffee beans if they consist of the same size and colour. Beans that are too dark are sorted out as they would otherwise reduce the quality of the roasted coffee at the customer's site.
- *Wet polishing.* This final step produces the highest quality of robusta coffee beans by improving and harmonising the bean's surface.

The selling price for the different qualities of robusta and purchasing price for robusta beans depend on the world market and the local supply. It varies from season to season or even shorter time scales because of international commodity trading. Assuming a high purchasing price of €1,000 per tonne, the premium for refinement ranges from less than €5 for cleaned beans up to €60 per tonne for wet polished robusta.

Coffee and the environment

Coffee is a typical example of a global commodity. It is mainly produced in emerging economy nations in tropical areas, but the majority of consumers can be found in industrialised countries. Large corporate wholesalers, roasters, and traders buy coffee from agricultural smallholders and distributors. The widely spread perception of the global value chain of coffee is one in which profits are made in industrialised countries at the expense of environmental and social problems in the emerging economy world. This has led to initiatives promoting fair trade and sustainable coffee farming, including organic, shade-grown, and bird-friendly coffee products. The market share of organic and fair trade coffee is continuously increasing; however, it is still less than 2 per cent of the world market (Ponte 2004).

The cultivation and processing of coffee has severe environmental consequences: deforestation, loss of biodiversity, eutrophication, depletion of water and energy resources, and erosion are examples of environmental impacts associated with the first steps of the coffee supply chain. Plentiful measures to reduce these impacts are available, for instance shade-grown and organic cultivation, diversification and alternating vegetation, fallowing, planting of grass under the coffee plants, recycling of wastewater, and composting of other waste. These measures are perceived as costly, therefore, the reasoning goes, the fierce price competition drives harmful practices (Clay 2004).

Admittedly, it cannot be concluded that less intense competition would automatically lead to less harmful practices. On the contrary, high world market prices and profit margins have encouraged Vietnamese authorities to promote coffee farming since the late 1980s and stimulated the interest of many Vietnamese to take their chance in coffee farming. As these Vietnamese farmers did not know much about coffee cultivation, harvesting and processing, this boost led to deforestation, soil degradation, overfertilisation, and other environmental impacts (Johnston 2002).

Whereas coffee cultivation, the supply chain's first step, is often in the spotlight of environmental attention, later steps of the value chain tend to be disregarded. However, life cycle assessments (LCA) of coffee production, conducted by Diers, Langowski, Pannkoke, and Hop (1999) and Salomone (2003), shows that another crucial step of the coffee life cycle is coffee consumption.

Company's motivation for using EMA

For several commodities Blowfield (2003) observed a gap between the sustainability or ethical standards of parts of the demand side and the values and priorities of producers in the chain. This is particularly true for the Vietnamese coffee chain. Neumann Vietnam's customers, international coffee roasters and traders, are exposed to environmental and sustainability concerns in the coffee-consuming countries. Many of the international roasters and traders have responded by establishing corporate social responsibility departments, launching codes of conduct, and offering fair trade and sustainable coffees. Neumann Vietnam's suppliers, in contrast, face almost no direct pressures and have few incentives to change their current way of coffee mass production.

Neumann Vietnam's options to increase its business performance are related to the margin between the purchase price and the selling price of coffee. Three basic options to increase the value added can be distinguished and are linked to environmental issues.

- *Option A: gain premiums for better qualities of coffee.* Neumann Vietnam is already refining robusta coffee to benefit from premiums. The export of sustainable coffees might be a further option to receive premiums; however, the supply and demand for sustainable, organic, or fair trade robusta coffee from Vietnam is negligible. Thus Neumann Vietnam would have to stimulate the demand and the supply at the same time. Neumann Vietnam could also try to export sustainable arabica coffee from Vietnam.
- *Option B: reduce company-internal costs.* Considering the purchasing and selling price of coffee as fixed, Neumann Vietnam could increase profits by reducing its costs of refining and exporting coffee. This includes measures to increase energy- and material-efficiency.
- *Option C: reduce purchase price.* Assuming unchanged selling prices, lower purchase prices of course add value to Neumann Vietnam's operations. Eco-efficiency improvements in the supply chain might enable suppliers to reduce their productions costs and prices.

The company's motivation for using EMA is to identify if and how environmental aspects are relevant for the business success. Option A has not been explored further, as the company considers itself not to be in a strong enough position to foster the development of a market for sustainable coffee from Vietnam. Neumann Vietnam's interest in analysing the relevance of environmental aspects on the production costs (Option B) can be characterised as an ad hoc, short-term-focussed analysis of available information. Referring to the EMA framework of Burritt, Hahn, and Schaltegger (2002) (Figure 13.1) this decision-making situation is found in Box 3, supported by some related physical information (Box 11). Option C requires external, supply chain-related information. Influencing the eco-efficiency of the suppliers requires a rather strategic, long-term-focussed approach. The EMA approach to provide adequate information for this decision-making situation refers to Boxes 4 and 12 of Figure 13.1.

EMA application

As elaborated above, the EMA application at Neumann Vietnam is expected to support two different decision-making situations: environment-related cost information on the refinement processes and eco-efficiency potentials within the supply chain (Options B and C above).

Material and energy flow-based cost accounting of the refinement processes

The business of refining and exporting coffee is not known for environmental problems such as air and water pollution or intensive energy and resource consumption. A rough analysis of Neumann's operations validated this presumption. Perceivable environmental issues at Neumann's site are energy consumption (electricity), solid waste, and water consumption. Transportation has not been considered as it is outsourced to suppliers. The low impacts of the on-site environmental issues are highlighted by the following comparisons. For refining and exporting a metric tonne of green beans, Neumann Vietnam uses 40 kWh of electric energy, whereas a Vietnamese company that cultivates and processes coffee consumes roughly 50 times more per tonne (Doan, Sturm, and Enden 2003). The water demand for one tonne of green bean is 35 litres on average, whereas the water demand for traditional wet processing of coffee can amount up to 70,000 litres per tonne (ICO 2001). An overview of material and energy inputs and outputs can be found in Table 13.1.

The consideration of inputs and outputs shows rather low raw material losses; dust and weight losses due to further drying of the beans account for 1 per cent of the total output only. Nevertheless, the financial relevance of

TABLE 13.1 Physical input/output table for one tonne of green bean input

Input		Output	
Item	*Physical amount*	*Item*	*Physical amount*
Green beans	1000 kg	Green beans Grade A	430 kg
Water	0.035 m³	Green beans Grade B	370 kg
Electric energy	40 kWh	Green beans Grade C	60 kg
		Green beans Grade D	55 kg
		Green beans for local market	75 kg
		Dust	2 kg
		Weight loss	8 kg
		Wastewater	0.035 m³

these losses is not to be neglected. One per cent loss equals 1 per cent of the purchasing costs of green beans, which account for more than 95 per cent of the total production costs. Furthermore, Grade D green beans and green beans for the local market need to be considered as unwanted products, as the selling price for these products is not higher but often rather lower than the purchasing price. There is no value added for these products, therefore Neumann Vietnam should aim at reducing the amount of these products as far as possible. To better understand the refinement process for the different grades, a product-specific material and energy flow-related cost accounting has been carried out to trace energy and water consumption as well as material losses to the different quality grades (see Table 13.2).

As expected, energy and water demand do not affect the profitability significantly. Material losses, and the generation of lower-quality grades, have financial implications. Assuming that it would be possible to produce Grade B without producing lower-quality grades and wastes, the profit would increase by 37 per cent or €10.50 per tonne of final product (best-case scenario in Table 13.2). These figures are fictive as it is not possible to fully eliminate lower-quality grades and waste. Nevertheless, the results imply that paying premiums for high-quality supplies, which lead to smaller amounts of unwanted products and wastes, is profitable within a certain margin. Furthermore, the results imply that only Grade A and B coffee beans contribute substantially to Neumann Vietnam's profits.

The material and energy flow-based cost accounting has proven most of Neumann Vietnam's assumptions, in particular that the financial importance of energy and water consumption is rather low and that the quality of the purchased coffee affects the profitability of the business. Eco-efficiency improvements in the supply chain, however, seem to be of higher importance for Neumann Vietnam's performance.

TABLE 13.2 Physical and monetary flows of green beans Grade B

		Current situation		Best-case scenario	
		Physical amount	Monetary equivalent (€)	Physical amount	Monetary equivalent (€)
Wanted product	Green beans Grade B	1,000 kg	1,040	1,000 kg	1,040
Unwanted product	Green beans Grade D	60 kg	60	0 kg	0
	Green beans for local market	10 kg	10	0 kg	0
Waste	Dust and weight loss	10 kg	0	0 kg	0
Raw material input	Green beans	1,080 kg	−1,080	1,000 kg	−1,000
Further input	Electric energy	25 kWh	−1.50	23 kWh	−1.40
Profit/loss[a]			28.50		39.00

a   Not including depreciation, labour costs, and overheads such as general administration costs and management salaries.

The state of the coffee supply chain's environment

The coffee supply chain starts with agricultural processes in tropical countries and ends with the consumption and disposal stages, predominantly in industrialised countries in cooler latitudes. The main steps are as follows (ICO 2001; Figure 13.2).

• *Coffee farming.* Coffee farmers and hired workers plant coffee trees, apply fertiliser, pesticides, and herbicides, irrigate the plants, and finally harvest coffee berries. These activities are associated with soil erosion and loss of biodiversity owing to the extension of agricultural land use, eutrophication, eco-toxicity and greenhouse effect due to fertilisation, mammal and aquatic life toxicity due to pesticide use, and resource depletion due to the fuel and water consumption required for farming.
• *Dry/wet processing.* The coffee berries have to be processed to release the green coffee beans. Robusta coffee berries are usually treated by using the dry processing method whereas most arabica coffees are wet processed. Dry processing can be achieved by solar power (sun-drying) or by the use of fuels; the latter is more common in Vietnam. After drying, the coffee berries are hulled to release the green coffee bean and then polished. The leftovers of this process, dried pulp and parchment skin, can be composted. Wet processing is more harmful from an environmental

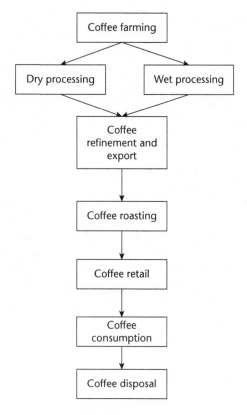

FIGURE 13.2 Main steps of the coffee life cycle.

point of view, but gains higher selling prices for the coffee beans. The traditional wet processing method requires 40,000 to 70,000 litres of water input per tonne of green bean; the mechanical mucilage removal method reduces this demand down to 1,000 litres. The organic pollutant load of the generated wastewater is similar in both cases. Biological oxygen demand (BOD) and chemical oxygen demand (COD) of wet-processing wastewater are extremely high, and the pH is low. Untreated wastewater from wet processing is therefore a major driver of environmental problems caused by the production of coffee.

- *Coffee refinement and export.* This part of the coffee life cycle has been described above.
- *Coffee roasting and retail.* To roast the green coffee beans, thermal energy is required. Its generation causes air emissions including greenhouse gases. Decaffeinated and soluble coffees in particular require water in the roasting process as well. After roasting, coffee needs to be packed; polyethylene foil (PET) ensures that no oxygen reacts with the coffee, to avoid ageing. Other packaging types are glass jars with screw caps for soluble coffees.

Roasting does not necessarily happen after export; it is also common to export roasted coffee.

- *Consumption.* Energy consumption is the most important environmental issue of this step of the coffee life cycle. The making of coffee requires energy, mainly electricity, for the percolator. The habit of leaving coffee on the hot plate of the percolator to keep it warm increases the energy demand further. Of course, coffee making involves a certain amount of water input as well.
- *Disposal.* Consumers need to dispose coffee grounds and filters as well as the packaging. Coffee grounds and filters are often composted, but have a comparatively long and uneven rotting process. Packaging, as well as jute and plastic bags from previous supply chain steps, is recycled, incinerated, or dumped. The common environmental problems related to waste treatment such as energy consumption, acidification, and greenhouse gas emissions are therefore present.
- *Transportation.* Transportation is not depicted in Figure 13.2 as it happens between almost all steps of the coffee life cycle. The biggest transportation distance concerns the shipping of green beans or roasted coffee from the producing to the consuming countries. Transportation is associated with the depletion of natural resources, in particular fossil fuels, and the environmental impacts of combusting the fuels, most prominently global warming.

From a decision-making point of view it is important to know at which steps of the coffee life cycle environmental improvements are most promising. As shown in the previous sub-section, energy-efficiency optimisation of the refinement processes might reduce Neumann Vietnam's production costs slightly but it would have almost no impact on the overall environmental performance of the supply chain. Life cycle assessments (LCAs) are a common tool of environmental accounting, conducted by companies as well as research organisations, governments, and the like (Schaltegger and Burritt 2000). An LCA can be used to highlight the environmental importance of different steps of a product's life cycle. Two LCAs have been conducted for coffee production (Diers *et al.* 1999; Salomone 2003). Looking for the highest overall improvement potential of the coffee life cycle, the conclusion of both LCAs is similar: the first and the last steps of the life cycle matter most.

Salomone (2003) identifies consumption as the single most important step, followed by cultivation. Cultivation accounts for more than 97 per cent of coffee's total eco-toxicity and eutrophication, whereas consumption, comprising mainly the water use and energy demand for preparing coffee, accounts for more than two thirds of the total air acidification, greenhouse effects, photochemical oxidant formation, depletion of ozone layer, human toxicity, and aquatic eco-toxicity. The importance of the consumption step for the overall environmental performance of coffee production is supported by the results of a sensitivity analysis. It reveals that, in terms of total eco-points, the impact of changing the coffee-making process, for example gas stove coffee making instead of an electric coffee machine, is substantially higher than the impact of avoiding pesticides or applying organic fertilisers in cultivation (Salomone 2003).

In the analysis of Diers and colleagues (1999), coffee cultivation and processing account for 49 per cent, and consumption and disposal for 41 per cent, of the environmental impacts. Furthermore, a comparison of best-case, worst-case, and the current situation places the current situation near to the worst-case scenario, meaning that the improvement potential of the coffee life cycle is rather high (Diers *et al.* 1999). The coffee-processing step has a higher impact in this analysis because wet and dry processing have both been considered, whereas Salomone considers dry processing only. Similarly, the analysis of Diers and colleagues (1999) stresses the waste disposal issue more than Salomone does, which leads to a slightly higher importance of the disposal stage. Both LCAs do not explicitly consider loss of biodiversity, which is likely to increase the environmental importance of the cultivation step even further.

The results of the two LCAs help decision-makers to prioritise options for environmental improvements of the supply chain (Diers *et al.* 1999; Salomone 2003).

- In cultivation, avoidance or reduction of fertiliser use is the most important concern followed by measures to avoid erosion. Preservation of biodiversity has not been considered in the LCAs, but is likely to be of importance in the Vietnamese coffee farming context as well.
- The impacts of wet processing can be substantially reduced by proper wastewater treatment and reduction of water consumption. In wet and dry processing, fuels are consumed for drying. Energy-efficiency measures could reduce environmental impacts such as global warming and resource depletion.
- Refinement, export, roasting, retail, and transportation are not the highest priority for environmental improvements of the coffee life cycle.
- In consumption, eco-efficiency can be improved by using electricity from renewable resources or by replacing coffee machines run on electricity with different devices, for instance plunger pots, which can make use of other and less polluting energy sources such as gas. A big improvement potential is the change of consumer habits, which includes the avoidance of pouring one cup of coffee per can on average and the use of thermos cans or bottles instead of leaving the coffee on the hot plate for several minutes.
- Coffee ground and coffee filters are the biggest contributors to environmental impacts of the disposal stage. Measures to ensure proper composting are likely to reduce these impacts substantially.

Environmental supply chain costing and management

Neumann Vietnam operates in a highly competitive market, thus financial implications of environmental supply chain improvements are of great interest. Gathering, analysing, and using supply chain cost information for managerial decision-making is not widely covered in the general management accounting literature. At least some authors have elaborated this topic in detail, in particular in the context of logistics (LaLonde and Pohlen 1996; Cullen, Berry, Seal, Dunlop, Ahmed, and Marson 1999).

Supply chain costing provides information to determine the overall effectiveness of the supply chain, identify improvement opportunities, evaluate alternative supply chain structures, and select supply chain partners. The implementation of supply chain costing is a difficult task as its benefits do not necessarily occur evenly throughout the chain (LaLonde and Pohlen 1996). 'The sharing of cost information may give away a hard-earned competitive advantage or provide negotiating leverage to their supply chain partners' (LaLonde and Pohlen 1996: 4).

The environmental improvement priorities elaborated in the previous sub-section can be used to analyse supply chain costs. As Neumann Vietnam does not consider itself in a position to affect the consumer behaviour or the disposal stage of the coffee life cycle, the environmental supply chain costing focuses on upstream stages, namely cultivation and processing. Robusta coffee processing uses the dry processing method, that is, in environmental terms the processing step is less important than the cultivation stage.

In cultivation, the use of fertilisers is costly and harmful for the environment. Figure 13.3 shows the 2003 composition of production costs at an average robusta coffee farm in Dak Lak province in Vietnam as investigated by

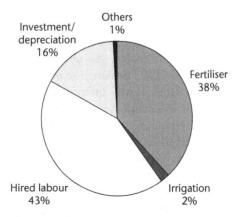

FIGURE 13.3 Composition of coffee cultivation costs (source: E.D.E. Consulting for Coffee 2003).

one of the authors (E.D.E. Consulting for Coffee 2003). Fertilisers account for 38 per cent of total production costs. Moreover, the majority of farmers have been found to use fertiliser inefficiently. Many farmers use more than twice as much fertiliser as necessary (E.D.E. Consulting for Coffee 2003). If farmers manage to use fertiliser in the best possible way they can reduce the costs of purchasing fertiliser by almost 50 per cent. This reduces their total production costs by roughly 20 per cent and doubles the average farmer's profits. Looking at these facts from a customer's perspective, the purchasing price for harvested coffee could be reduced significantly without compromising the farmer's profits.

An environmental supply chain costing can also be used to reveal the additional benefits and costs of alternative, less damaging cultivation methods, for instance by comparing the premiums paid for organic, shade-grown coffee and the consequent reduction of production costs with the reduced yields. In processing, the saving potential of more energy-efficient drying devices could be of interest, too.

The availability of supply chain cost information does not solve one major problem: '[r]estructuring the supply chain to exploit efficiencies or seize competitive advantages requires a mechanism capable of equitable allocating cost benefits and burdens between supply chain partners' (LaLonde and Pohlen 1996: 8). Obviously, most Vietnamese farmers have not adapted methods for efficient fertiliser use by themselves. If one supply chain actor, such as Neumann Vietnam, starts to train farmers on more efficient use it is not necessarily Neumann Vietnam that benefits. The farmers may as well sell their coffee to other middlemen and exporters or just keep the farm-gate price on the same level to make more profit. At first glance, the incentive for Neumann Vietnam to facilitate eco-efficiency improvements within the supply chain is rather low. Environmental supply chain management is considered to be a solution for this problem.

For Cooper, Ellram, Gardner, and Hanks (1997: 68) supply chain management is 'an integrative philosophy to manage the total flow of a channel from earliest supplier of raw materials to the ultimate customer, and beyond, including the disposal process'. When taking the perspective of one company within the chain, the challenge is slightly different, though. In this perspective, according to the author of the definition above, the supply chain looks not like a chain, but rather like an uprooted tree. The company needs to decide how many of the roots and branches it wants to manage (Cooper, Lambert, and Pagh 1997: 9). In this connection, Seuring (2004) has compared different concepts of environmental management that address the flow of material and information along life cycles or supply chains. He concludes that environmental supply chain management is the most management-orientated approach of all the approaches assessed.

For Neumann Vietnam, the supply chain management challenge is to foster eco-efficiency improvements, in particular reduced use of fertiliser, at the coffee farming stage and to ensure participation in the financial benefits. According to Williamson (1975, 1985) the three basic options for coordinating supply chains are price (market arrangement), command and control (hierarchical arrangement), and negotiation (cooperative arrangement).

- Neumann Vietnam could use market arrangements to provide incentives, or more precisely premiums, to its supplier to receive higher qualities or special types of coffee, for instance organic, fair trade coffees, if there is a customer demand for them. For the reduction of fertiliser use or other eco-efficiency measures in the upstream supply chain, market arrangements are not a promising option.
- Establishing hierarchical arrangements is nearest to the original understanding of supply chain management, whereby rather large enterprises purchase key suppliers and own or control distribution channels. However, Neumann Vietnam does not intend to buy suppliers and is also not in a position to dominate the chain.
- Cooperative arrangements are the most promising option for Neumann Vietnam. For instance, the company can offer its suppliers training and support on implementing eco-efficiency measures. In return, the suppliers need to agree to either pay Neumann Vietnam for these services or share their financial benefits. This kind of vertical cooperation is, however, difficult to achieve as it requires monitoring of the success of eco-efficiency measures and the adherence to contracts by all partners involved. Traders and distributors or farmers might take the opportunity to underestimate the savings or to sell parts of the harvest to other traders and exporters without Neumann Vietnam's knowledge. Thus, horizontal cooperation seems to be the best available option. Higher energy-efficiency in dry processing and appropriate use of fertilisers lead to higher profitability and/ or competitiveness for the Vietnamese coffee industry as a whole. Having this in prospect, Vietnamese coffee exporters, traders, and related organisations such as the Vietnam Coffee and Cocoa Association (VICOFA) could share the costs of training programmes for coffee farmers and companies of the processing step. Neumann Coffee could try to initialise and lobby such an eco-efficiency programme.

The findings above are in line with the results of a comprehensive analysis of sustainable cotton supply chains conducted by Goldbach, Seuring, and Back (2003). The authors have observed that the initial phase of environmental and sustainability supply chain management is characterised by cooperative or even hierarchical arrangements, whereas at later stages market arrangements gain importance. Furthermore, they conclude that environmental supply chain management cannot be viewed as a technical matter only. It is rather an interorganisational concept (Goldbach *et al.* 2003). It implies a 'change from managing supply chains based on serial dependence and power to recognising and managing the reciprocal dependence' (Cullen *et al.* 1999: 31).

Conclusion

Neumann Vietnam is one of many actors in the Vietnamese coffee industry and supply chain. Neumann Vietnam's business, the refinement and export of green robusta coffee beans, is not causing huge environmental impacts. EMA has been used to prove this presumption, but it has also ascertained the financial relevance of even small raw material losses such as dust and weight loss due to evaporation.

In contrast to the rather low environmental importance of its refinement and export operations, the supply chain in which Neumann Vietnam operates is exposed to various substantial environmental concerns. Using LCA information in the context of EMA has helped to identify those steps within the coffee supply chain that have the highest environmental impacts and the greatest potential for environmental improvement measures. Cultivation and consumption are the most important steps from an environmental perspective. Some of the environmental concerns in the supply chain have direct financial consequences. Energy inefficiencies and the overuse of fertiliser diminish the overall supply chain profits or lead to less competitive market prices. Neumann Vietnam can gain a better understanding of these interdependencies by applying supply chain costing. Measures to increase the supply chain eco-efficiency need supply chain management efforts, in particular horizontal cooperation.

Besides Neumann Vietnam, further actors within the supply chain can contribute to environmental and related financial improvements. Coffee consumers have an even bigger role in this than expected. By demanding alternative types of coffees such as organic, fair trade or sustainable coffee, consumers influence the supply chain indirectly, in particular the cultivation step. However, consumers can also directly reduce the environmental burdens of the coffee life cycle, for instance by not making more coffee than is consumed, by using insulated coffee pots rather than leaving coffee on the percolator stove, by purchasing electricity from renewable sources, or by replacing their electric coffee machines.

This case study reveals the importance of environment-related supply chain information for corporate decision-making. EMA can make use of tools such as LCA to satisfy this demand. In combination with concepts such as supply chain costing, this analysis leads to the identification and prioritisation of eco-efficiency improvements along the chain. In contrast to still-growing niche market solutions such as fair trade or organic coffee farming, supply chain eco-efficiency measures show a potential to directly enter the mass market of Vietnamese coffee production.

References

Blowfield, M. (2003) 'Ethical supply chains in the cocoa, coffee and tea industries', *Greener Management International*, 43: 15–24.

Burritt R., Hahn, T., and Schaltegger, S. (2002) 'Towards a comprehensive framework for environmental management accounting: links between business actors and environmental management accounting tools', *Australian Accounting Review*, 12: 39–50.

Clay, J. (2004) *World agriculture and the environment: a commodity-by-commodity guide to impacts and practices*, Washington, DC: Island Press.

Cooper, M.C., Ellram, L.M., Gardner, J.T., and Hanks, A.M. (1997) 'Meshing multiple alliances', *Journal of Business Logistics*, 18: 67–87.

Cooper, M.C., Lambert, M.L., and Pagh, J.D. (1997) 'Supply chain management: more than a new name for logistics', *International Journal of Logistics Management*, 8: 1–14.

Cullen, J., Berry, A.J., Seal, W., Dunlop, A., Ahmed, M., and Marson, J. (1999) 'Interfirm supply chains: the contribution of management accounting', *Management Accounting*, 77 (6): 30–32.

Diers, A., Langowski, H.C., Pannkoke, K., and Hop, R. (1999) *Produkt-ökobilanz vakuumverpackter Röstkaffee*, Bayreuth: Eco-Informa Press.

Doan, T., Sturm, A., and Enden, J.v. (2003) *First environmental report of Tan Lam company*, unpublished document.

E.D.E. Consulting for Coffee (2003) *Project results from Dak Lak area*, unpublished document.

Flexnews – Business News for the Food Industry (2007) 'Vietnam's coffee sales soar, dryness hits some areas', 26 March [online – accessed on 14 January 2008]. Available from Internet: http://www.flex-news-food.com/console/PageViewer. aspx?page=7959.

Goldbach, M., Seuring, S., and Back, S. (2003) 'Co-ordinating sustainable cotton chains for the mass market: the case of the German mail-order business OTTO', *Greener Management International*, 43: 65–78.

ICO – International Coffee Organization (eds) (2001) *Environmental issues relating to the coffee chain within a context of trade liberalization, through a life-cycle approach*, London: ICO.

Johnston, J. (2002) 'Bountiful harvests of despair: Vietnam and the global coffee crisis', *TED Case Studies*, 12 (1) [online – accessed on 2 April 2007]. Available from Internet: http://www.american.edu/TED/class/all.htm#Jan2002.

LaLonde, B.J. and Pohlen, T.L. (1996) 'Issues in supply chain costing', *International Journal of Logistics Management*, 7: 1–12.

Lewin, B., Giovannucci, D., and Varangis, P. (2004) *Coffee markets – new paradigms in global supply and demand, agriculture and rural development*, Discussion Paper 3, Washington, DC: World Bank.

People's Daily Online (2006) 'Vietnam coffee industry still ailing', 9 May [online – accessed on 18 June 2010]. Available from Internet: http://english.peopledaily.com. cn/200605/09/eng20060509_264116.html.

Ponte, S. (2004) *Standards and sustainability in the coffee sector: a global value chain approach*, Winnipeg: IISD.

Salomone, R. (2003) 'Life cycle assessment applied to coffee production: investigating environmental impacts to aid decision-making for improvements at company level', *Food, Agriculture and Environment*, 1: 295–300.

Schaltegger, S. and Burritt, R. (2000) *Contemporary environmental accounting: issues, concepts and practice*, Sheffield: Greenleaf.

Seuring, S. (2004) 'Industrial ecology, life cycles, supply chains: differences and interrelations', *Business Strategy and the Environment*, 13: 306–319.

Williamson, O. (1975) *Markets and hierarchies: analysis and antitrust implications*, New York: Free Press.

Williamson, O. (1985) *The economic institutions of capitalism*, New York: Free Press.

14

ENVIRONMENTAL AND QUALITY IMPROVEMENTS AS JUSTIFICATION FOR HIGHER CAPITAL EXPENDITURE AND LAND USE IN SHRIMP FARMING

Chau Thanh Tam Shrimp Farm, Vietnam

Introduction

Aquaculture, and especially semi-intensive shrimp farming, is a fast-growing industry in Vietnam, promising better income and employment to rural communities along the coast. Chau Thanh Tam, a former rice farmer, started his business in 2000. His shrimp farm is situated a few kilometres outside Ca Mau City in the centre of the Mekong river delta in the far south of Vietnam. The Chau Thanh Tam Shrimp Farm (shortened to CTT in the following discussion) buys the larvae of black tiger shrimp (*Penaeus monodom*) from specialist larvae hatchers and grows them to a marketable size. Mr Tam sells his shrimp to wholesalers, who export them to the United States. The shrimp farm is a small enterprise providing an income for Tam's family and eight employees. Mr Tam is also the chairman of the shrimp farm club in Ca Mau City.

Shrimp farming has severe ecological consequences; in particular, deforestation of coastal areas, salination of fertile soil, and water pollution. It is a potentially profitable but risky business from a financial perspective and often leads to insolvency because of high capital costs for land, shrimp larvae, feed, aeration, and pesticides. Any outbreak of pests devastating a farmer's yield can threaten the farm's existence.

This case study assesses the financial and environmental performance of CTT through a retrospective comparison with neighbouring farms over a period of five years (see Figure 14.1: Boxes 10 and 2).

Decision setting

At first glance, CTT looks similar to other shrimp farms in the Ca Mau Province, with one important difference: Mr Tam established two additional

		Monetary EMA		Physical EMA	
		Short-term	Long-term	Short-term	Long-term
Past-orientated	Routinely generated	Environmental cost accounting [1]	Environment-induced capital expenditure and revenue [2]	Material and energy flow accounting [9]	Environmental capital impact accounting [10]
Past-orientated	Ad hoc	Ex-post assessment of relevant environmental costing decisions [3]	Ex-post inventory assessment of projects [4]	Ex-post assessment of short-term environmental impacts [11]	Ex-post inventory appraisal of physical environmental investments [12]
Future-orientated	Routinely generated	Monetary environmental budgeting [5]	Environmental long-term financial planning [6]	Physical environmental budgeting [13]	Environmental long-term physical planning [14]
Future-orientated	Ad hoc	Relevant environmental costing [7]	Monetary environmental investment appraisal [8]	Tools designed to predict relevant enviromental impacts [15]	Physical environmental investment appraisal [16]

FIGURE 14.1 Application of the EMA framework (Burritt, Hahn, and Schaltegger 2002) to CTT shrimp farm.

Note: Dark (light) grey boxes represent the major (minor) EMA applications.

ponds for recycling water when he started his business. He believed that by doing so he could reduce the risk of pest epidemics and increase the quality of his shrimp. To establish the additional ponds he had to buy more land than his competitors. To assess the environmental and financial advantages of Mr Tam's business decision, it is necessary to take a closer look at the environmental and economic conditions of shrimp farming in the Mekong delta and to understand Mr Tam's shrimp farming approach.

Environmental and economic conditions of shrimp farming in the Mekong delta

The Mekong delta is a tropical area with two seasons, dry and wet. The whole delta is extremely flat and influenced by tides. Depending on the tides, either the numerous river streams of the delta carry freshwater from the Mekong into the ocean or saltwater is pushed upstream from the coast. Thus, the streams contain a brackish mixture of freshwater and saltwater. Ca Mau province, which contains almost 50 per cent of the Mekong delta, is affected by salinity for more than six months per year (Brennan, Preston, Clayton, and Be 2002). The abundance of brackish water is sufficient to rear shrimp inland, in particular tiger shrimp, which are less vulnerable to changing salinity levels than other shrimp species.

The possibility of growing shrimp inland has contributed to the growth of the shrimp farming industry in the south of Vietnam. According to statistics from the Food and Agriculture Organization of the United Nations (FAO), Vietnam has become the world's third largest producer of aquaculture shrimp, with an annual production of 327,000 tonnes in 2005, which is roughly quadruple the volume of 2000 (FAO 2008).

Such rapid growth is certain to lead to environmental damage. Pollution and eutrophication of fresh and marine water, salination of soil, and destruction of ecosystems such as mangrove forests are severe consequences of this form of aquaculture (e.g. Rönnbäck 2001; Brennan *et al.* 2002; Thornton, Shanahan, and Williams 2003; Public Citizen 2004). The growth of production is accompanied by a move from extensive to semi-intensive shrimp farming (Nhuong, Phillips, and van Anrooy 2002). Extensive shrimp farming is known to be less polluting; however, the farming area required for semi-intensive shrimp farming is substantially lower (for an overview and classification of farming techniques and their environmental, social, and economic consequences, see Rönnbäck 2001).

Shrimp farming approach of Chau Thanh Tam

CTT is located in a former rice farming area a few kilometres inland. Mr Tam farms his shrimp in a semi-intensive way. He buys larvae and grows a dense monoculture which requires feeding, aeration, water pumping, and the use of fertilisers and pesticides. Semi-intensive shrimp farming promises high yields and, therefore, better income than conventional extensive shrimp farming or rice farming, but it also brings high costs and increased risks of shrimp pests and diseases.

The shrimp farming approach of conventional, semi-intensive shrimp farms in the Ca Mau area is depicted in Figure 14.2. Twice a year farmers take in brackish water from nearby rivers and pre-treat it with chemicals, to destroy, in particular, organic matter including small animals such as wild shrimp (see Step 1 in Figure 14.2). The brackish water is used in several ponds for growing shrimp from the larval state to harvesting (Step 2). Farmers monitor the water quality constantly, adding fertilisers and aeration. To harvest shrimp, the ponds are emptied into a sedimentation pond where solid matter settles (Step 3). Sewage is finally discharged to a river or channels (Step 4).

The conventional approach works well during the dry season but causes problems during the wet season. In the dry season, the salinity of the river water is sufficient. Water losses in the shrimp ponds caused by evaporation can easily be balanced by adding brackish river water. At the transition from dry to wet season, farmers have to quickly fill the shrimp ponds with water before the massive rainfall turns the brackish river water fresh, which is not suitable. Even if the farmers manage to take in enough brackish water, rainfall and run-off directly into the ponds reduces the salinity still further. In addition,

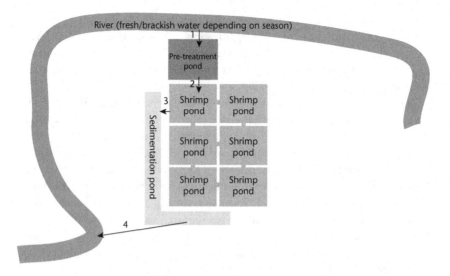

FIGURE 14.2 Conventional shrimp farming approach in Ca Mau province.

the farmers are forced to pre-treat the water quickly. As the sewage is usually discharged to the same river the water is taken from, the risk of spreading pests and diseases rises. As a consequence, the quantity and quality of the second season yield is substantially lower.

Mr Tam modified this conventional approach and installed a semi-closed system (as shown in Figure 14.3 and Figure 14.4) by adding two ponds, a fish pond and a recycling pond. During the dry season, he takes in brackish water from the nearby river and pre-treats it. As an additional treatment step, he feeds the pre-treated water into a fish pond, where he grows a food fish species that improves the water quality further. At the end of the dry season he empties the shrimp pond water into a sedimentation pond. Instead of discharging the sewage into the river, it fills up a recycling pond (see Step 5 in Figure 14.3). Between the dry and wet seasons, the water is treated in the recycling pond and processed to the fish pond, where it provides feed for growing fish (see Step 1 in Figure 14.4). The salinity of the recycled water in the recycling and fish pond provides good conditions for shrimp farming independent of the river's salinity. A small amount of river water is still added but, in contrast to the neighbouring farmers, CTT can pre-treat this intake properly without time pressure. After the wet season harvest, CTT discharges the water to the river like all conventional farmers. According to CTT's observations, the recycling pond increases salinity and reduces the risk of pests during the wet season, and the fish pond increases the water quality during both seasons and provides additional income from selling fish. However, the CTT approach requires additional acreage.

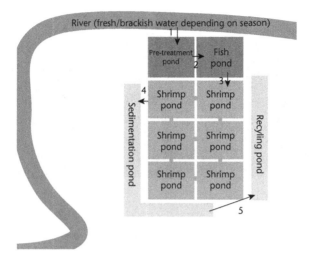

FIGURE 14.3 CTT's dry season approach: first season (dry season, no rain, high salinity in river water).

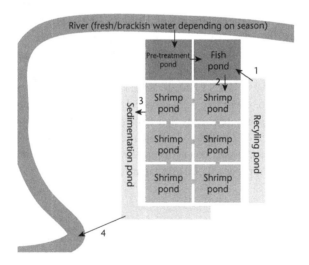

FIGURE 14.4 CTT's wet season approach: second season (wet season, monsoon, low salinity in river water).

Figure 14.5 illustrates some aspects of CTT shrimp farming. The picture to the left shows a half-emptied shrimp pond with aeration devices. In the middle picture Mr Tam monitors the quality and size of shrimp by visual inspection, and the right picture shows the additional recycling pond.

FIGURE 14.5 CTT shrimp farm.

Company's motivation for using EMA

After five years of operation, Mr Tam is convinced that his approach is superior to conventional farming. Thus, he wondered whether to become a consultant for other farmers and promote his methods further. Although his initial rationale for the superiority of his approach was based on 'gut instinct', he hoped that analysis of the environmental and economic effects of his business would support his argument with reliable and quantifiable facts. It should be noted, though, that his primary motivation was to further analyse the economic benefits.

Figure 14.1 depicts CTT's EMA decision situation as being past-orientated, long-term-focussed monetary and physical analysis of routinely generated information. Routine here means that almost all the information to conduct the analysis has been collected by CTT on a regular basis, although it has never been combined and assessed in a systematic way to help review the benefits of CTT's alternative approach to shrimp farming.

EMA application

Discussion with a local EMA expert and consultant, who is also a shrimp farming expert, and a visit to his shrimp farm identified the assumptions underpinning the environmental and financial drawbacks and benefits of his approach (see Table 14.1).

Next, to analyse the situation more precisely, data for five years were traced back on the basis of written and oral records provided by CTT. To compare Mr Tam's farm performance with neighbouring shrimp farms, yields were assessed on the basis of estimates provided by three people involved in the case study: a representative of the local office of the Vietnam Ministry of Fisheries who joined the initial case study discussion at CTT, Mr Tam in his function as the chairman of the local shrimp farm club, and Mr Thi, EMA trainer and

TABLE 14.1 Benefits and drawbacks of the CTT approach

	Benefits	*Drawbacks*
Financial	Increased yield in second season (approximately 1 tonne per pond) Reduced risk in second season (up to 70% risk of complete harvest loss versus estimated 0% for new system) Increased size of shrimp in second season (bigger shrimp get higher prices per kg)	High investment costs (buying new land, digging new ponds, building new pipes) High interest rates (1.1% per month)
Environmental	Less river water consumption Less sewage discharge Reduced organic matter in sewage due to lower shrimp mortality	Increased acreage for shrimp farming (6.85 ha instead of 5.8 ha)

consultant and shrimp farming expert. It was assumed that CTT and a comparable conventional farm use the same size and number of shrimp ponds.

In the following, detailed physical and monetary information for both systems is unveiled, assessed, and compared. To ensure confidentiality, some of the figures have been generalised and/or aggregated and financial figures have been rounded.

Land use

CTT shrimp farm covers an area of 6.85 hectares (ha) (68,500 m²) with shrimp ponds accounting for 60 per cent or 4.2 ha. The additional fish pond (0.45 ha) and recycling pond (0.6 ha) account for 15 per cent of the total area. Embankments between the different types of ponds, sheds, appliance rooms, and footways cover the remaining 1.6 ha. A comparable conventional shrimp farm requires only 5.8 ha (58,000 m²). CTT bought the additional 1.05 ha for VND30,000/m² (Vietnamese dong, approximately €1.5/m²), that is VND315 million (roughly €16,000) in total. (Strictly speaking, Mr Tam does not own the land; rather he is leasing it from the Vietnamese government for almost 100 years.)

The land use is important from an environmental perspective. As mentioned above, the rapid growth of shrimp farming threatens coastal ecosystems including mangrove forests, and leads to salination of formerly fertile land. Mr Tam's farm contributes directly to these problems. The shrimp farm's soil had been suitable for other types of agricultural use before the farm was built. Indirectly, CTT may contribute to coastal ecosystem destruction despite being located inland. If growth continues as expected, further land will be used for shrimp farming. If CTT requires more acreage to produce shrimp than conventional farming, this will compound the problem.

From both perspectives, environmental and financial, land use is a critical issue. CTT's alternative method of shrimp farming will be accepted only if it improves eco-efficiency, that is, if revenues per hectare of land are substantially higher than with a conventional farm (for a general discussion of eco-efficiency in the context of accounting, see Schaltegger 1998).

Shrimp yield and revenues

Because of the different weather and salinity conditions, harvest in the dry season is higher than in the wet. This is one reason why agricultural and environmental experts promote the idea of rice-shrimp farming, whereby the farmer grows shrimp in the dry season and rice in the wet (Brennan *et al.* 2002). However, rice-shrimp farming requires extensive shrimp farming techniques, whereas Mr Tam applies semi-intensive shrimp farming, which is much closer to intensive than to extensive farming. He is clearly focussing on maximising the wet season's yield rather than substituting it by growing rice.

In the dry season, CTT harvests about 3.5 tonnes of shrimp per pond (21 tonnes in total). In the wet season he runs five of the six ponds, the sixth being available for reconstruction. This allows CTT to reconstruct a pond every six years. Since 2002, the harvest of the second season has resulted in about three tonnes of shrimp per pond (15 tonnes in total). In the first few years of operation, Mr Tam had to optimise his water-recycling system. At this time the harvest of the second season was lower (seven tonnes in 2000, 10 tonnes in 2001).

A comparable conventional shrimp farm harvests the same amount and quality of shrimp in the first season (21 tonnes in total). In the second season the results are different. Because of the quick intake of river water and limited time for pre-treatment, the risk of low salt levels and diseases such as white spot disease are high. Many farmers in the area lose their whole second season harvest. The experts estimated that, on average, a conventional shrimp farmer harvests only about 10 tonnes of shrimp (assuming that only five of the six ponds are used). Even worse, the shrimp are comparatively small: 38–40 pieces per kilogram. In contrast, Mr Tam's shrimp grow bigger and yield 27–29 pieces per kilogram. The market price for bigger shrimp is higher, about VND120,000/kg (€6/kg) compared with VND90,000/kg (€4.5/kg) for small shrimp.

Table 14.2 presents the yields and revenues of CTT in comparison with a conventional farm. It confirms that in the wet season CTT is more productive than a conventional farm.

Water use and sewage generation

The river water intake for both CTT and a conventional shrimp farm is about 50,000 m³ for the dry season. In the wet season, CTT requires only 10,000 m³

TABLE 14.2 CTT versus conventional farm: yields and revenues 2000–2004

| Season | CTT | | | Conventional | | |
	Yield (tonnes)	Revenue (€/kg)	Revenue (€)	Yield (tonnes)	Revenue (€/kg)	Revenue (€)
Dry 2000	21	5	105,000	21	5	105,000
Wet 2000	7	6	42,000	10	4.5	45,000
Dry 2001	21	5	105,000	21	5	105,000
Wet 2001	10	6	60,000	10	4.5	45,000
Dry 2002	21	5	105,000	21	5	105,000
Wet 2002	15	6	90,000	10	4.5	45,000
Dry 2003	21	5	105,000	21	5	105,000
Wet 2003	15	6	90,000	10	4.5	45,000
Dry 2004	21	5	105,000	21	5	105,000
Wet 2004	15	6	90,000	10	4.5	45,000

of river water in addition to the re-used water from the dry season. A conventional farm takes in 40,000 m³ of river water in the wet season (the difference from the dry season of 10,000 m³ results from rainwater supply and use of five instead of six ponds). The river water is available free of charge.

At harvest, while the water from the shrimp ponds flows into a sedimentation pond, shrimp are caught with a net. The sewage contains leftovers of feed, chemicals such as chlorine, dead shrimp not captured by the net, and other organic matter. A quantitative comparison of the pollutants within the wastewater has not been carried out. The following qualitative comparison shows the main differences between the two systems.

- The sewage volume is higher for a conventional shrimp farm. In the dry season, a conventional shrimp farm discharges all the wastewater into the river after the ponds have been harvested. Mr Tam, however, pumps the wastewater at the end of the first season into his recycling pond. In the second season the wastewater of both systems is discharged into the river channel.
- The total amount of chemical pollutants within the wastewater is likely to be the same for both systems. Instead of pre-treating river water, CTT treats the recycled water and uses almost the same amount of chemicals as a conventional shrimp farm. A fully closed shrimp farming system would be the best solution to reduce damage caused by chemical pollutants, but is not a feasible option for CTT.
- The total amount of organic matter is lower for CTT. Some of the matter is eaten by the fish in the fish pond. More importantly, shrimp mortality

is lower in the wet season than on the conventional farm. Therefore, the sewage contains less unused feed, fertilisers, and dead shrimp.

Cost of goods sold

Both shrimp farming systems cause comparatively high costs at the beginning of each growing season. Hatching of shrimp larvae is difficult and requires high purchasing costs for the larvae. Feed is another, and higher, recurring cost item. In addition, the purchase of chemicals and admixtures, diesel fuel (for aeration and pumping), and hired labour contribute to the cost. The composition of CTT's cost of goods sold in 2004 is depicted in Figure 14.6 and shows that feed is by far the biggest cost factor. The conventional farm's composition is very similar to CTT's. The total cost of goods sold is slightly lower because of the production of smaller and fewer shrimp in wet season which reduces the demand for feed. An overview of the cost of goods sold for 2000–2004 is shown in Table 14.3.

Capital expenditure

When setting up his shrimp farm, Mr Tam invested €104,000 to purchase the land and €75,000 to buy equipment and dig the ponds. A conventional farm with the same number of shrimp ponds but no additional recycling facilities requires less investment in land (€88,000) and in equipment and pond digging (€60,000).

CTT and the conventional shrimp farm cannot be sure if shrimp farming is profitable in the long run, that is, after 10 years of operation. If not, the salinated land is of no other use in the future or has to be completely redeveloped. It is estimated that the land loses half of its value in this period. Therefore, a redevelopment reserve is needed. Redevelopment reserves of €52,000 for

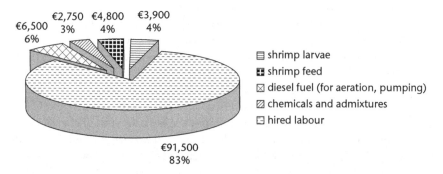

FIGURE 14.6 Composition of CTT's cost of goods sold in 2004.

TABLE 14.3 Total cost of goods sold, CTT versus conventional shrimp farm 2000–2004

Season	CTT (€)	Conventional farm (€)
Dry season 2000	60,000	56,000
Wet season 2000	37,000	40,000
Dry season 2001	60,000	56,000
Wet season 2001	42,000	40,000
Dry season 2002	60,000	56,000
Wet season 2002	50,000	40,000
Dry season 2003	60,000	56,000
Wet season 2003	50,000	40,000
Dry season 2004	60,000	56,000
Wet season 2004	50,000	40,000

CTT and €44,000 for the conventional farm are accumulated over a 10-year period.

Equipment and pond-digging assets are depreciated within six years, because each pond has to be reconstructed completely after this period. The straight-line annual depreciation is €12,500 for CTT and €10,000 for the conventional farm.

Both CTT and the conventional farm raised a credit to buy land and equipment. The interest rate for credit is 1.1 per cent per month (14 per cent per year). The amortisation scheme of both farms was scheduled for five years on a six-monthly basis with instalments at the end of both harvesting seasons (see Table 14.4).

Further relevant information

Comparing conventional and CTT's shrimp farming, the difference in energy consumption for pumping and aeration is negligible. An additional benefit of Mr Tam's approach is the possibility of raising fish. Most of the catch is consumed by Mr Tam, his family, and his employees; however, some of it can be sold. The yield is negligible in financial as well as in physical terms compared with the yield from shrimp farming. Operational expenditure such as marketing, research and development, travel, and office expenses are comparatively low. Both Mr Tam and the conventional farmer are responsible for all these activities by themselves and do not rent offices, employ extra staff, or pay consultants. The estimate of total annual operational expenditure was €4,000 for both types of farm.

TABLE 14.4 CTT versus conventional farm: amortisation scheme

	CTT (€)	Conventional farm (€)
Initial debt	177,750	147,000
Six-month instalment	25,056	20,721
Interest rate (6 months)	6.8%	6.8%

	CTT (€)		Conventional farm (€)	
Date	Interest	Remaining debt	Interest	Remaining debt
Jun 2000	12,059	164,753	9,973	136,252
Dec 2000	11,177	150,875	9,244	124,774
Jun 2001	10,236	136,055	8,465	112,518
Dec 2001	9,230	120,229	7,633	99,430
Jun 2002	8,157	103,330	6,746	85,454
Dec 2002	7,010	85,284	5,797	70,530
Jun 2003	5,786	66,014	4,785	54,594
Dec 2003	4,479	45,437	3,704	37,577
Jun 2004	3,083	23,464	2,549	19,405
Dec 2004	1,592	0	1,316	0

Income statements

Based on the financial information provided, income statements for both types of farm have been derived for a five-year period covering 10 harvesting seasons (Table 14.5). They confirm that CTT has generated higher net income before taxes than a conventional farm in the wet season. However, the comparison also shows that CTT's income is slightly lower in the dry season because of higher expenditures and that the new shrimp farming system generated slightly less income within the first three years of operation because of teething problems. Differences in cost of goods sold are mainly caused by expenses for shrimp feed. If shrimp grow to a smaller size each, or a smaller volume in total, less feed is needed. This explains the differences between CTT and a conventional farm as well as between the dry and wet seasons. CTT's expenses are slightly higher because of debt levels and interest rates (see 'Capital expenditure' above). To stop production in the wet season is not an option because of the high fixed costs of land, equipment, and labour. The fixed costs cannot be avoided in the wet season, so stopping shrimp farming in the second season would increase the net loss in all five years (expenses would equal net loss). As a consequence another strategy is needed.

In the long run, the additional wet season income outweighs the lower

TABLE 14.5 Income statements for CTT and conventional shrimp farm

	Dry season 2000	Wet season 2000	Dry season 2001	Wet season 2001	Dry season 2002	Wet season 2002	Dry season 2003	Wet season 2003	Dry season 2004	Wet season 2004
CTT shrimp farm										
Revenues	105,000	42,000	105,000	60,000	105,000	90,000	105,000	90,000	105,000	90,000
Minus cost of goods sold (feed, larvae, hired labour, etc.)	60,000	37,000	60,000	42,000	60,000	50,000	60,000	50,000	60,000	50,000
Gross profit	45,000	5,000	45,000	18,000	45,000	40,000	45,000	40,000	45,000	40,000
Minus expenses (bank interest, redevelopment reserve, depreciation of equipment, operational expenditure)	25,000	25,000	24,000	23,000	22,000	20,000	19,000	18,000	17,000	15,000
Net income before taxes	20,000	**−20,000**	21,000	**−5,000**	23,000	20,000	26,000	22,000	28,000	25,000
Conventional shrimp farm										
Revenues	105,000	45,000	105,000	45,000	105,000	45,000	105,000	45,000	105,000	45,000
Minus cost of goods sold (feed, larvae, hired labour, etc.)	56,000	40,000	56,000	40,000	56,000	40,000	56,000	40,000	56,000	40,000
Gross profit	49,000	5,000	49,000	5,000	49,000	5,000	49,000	5,000	49,000	5,000
Minus expenses (bank interest, redevelopment reserve, depreciation of equipment, operational expenditure)	21,000	21,000	20,000	19,000	18,000	17,000	16,000	15,000	14,000	13,000
Net income before taxes	28,000	**−16,000**	29,000	**−14,000**	31,000	**−12,000**	33,000	**−10,000**	35,000	**−8,000**

dry season results (Figure 14.7). At the end of the wet season in 2004, the accumulated net income of CTT (€160,000) was almost 70 per cent above the conventional farm's accumulated net income (€96,000).

Key comparative indicators

Mr Tam's motivation to apply EMA was to promote his idea to other farmers. He required reliable and quantifiable facts concerning the financial and ecological superiority of his approach. In the following discussion, some key comparative indicators are derived from the information provided above. The first three indicators aim at convincing other shrimp farmers that the CTT system is beneficial, whereas the last two indicators are orientated towards authorities and other organisations involved in shrimp farming policy-making.

- *Annual revenues per hectare of land.* Despite the higher demand for land, CTT generates greater revenues per hectare of land than a conventional farm (Table 14.6). Other farmers applying the CTT approach could gain a 10 per cent increase in revenues per hectare, assuming that they would not have to undergo the same initial problems as CTT.
- *Net income per year.* The computation of net income before taxes (Table 14.6) includes capital expenditure for buying land and equipment, that is, higher initial investments and debts are incorporated already. The annual net income comparison reveals that CTT earned about twice as much before taxes.
- *Initial debt and annual gross profit.* CTT's system requires more land and equipment and thus a higher initial debt than the conventional system. The ratio between initial debt and gross profit shows that a conventional farm needs the gross profit from almost three years to refund the initial

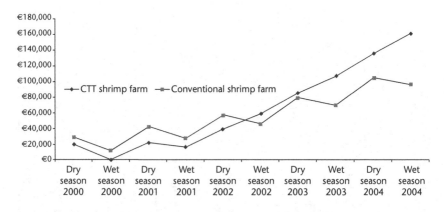

FIGURE 14.7 Accumulated net income before taxes 2000–2004.

TABLE 14.6 Key comparative indicators

	CTT	Conventional	Difference (%)
Revenues/ha/year (2000–2004)	€26,190	€25,862	1.3
Revenues/ha/year (2002–2004)	**€28,467**	**€25,862**	**10.1**
Net income/year (2000–2004)	€32,000	€19,200	66.7
Net income/year (2002–2004)	**€48,000**	**€23,000**	**108.7**
Initial debt/annual gross profit (2000–2004)	2.42	2.72	–11.3
Initial debt/annual gross profit (2002–2004)	**2.09**	**2.72**	**–23.2**
Wastewater/shrimp yield (m³/t)	**1,389**	**3,226**	**–56.9**
Water intake/shrimp yield (m³/t)	**1,667**	**2,903**	**–42.6**
Additional farm land required in Ca Mau Province to meet 2010 export targets (ha)	**13,173**	**14,500**	**–9.2**

debt, whereas the CTT system needs a little more than two years (Table 14.6, again assuming that CTT's teething problems do not recur).

- *Wastewater and water intake per shrimp yield.* The CTT system is clearly superior in terms of wastewater discharge and water intake. Per tonne of shrimp yield the CTT system requires about 40 per cent less water and discharges roughly 60 per cent less wastewater (Table 14.6). It should be noted that the total pollutant load is not lower for CTT, although the total amount of organic matter is substantially lower (see 'Water use and sewage generation' above).
- *Farm land required to meet export targets.* As mentioned earlier, the local government planned to double shrimp exports from 2005 to 2010. That equals additional revenues of €375 million. In order to reach this goal, 14,500 ha (145 km²) of land would have to be used for shrimp farming if the conventional approach were applied, whereas in comparison the CTT approach would require 9 per cent less land (Table 14.6). The table reveals that CTT is the preferred option in all aspects considered. The indicators are even more decisive if the first years of operation (2000 and 2001) are left out. At that time the newly established system had some teething problems, which have not occurred again (for reasons of completeness, indicators are given for 2000–2004 and for 2002–2004).

Data quality

As mentioned earlier, the data for this case study are based on CTT's written records, interviews with Mr Tam, and estimates provided by experts involved in the study. The data has been compared with figures available in shrimp publications (Rönnbäck 2001; Brennan *et al.* 2002). The order of magnitude and the general direction of the results derived from the data available are confirmed by these comparisons. However, the overall precision and data quality of the EMA application have to be classified as low and reflect the reality of data availability in small- to medium-sized enterprises (SME) and emerging countries. Nevertheless it provides support for SME decision-making and basic evidence that the recycling system is economically and ecologically superior to the conventional approach.

Discussion and conclusion

The EMA application at CTT confirms that Mr Tam's gut instincts were right: adding a recycling system in order to re-use the dry season's water with a proper level of salinity, instead of wet season water intake, pays off in financial and ecological terms. By gathering and assessing physical and monetary information for a period of five years and by comparing these with a conventional farm, the environmental and financial superiority of Mr Tam's system has been demonstrated. Mr Tam can use the EMA information for his consulting activities and assess new ideas for improving his shrimp farming system. For instance, he is considering coating the pond grounds with special foil to increase shrimp quality and further decrease mortality. The quantitative assessment made in this EMA study can serve as a basis for appraising the perceived benefits and expected expenses of such investments.

Many EMA case studies and approaches focus on short-term aspects such as cost savings and efficiency improvements. This case study highlights the necessity of including long-term considerations, for instance capital expenditure, in EMA-based decision-making. In this context, another important aspect to consider in EMA is risk. The CTT recycling system reduces the risk of shrimp diseases and total loss of harvest caused by low levels of salinity. This risk reduction has been quantified in terms of lower wet season yields for conventional farms. However, the inclusion of additional risk abatement for conventional farms would also have been adequate. Wet season extinction of stock in the first years of shrimp farm operations can cause severe financial consequences or even lead to bankruptcy if debts cannot be redeemed. This risk and its consequences could not be quantified accurately because of data quality issues and have been disregarded. This is nevertheless a real risk worth considering in decision-making.

This case study provides a past-orientated benchmark for two shrimp farm systems in financial and environmental terms. The results suggest that the CTT system is more efficient, less polluting, and more profitable than a conventional system. Other systems, for example rice-shrimp farming or closed-looped intensive farming, might well be less harmful to the environment or more profitable. This case study does not imply that the CTT system is the most effective or efficient system for shrimp farming in Ca Mau province and it does not state that Mr Tam's business is contributing significantly to sustainable development. Given that the Ca Mau authorities continue to promote rapid growth of the shrimp farming industry, more semi-intensive shrimp farming is likely to be the consequence. With this in mind, the CTT approach is likely to be one of the few feasible solutions for reducing environmental impacts and ensuring profits of shrimp farming in Ca Mau province.

References

Brennan, D., Preston, N., Clayton, H., and Be, T.T. (2002) *An evaluation of rice-shrimp farming systems in the Mekong Delta*. Report prepared under the World Bank, NACA, WWF and FAO Consortium Program on Shrimp Farming and the Environment. Work in progress for public discussion. Washington, DC: the Consortium.

Burritt, R., Hahn, T., and Schaltegger, S. (2002) 'Towards a comprehensive framework for environmental management accounting: links between business actors and environmental management accounting tools', *Australian Accounting Review*, 12: 39–50.

FAO (Food and Agriculture Organization of the United Nations) (2008) *Fishery and aquaculture statistics 2006: FAO yearbook*, Rome: FAO.

Nhuong, T.V., Phillips, M.J., and van Anrooy, R. (2002) *Coastal shrimp aquaculture: searching for better management practices*. Report prepared under the World Bank, NACA, WWF and FAO Consortium Program on Shrimp Farming and the Environment. Work in progress for public discussion. Washington, DC: the Consortium.

Public Citizen (ed.) (2004) *Shell game: the environmental and social impacts of shrimp aquaculture*, Washington, DC: Public Citizen Food Program.

Rönnbäck, P. (2001) *Shrimp aquaculture: state of the art*, Uppsala: Swedish University of Agricultural Sciences.

Schaltegger, S. (1998) 'Accounting for eco-efficiency', in Nath, B., Hens, L., Compton, P., and Devuyst, D. (eds) *Environmental management in practice, volume I: instruments for environmental management*, London: Routledge, pp. 272–287.

Thornton, C., Shanahan, M., and Williams, J. (2003) 'From wetlands to wastelands: impacts of shrimp farming', *Society of Wetland Scientists Bulletin*, March: 48–53.

15

MATERIAL AND ENERGY FLOW ACCOUNTING IN BEER PRODUCTION

Sai Gon Beer, Vietnam

Introduction

Beer has an ancient history dating back to 6000 BC in Babylonia and Sumer. It was one of the first products to be mechanised during the industrial revolution. Beer brewing makes use of natural products such as water, hops, barley, rice, and malt. Its contribution to environmental pollution and other ecological problems is usually not considered to be of particular importance. However, beer brewing on an industrial scale requires a substantial amount of energy and large amounts of water and natural products. In recent years the notion of 'green' beer has been developed by some brewers.

This case study focuses on the application of environmental management accounting (EMA) at Sai Gon Beer, a brewery in central Vietnam. It examines the relevance of material and energy flow accounting for corporate decision-making and reveals options for improving eco-efficiency at the site level (see Figure 15.1: Boxes 9, 1, 16, 8).

Decision setting

Sai Gon Beer is a producer of beer in central Vietnam, founded as a joint venture by two parent companies: an alcohol and beverage corporation and an import–export company. The total capital investment of Sai Gon Beer is €7.4 million. The joint venture company started production of bottled and barrelled beer in 1999. It is certified under ISO 9001 and ISO 14001 for quality and environmental management systems and has won several Vietnamese quality awards for its products. With the help of its 200 employees, the brewery has increased beer output annually up to almost 200,000 hectolitres (hl) and plans to continue growing in the future.

		Monetary EMA		Physical EMA	
		Short-term	Long-term	Short-term	Long-term
Past-orientated	Routinely generated	Environmental cost accounting [1]	Environment-induced capital expenditure and revenue [2]	Material and energy flow accounting [9]	Environmental capital impact accounting [10]
Past-orientated	Ad hoc	Ex-post assessment of relevant environmental costing decisions [3]	Ex-post inventory assessment of projects [4]	Ex-post assessment of short-term environmental impacts [11]	Ex-post inventory appraisal of physical environmental investments [12]
Future-orientated	Routinely generated	Monetary environmental budgeting [5]	Environmental long-term financial planning [6]	Physical environmental budgeting [13]	Environmental long-term physical planning [14]
Future-orientated	Ad hoc	Relevant environmental costing [7]	Monetary environmental investment appraisal [8]	Tools designed to predict relevant enviromental impacts [15]	Physical environmental investment appraisal [16]

FIGURE 15.1 Application of the EMA framework (Burritt, Hahn, and Schaltegger 2002) to Sai Gon Beer.

Note: Dark (light) grey boxes represent the major (minor) EMA applications.

Environmental issues

In comparison with pharmaceutical, petrochemical, or other industrial products, brewing beer is usually not considered to be particularly harmful to the environment as it requires only natural ingredients such as malt, barley, hops, water, or rice. However, a closer look at the environmental life cycle of beer reveals its environmental importance (Talve 2001; Narayanaswamy, Altham, van Berkel, and McGregor 2005; Cordella, Tugnoli, Spadoni, Santarelli, and Zangrando 2008). By far the largest ecological impact is caused by agricultural processes to produce the basic ingredients of beer. According to Talve (2001: 297), agriculture contributes almost 80 per cent to the total environmental impact of the beer life cycle, followed by transportation (8 per cent), production of auxiliary materials (6 per cent), and beer production (5 per cent). From a life cycle perspective, brewers such as Sai Gon Beer are not the focal point for environmental improvement: 'beer production did not seem to be a worrying stage, consistently with the widely held opinion that breweries have to be considered among the less energy consuming and less polluting activities in the industrial sector' (Cordella *et al.* 2008: 137). On the other hand, all life cycle assessment (LCA) studies on beer conclude that certain aspects of beer production are important, in particular energy consumption and the contribution to global warming. A weighted assessment of all environmental impacts by Talve (2001: 297) shows that the global warming contribution (GWC) is the most important environmental impact of brewing, contributing roughly one third of the overall life cycle's GWC. Given that other life cycle steps are more important in general and energy use is the crucial issue for brewers, Cordella and colleagues (2008: 139) arrive at the following recommendations for environmental management measures of breweries:

> monitoring, registering and analysing the input and the output streams of the brewery system; choosing carefully the suppliers, especially those of barley and glass bottle; improving energy saving policies; optimizing solutions for the product delivery; setting up marketing strategies in favour of reusable packaging rather than non-returnable ones.

From its own perspective, Sai Gon Beer is an environmental flagship company for the central Vietnam region. The company uses state-of-the-art brewing equipment and has implemented an environmental management system which led to proper waste separation, recycling of broken bottles and other materials, wastewater treatment, and so forth. Consequently, Sai Gon Beer received its ISO14001 certification with ease and does not face any legal problems relating to environmental issues. The environmental targets of Sai Gon Beer stated in its environmental management report are of a rather general nature and not particularly ambitious. In 2004, for instance, the targets comprise a reduction of the relative use of water (freshwater per unit of product) and relative energy use (electric power per unit of product) by 1 per cent compared with 2003. Other targets listed in internal company documents relate to noise, dust, and certain pollutants within the wastewater.

Economic situation

The Vietnamese beer industry is rapidly growing in terms of production and consumption. Annual beer output grew from 8.7 million hl in 2002 to 17 million hl in 2006, an annual growth rate of 18 per cent. The Ministry of Industry announced plans to double this output by 2010 up to 35 million hl. It also predicted a beer consumption of 28 litres per capita by 2010, which would almost double the 2006 consumption of 15 litres (all figures taken from Mekong Securities 2007; see also Datamonitor 2008).

This fast growth of the beer industry is strongly supported by the Vietnamese government. The government has privatised the biggest breweries and encouraged international brewing companies such as Carlsberg and Anheuser Busch to establish joint ventures as the Vietnamese laws do not allow for 100 per cent foreign investment (Mekong Securities 2007). Sai Gon Beer was established at an early stage of this development as an equity joint venture of one of the biggest and former state-owned brewing companies and a newly privatised Vietnamese import–export company.

As an independently run company with fewer than 300 employees Sai Gon Beer can be classified as a small- to medium-sized enterprise (SME) according to the Vietnamese government (2001). In line with the general development of the Vietnamese beer industry, Sai Gon Beer has set a target of more than doubling production from 200,000 hl in 2004 to 500,000 hl in 2010. This required the construction of an additional brewing facility nearby, which was being planned at the time the case study was conducted.

As a first impression of its economic performance, Sai Gon Beer provided the budgeted and the actual figures for sales and net profit in 2004 (Table 15.1). Although the company met its sales targets, it failed to meet the net profit target. According to the accounting department, the cause was mainly higher than expected operational expenses on raw materials and energy.

Brewing technology

The production facilities of Sai Gon Beer were constructed in 1998. Almost all brewing machinery and equipment was imported from German suppliers and installed by a German engineering company. Sai Gon Beer produces beer in bottles and kegs and delivers these products to retailers, with a small portion going to large customers, for instance restaurants in the same province. The company operates a return system for bottles and kegs, that is, empty bottles and kegs are collected, sorted, and washed.

The main production steps for Sai Gon Beer are grinding (of malt and rice), brewing, fermentation, filtration and storage, and keg and bottle filling. All these steps comprise further separable processes and activities, which are not considered in the following discussion. Unlike most European and North American breweries, Sai Gon Beer uses rice instead of barley as one of the main beer ingredients. Important supply or utility processes from an environmental point of view are chilling, air compressing, heat supply (boiler), and wastewater treatment. All these activities involve further facilities and devices such as the office building and the air conditioning system of the factory building.

TABLE 15.1 Sai Gon Beer 2004 sales and profit

Sai Gon Beer 2004	Budget figure	Actual figure	Actual performance relative to target (%)
Sales (hl)	200,000	203,000	101.5
Sales (€)	7,250,000	7,299,100	100.7
Net profit before taxes (€)	475,600	180,000	37.8

Source: Sai Gon Beer records.

Decision situation and company's motivation for using EMA

Given Sai Gon Beer's ISO 9001 and ISO 14001 certification, its quality awards, and its comparatively new equipment, a state-of-the-art brewery might be expected. The production manager was alarmed by international benchmark figures for electricity and water consumption of beer brewing. He noticed that Sai Gon Beer exceeded these benchmarks and did not seem to perform well in this regard. In fact, he noticed that Sai Gon Beer's total water and energy demand per hectolitre of beer produced was at least twice the international benchmark. Hence, particularly to get a better idea of the drivers of energy and water consumption and to develop improvement options, the production manager announced his interest in applying EMA. Interestingly, the manager had a focus on the improvement of physical performance, knowing that this would also affect financial performance. The manager and environmental manager were keen to link these physical performance issues to environmental management activities, in particular continuous improvement, as required by their environmental management system. Both managers showed a strong interest in monitoring performance on a regular basis and gathering ideas for the new plant which was being constructed.

Analysis of the decision situation showed that the managers need information that is generated routinely (to monitor improvements in performance), relates to the past (consumption of previous month, year, etc.), takes a short-term perspective (monthly or at most annually), and, is measured in physical units. The decision-making situation is therefore linked to Box 9 of the EMA framework (see Figure 15.1) as well as, in part, to Box 1 as any improvement in energy and water efficiency has regular financial consequences period by period. Taking the plans for a new plant into consideration, a long-term, future-orientated perspective would also be relevant for Sai Gon Beer's long-term decision-making (Figure 15.1: Boxes 8 and 16). However, the interest of the managers was clearly focussed on current plant performance. As a matter of course, any conclusions drawn from the assessment of current operations would be included in the planning process for the new plant (Figure 15.1: Boxes 6 and 14). (The application of these tools was not further analysed and thus not highlighted in the framework in Figure 15.1.)

EMA application

To fulfil the environmental and production managers' need for information and to get a better understanding of Sai Gon Beer's operations in general and the drivers of environmental performance in particular, a material and energy flow accounting system (Figure 15.1: Box 9) was agreed upon. This system could then be linked to financial performance (Box 1) and assessed in terms of options for improvement (Boxes 8, 16). Sai Gon Beer's database required for establishing material and energy flow accounting was comparatively good, that is, most data were available, but scattered between different sources. The accounting, environmental management, quality management, and engineering/production departments all contributed some data towards this type of accounting.

Material and energy flow accounting

To develop material and energy flow accounting, the following main production steps were identified (Figure 15.2).

- *Grinding (or milling).* Malt and rice are crushed into smaller pieces.
- *Brewing.* The grist (ground material) is mashed (mixed with water), heated up and mixed with hop in kettles, and finally cooled down. The brewing process generates trub, a bitter mixture of suspended proteins, oils, and so on, which can be used as fertiliser on farmland.
- *Fermentation.* Yeast is added to convert the sugars in wort into alcohol in order to produce unfiltered beer (also called young or green beer).
- *Filtration and storage.* Fermentation continues at slow speed and low temperatures to remove undesired compounds. The beer is then filtered through diatomaceous earth to take out yeast and other leftovers.
- *Bottling.* Beer is mainly bottled into 33-centilitre bottles. The bottle-filling step also includes pasteurisation of filled beer bottles and cleaning of returned bottles.
- *Barrelling.* Beer is filled into kegs (barrels) of various sizes, for example 30 litres, 50 litres, or 100 litres.

In addition to these production steps, several supply processes were considered to be relevant.

- *Steam supply.* Fuel oil is burned in a boiler to produce steam.
- *Air supply.* An air compressor run by electric energy provides the required air pressure.
- *Chiller.* Electric energy is used to provide cooling for several production steps.
- *Wastewater treatment.* All wastewater is collected and treated bio-mechanically before being drawn into public drainage.
- *Other facilities.* This includes the electricity demand of offices, the factory building air conditioning, and other overhead electricity consumption.

For all of the above processes, input–output tables were created listing the inputs of energy (electricity, steam, compressed air, cooling), water, raw material, and intermediates as well as outputs of intermediates, products, solid

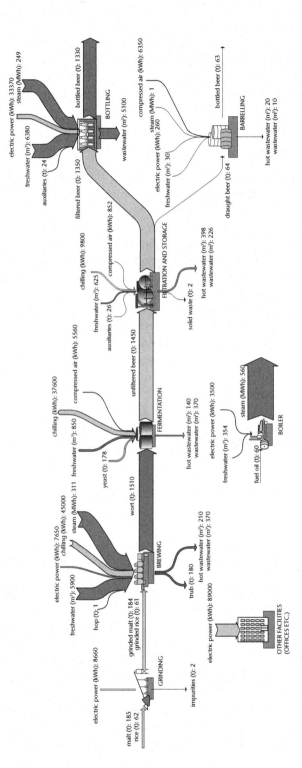

FIGURE 15.2 Sai Gon Beer material and energy flow chart (monthly average Jan–Jun).

wastes, wastewater, and other items. Input–output tables cover a period of six months, but are averaged to one month to assist comparison.

Finally, inputs and outputs of each process were mapped on to a production flow chart using Sankey diagrams, which enabled the depiction of flows in terms of physical proportionality (see Schmidt 2008). Figure 15.2 shows the material and energy flows of Sai Gon Beer for one month (average). The supply process of wastewater treatment was not considered as its energy demand is negligible and the bio-mechanical treatment processes fulfil all legal requirements for wastewater treatment. The main input to the chiller and the air compressor is electricity. The electricity demands of air compressors and chillers were allocated to the various production steps without considering any inefficiency within the devices. This is because the electricity consumption of those devices was known, but not the distribution to production steps. The distribution was estimated on the basis of technical manuals.

All mass flows (in tonnes) were depicted proportionally. Accordingly this applies for volume flows (in m³). For energy flows one exception is made. The flows for steam (in megawatt hours, MWh) are not proportional to all other energy flows (in kilowatt hours, kWh) because the magnitude of the steam flows would otherwise dominate all other flows graphically.

The overall relevance of steam for the energy-related environmental performance of Sai Gon Beer is highlighted in Figures 15.3 and 15.4. Figure 15.3 depicts the total energy demand of all production steps and other facilities and Figure 15.4 shows the resulting GWC for each of these steps. The GWC was calculated based on the following assumptions.

The global warming potential (GWP) for electricity is 0.7 kg CO_2eq per kWh. This value was computed on the basis of the Vietnamese electricity mix (roughly 50 per cent hydro and 50 per cent fossil fuel power, see EIA 2007) using Ecoinvent data sets. The GWP for fuel oil is 3.15 kg CO_2eq per kilogram (see Jardine 2005: 4), that is, 0.34 kg CO_2eq per kWh of steam at Sai Gon Beer.

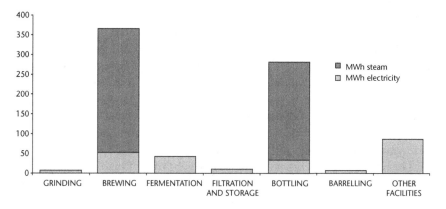

FIGURE 15.3 Sai Gon Beer energy breakdown.

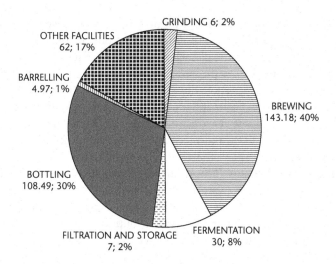

FIGURE 15.4 Sai Gon Beer GWC breakdown (tonnes of CO_2eq; percentage of total).

Water and energy costs

Physical information was the main interest of Sai Gon Beer's production and environmental managers, and the direct financial implications were given a slightly lower priority (see previous section; for more comprehensive case studies on cost accounting in breweries see Jasch and Schnitzer 2003: 71–96; see also Jasch 2006).

According to information provided by the accounting department, purchasing costs were VND1,000/kWh of electric energy, VND3,400/kg of fuel oil and VND3,500/m³ of freshwater (VND20,000 equalled €1 at the time the case study was conducted). Figure 15.5 displays a Sankey diagram of purchasing costs and aggregated costs for Sai Gon Beer. The unit price for chilling and compressed air was assumed to be the same as for electric energy.

Figure 15.5 shows that the total energy and water costs sum to roughly €21,000 per month. This equals 'only' about 4 per cent of total sales and had therefore not been of the highest importance for decision-making in the past. It should be noted, though, that by far the biggest portion of production costs cannot be affected by management action. For instance, the options for reducing raw material purchase costs are very limited as solid waste and other unwanted output is already very low (see Figure 15.2) and, according to the managers of Sai Gon Beer, not avoidable.

The relevance of energy and water costs can be further highlighted by comparing them with labour costs. In rough terms, the total of monthly energy and water costs equals the monthly labour costs of 100 full-time workers, half of Sai Gon Beer's total work force.

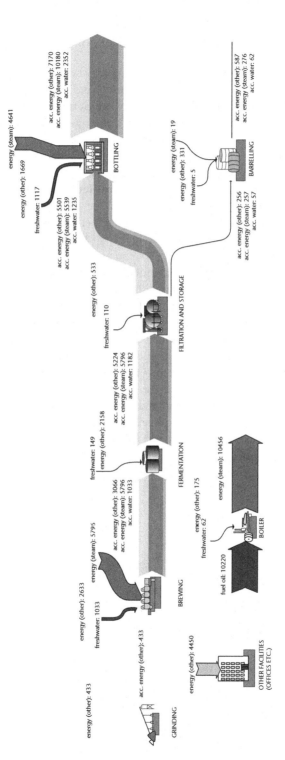

FIGURE 15.5 Sai Gon Beer energy and water costs (€; monthly average Jan–Jun).

Assessment

Sai Gon Beer's production manager was alarmed by benchmark figures found on the Internet (see previous section). For instance, Friesisches Brauhaus zu Jever GmbH and Co. KG, a medium-sized to large Germany brewery, reported its energy and water demand per hectolitre of output in its 2004 environmental report (Jever 2004: 17). Figure 15.6 compares these indicators with Sai Gon Beer's indicators derived from Figure 15.2. Clearly, this benchmark must have been shocking for Sai Gon Beer's production manager because the demand for electric power was about 90 per cent above Jever's resource consumption, for thermal energy 40 per cent above, and for water 130 per cent above. Despite the company's willingness to compare its performance with a German brewery, this type of benchmark can provide only a first orientation because of climate and technological differences.

The material and energy flow accounting results astonished the company's manager in another respect. Previously, the managers did not expect the bottling step to be the biggest consumer of freshwater (see Figure 15.2) and the second biggest consumer of energy (see Figure 15.3). Once it was known, they found an explanation for the high energy and water demand related to this step: bottling includes the washing of returned bottles, which occurs in several steps using different water temperatures and detergents. The heating of water for washing consumed a huge amount of thermal energy and the water demand for washing turned out to be crucial. The benchmark in Figure 15.6 includes indicators for Sai Gon Beer, excluding the bottling step, which highlights the relevance of this step for overall energy and water efficiency. Water and energy efficiency are the relevant categories of eco-efficiency for Sai Gon Beer (for a general introduction to the concept of eco-efficiency in an

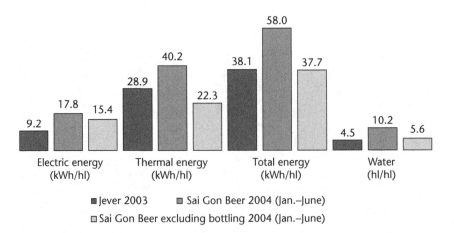

FIGURE 15.6 Energy and water benchmarks.

accounting context see Schaltegger 1998). Their calculation supports management to focus on simultaneous reductions of costs as well as water and energy consumption at Sai Gon Beer. In terms of electricity, Sai Gon Beer remains behind the benchmark even if the bottling step is excluded. Of course, Sai Gon Beer cannot simply outsource the bottling step but this comparison highlights the importance of bottling for overall environmental performance.

Besides bottle washing, heat losses have been identified as important energy consumption drivers. Given the high outside temperatures of a sub-tropical setting, cooling processes and storage of cooled beer require special care. The chilling demand from brewing, fermentation, and filtration and storage accounts for almost 40 per cent of total electricity consumption (see Figure 15.3; in addition Figure 15.7 shows two examples of energy losses caused by poor insulation of chilling and freezing devices). Another third of the total electricity consumption is driven by office and production buildings as well as other overhead electricity demand; most of it the result of air conditioning devices. It can therefore be assumed that two thirds of total electricity consumption is driven by the need for cooling. There are also heat losses to consider. Besides bottling, brewing is the biggest consumer of steam.

The inclusion of energy and water costs into the EMA assessment supports the findings from applying material and energy flow accounting. Brewing and

FIGURE 15.7 Energy losses caused by weak insulation at Sai Gon Beer.

bottling are the most important production steps in terms of energy and water costs, too. To reduce overall costs effectively, these production steps and/or the steam supply needs to become more efficient. Overhead electricity consumption for air conditioning devices is another important contributor to total energy costs (see Figure 15.5). Sai Gon Beer was recommended to analyse the air compressors and chilling units in detail to find further improvement potentials.

The material and energy flow analysis including energy and water costs allows comparison of bottled and draught beer. Table 15.2 is derived from Figure 15.2, Figure 15.4, and Figure 15.5 and confirms the advantage of draught beer in comparison with bottled beer from an environmental point of view. Sai Gon Beer's draught beer performs better in environmental terms. The different energy sources explain why energy and water costs of draught beer are nevertheless not much lower than those of bottled beer. Bottled beer requires more thermal energy (steam) per hectolitre whereas draught beer consumes greater quantities of electric energy, which is more expensive. In any case, comparison supports the conclusion of an Italian LCA study on lager beer: '[f]rom the previous analysis it turned out that the most effective actions to reduce the environmental burdens of the beer life cycles have to be promoted in the consumption phase, preferring draught beer to bottled one' (Cordella *et al.* 2008: 138).

Improvement options

Based on the material and energy flow assessment, two improvement options were discussed and presented to Sai Gon Beer's top management:

• A cascade water-recycling system could be installed to reduce the water and energy consumption in bottling. The system in place did not re-use any water. For each of the four separate washing steps, freshwater had to be taken from the tap, heated up by steam or electric energy, and discharged to wastewater treatment. A cascade system would use freshwater only for the final washing step and re-use the lightly polluted wastewater of this step as water input to the second-last washing step, the wastewater

TABLE 15.2 Comparison of bottled and draught beer at Sai Gon Beer

	CO_2eq (kg/hl)	Water (hl/hl)	Costs (VND/hl)	Total energy (kWh/hl)
Bottled beer	8.16	4.80	29,600	21.23
Draught beer	7.89	0.48	29,400	12.08
% bottled to draught	3.4%	907.4%	0.9%	75.8%

from that step as input for the third-last step, and so on, thereby enabling freshwater, wastewater, and the steam demand to heat water to be reduced.

- A large energy-saving potential lies in the proper insulation of pipes and tanks, in particular where large temperature differences from the surrounding environment occur. For instance, some large beer tanks of Sai Gon Beer were situated outside and exposed to direct sunlight, while the beer inside had to be kept a temperature below 2°C (Figure 15.8). Installing a roof over these tanks and improving the tank insulation seemed to be a profitable and energy-saving option, but required further examination after conduct of the case study.

- The biggest part of energy consumption is caused by supply processes, in particular the fuel oil-fired boiler, air compressors, and chilling devices. It was recommended that the efficiency of these processes be checked and measured. The boiler, for instance, could make use of exhaust heat for pre-heating rather than using electric energy for this purpose. Furthermore, the water required to produce steam could be pre-heated by solar power (tank or black hose on the company's roof).

- Heat exchangers promise to be a valuable option for several processes in the brewing step and could also be used to reduce the loss of thermal energy in air conditioning by using the cooler temperature of exhaust air that leaves the office and production buildings to pre-cool the incoming air.

FIGURE 15.8 Unsheltered cooled storage tanks at Sai Gon Beer.

- The environmental management system could be enhanced by including specific indicators concerning energy and water consumption and by basing the overall environmental targets on the results of material and energy flow accounting. Targets such as the annual 0.5 per cent reduction of energy consumption per unit of product could easily be increased to more ambitious targets.
- The senior managers of Sai Gon Beer agreed to consider these recommendations and to conduct further measurements and assessments where necessary. They insisted on continuing material and energy flow accounting on a regular basis and including it in the planning process of the new plant. Furthermore Sai Gon Beer commissioned a Japanese company to conduct a feasibility study for energy efficiency measures at its new plant. The commissioned company recommended the establishment of a so-called total energy management system in combination with cleaner development mechanism measures.

Data quality

This case study is based on Sai Gon Beer's written records (environmental report according to ISO 14001, books of account, etc.) and on oral information provided by the environmental, production, and accounting departments Data obtained were compared with figures available in several publications on brewing that are referenced throughout this study. Based on these publications the order of magnitude and the general direction of the results derived from the data available can be considered as reliable. The overall completeness and data quality of the EMA application can be classified as only medium to low. In particular, the breakdown of material and energy flows to production and supply processes is based on estimates and computations by production managers and engineers. To improve the reliability of the information actual measurements could be carried out.

Conclusion and outlook

Applying EMA at Sai Gon Beer has helped the production, environmental, and accounting department to identify drivers of environmental performance and related costs. The managers were surprised that bottle filling and bottle washing in particular were amongst the most important drivers of water and energy consumption. As the existing environmental management system did not break down the physical inputs and outputs to single production steps and supply processes, this fact had been overlooked before the EMA analysis took place. A cascade water-recycling system and several other environmental improvements were identified which would easily exceed the environmental goals of Sai Gon Beer stated in its environmental reports. Thus, the case study shows that EMA can create benefits for environmental management systems such as ISO 14001 by providing a detailed information basis for goal setting, planning of improvement measures, and performance monitoring.

The case study confirms the importance of considering both production processes and supply processes and utilities. Most of the energy required at Sai Gon Beer is supplied as steam from a boiler, chilling from refrigerating units, and compressed air from compressors. Increased energy efficiency in production processes reduces the demand for such supplies, but also the supplying devices should undergo permanent energy efficiency improvements.

The application of EMA at Sai Gon Beer was comparatively simple, comprising basic material and energy flow accounting and a breakdown of related energy and water costs. Nevertheless, it led to several improvement options and made the top management rethink its environmental targets. This case study highlights the importance of a systematic material and energy flow-accounting approach which enables managers and engineers to break down relevant physical information to separate production steps and supply processes. This helps to meet the accounting criteria of materiality; to phrase it in a more colloquial manner, it helps to focus on hot-spots, that is, those steps and processes with the highest potential for improvement and the greatest effect on overall (environmental) performance.

Overall, the EMA application at Sai Gon Beer supports the findings of other studies dealing with beer production and the beer life cycle:

> At the process level, improving the energy and material use efficiency of energy intensive equipment could enhance efficiency of production and processing. There is a clear need to expand the focus of the past and existing cleaner production efforts, which were mainly focusing on solid waste and dust control towards enhancing energy and resource use efficiency.
>
> *(Narayanaswamy et al. 2005: 15–16)*

Similarly Peter (1996) and Schaltegger (1997) highlight the importance and advantages of site-specific measures compared with mere life cycle approaches.

References

Burritt, R., Hahn, T., and Schaltegger, S. (2002) 'Towards a comprehensive framework for environmental management accounting: links between business actors and environmental management accounting tools', *Australian Accounting Review*, 12: 39–50.

Cordella, M., Tugnoli, A., Spadoni, G., Santarelli, F., and Zangrando, T. (2008) 'LCA of an Italian lager beer', *International Journal of Life Cycle Assessment*, 13: 133–139.

Datamonitor (2008) *Beer, cider and FABs in Vietnam to 2011*, London: Datamonitor.

EIA (Energy Information Administration) (eds) (2007) *Vietnam energy data, statistics and analysis: oil, gas, electricity, coal*, Washington, DC: EIA.

Jardine, C.N. (2005) *Calculating the environmental impact of aviation emissions*, Oxford: Oxford University Centre for the Environment.

Jasch, C. (2006) 'How to perform an environmental management cost assessment in one day', *Journal of Cleaner Production*, 14: 1194–1213.

Jasch, C. and Schnitzer, H. (2003) *EMA – environmental management accounting – Fallstudienreihe zur Umweltkosten- und Investitionsrechnung [Environmental management accounting – case studies on environmental cost accounting and investment appraisal]*, Vienna: Bundesministerium für Verkehr, Innovation und Technologie, available in German only.

Jever (2004) *Umwelterklärung 2004 [Environmental report 2004]*, Jever (Germany): Friesisches Brauhaus zu Jever GmbH and Co. KG.

Mekong Securities (2007) *Industry Research Beer in Vietnam*, Hanoi: Mekong Securities.

Narayanaswamy, V., Altham, W., van Berkel, R., and McGregor, M. (2005) 'Application of life cycle assessment to enhance eco-efficiency of grains supply chains', paper presented at the 4th Australian LCA Conference, Sydney, February.

Peter, D. (1996) 'Case Study Feldschlösschen', in Schaltegger, S. (ed.) *Life cycle assessment (LCA) – quo vadis?*, Basel: Birkhäuser, pp. 93–130.

Schaltegger, S. (1997) 'Economics of life cycle assessment: inefficiency of the present approach', *Business Strategy and the Environment*, 6: 1–8.

Schaltegger, S. (1998) 'Accounting for eco-efficiency', in Nath, B., Hens, L., Compton, P., and Devuyst, D. (eds) *Environmental management in practice, volume I: instruments for environmental management*, London: Routledge, pp. 272–287.

Schmidt, M. (2008) 'The Sankey diagram in energy and material flow management. Part II: methodology and current applications', *Journal of Industrial Ecology*, 12: 173–185.

Talve, S. (2001) 'Life cycle assessment of a basic lager beer', *International Journal of Life Cycle Assessment*, 6: 293–298.

Vietnamese Government (2001) Decree 90/2001/CP-ND – Decree of the Government of the Socialist Republic of Vietnam on Supporting for Development of Small and Medium Enterprises, 23 Nov 2001.

Part III

Findings, discussion, and conclusion

16

RATIONALE BEHIND AND REASONS FOR APPLYING EMA IN CORPORATE PRACTICE

The 12 exploratory South-East Asian case studies presented in Part II of this book reveal a great variety of environmental management accounting (EMA) applications, tools, and outcomes. The findings are valuable to individual case study companies and contribute to a better understanding of EMA practice. This part of the book undertakes a comparative review of the case studies and elaborates upon generalisable results in order to address one potential pitfall of qualitative management accounting research, the presentation of results in 'a loose assembly of calculative practices that are used selectively, in a bewildering variety of ways, by a multitude of agents within a broad range of organisational processes and situations' (Vaivio 2008: 67).

This and the following chapters compare the findings from all case studies based on the comparative case study design and the research questions elaborated on in this part. Chapter 16 looks into the reasons why managers decide to implement EMA as a part of their corporate practice. This analysis is followed by an exploration of EMA patterns which reveal how companies can use and combine tools out of a set of various EMA tools to make better-informed decisions. The comparison across cases also leads to further research questions including the demand for generalisable conclusions. This final part of the book thus concludes with an executive summary including management and policy implications for decision-makers in business, government, and not-for-profit organisations.

The research questions will now be discussed in the light of the case studies previously examined.

How do environmental and institutional settings influence the implementation of EMA in South-East Asia? This first research question seeks the *rationality, motivations, and reasons behind, as well as organisational circumstances and* ·

institutional settings which influence, the decision to establish EMA and to design it in a specific way. The factors influencing the implementation of EMA by companies in South-East Asia are expressed through the choice of EMA tools and the logic behind the introduction of EMA procedures and responsibilities. Very often the reasons for conducting EMA are related to the business environment and success factors that managers need to address. Specific characteristics of the environment and institutional settings can support or discourage the implementation of EMA tools. Comparison of the case studies provides insight into the links and relationships between EMA implementation, on the one hand, and, on the other hand, economic, socio-cultural, technical, and ecological issues and institutional arrangements such as political power, regulations, and governing and self-governing structures.

An overwhelming body of research into EMA, as well as EMA standards, guidelines, and case studies, considers economic rationality as the dominating rationale for applying EMA and its specific concepts such as material flow cost accounting (e.g. Onishi, Kokubu, and Nakajima 2008; Jasch 2009), environmental cost accounting (Schaltegger and Wagner 2005), eco-efficiency (e.g. Schaltegger 1998; Schaltegger, Bennett, Burritt, and Jasch 2008), health and safety (e.g. Rikhardsson 2006), or risk (e.g. Burritt 2005). Not surprisingly, economic rationality is a main driver for the implementation of EMA in most of the 12 case studies presented here. Environmental information, in particular on material and energy flows, is combined with monetary figures to assess the potential economic benefits of cleaner production and environmental protection measures. This is the case for all sizes of company and all four countries. Economic efficiency represents a core motivation of owners and senior managers, as well as internal stakeholders such as environmental or quality managers for applying EMA. Thus EMA is used to confirm the economic advantages of:

- operational measures and investments for increasing material and energy efficiency, for example by means of cleaner production, waste minimisation, and energy saving (see Indah Jaya, JBC Food, Tan Loc Food, Sai Gon Beer, Classic Crafts);
- strategic investments into new environmental technologies and assets which help to reduce costs and/or increase revenues (see Oliver Enterprises I and II, Thai Cane Paper, CTT, Tan Loc Food); and
- supply chain-related eco-efficient measures and improvements (see Neumann Vietnam, Bisma Jaya).

Many of these economic considerations are closely linked to scientific and technical issues and rationality. EMA is used to assess the effectiveness of new investments, cleaner production measures, and so forth, in terms of achieving an actual reduction of environmental impacts or an increase in environmental quality. In several case studies technical rationality is the initial driver for environmental measures and EMA has had to confirm the effectiveness of these measures prior to establishing their economic efficiency. Environmental effectiveness is a separately identifiable decision-making rationale which comes particularly to the fore when environmental or quality managers are the most important EMA activists. Such effectiveness is often influenced by scientific knowledge and logic as well as by technological progress, possibilities, and innovation. Examples whereby these issues influence the establishment of EMA are as follows.

- The reduction of freshwater consumption is a technical goal of increasing importance in many countries. Indah Jaya's management representative was eager to reduce freshwater consumption substantially by introducing a water-recycling technology, no matter if this made sense from an economic point of view. Tan Loc Food evaluated options to store rainwater in a tank to bridge the water shortages of the dry season, and Thai Cane Paper assessed the benefit from water availability through a pond to store water to deal with dry periods and avoid production stoppages.
- To reduce overall environmental impacts can be a further goal defined in a technical way. The environmental task force at JBC Food constantly tries to apply new ideas to reduce overall environmental impacts. Economic assessment of these new ideas is needed to convince top management and to decide on priorities because of limited budgets.
- More specifically, the reduction of carbon emissions is a goal that is often internally driven. The two owners of Oliver Enterprises were committed to resolving problems associated with a challenge to their legitimacy in the local community, as the burning of rice husk in open fields led to severe accidents for children and the local populace. A technical solution was sought whereby new carbonisation machinery was acquired and installed, thereby avoiding the need to transport and burn rice husk in the open. Furthermore, technical rationality was extended in a sequential way as energy generated from the company's newly installed carbonisation process was eventually fed back into the grid for an economic return.
- In some cases, reducing local pollution, such as toxic waste (water) or smoke, can be a technically defined goal. Well-Ever represents a case in point, as attempts were made to clean up the emissions of fumes and wastewater associated with electroplating in order to assuage environmental concerns of the local community and local government.
- Technically defined health and social issues can be a driving issue such as in the case of Bisma Jaya, where the accident rate was considered to be too high, or at Oliver Enterprises, which aimed at reducing and preventing cases of burnt hands and damaged eyes among people digging for rice leftovers in the burning rice husk heaps.

Some case studies highlight the strong link between EMA and legal and regulatory rationality. By quantifying and assessing whether cleaner development mechanism requirements, limit values, and other regulations are met or will be met by future measures and technology, EMA helped some of the case study companies to maintain, or regain, legal capacities, reduce corresponding risks and uncertainties, or react to international regulatory settings.

- Compliance with and adaptations on basis of regulations can be a reason to introduce EMA. Well-Ever, for example, used EMA as the basis for obtaining information about environmental impacts that would assist it to obtain a licence to operate in a previously non-industrial zone. EMA helped Well-Ever to demonstrate that it had met local council regulations.
- International regulatory settings such as clean development mechanism (CDM) or joint implementation projects can support the introduction of EMA to assess the physical effects and the financial viability of cleaner production projects. Oliver Enterprises applied EMA to help understand the environmental advantages of a new technology for decarbonising rice husk. In a second step these improvements were checked against the rules and requirements of the cleaner development mechanism regime.
- Audits and other quasi-legal or standard-based approaches conducted by the main customer may have an effect similar to that of legal requirements. The Bisma Jaya case shows the strong pressure the main customer can exert with criteria-based audits which influence corporate behaviour and the collection of date in line with the required key performance data. Similarly, Well-Ever responded to supply chain pressure from the purchaser by an international company of automotive parts, in order to establish the credibility of environmental management.

Socio-cultural, normative rationality and questions of morality, reliability, and social purposes of a company are a very important issue for larger corporations and can be associated with popular concepts and approaches such as corporate social responsibility or corporate citizenship. In accounting this is reflected in the growing market for sustainability reporting, the use and usefulness of measurement to legitimise corporate activities, and the internal company communication and awareness-raising effects of data collection. For smaller companies, and in the emerging economies context, this type of rationality seems to be less evident, especially when considering the internal decision-making notion of EMA. Nevertheless some case studies did reveal aspects of normative rationality.

- Documenting responsibility towards employees may be a reason to implement EMA. For example, JBC Food's environmental task force was keen to reduce environmental and social impacts, for example the health

problems of poor people using JBC Food's used frying oil, for normative reasons (but required economic rationality to get top management
approval).

* EMA can serve as an approach of organisational learning to establish a
momentum or project which motivates various employees to engage
and to exchange ideas, information, views, and assessments. In the case
of Sai Gon Beer, EMA led to the gathering of managers from very different departments (production, environment, quality, finance, strategy,
and accounting) to discuss learning and the design criteria for building
a new production plant which extends the existing production facilities
threefold.

* Signalling responsibility to the public to secure legitimacy is usually
mainly referred to in the context of large companies, but can also be an
issue of small- to medium-sized enterprises. Tan Loc Food used a pilot
EMA assessment exercise as an opportunity to invite the local television
company to report on its environmental quality measures.

Within the concept of socio-economic rationality, the fifth sphere is politics; this considers the power and importance of stakeholders. Companies try
to assert their political interests to maintain freedom of action. The case studies reveal that external environmental stakeholders are comparatively weak in
many South-East Asian countries. In no case were the claims of environmental
non-government organisations of significant importance. Nevertheless, in
Vietnam authorities and the political bureau did play a crucial role for managers and substantially influenced their way of thinking. In all South-East Asian
countries environmental authorities as executives of environmental law and
regulation had some impact, for instance in the cases of Well-Ever or Tan Loc
Food. However, these and other cases also show that the enforcement of environmental regulation was rather weak. Open rice husk burning (see Oliver
Enterprises case study), for instance, was a common practice despite govern-
mental decrees prohibiting it. Several of the case study companies mentioned
that corruption was a widespread approach in their respective industries to
ensure political interests and established an undesirable type of legal rationality
that led to suppression of environmental development and improvements.

Here are some case study examples on the role EMA can play with regard
to politics.

* Convincing authorities, and associations or political bureaus and parties,
about legitimacy and conformity with political expectations can be an
important success factor in many countries, not just in South-East Asia. As
an example, Tan Loc Food used EMA as an assessment exercise and as an
opportunity to invite representatives of the political office and local television to report on its environmental quality measures. Oliver Enterprises

engaged in development of EMA calculations with PhilRice, the Philippine government research institution, as a foundation for analysing whether investment in new rice husk-processing technology, promoted by the government agency, is justifiable. Pre- and post-assessments of the ACS investment served the government research body to examine the practical problems of implementation and roll out the technology in the Philippines.

- Promoting superior techniques and practices is not just a question of technical or economic rationality but can be supported and influenced by business associations and political organisations to a large extent. The case of CTT was illustrative because EMA information was gathered and assessed to convince crucial stakeholders such as the local fishing authority and the local shrimp farming association that the new and different shrimp farming approach made sense from an environmental and economic point of view.

Socio-economic rationality requires balanced management of all these spheres of rationality (Schaltegger, Burritt, and Petersen 2003: ch. 7). The case studies showed that EMA can support managers in very different ways and with regard to different rationales, success factors, and requirements defined in the socio-economic business environment. Thus, EMA can help managers achieve such a balanced approach. In fact, in most of the case studies several types of rationality are combined and integrated.

- Tan Loc Food used EMA to assess the consequences of a new wastewater regulation for its operations, which led to changes in the company's wastewater treatment approach (legal, technological, political, and economic rationality).
- Sai Gon Beer applied EMA in a way which supported interdepartmental learning processes and the improvement of economic goals (improved eco-efficiency) by aiming at technical progress (less energy consumption).
- In the case of JBC Food, EMA was used to legitimise the work of the environmental taskforce and manager within the company and to expand their freedom of action by achieving cost reductions and improving energy efficiency. In addition, at JBC Food the environmental group was keen to improve working conditions for employees in plant where temperatures were high and it built upon this social rationality to develop performance-based information which demonstrated how the installation of air-conditioning led to increased productivity and, using economic rationality, increased profitability (political, social, and economic rationality).
- Oliver Enterprises engaged in development of EMA calculations with PhilRice, the Philippine government research institution, as a foundation for securing a linkage with the overseas company transferring and

subsidising, in the first instance, Japanese technology needed to make the carbonisation process work in terms of economic rationality (political and economic rationality).

With regard to the reasons to use EMA, the case studies provided a rich variety of motivations and rationales to respond to requirements and circumstances in the social and business environment. The rationale behind EMA implementation is also expressed in the choice of EMA tools and patterns of tool use, that is, combinations of tools applied in each company.

References

Burritt, R.L. (2005) 'Environmental risk management and environmental management accounting. developing linkages', in Tukker, A., Rikhardsson, P.M., Bennett, M., Bouma, J.J., and Schaltegger, S. (eds) *Implementing environmental management accounting: status and challenges*, Dordrecht: Kluwer.

Jasch, C. (2009) *Environmental and material flow cost accounting: principles and procedures*, Dordrecht: Springer.

Onishi, Y., Kokubu, K., and Nakajima, M. (2008) 'Implementing material flow cost accounting in a pharmaceutical company', in Schaltegger, S., Bennett, M., Burritt, R.L., and Jasch, C. (eds) *Environmental management accounting for cleaner production*, Dordrecht: Springer, pp. 395–409.

Rikhardsson, P.M. (2006) 'Accounting for health and safety costs: review and comparison of selected methods', in Schaltegger, S., Bennett, M., and Burritt, R. (eds) *Sustainability accounting and reporting*, Dordrecht: Springer, pp. 129–153

Schaltegger, S. (1998) 'Accounting for eco-efficiency', in Nath, B., Hens, L., Compton, P., and Devuyst, D. (eds) *Environmental management in practice, volume i: instruments for environmental management*, London: Routledge, pp. 272–287.

Schaltegger, S. and Wagner, M. (2006) 'Integrative management of sustainability performance, measurement and reporting', *International Journal of Accounting, Auditing and Performance Evaluation*, 3: 1–19.

Schaltegger, S., Burritt, R., and Petersen, H. (2003) *An introduction to corporate environmental management: striving for sustainability*, Sheffield: Greenleaf.

Schaltegger, S., Bennett, M., Burritt, R.L., and Jasch, C. (2008) *Environmental management accounting for cleaner production*, Dordrecht: Springer.

Vaivio, J. (2008) 'Qualitative management accounting research: rationale, pitfalls and potential', *Qualitative Research in Accounting and Management*, 5: 64–86.

17

REVEALING PATTERNS OF EMA APPLICATION

Analysing the relationship between tools

Environmental management accounting (EMA) represents a concept that embraces a large range of tools. The application of these tools supports managers with information to understand, manage, control, and report the company's impacts on the natural environment in a better way, as well as improve its environmental and/or financial performance. Whereas the EMA framework provides an overview of possible decision situations and EMA tools, it does not show the tools, and combination of tools, which may be most useful in corporate practice.

This chapter compares and contrasts the main findings across all 12 case studies in relation to the second research question: *How do EMA tools interact and complement each other as support for managers in decision-making?* The chapter considers the identified application and applicability of various EMA tools and how they are linked with each other in different decision settings. The comparison of case studies shows what EMA tools were relevant and that coupling of certain types of EMA tools can provide management with useful information in different decision settings. Across the set of case studies various patterns of using EMA tools emerge. The following sections reveal a consolidated view on the uses of and relationships between EMA tools to support decision-making.

Several contrasting contexts are examined within which different EMA patterns emerge. These are discussed in two steps. First, four simple relationships between EMA tools are introduced based on the comprehensive EMA framework, that is, the uses and relationships of related pairs of EMA tools are presented (next section). The patterns examined highlight two complementary tools in settings where other aspects of EMA decision-making remain the same. The pairs are past/future, physical/monetary, short- and long-term decisions, and provision of information on a regular or ad hoc basis. Second, two generic sets of more complex patterns of EMA use which emerge from the case study findings are discussed. These patterns represent complex interrelationships between a broader set of EMA tools, and advance either environmentally sound physical environmental management accounting (PEMA) or eco-efficient physical environmental management accounting/ monetary environmental management accounting (PEMA/MEMA) decision-making. For each EMA pattern one example is provided.

Four main *simple* relationships between different EMA tools are illustrated:

*   *Physical/monetary EMA tools.* CTT represents a retrospective assessment and comparison of the environmental and financial performance of a capital investment.
*   *Past/future EMA tools.* Oliver Enterprises I portrays an ex-post appraisal as an ongoing check on the assumed costs and benefits of an environmental investment calculation.
*   *Short-term/long-term EMA tools.* Classic Crafts shows the advancement of long-term investment appraisal through short-term related environmental cost analysis.
*   *Application of EMA tools on a regular/ad hoc basis.* Thai Cane Paper demonstrates the mobilisation of ad hoc information about the effects of different environmental investment options to advance integration of difference scenarios for water supply into regular environmental long-term planning.

These sets of complementary tools illustrate the main four characteristics of the comprehensive EMA framework central to the book.

In many instances a larger number of tools are used, revealing the complex interrelationships between EMA tools and the potential for EMA as a whole. The focus in the following examples is on ecological-effectiveness and eco-efficiency.

*   *Set of PEMA tools to assist in the transparency of ecological effectiveness.* Well-Ever presents a complex relationship between three PEMA tools which help in the management of ecological effectiveness, starting with an ex-post analysis of environmental impacts caused by the organisation's operations for better prediction of expected future impacts and development of a system to account for material and energy flows in a regular way, coupled with occasional ad hoc assessments of short-term environmental impacts.
*   *Indah Jaya – a complex relationship between MEMA and PEMA tools to support eco-efficiency improvements.* Indah Jaya starts with material and energy flow accounting as a basis for comprehensive environmental cost accounting. This information is used for several assessments of technical measures for improving eco-efficiency, for an improved consideration of material

and energy flow impacts on pricing decisions, and for regular reporting of eco-efficiency performance.

Simple relationships between EMA tools

Patterns of physical and monetary tools

The first EMA patterns examined address simple relationships between physical and monetary EMA tools. Here, monetary environmental information is created through linking physical environmental information, derived from the corresponding PEMA tool, with monetary figures.

An illustration of this first type of EMA pattern is CTT (Figure 17.1). Here, the environmental and financial performance of a capital investment (semi-closed shrimp farming system) is assessed through a retrospective assessment and comparison with conventional shrimp farming over a five-year period. CTT's shrimp farming approach was deemed to be environmentally beneficial and data generated over the five-year period primarily aimed at analysing the economic effects of the capital investment. Hence, building upon information from Box 10 of the EMA framework (Figure 17.1), there is strong emphasis on the corresponding MEMA Box 2.

A related EMA pattern can be found in the case of Oliver Enterprises II. The owners of the company use physical environmental investment appraisal (Figure 17.1: Box 16) to calculate CO_2 emission reductions from investment

		Monetary EMA		Physical EMA	
		Short-term	Long-term	Short-term	Long-term
Past-orientated	Routinely generated	Environmental cost accounting [1]	Environment-induced capital expenditure and revenue [2]	Material and energy flow accounting [9]	Environmental capital impact accounting [10]
Past-orientated	Ad hoc	Ex-post assessment of relevant environmental costing decisions [3]	Ex-post inventory assessment of projects [4]	Ex-post assessment of short-term environmental impacts [11]	Ex-post inventory appraisal of physical environmental investments [12]
Future-orientated	Routinely generated	Monetary environmental budgeting [5]	Environmental long-term financial planning [6]	Physical environmental budgeting [13]	Environmental long-term physical planning [14]
Future-orientated	Ad hoc	Relevant environmental costing [7]	Monetary environmental investment appraisal [8]	Tools designed to predict relevant enviromental impacts [15]	Physical environmental investment appraisal [16]

FIGURE 17.1 CTT Shrimp Farm as an example of a simple pattern of PEMA and MEMA tools. Dark grey boxes represent the major EMA applications.

in a rice husk-fired cogeneration plant. Then, through a monetary environmental investment appraisal (Figure 17.1: Box 8), the additional revenues are calculated and these may be obtained from emissions reductions through the clean development mechanism scheme. Besides these patterns, information generated through routine and ad hoc means through the combined use of PEMA and MEMA tools may also occur when coupling short-term EMA tools (Figure 17.1: Boxes 11 and 3 or 13 and 5).

Patterns of past- and future-orientated EMA tools

The second simple relationship between EMA tools refers to organisational contexts within which the interrelationship between ex-post and ex-ante analysis of physical monetary environmental information is clarified. Different tool combinations can emerge and the EMA pattern of Oliver Enterprises I is described (Figure 17.2).

Oliver Enterprises utilises ex-ante monetary environmental investment appraisal to promote cleaner production technology and draws conclusions in the context of an ex-post assessment of the actual costs and savings observed in the pilot phase of the investment. The configuration provides a classic example of ex-post appraisal as ongoing checks on the assumed costs and benefits of an environmental investment calculation. An opportunity to acquire rice husk carbonisation technology from Japan meant that the owners

		Monetary EMA		Physical EMA	
		Short-term	Long-term	Short-term	Long-term
Past-orientated	Routinely generated	Environmental cost accounting [1]	Environment-induced capital expenditure and revenue [2]	Material and energy flow accounting [9]	Environmental capital impact accounting [10]
	Ad hoc	Ex-post assessment of relevant environmental costing decisions [3]	Ex-post inventory assessment of projects [4]	Ex-post assessment of short-term environmental impacts [11]	Ex-post inventory appraisal of physical environmental investments [12]
Future-orientated	Routinely generated	Monetary environmental budgeting [5]	Environmental long-term financial planning [6]	Physical environmental budgeting [13]	Environmental long-term physical planning [14]
	Ad hoc	Relevant environmental costing [7]	Monetary environmental investment appraisal [8]	Tools designed to predict relevant enviromental impacts [15]	Physical environmental investment appraisal [16]

FIGURE 17.2 Oliver Enterprises I as an example of a simple pattern of past- and future-orientated EMA tools. Dark grey boxes represent the major EMA applications.

of Oliver Enterprises in the Philippines examined the investment cash flows associated with acquisition. With a 50 per cent capital contribution from the Japanese manufacturing company the ex-ante, one-off decision-making data indicated that the investment decision should go ahead (Figure 17.2: Box 8). Following the introduction of carbonisation units Oliver Enterprises needed to decide whether further units should be acquired and an ex-post assessment of the initial investment provided a certain level of confidence that the further investment should take place (Box 4).

Other cases include Classic Crafts, where an investment in water tanks to improve water quality required prediction of the future prospects of the investment and ex-post realisation of the net benefits from the investment. A similar example was provided by Tan Loc Food.

Patterns between EMA tools focussing on ad hoc and routinely generated information

The third type of simple EMA pattern utilises the linkage between ad hoc and routinely generated environmental information.

Thai Cane Paper occupies a future and long-term perspective on the assessment of environmental impacts. Here, the dynamic relationship between two long-term future-orientated physical EMA tools is explored. The use of a long-term environmental planning system (Figure 17.3: Box 14) and ad hoc-generated information about the effects of different environmental

		Monetary EMA		Physical EMA	
		Short-term	Long-term	Short-term	Long-term
Past-orientated	Routinely generated	Environmental cost accounting [1]	Environment-induced capital expenditure and revenue [2]	Material and energy flow accounting [9]	Environmental capital impact accounting [10]
Past-orientated	Ad hoc	Ex-post assessment of relevant environmental costing decisions [3]	Ex-post inventory assessment of projects [4]	Ex-post assessment of short-term environmental impacts [11]	Ex-post inventory appraisal of physical environmental investments [12]
Future-orientated	Routinely generated	Monetary environmental budgeting [5]	Environmental long-term financial planning [6]	Physical environmental budgeting [13]	Environmental long-term physical planning [14]
Future-orientated	Ad hoc	Relevant environmental costing [7]	Monetary environmental investment appraisal [8]	Tools designed to predict relevant enviromental impacts [15]	Physical environmental investment appraisal [16]

FIGURE 17.3 Thai Cane Paper as an example of a simple pattern of ad hoc and routine EMA tools. Dark grey boxes represent the major EMA applications.

investment options to reduce any predicted shortages in water supply (Box 16) is mobilised to advance the integration into environmental long-term planning of different scenarios for water supply and demand with different investment options.

Another example of a simple pattern of ad hoc and routine EMA tools is Well-Ever. However, in contrast to Thai Cane Paper it mobilises short-term and past-orientated PEMA tools (Figure 17.3: Boxes 11 and 9). More generally, this third pattern of EMA use is not limited to PEMA tools and may also occur when there is interest in past- or future-orientated monetary environmental information (e.g. Figure 17.3: Boxes 1 and 3, Boxes 5 and 7).

Patterns between EMA tools focussing on short-term and long-term decision-making

The comparative case study reveals a fourth type of tool linkage which bring to the fore the interrelated aspects of short- and long-term decision-making.

In the case of Classic Crafts, the consecutive application of two ad hoc and future-orientated monetary EMA tools (Figure 17.4: Boxes 7 and 8) enhances the company owners' long-term thinking and supports them in deploying their cost reduction strategy. This approach to EMA provides support by making visible inappropriate short-term decisions in relation to the use of a by-product. Based on a short-term-related cost analysis and the improved

		Monetary EMA		Physical EMA	
		Short-term	Long-term	Short-term	Long-term
Past-orientated	Routinely generated	Environmental cost accounting [1]	Environment-induced capital expenditure and revenue [2]	Material and energy flow accounting [9]	Environmental capital impact accounting [10]
Past-orientated	Ad hoc	Ex-post assessment of relevant environmental costing decisions [3]	Ex-post inventory assessment of projects [4]	Ex-post assessment of short-term environmental impacts [11]	Ex-post inventory appraisal of physical environmental investments [12]
Future-orientated	Routinely generated	Monetary environmental budgeting [5]	Environmental long-term financial planning [6]	Physical environmental budgeting [13]	Environmental long-term physical planning [14]
Future-orientated	Ad hoc	Relevant environmental costing [7]	Monetary environmental investment appraisal [8]	Tools designed to predict relevant enviromental impacts [15]	Physical environmental investment appraisal [16]

FIGURE 17.4 Classic Craft as an example of a simple pattern combining short-term and long-term EMA tools. Dark grey boxes represent the major EMA applications.

quality of environmental information, it advances the application of a long-term investment appraisal.

The mobilisation of the relationship between short- and long-term decision-making is also evident in the Thai Cane Paper case study. Physical environmental stock and flow information aims to monitor changes in the condition of the environment (water supply) and to support the company in avoiding water scarcity within its operation and the surrounding environment. The development of a long-term environmental planning system and a related short-term budgeting system (Figure 17.4: Boxes 13 and 14) supports the company in forecasting and addressing environmental, social, and economic risks in production planning and control.

Other possible patterns may address Boxes 5 and 6 or Boxes 15 and 16 of the EMA framework. They may also consist of two ad hoc and past-orientated MEMA or PEMA tools.

Variations and combinations of EMA patterns

The discussion of EMA patterns concentrates on relationships between two complementary EMA tools which differ in only one characteristic (e.g. ad hoc versus routinely generated environmental information). Our case studies also provide evidence for the usefulness of coupling EMA tools in settings where information is needed which differs in more than one aspect (variations of simple EMA patterns). One example is provided by routinely generated monetary information from an environmental costing system (Figure 4.1: Box 1) being used by Indah Jaya as input to a one off investment in a new boiler which would increase energy efficiency by reducing waste heat (Figure 4.1: Box 8). This case illustrates the use of two MEMA tools providing and coupling routinely generated, and short-term, past-orientated information with an ad hoc long-term appraisal of an eco-efficient investment project. Another good case in point is Bisma Jaya. The case study demonstrates the usefulness of the ex-post assessment of short-term health, safety, and environmental (HSE) impacts (PEMA tool, Figure 5.1: Box 11) and how this information can flow into a costing approach, supporting the implementation of HSE measures in the most cost-efficient way (MEMA tool, Figure 5.1: Box 7). It illustrates how short-term and past-orientated non-monetary information about HSE which is gathered on an ad hoc basis (HSE audit) can be combined with a short-term and future-orientated ad hoc monetary assessment of HSE measures.

Besides these variations of simple EMA patterns which are based on two EMA tools, the coupling of more than two tools can further increase the complexity of relationships between EMA tools. Our case studies show how EMA tools can provide support to management in more complex decision settings by combining some of the EMA patterns which have been discussed before. Two generic sets of more complex EMA patterns are described next.

More complex relationships between EMA tools

Eco-efficiency orientation by combining PEMA and MEMA

The first complex approach to combining EMA tools is aimed at improving decision-making to improve eco-efficiency. In the context of the 12 South-East Asian case studies, several decision settings were explored within which the interplay between MEMA and PEMA tools has been useful for eco-efficient decision-making. There have been varying uses and different numbers of EMA tools; see for example Classic Craft and JBC Food. One example strongly orientated towards eco-efficiency is discussed next: Indah Jaya (Figure 17.5). The EMA approach of this case study is complex MEMA and PEMA interaction.

The case of Indah Jaya represents a 'classic' EMA pattern studied in length in the literature (e.g. Schaltegger and Burritt 2000; Strobel and Redmann 2002; Jasch 2006, 2009; Wagner and Enzler 2006; Kokubu, Campos, Furukawa, and Tachikawa 2009). It combines regular gathering of past-orientated, short-term (material and energy flow) information and related cost information with future-orientated information required to assess short- and long-term ad hoc decisions. Within this EMA approach, the implementation usually starts with the identification, collection, measurement, and assessment of all kinds of physical information relevant to the mapping of the company's environmental

		Monetary EMA		Physical EMA	
		Short-term	Long-term	Short-term	Long-term
Past-orientated	Routinely generated	Environmental cost accounting [1]	Environment-induced capital expenditure and revenue [2]	Material and energy flow accounting [9]	Environmental capital impact accounting [10]
Past-orientated	Ad hoc	Ex-post assessment of relevant environmental costing decisions [3]	Ex-post inventory assessment of projects [4]	Ex-post assessment of short-term environmental impacts [11]	Ex-post inventory appraisal of physical environmental investments [12]
Future-orientated	Routinely generated	Monetary environmental budgeting [5]	Environmental long-term financial planning [6]	Physical environmental budgeting [13]	Environmental long-term physical planning [14]
Future-orientated	Ad hoc	Relevant environmental costing [7]	Monetary environmental investment appraisal [8]	Tools designed to predict relevant enviromental impacts [15]	Physical environmental investment appraisal [16]

FIGURE 17.5 Indah Jaya as an example of a more complex pattern combining PEMA and MEMA. Dark (light) grey boxes represent the major (minor) EMA applications.

and financial performance. This process is called material and energy flow accounting (or material flow accounting; see, for example, Möller 2005; Figure 17.5: Box 9).

Material and energy flow accounting serves two functions. First, it supports the measurement, assessment, and monitoring of a company's environmental performance and the identification of areas most relevant to the company's (actual and potential) environmental impacts. As also shown in some of the other case studies (Sai Gon Beer, JBC Food), material and energy flow accounting has been useful in the identification and implementation of improvement measures and appropriate control mechanisms. There were also close links to the operation of existing systems such as environmental management or performance indicator systems (see also, for example, Wilmshurst and Frost 2001; Schaltegger, Burritt, and Petersen 2003; Jasch 2009).

Second, material and energy flow accounting is an important element of the analysis of the material and energy flows' financial implications. Linking material and energy flow information to business performance is related to Box 1 of the EMA framework (Figure 17.5), the routinely generated, short-term and past-orientated environmental cost information. In the case of Indah Jaya, the EMA analysis focussed on the quantification and visualisation of material losses and the reduction of waste-induced inefficiencies through improved decision-making. This specific environmental cost-accounting approach is called material flow cost accounting (also resource efficiency accounting or flow cost accounting; see, for example, Schaltegger and Müller 1998; Jasch 2009). Irrespective of the specific environmental cost-accounting approach, the combination of regularly gathered physical and monetary environmental information enhances the understanding and control of the eco-efficiency of processes and products. It also builds a basis for the application of other EMA tools.

In the case of Indah Jaya and other similar cases (JBC Food, Sai Gon Beer), evidence is found for the discussion and assessment of improvement options which were building upon the information gathered through the application of Boxes 9 and 1 of the EMA framework (Figure 17.5). In conformity with the overriding principle of improving eco-efficiency, these ad hoc assessments were orientated towards the analysis of both environmental and financial consequences of ad hoc decisions and enabled the companies to improve the eco-efficiency of processes and products. At Indah Jaya, two types of ad hoc assessments were carried out: investment appraisal and job costing/pricing decisions. In a more environment-specific sense, investment appraisal represents a cost–benefit analysis of projects. The EMA application built upon the information provided by Boxes 9 and 1 of the EMA framework and generated future-orientated and long-term ad hoc information in physical and monetary terms to assess options for improving eco-efficiency at site level. Examples are Indah Jaya (Figure 4.1: Boxes 16 and 8) and Sai Gon Beer (Figure 15.1: Boxes 16 and 8). The Indah Jaya case also explored how regular short-term past-orientated information can be linked with the company's approach to assessing short-run environmental impacts and related pricing (Figure 4.1: Boxes 15 and 7). This particular configuration enabled the company to analyse environmental impacts and environmentally induced production costs of customer orders in order to provide support to the sales department in making eco-efficient decisions on customer orders.

Another company example which follows a similar logic is the aforementioned case of Sai Gon Beer. At Sai Gon Beer, the development of a material and energy flow-accounting system aimed at providing past-orientated, short-term information on material losses and the identification of related potential cost savings through the reduction of waste-induced inefficiencies. Future-orientated information was required to assess long-term ad hoc decisions in the form of physical and monetary environmental investment appraisals; based on this information, physical and monetary long-term planning (Figure 15.1: Boxes 6 and 14, see also p. 272) was introduced for the construction of a new, more eco-efficient plant/site using the experience previously gained through the application of the EMA tools. Whereas this case study extends the possible use of EMA tools compared with the Indah Jaya case, JBC Food emphasised the use of the two basic EMA tools of Indah Jaya (Figure 4.1: Boxes 9 and 1) without elaborating on further possible EMA applications. There were also other cases which at least partially used eco-efficiency-related information from these two EMA applications, reinforcing its importance for the implementation of EMA.

However, not all complex relationships of EMA applications found across the 12 case studies were building upon the 'classic' approach to EMA for improving eco-efficiency. Tan Loc Food is an example where a future change of environmental legislation – the introduction of wastewater fees – is anticipated and evaluated in terms of financial consequences (Figure 12.1: Boxes 7 and 15). Measures to cope with the new legislation are finally assessed on the basis of these anticipated physical and related monetary consequences and the potential savings of the measures.

The EMA pattern illustrated in this section refers to decision settings within which physical environmental information may support the making of environmentally benign decisions but primarily serves further analysis of the decision's financial implications (predominantly an instrumental role of PEMA tools). Accordingly, across all cases, the systematic integration of environmental aspects into management decision making was dominated by the aim of increasing eco-efficiency, and most calculations helped management to meet expectations about minimising costs through the reduction of material and energy flows. This is mirrored in the strong coupling of the corresponding

PEMA and MEMA tools within the EMA framework (e.g. Figure 17:5: Boxes 9 and 1; Boxes 16 and 8; Boxes 15 and 7).

A contrasting EMA pattern portrays the use of a set of PEMA tools mobilised by companies to account for the ecological effectiveness of their processes and products. This sixth and final pattern is described next.

PEMA patterns combining tools of pursuing ecological effectiveness

This sixth approach to EMA concentrates on the analysis of the impacts of companies' activities on the natural environment and their environmental performance. The EMA patterns are characterised by the use of physical EMA tools which serve internal decision-making through the generation of environmental performance and impact information expressed in physical units.

The Well-Ever case study is a good case in point (Figure 17.6). Within the context of an environmental impact assessment at Well-Ever, ex-post analysis of environmental impacts caused by the organisation's operations was used to provide a better understanding of and to predict expected future impacts with greater accuracy (Figure 17.6: Boxes 11 and 15). Then, the environmental manager of Well-Ever investigated the link between EMA information gathered for the purpose of a one-off report to be submitted to a local authority (Box 11) and subsequent gathering of EMA information on a regular basis (Box 9), supporting continuous recording and disclosure of environmental information. EMA implementation takes place in the context of a regulatory

		Monetary EMA		Physical EMA	
		Short-term	Long-term	Short-term	Long-term
Past-orientated	Routinely generated	Environmental cost accounting [1]	Environment-induced capital expenditure and revenue [2]	Material and energy flow accounting [9]	Environmental capital impact accounting [10]
	Ad hoc	Ex-post assessment of relevant environmental costing decisions [3]	Ex-post inventory assessment of projects [4]	Ex-post assessment of short-term environmental impacts [11]	Ex-post inventory appraisal of physical environmental investments [12]
Future-orientated	Routinely generated	Monetary environmental budgeting [5]	Environmental long-term financial planning [6]	Physical environmental budgeting [13]	Environmental long-term physical planning [14]
	Ad hoc	Relevant environmental costing [7]	Monetary environmental investment appraisal [8]	Tools designed to predict relevant enviromental impacts [15]	Physical environmental investment appraisal [16]

FIGURE 17.6 Well-Ever as an example of a more complex pattern focussing on PEMA tools. Dark grey boxes represent the major EMA applications.

policy mix whereby the company was trusted to self-control and self-report environmental information. However, this tool configuration may also be useful in other decision settings such as internal accountability. For example, ex-post assessment of short- or long-term environmental impacts may be used in the implementation stage of a new environmental management system. The initial analysis of environmental impacts and identification of critical areas (environmental audit) is usually intended to set up environmental targets and appropriate accounting systems which ensure control for achievement of these goals on a regular basis.

A further example is Thai Cane Paper, which mobilises a set of interlinked PEMA tools to support management in future-orientated, long-term decision-making to improve the management of environmental risk associated with concern over growing water scarcity (see Figure 11.1).

Synthesis of EMA patterns

The comparison of cases reveals that no generic EMA tool or EMA approach is applicable for all companies. Although it has become increasingly popular to promote a few specific EMA tools, such as environmental cost accounting (Box 1) and environmental investment appraisal (Box 8), our comparative case studies demonstrate that it is not possible to apply one tool to all companies unless heroic and unrealistic assumptions are made about the relationships between past- and future-orientated, physical and monetary, short- and long-term, and regular and ad hoc information in any setting. From a management perspective, the business view of EMA starts with thinking about the decision situation and the processes, and then moves to choice of the tools which consider the decision situation and the organisational processes. As the last two examples show, in practice a complex mix of tool identification and use can be developed over time in the context of a particular decision setting such as the need to calculate eco-efficiency or manage and control environmental performance.

Further observations emerge from the examination of patterns of EMA use. First, EMA tools are used to complement conventional accounting techniques, for example by exhibiting a close fit with conventional budgeting techniques whereby past data are used as the basis for making predictions about the future in order that regular and ad hoc decisions can be made. The substantive difference is that environmental efficiency and effectiveness are frequently the focus of attention rather than pure monetary net gains.

Second, patterns reveal that different actors are using EMA often in sequence rather than at a single point in time as attention shifts from one aspect of an environmental issue (e.g. technical logic) to the monetary benefits (e.g. economic logic) and back again in an ongoing sequence of discovery, innovation, and application.

Third, patterns of use confirm that each company situation is different, indeed unique, overall; however, in incremental terms, EMA tools can be seen to be useful for analysing specific decision settings, such as an environmental investment in wastewater machinery, or the calculation of carbon emissions and their reduction.

Fourth, patterns of use always take place within a specific context composed of various rationalities, including political settings, there being no neutral application of EMA divorced from the interrelations between people, planet, and profits.

Finally, the search for regularities in patterns of EMA use also reveals the lack of regularity in the complex decision milieu in corporations, the need for EMA to be collected and distributed to managers with their own information needs, and the need for trade-offs in decision-making to be supported by EMA when perspectives of different managers are juxtaposed. EMA patterns reveal the manifold ways in which EMA bring information to managers concerned to improve decision-making, which involves cross-overs between past and future, short- and long-term thinking, different disciplinary logics and perspectives, decisions made at different levels in organisations, decisions made frequently and infrequently, as well as metrics which go beyond the monetary.

References

Burritt, R., Hahn, T., and Schaltegger, S. (2002) 'Towards a comprehensive framework for environmental management accounting: links between business actors and environmental management accounting tools', *Australian Accounting Review*, 12: 39–50.

Jasch, C. (2006) 'How to perform an environmental management cost assessment in one day', *Journal of Cleaner Production*, 14: 1194–1213.

Jasch, C. (2009) *Environmental and material flow cost accounting: principles and procedures*, Dordrecht: Springer.

Kokubu, K., Campos, M.K.S., Furukawa, Y., and Tachikawa, H. (2009) 'Material flow cost accounting with ISO 14051', *ISO Management Systems*, January–February: 15–18.

Möller, A. (2005) 'Dynamic material flow analysis in the life cycle assessment tool chain', in Treitz, M., Schollenberger, H., Entz, O., and Geldermann, J. (eds) *Challenges for industrial production*, Karlsruhe: University of Karlsruhe.

Schaltegger, S. and Burritt, R. (2000) *Contemporary environmental accounting: issues, concepts and practice*, Sheffield: Greenleaf Publishing.

Schaltegger, S. and Müller, K. (1998) 'Calculating the true profitability of pollution prevention', in Benett, M. and James, P. (eds) *The green bottom line: environmental accounting for management: current practice and future trends*, Sheffield: Greenleaf, pp. 86–99.

Schaltegger, S., Burritt, R., and Petersen, H. (2003) *An introduction to corporate environmental management*, Sheffield: Greenleaf Publishing.

Strobel, M. and Redmann, C. (2002) 'Flow cost accounting, an accounting approach based on the actual flows of materials', in Bennett, M., Bouma, J.J., and Wolters, T. (eds) *Environmental management accounting: informational and institutional developments*, Dordrecht: Springer, pp. 67–82.

Wagner, B. and Enzler, S. (eds) (2006) *Material flow management: improving cost effi-ciency and environmental performance*, Heidelberg: Physica.

Wilmshurst, T.D. and Frost, G.R. (2001) 'The role of accounting and the accountant in the environmental management system', *Business Strategy and the Environment*, 10: 135–147.

18

CONCLUSIONS AND OUTLOOK

Our analysis has several consequences for practice and policy in the area of environmental management accounting (EMA).

Management consequences

Patterns of EMA use illustrated in the cases explored range from the simple to the complex depending on the decision settings facing individual companies, and on the individuals within companies whose decisions can be supported. The different decision-making situations stylised by Burritt, Hahn, and Schaltegger (2002) and examined in Chapter 17 reflect various aspects of the relevance of EMA to decision-making: physical/monetary EMA tools; past/future EMA tools; short-term/long-term EMA tools; application of EMA tools on a regular/ad hoc basis; and complex tool combinations to measure eco-efficiency and eco-effectiveness. Given the variety of patterns of EMA application, no generally valid, concrete management consequences can be justified. Although popular and an aspiration, any promotion of one EMA method or a limited choice of EMA tools needs to be rejected as having too narrow a focus because it does not take into account the different rationales, motivations, and decision situations leading managers to implement EMA. Instead, the case studies showed that a thorough analysis of the decision situation and reflection on goals, motivations, and rationales are needed in the design of useful and applicable EMA patterns which best support managers in their desire to achieve individual and corporate goals.

The conventional perception of EMA is one of improving the consideration of physical aspects in order to reduce costs. This extension of thinking is often very important and valid as a relevant driver of economic benefits secured through cost reduction. However, EMA practice has several additional benefits, including securing social acceptance, resource availability, and political support, improving internal collaboration, or meeting audit requirements.

Depending on specific goals and company size, different actors and different numbers of actors were involved in EMA. Medium-sized and medium to large companies such as Indah Jaya, JBC Food, Sai Gon Beer, and Thai Cane Paper shared responsibilities among different managers and staff. These companies tended to assign EMA to environmental managers or environmental departments, who are the practical driving force behind its application. Quite often, production and quality management were involved as well. The conventional accounting function contributed necessary information but very often had no or only a limited interest. Top managers, in contrast, received and used the results of EMA but did involve themselves in the data-gathering process. In these companies EMA, once established, is likely to be conducted continuously and routinely. EMA often serves as an approach to management control, to increase transparency and rationalise and justify decisions.

Small- to medium-sized enterprises (SMEs) were dominated by their owners or a small group of senior managers (e.g. Classic Crafts, Chau Tanh Tam, Oliver Enterprises, and Tan Loc Food), leading to the general observation that, as smaller companies can lack formalised accounting and management accounting, easier and ad hoc EMA approaches are applied more often. With SMEs, EMA often seemed to serve as a project to improve the understanding of cause and effect links and business logics, and the evaluation of opportunities (e.g. of cost reduction).

This case study research strengthens the perception of EMA as a multi- and inter-disciplinary task that benefits from or even requires the involvement of intermediaries, particularly in smaller companies without formal environmental managers and departments. Gathering and measuring physical or ecological information is one of the bigger challenges of applying EMA. Therefore, existing environmental information or management systems facilitate the introduction of EMA and can, in fact, be considered as part of EMA provided that they are used for environmental measures, decisions, and control and not just maintained for the purpose of customer satisfaction or fulfilment of legal requirements.

Policy consequences

This study also has several implications for policy in the area of EMA, which also influence environmental information management in general.

So called *smart regulations* that combine voluntary and mandatory approaches to corporate environmental management and reporting have become more important in recent years (Herzig and Schaltegger 2011). They make use of a variety of forms for regulating environmental and sustainability accounting and see these forms as a spectrum rather than conflicting positions. Our study shows that the promotion of an EMA-based information strategy can indeed help policy-makers to design a balanced policy mix (Burritt, Herzig, and Tadeo 2009) and complement command-and-control regulation, which is often not effective in emerging economy countries (Desai 1998; Winbourne 2002; Shi, Peng, Liu, and Zhong 2008). Through improved management of environmental information, governments can help companies in assessing the ecological effectiveness and economic profitability of cleaner production investments and other environmental improvement measures (e.g. Schaltegger, Hahn, and Burritt 2002, 2005). Information-based EMA strategies may include capacity-building programmes (Viere, Herzig, Schaltegger, and Leung 2006), support in research and development (Burritt *et al.* 2009), or the establishment of guidelines (e.g. EMB 2003).

Relatedly, regulations by a variety of institutional bodies such as governments, accounting regulators, or security regulators can probaby fulfil their highest potential when designed as complementary approaches to enhancing the generation and sharing of relevant environmental information. The relevance of professional influences (e.g. the qualification of environmental managers or consultants) on the development of EMA was particularly evident in many of our cases. Besides regulatory pressures and support, professional structures and interprofessional communication may thus provide an important impetus to the advancement of EMA practices (Kuasirikun 2005; Qian and Burritt 2008). It appears that regulatory institutions have to play an important role in this to support environmental managers, accountants, and others in overcoming the obstacles related to conventional professional values, norms, and practices.

Finally, governments' initiatives to enhance environmentally sound business through the promotion of environmental management concepts and systems can be reinforced through measures discussed above. The study has shown various strong linkages between EMA, on the one hand, and, on the other hand, environmental management systems, environmental performance indicator systems, cleaner production, or quality management systems (for a general discussion of possible linkages see Schaltegger *et al.* 2002, 2005). As environmental accounting systems have not yet been institutionally developed and implemented in a sufficiently broad manner in the countries under study, this may be an answer to the question why the implementation of environmentally sound management concepts has often been slow and reactive (Schaltegger, Bennett, Burritt, and Jasch 2008). Strong support of companies in establishing EMA through professions, networks, information campaigns, and so on may contribute to better understanding of the usefulness of environmental management policies and concepts and increase the number of adopters and innovators in this field.

Concluding comments and outlook

In showing why and how EMA is and could be used, this book can support both practitioners aiming at reducing environmental impacts of business operations within and beyond company borders as well as researchers seeking the further development of pragmatic (E)MA theories as not 'totally new conceptualizations, but a coherent set of propositions regarding some practitioner-related problem' (Malmi and Granlund 2009: 602).

Overall, the case studies showed that the framework and toolbox of EMA provides a set of opportunties and possibilities to support managers in achieving different goals. Some observations from the case studies may puzzle conventional managers when assessing why and how EMA was introduced. The 'why' may be a first puzzle. Economic reasons why manages introduce EMA may be expected to be dominant. In fact, economic rationality was a core issue in the majority of the cases, but clearly not the only issue. Scientific-technical and legal rationality were also important, as well as socio-cultural and political rationality to manage relationships with internal and external stakeholders. The observation that other issues, beyond the market, can play an important role to introduce EMA was not limited to one country but could be observed in all case study countries.

A second surprise may be the 'how'. With regard to the organisational processes to support the introduction of EMA generally, three approaches to EMA can be distinguished: inside-out, outside-in, and twin-track (Schaltegger and Wagner 2006; Schaltegger and Burritt 2010). The inside-out approach follows the logic that management defines goals, implements EMA and measures of improvement, and then reports to stakeholders. The outside-in approach, as a contrast, is a reaction to outside pressures from stakeholders, transferring these pressures into key indicators, measures, and EMA approaches to meet expectations. The twin-track approach is a combined process following both procedures.

Given that EMA is about internal decision-making, one would expect that EMA would follow an inside-out perspective. The case studies show that this is true for many cases but that several exceptions exist where an outside-in approach could be observed. This means that the establishment of EMA with its internal accounting procedures and methods is often initiated by changing stakeholder requirements and expectations. In order to align internal goals with external expectations, a twin-track approach may be applied, by, first, thinking through which EMA methods can support internal management decisions best and, second, analysing on the basis of the EMA framework which EMA approaches can generate information as a basis for external uses and methods.

Less surprising, but often undesirable, is the result that differentiation is key to successful EMA implementation and design in the company. The successful dissemination of EMA at an international, regional, or industry-specific level and the actual implementation of EMA within companies of different sizes and complexities thus need to compromise between the desire to promote and apply a straightforward, 'one size fits all' approach and the need for contextual EMA solutions, which consider cultural differences, distinguish rationalities, and analyse specific decision settings. The forthcoming ISO Standard 14051 on Material Flow Cost Accounting is an example of a 'one size fits all' approach and will presumably lead to eco-efficiency improvements in most of the companies that apply it. There will be companies where the approach does not fit at all, as well as companies that could gain more from other and more comprehensive patterns of use of EMA tools. Optimistically speaking, the use and promotion of such 'one size fits all' approaches might serve as a starting point for comprehensive applications of EMA in corporate practice.

Although South-East Asia was the focus of the case studies, the results are relevant for a larger audience of EMA researchers and practitioners, following the conclusion of Hopper and colleagues (2009: 495–496) concerning their research on management accounting in less developed countries (LDCs): '[h]owever, many contextual factors and issues are not unique to LDCs – it is wrong to ghettoize LDC research as exotic and irrelevant to mainstream accounting research'. Thus, we hope that the case study results and implications provide useful insights and new ideas for researchers and practitioners beyond the South-East Asian region to reveal the actual and potential contribution EMA can make to sustainable development.

References

Burritt, R., Hahn, T., and Schaltegger, S. (2002) 'Towards a comprehensive framework for environmental management accounting: links between business actors and environmental management accounting tools', *Australian Accounting Review*, 12: 39–50.

Burritt, R.L., Herzig, C., and Tadeo, B.D. (2009) 'Environmental management accounting for cleaner production: the case of a Philippine rice mill', *Journal of Cleaner Production*, 17: 431–439.

Desai, U. (ed.) (1998) *Ecological policy and politics in developing countries: economic growth, democracy, and environment*, New York: State University of New York Press.

EMB (Environmental Management Bureau) (2003) *Guidebook on environmental management system, pollution prevention/cleaner production and environmental cost accounting*, Quezon City, Philippines: EMB.

Herzig, C. and Schaltegger, S. (2011) 'Corporate sustainability reporting', in Godemann, J. and Michelsen, G. (eds) *Sustainability communication: interdisciplinary perspectives and theoretical foundations*, Berlin: Springer, pp. 151–169.

Hopper, T., Tsamenyi, M., Uddin, S., and Wickramasinghe, D. (2009) 'Management accounting in less developed countries: what is known and needs knowing', *Accounting, Auditing & Accountability Journal*, 22: 469–514.

Kuasirikun, N. (2005) 'Attitudes to the development and implementation of social and environmental accounting in Thailand', *Critical Perspectives on Accounting*, 16: 1035–1057.

Malmi, T. and Granlund, M. (2009) 'In search of management accounting theory', *European Accounting Review*, 18: 597–620.

Qian, W., and Burritt, R. (2008) 'The development of environmental management accounting: an institutional view', in Schaltegger, S., Bennett, M., Burritt, R.L., and Jasch, C. (eds) *Environmental Management Accounting for Cleaner Production*, Dordrecht: Springer, pp. 233–248.

Schaltegger, S. and Burritt, R. (2010) 'Sustainability accounting for companies: catch-phrase or decision support for business leaders?', *Journal of World Business*, 45: 375–384.

Schaltegger, S. and Wagner, M. (2006) 'Integrative management of sustainability performance, measurement and reporting', *International Journal of Accounting, Auditing and Performance Evaluation*, 3: 1–19

Schaltegger, S., Hahn, T., and Burritt, R. (2002) *EMA – links: government, management & stakeholders. improving governments' role in promoting environmental management accounting (EMA)*, UN Workbook 2, New York: UNDSD.

Schaltegger, S., Hahn, T., and Burritt, R. (2005) 'Analysis of promotion paths promising success for environmental policies: stakeholder links between government, management and intermediary stakeholders – the example of corporate environmental accounting', *Journal of Environmental Law and Policy*, 2: 193–210.

Schaltegger, S., Bennett, M., Burritt, R.L., and Jasch, C. (2008) *Environmental management accounting for cleaner production*, Dordrecht: Springer.

Shi, H., Peng, S.Z., Liu, Y., and Zhong, P. (2008) 'Barriers to the implementation of cleaner production in Chinese SMEs: government, industry and expert stakeholders' perspectives', *Journal of Cleaner Production*, 16: 842–852.

Viere, T., Herzig, C., Schaltegger, S., and Leung, R. (2006) 'Partnerships for sustainable business development: capacity building in South-East Asia', in Welford, R., Hills, P., and Young, W. (eds) *Partnerships for sustainable development: perspectives from the Asia-Pacific Region*, Hong Kong: University of Hong Kong, pp. 4–15.

Winbourne, S. (2002) *Corruption and the environment*, Washington, DC: Management Systems International/United States Agency for International Development [online – accessed on 1 July 2011]. Available from Internet: http://pdf.usaid.gov/pdf_docs/PNACT876.pdf.

INDEX

Printed in the United States
by Baker & Taylor Publisher Services